S P Oliner

Toward the Understanding
and Prevention of Genocide

DR. S. P. OLINER
The Study of the Altruistic Personality
Department of Sociology
Humboldt State University
Arcata, California 95521

Westview Replica Editions

The concept of Westview Replica Editions is a response to the continuing crisis in academic and informational publishing. Library budgets for books have been severely curtailed. Ever larger portions of general library budgets are being diverted from the purchase of books and used for data banks, computers, micromedia, and other methods of information retrieval. Interlibrary loan structures further reduce the edition sizes required to satisfy the needs of the scholarly community. Economic pressures on the university presses and the few private scholarly publishing companies have severely limited the capacity of the industry to properly serve the academic and research communities. As a result, many manuscripts dealing with important subjects, often representing the highest level of scholarship, are no longer economically viable publishing projects--or, if accepted for publication, are typically subject to lead times ranging from one to three years.

Westview Replica Editions are our practical solution to the problem. We accept a manuscript in camera-ready form, typed according to our specifications, and move it immediately into the production process. As always, the selection criteria include the importance of the subject, the work's contribution to scholarship, and its insight, originality of thought, and excellence of exposition. The responsibility for editing and proofreading lies with the author or sponsoring institution. We prepare chapter headings and display pages, file for copyright, and obtain Library of Congress Cataloging in Publication Data. A detailed manual contains simple instructions for preparing the final typescript, and our editorial staff is always available to answer questions.

The end result is a book printed on acid-free paper and bound in sturdy library-quality soft covers. We manufacture these books ourselves using equipment that does not require a lengthy make-ready process and that allows us to publish first editions of 300 to 600 copies and to reprint even smaller quantities as needed. Thus, we can produce Replica Editions quickly and can keep even very specialized books in print as long as there is a demand for them.

About the Book and Editor

Toward the Understanding and Prevention of Genocide:
Proceedings of the International Conference
on the Holocaust and Genocide
edited by Israel W. Charny

The historic International Conference on the Holocaust and Genocide took place in 1982 in the face of opposition from the government of Israel, following threats from the Turkish government over Armenian participation. This book brings together transcripts of the round table discussions from the conference and emphasizes proposals for the prevention of future acts of genocide. The contributors provide case studies, look at the emergence of nuclear and other threats to the survival of the human race, and consider the role of the arts, religion, and education in understanding and preventing genocide.

Israel W. Charny, associate professor of psychology at the School of Social Work, Tel Aviv University and executive director of the Institute of the International Conference on the Holocaust and Genocide, is the author of *How Can We Commit the Unthinkable? Genocide: The Human Cancer* (Westview, 1982).

A Publication of the Institute
of the International Conference
on the Holocaust and Genocide

Toward the Understanding and Prevention of Genocide

Proceedings of the International Conference on the Holocaust and Genocide

edited by Israel W. Charny

Westview Press / Boulder and London

Published in 1984 in the United States of America by
    Westview Press
    5500 Central Avenue
    Boulder, Colorado 80301
    Frederick A. Praeger, Publisher

Library of Congress Cataloging in Publication Data
International Conference on the Holocaust and Genocide
    (1st: 1982: Tel Aviv, Israel)
    Toward the understanding and prevention of genocide.
    (Westview replica edition)
    1. Genocide--Congresses. 2. Holocaust, Jewish (1939-1945)--Congresses.
I. Charny, Israel W.   II. Title
JX5418.I57   1982   341.7'7   84-15241
ISBN 0-86531-843-3

Printed and bound in the United States of America
10 9 8 7 6 5 4 3 2 1

Contents

The author of "Accounting for Genocide" develops a
remarkable series of fictional scenarios or scripts
depicting both familiar and potential new patterns
of genocide under different conditions of historical,
political and social organization. These "templates"
of future events of mass murder are gripping reading
for both scholars and world leaders, and an exceptional
teaching tool. In a concluding section on "critical
responses to genocide," Fein also discusses strategies
for aborting or reversing "deadly endings."

A typology of genocide: against indigenous peoples;
following decolonization of a two-tier structure of
domination; in the process of struggle for power by
ethnic, racial or religious groups, or struggles for
autonomy or secession; against hostage or scapegoat
groups; and mass murder of political groups.

PART II
CASE STUDIES

3   Pol Pot's Cambodia: Was It Genocide?
David Hawk, Former Executive Director,
  Amnesty International, (U.S.A.)

51

Even under a restricted definition of genocide the
mass murders in Cambodia were genocide, since there
were target groups such as the Chams - an Islamic
minority - and the Buddhist monks. Were it not for
political cynicism and indifference, Cambodia, which
is a signator to the Genocide Convention, <u>could</u> be
an instructive instance of enforcement of the
Convention.

4   The Soviet Gulag: Is It Genocidal?
Lyman H. Legters, Ph.D., University of Washington

60

Genocide is a specific type of crime and does not
embrace <u>all</u> forms of mass murder. Nonetheless, if
the Soviet slaughter of fifteen million peasants is
omitted, it will "weaken and even trivialize the
judicial concept of genocide."

5   The Man-Made Famine of 1933 in the Soviet Ukraine:
What Happened and Why?
James E. Mace, Ph.D., Harvard University

67

Five to seven million Ukrainians died in a man-made
famine whose purpose was "to destroy the Ukrainian
nation as a political factor and social organism."
Churchill reported that Stalin, who otherwise disclaimed reports of starving dead as fairy tales,
admitted in a conversation with him to ten million
dead.

6   Genocide and Denial: The Armenian Case
Richard G. Hovannisian, Ph.D., University of
  California, Los Angeles

84

The denial of the Armenian genocide by Turkey is an
effort to avoid responsibility and the moral, material,
and political consequences of admission. Turkish
writers and scholars are unable to deal with their
national past honestly and are drawn into wheels of
falsification and rationalization.

7   What Genocide? What Holocaust? News From Turkey,
1915-23: A Case Study
Marjorie Housepian-Dobkin, M.A., Litt. D., Office
  of the Dean of Studies, Barnard College,
  Columbia University

100

The evidence of the Turkish extermination of the
Armenians "alas, is irrefutable," said Alan Dulles,

then Chief of Staff to the American High Commissioner
in Constantinople. Yet before too many years passed,
the American press was often treating the "two sides"
of the story evenhandedly. "Denying the crime of
genocide can only encourage and indeed ensure the
repetition of genocide."

8 Gypsies and Jews: Chosen People
   Leita Kaldi, Romania of Massachusetts

Like the Jews, the Gypsies were the objects of
genocide by the Nazis. A touching description of
the Gypsy people - at once a lusty "outdoor people...
who resist temptations of power," and a people who
"live in the shadows of our societies, shrouded in
fear, suspicion and secrecy."

9 Tibet: A Case of Eradication of Religion Leading
   to Genocide
   *Phuntsog Wangyal, M.A., M. Phil., Office of the
     Dalai Lama, London*

The genocidal killings of the Tibetans are on a
scale that may match those of Pol Pot. It is likely
that Tibetans "will finally vanish as an ethnic
group...The Tibetan people now undergoing genocide
would like to hope that their suffering could
contribute to the prevention of similar human
suffering."

PART III
DYNAMICS OF GENOCIDE

10 From Holocaust to Genocides
    Monty N. Penkower, Ph.D., Touro College, New York

The West could have checked the tempo of the Final
Solution. "An obtuse world persists in disregarding the warning signals that came from the
smokestacks of the crematoria; power-politics-as-
usual tolerates genocides and mass murders."

11 Societal Madness: Impotence, Power and Genocide
    *Ronald Aronson, Ph.D., Division of Humanities,
      Wayne State University*

An integrated analysis of three genocides - the
Holocaust, the liquidation of twenty million Soviets
by Stalin, and the American war campaign in Vietnam.
"Each instance comes from the depths of a society,"
and is an irrational or "mad" effort to rid the society
of its impotence through a deranged sense of omnipotence.

have experienced in my country all my lifetime.
Seldom have I heard a word of sympathy for the Jews."

Niemoller minimized its extent. When the
Protestant churches were directly affected, some
churchmen responded in a heroic fashion. "An
earlier recognition that Jews and Gentiles were
integral parts of the same body might have avoided
the occasion for largely ineffective heroism."

It is not an accident that the "death of God"
thinking should have historically succeeded the
Holocaust. This is a Midrash on kivyuchol (as it
were) divine sin. "The penultimate height of
faith is to find oneself genuinely sorry for God."

The minimum task of the Holocaust pedagogy is to
rediscover the sanctity of life. "Death camps
and crematoria bear horrendous witness to the truth
that imaginative capacity which is not grounded in
a firm sense of human obligation imperils life
itself." A pedagogy of paradox demonstrates a
willingness to accept the limitations of human
existence.

PART V
TOWARD   INTERVENTION AND PREVENTION

The organizer of Amnesty International's Conference
on Extrajudicial Executions in 1982 in Amsterdam
calls for a worldwide information campaign to
increase the "willingness of individuals and
institutions to act when confronted with murders
by governments."

The bottom line in preventing future holocausts "is
how do we appeal to the minds and hearts of the bulk

of people not to yield to their baser impulses and
follow leaders on the road to mass murder?"

PART VI

EPILOGUE: THE INTERNATIONAL CONFERENCE ON THE HOLOCAUST
AND GENOCIDE, JUNE 1982

Editor's Preface

The papers assembled in this volume were selected from the rich gathering of work accepted for the historic International Conference on the Holocaust and Genocide in 1982 on the basis of two main criteria.

The first criterion was that we want to present works that develop possibilities of reduction and prevention of genocide in the future.

We are proud to present papers by such outstanding scholars of genocide as Helen Fein, author of Accounting for Genocide, and Leo Kuper, author of Genocide, both of whom develop guides to the varieties of ways in which genocides historically have unfolded and are likely to develop in the future. The featured chapter by Helen Fein presents an unusual series of templates or scenarios of future genocides by using a device of retranslating past historical events into fictionalized versions. Removed from their old too-familiar factual contexts, these scenarios bring home to us the truth of how a genocidal potential lurks in so many societies, nearly everywhere on our planet.

Leo Kuper's work appears in two separate chapters (which the reader may wish to read sequentially): the first presents a comprehensive conceptual classification of different types of genocide; and the second - in a later section of the book which is specifically devoted to proposals of new political legal, social science, and communication projects for reducing and preventing genocide - discusses existing and possible new international initiatives, including a new proposal for INTERNATIONAL ALERT.

The reader will also find throughout the book that many of the papers that are not directly concerned with proposals for prevention nonetheless are relevant to this central issue.

The second criterion was to provide a representative selection of the diverse fields that participated in the remarkable interdisciplinary gathering of the conference.

Clearly, there is not much immediate or tangible relevance of the poetry of a survivor of the Holocaust to our long-range concern with prevention. Similarly, even essays on secular and religious education of people not to acquiesce to be destroyers are also, to a large extent, intellectual exercises by decent-minded people who, in truth, have little influence on the real power politics and decisions of state, or the foreboding dynamics of historical inevitability in a world that is armed to its teeth with a possible capacity to destroy all life. It also has to be clear to all of us by now that, notwithstanding the hopes of many earlier philosophers, simply knowing the historical facts of the past does not in itself free humankind to change the future.

Nonetheless, every level of the tapestry that is "civilization" must be involved in any serious efforts to explore the possibilities of developing a new consensus to reduce mass extermination, and there is also no question that fuller knowledge of the historical process is a very necessary, even if insufficient step, in confronting genocide. (It is hardly coincidental that the reader will enjoy in some of these scholarly chapters philosophical or literary experiences that are in the best intellectual tradition of the very civilization we are so reluctant to see destroyed.)

The section of the book "Case Studies" includes studies of genocide in Cambodia, Tibet, the Soviet Union, the Armenian genocide at the hands of the Turks, and the genocide of the Gypsies by the Nazis. Many of the authors also note the incredible resourcefulness and dedication of the murderers to conceal their actions, and in the case of the Armenians - which became the cause celebre of the First International Conference on the Holocaust and Genocide - we learn of incredible efforts to deny and actually rewrite history even many years after the events.

Following these case histories, we move to a series of studies of some of the dynamics of genocide by an impressive variety of scholars from the fields of history, psychology, philosophy, theology, and linguistics. One of the problems that is tackled with remarkable consensus by several authors is whether people and societies who commit genocide really ought not be considered "insane," and just what the nature of such madness is. The intellectual product of these analyses too may not really save lives in any immediate way, but there is at least some satisfaction in committing our learned professions (heretofore often strangely "impartial" in the face of evils that invariably destroy all learned professions as well) to a value position that, unambiguously, opposes genocide. (Mass murder and death, after all, are inherently not good for living people, the improvement of whose lives is the raison-d'etre of the professions to begin with).

Regretfully, a good deal of the fine work presented at the conference could not be accepted for publication. Some of the papers that could not be included are truly outstanding scholarship on one or another aspect of the Holocaust or other events of genocide, but their focus was on specific subjects that are better placed in other academic publications. There were also several instances where excellent material was not accepted because the same subject was already dealt with by other authors. The other side of the coin that also should be acknowledged is that in a few instances papers that are relatively weak in scholarship nonetheless are included in the book because they were judged to be efforts to deal with an important theme that otherwise has not been sufficiently developed in the literature and research of the Holocaust and genocide.

One major area of study at the conference that regrettably is not represented in this volume - other than in some of the fascinating remarks of conference leaders and participants in round tables in the Opening and Summary Sessions - is the subject of the dynamics and treatment of survivors of genocide, their families, and their children. This very significant subject played a moving part in the experience of the conference for all of us. The reason for its omission from this book is our hope that a separate volume devoted to this topic, under the editorship of Professor Shamai Davidson, may be forthcoming.

It remains for me now to express appreciation to a number of people for their helpfulness in creating this volume. My experiences, working with colleagues to create the International Conference on the Holocaust and Genocide, and inaugurating the non-profit Institute of the International Conference on the Holocaust and Genocide, which is the sponsoring body for this volume (like its predecessor, Book I: The Conference Program and Crisis), have been remarkably warm and enriching. The same unusually good spirit has accompanied the detailed, time-demanding collaboration required for the preparation of this book.

Lynne Rienner, Editor-in Chief and Associate Publisher at Westview Press which published my recent major book on genocide, How Can We Commit The Unthinkable?: Genocide, The Human Cancer, and my earlier edited book, Strategies Against Violence, understood the imperatives of this project and gave her support from the outset. As in the past, I appreciate the first-rate professionalism at Westview and the unfailing graciousness and warmth of the Westview staff.

Elchanan Rosenheim, who heads the Tel Aviv firm of Bamberger-Rosenheim which represents the Lanier Business Equipment Company in Israel, deserves a special thank you, not simply for the excellent word-processing equipment, but for his thoughtfulness and, in effect, contribution to the work of our Institute and the creation of this book at times when the budget we were working from was badly strained.

I also want to acknowledge once again the helpfulness of the firm Kenes, Congress Organizers, under the direction of owner Gideon Rivlin who played such a major role in making possible the continuation of the International Conference in 1982 when we were being pressured by the Israeli government to cancel the proceedings because of threats by the government of Turkey if Armenians were allowed to speak of their genocide at the conference.

Preparation of the manuscript has been the tireless province of my friend and secretary Sonia Neu of Herzliya Pituach, Israel to whom I am grateful, as in many years past, for encouragement as well as skillful and hard work.

Finally, I note with colleagueal appreciation the many contributions of my wife Judy Katz-Charny to the preparation of the manuscript, and most of all, on an entirely personal level, I dedicate this book to her with deep love.

Israel W. Charny
Jerusalem
March 1984

Part I

Scenarios of Genocide
Past and Future

1. Scenarios of Genocide: Models of Genocide and Critical Responses

Helen Fein

Helen Fein is an historical sociologist concerned with collective violence for over a decade who was puzzled by the unasked (thus unaswered) questions about the Holocaust. She is the author of IMPERIAL CRIME AND PUNISHMENT: THE JALLIANWALLA BAGH MASSACRE AND BRITISH JUDGMENT, 1919-1920 (1977), and ACCOUNTING FOR GENOCIDE: NATIONAL RESPONSES AND JEWISH VICTIMIZATION DURING THE HOLOCAUST (1979), winner of the 1979 Sorokin Award of the American Sociologist Association, and which will be reprinted in paperback by the University of Chicago Press in 1984. She views the sociological imagination as a lens to understand how good and evil emerge from social action. She lives in New Paltz, New York.

How is one to begin to think about futures in genocide? One way to use the sociological imagination is to construct scenarios based on ideal-types and typical processes abstracted from the past, assuming not that the future repeats the past mechanically but that social facts, structures, systems of belief and conflicts which have led to deadly endings before still have the potential of doing so again if neither reversed nor deterred. To focus upon typological patterns rather than particular events in the past, scenarios will be drawn as scripts to be enacted by fictive states.

It must be understood there is no assumption that the future can be apprehended as a simple extrapolation or projection of images of events from the past, for forms may vary, be recreated, or be transposed to fulfill similar functions. Since past and future are conceived of as continuous, no distinction is made between scenarios based on models that have occurred once or repeatedly and those that have not and are latent. New variables integrated in the scenarios include the possibility of superpower confrontation which is related to my assumption that all states are part of a world system.

To apprehend deadly endings and consider whether they can be prevented, aborted, alleviated, or counteracted, we need first to be aware of the preconditions and processes that lead toward genocide. For clarity, I am restricting the term to its definition under the United Nations Genocide Convention although this differs from the original definition of the author of the concept, Raphael Lemkin. [1]

The most serious problem in restricting oneself to the usage of the Convention is the Convention's exclusion of mass murder when the victims are annihilated solely on political grounds - membership in a suspect party or class – rather than in a "national, ethical, racial or religious group." Thus, using the UN definition, the massacres by Indonesia of victims labeled as communists in 1965 – 1966 when collective death was dispensed to an estimated 200,00 – 500,000 "communists" by the Indonesian Army aided by local religious authorities (Crouch, 1978, pp. 151-157) could not be called genocide and it is questionable if the mass deaths meted out directly and indirectly in Kampuchea from 1975 to 1978 by the Khmer Rouge would be called genocide, although many label this a case of "autogenocide." While anticommunist states label the victims they slaughter as communists, communist states call them enemies of the people or counter-revolutionaries, assuming the states represents "the people." A Soviet concentration camp official is recalled to have replied to a geologist protesting the treatment of prisoners in Siberia, a treatment calculated to kill them, by denying the victims were people: " 'These are the enemies of the people'" (Conquest, 1978, p. 78). I will call these ideological slaughters but do include them in the discussion as the processes and causes are so similar to those of genocide. Kuper calls them genocidal massacres (1981, p. 10) and Horowitz (1976) includes them among genocides. The theory to be presented can explain these also with slight amendation.

Genocides may be conceptually related to other forms of collective or intergroup violence such as pogroms, lynching, collective punishments and massacre in which the victims are selected as members of a social collectivity or category. These forms are more apt than genocide to be instances of collective behavior rather than organized state actions. Twentieth century genocide is predominately an act of state. Horowitz (1976, p. 42) sees it as the ultimate means of state control over deviant or dissident behavior.

Although genocides differ in function (which will be discussed), I believe one underlying explanation can encompass all types. Genocide is the calculated murder of a segment or all of a group defined outside of the universe of obligation of the perpetrator by a government, elite, staff or crowd representing the perpetrator in response to a crisis or opportunity perceived to be caused by or impeded by the victim. The universe of obligation is the range of people to whom the common conscience extends: the people toward whom rules and obligations are binding, who must be taken into account, and by whom we can be held responsible for our actions. The range of the common conscience is defined by the class and collectivities to which one belongs (or to which one may aspire) through primary and secondary socialization. While social structure is often the basis of ideologies justifying exclusion of the other from the universe of obligation (such as racism), ideology may preceed and justify the establishment of social structures based on exclusion as in Nazi Germany in which Jews were first decreed noncitizens to be regulated and segrated by the state before any plans for their annihilation were advanced.

Reformulating Durkheim's theory of the functions of crime and punishment, it was shown that offenses against people within our universe of obligation in an exclusionary social order will generate a need for collective punishment of the other (revenge, vengeance, reprisal): however, offenses against the other will not be socially recognized, labeled, and sanctioned as crime. Collective violence is an offense against a class whose members are outside the universe of obligation. Genocide is the apotheosis of collective violence, the annihilation of the other (Fein, 1977, Ch. 1).

Genocides vary in motives, justifications, structural relationships between victims and perpetrators, precipitants or triggers, facilitating conditions, accounting strategies used by the perpetrator, strategies or processes or annihilation, social organization of the perpetrators, and the responses of the victims and of the "bystanders." Crises and opportunities may be a result of war, challenges to the structure of domination, the threat of internal breakdown or social revolution and economic development. Motives may be ideological - to eliminate a group which is defined as the New Order, economic - to eliminate a group competing for space or resources - and/or political - to eliminate a threat to the present governing class from a group perceived as loyal to another state, and to reinforce cohesion by restructuring the population. Genocide, as our other murders, may be premeditated or an ad hoc response to a problem or opportunity.

Ideational justifications excluding the other from the universe of obligation include religious doctrines defining the nonbeliever outside the sanctified circle of belief or an adversary (rejecting the message or messenger), folk beliefs ascribing different origins to different peoples, ideologies based on racism or ethnocentrism, or political missions that assign exclusive rights to one group or class. The other need not be viewed as inferior but must be seen as alien. Kuper notes that the need for ideological legitimation itself depends on our "assumption that massive slaughter of members of one's own species is repugnant to man" but this may not be a trans- historical constant:

> One must allow for the possibility that there are histori-
> cal situations or periods in which genocide is taken for
> granted. Either it was customary under certain condi-
> tions, in which case tradition would be the legitimation,
> or it raised no ethical problem which might evoke an ideo-
> logy of legitimation (Kuper 1981, pp. 84-85).

Psychological justification of genocide includes production of images of the other which justify their victimization. Many have labeled this process dehumanization (Kelman, 1973; Charny, 1982; Kuper, 1981) while Erikson, (1964) called it "pseudo-speciation." The labeling is itself a product of the moral universe of the labelers which is based on the assumption one must justify behavior ward all people by a categorical ethic: thus, to kill the other they must be seen as nonhuman or of another species. But the perpetrator of genocide may incorporate different assumptions, excluding the other from the universe of obligation without any presumption the other is nonhuman. This may account for the superficially anomalous rapidity with which people who have lived as neighbors side by side for years may murder each other one year and be united against the violence by a charismatic leader the next as the people of Calcutta – Muslims and Hindus – were united by Gandhi a year after the great "Calcutta killings" of 1946 (Collins and LaPierre 1975, pp. 41-42, 96, 310-311, 362-367).

Images of the other which justify their victimization include their depiction as adversaries, violators, criminals, and enemies. These evoke the conventional paradigms of punishment – and allow the perpetrators to project their aggression onto the victim so they may kill without guilt.

These processes draw upon and reinforce the preexistant definition of the other as outside the universe of obligation in most cases. However, there are instances where people of the same "kind" become polarized on the basis of political differences alone and respond to their suspected ideological opponents as enemies belonging to another tribe as in Columbia during "La Violenza" (Weinert, 1966) and in civil wars. Prior dehumanization does not always lead to genocide but may be used by authorities to incite or justify "guilt-free massacres" (Duster, 1971).

Dehumanization is often exhibited as degradation of the other, imputing their inferiority or worthlessness. The other may also be dehumanized or objectified by comparing or equating them to animals – rats, dogs, pigs – and nonhuman forms of life: lice, bacteria, cancer. But at the same time the image of the other is degraded, it may also be magnified to appear as a threat in order to justify their victimization. Dehumanization, so often noted in pre-Holocaust Nazi imagery of the Jew, both dehumanizes and magnifies the other at the same time, thus justifying the necessity for violence against them.

Structural relationships most conducive to genocide are orders based on ethnic stratification in which state power is not effectively constrained by internal or external checks. The other or victim may be the natives formally incorporated into the empire of the colonizer but without power or effective participation; a tribal or ethnic minority incorporated but not integrated in a multiethnic state after decolonization; the indigenous people of the hinterlands who have never been part of state or society; or a middleman-minority devoid of political rights, because they are not citizens which is dependent on the tolerance of the ruling elite. Most victims of genocide in the twentieth century surveyed by Kuper (1981) are part of plural societies in Africa, Asia, and Latin America (though, clearly, the Holocaust proves European – "enlightened" societies are very much in the picture). Some plural societies that have integrated different groups into a democratic state such as Canada and Belgium have not been marked by intergroup violence despite longstanding intergroup conflicts. Thus, the charter and structure of the state itself may warrant or negate genocide.

Structures of totalitarian rule render all citizens equally powerless and thus potential victims of genocide may be snatched from
home and community and "disappear" into concentration camps. The
potentials for genocide may also be related to the motives of the
perpetrator, strains within the state, and deterrents (if not within
then outside the state).

Precipitants triggering genocidal responses include challenges
to the structure of domination by the victim, opportunities for internal development impeded by the presence or habitual mode of life
of the victim, and ideological strains within the worldview or utopia of the victim which demand social homogeneity and sacrifice of
groups which do not fit the idealized image of the people.

Facilitating conditions favoring genocide include wars which
both diminish the visibility of the killing and the will or ability
of other states to protest and impose sanctions, thus altering the
calculus of genocide which precedes the act, assuming that it is
state-organized. The invisibility of the victims may also be a
function of their distance from the core of the state and/or the
lack of communications and absence of disinterested or sympathetic
witnesses in their region. Invisibility may be created by removing
the victims to special camps in remote areas before their murder.
But visibility can never be reduced to zero as long as there are
many personnel involved and evaders who become refugees flee over
borders. Another significant variable related to visibility is the
length of time before the genocide is revealed to significant
others. The continued invisibility or lack of recognition of genocide depends both on the lack of observability of the crime and the
inability or unwillingness of significant others to credit reports
and imputations of a pattern of genocide rather than individual
"excesses" or another interpretation or label for such events.

The most common way for the perpetrator to account for genocide
is to deny it. Diminishing the visibility of the victims by first
incarcerating them after phasing their disappearance in stages
allows both the authorities and the neighbors of the victims to deny
it longer. Sometimes there are few pretenses; indeed, complete invisibility is not functional for the perpetrators if their intent is
to terrorize other citizens. Another way to account for genocide is
to declare state actions as defensive responses to attacks by the
victims. The state's right to self-defense is the most recognized
human right in practice. One may also explain to one's own constituency that it was a prophylactic act of self-defense: we did it to
them before they could do it to us.

Genocides may be executed by a special operational force and an
ad hoc bureaucracy or may depend on the local militia and general
state bureaucracy. The dominant party may have its own paramilitary, party cadres, or youth organization to do the dirty work.
A high-participation genocide, such as the Turkish annihilation of
the Armenians in 1915, depends on and evokes mass complicity, inciting to murder by sanctioning the looting of the victims' property.

8

The responses of the victims depend upon their perception of the nature of threat which in turn is related to their acculturation and context, the openness of escape routes, the likelihood of their neighbors helping them and the viability of resistance or other alternatives to flight. Flight is the most common (and most effective) response when escape routes are open and the victims apprehend a threat. Trapped victims and victims not understanding they are threatened have often been described as appearing numbed and frozen, conforming mechanically to orders.

SCENARIOS OR MODELS OF GENOCIDE

A. DEVELOPMENTAL GENOCIDES: CLEARING THE WAY

Scenario 1. The Agape - A Hunting Tribe in Amerinda

The prototype for developmental genocides may have occurred in the interaction between European settlers and the natives of the Americas, Australia, New Zealand, and South Africa. Settlers at times negotiated with the natives, at times fought them, and at times attempted to annihilate them. Some historians and anthropologists comparing systems of slavery stress how the colonizers were checked from total oppression or annihilation of the natives and imported slaves by their own religious doctrines and by the intervention of state and church of their homeland, supervisory organizations that came with the colonists often.[2]

Another effective check on their violence was the physical limits of the colonizers' weaponry and manpower and the extent of space into which the indigenous people could retreat which curtailed the ability of the colonizers to eliminate them. Such "utilitarian" genocides as occurred may be seen as instrumental acts to get rid of peoples outside their universe of obligations who stood in the way of economic exploitation. "Latent genocide," deaths not intended by the settlers, occurred without planning as the settlers imported diseases to which the natives had no resistance. (This typology is taken from Dadrian (1975)). Insofar as these were not intended, they would not today be construed as genocide under the U.N. Convention but they decimated the indigenous population.

Such genocides still occur today in the sequestered jungles and rain-forests where so-called "Fourth World" peoples, unintegrated in any nation-state, live. We will trace this process through a tribe I shall call the Agape who are located in the State of Amerinda. Permission to exploit minerals in the interior - bauxite and aluminium are suspected - has been leased to a multinational corporation by the government of Amerinda, intent on extracting saleable commodities on the world market in order to offset the growing national imbalance of payment and enrich the ruling class. Permission, in turn, is contracted to local companies who are joined in the exodus to the new settlements by small shareholders, granted land by the government to raise cattle and sufficient crops to feed themselves and the mining and road workers.

The Agapé, a hunting tribe living as they did in the paleolithic age in a world without borders or property, are accused of stealing several cows that have disappeared. In one incident, two shareholders shot at an aborigine fleeing in the jungle and their prey returned their fire with an arrow which pierced the thigh of the shareholder and caused his death, apparently by poison. This triggers open season on the Agapé who are called by the name of a local rodent in the Amerindan tongue. A local army commander arrogates to himself the responsibility of taking care of the "Indian problem:" the frequency of shooting among shareholders at any sign of intrusion has caused casualties among laborers and soldiers. Shooting parties are a welcome diversion for the army from the boredom of frontier life away from the amusements of the metropolis. The possibility of owning a class of female slaves suggests to them other amusements. The Agapé women and children are kept alive and the women induced to serve in the army brothel. Noncooperative and excess women (and their children) are sold as slaves in the metropolis, thus supplementing the meager pay of the army and allowing them to have a bar in the brothel stocked with international namebrands rather than homebrewed liquor.

Stories filter back to the metropolis: visiting anthropologists and engineers as well as priests are a source of news. One impediment in this scenario is protest by the dominant national church or sympathetic citizens of Amerinda and intervention by the Amerindian authorities. If the commander authorizing the genocide is an integral member of the elite supporting the ruler, intervention does not have to be feared. The national church, concerned with integrating the indigenous people in its midst, may condemn the genocide but its preachings can be ignored.

The response of the Agapé, unmediated by language or any previous communication with their attackers, is to flee. But as the zones of drilling surround them and their attackers roam the forest by road and survey it by air, they must survive by stealth in smaller groups. They become victims of trauma and social disorganization as their society has been displaced and arbitrarily divided, youngsters isolated from their age mates whom they knew as brothers and sisters, as well as parents. These groups in hiding become demoralized and are likely to die soon despite their knowledge of the forest as they can neither look back or look forward.

The disappearance of the Agapé from the world is of interest to few people in their land or abroad: there are no Agape communities or foreign students to plead their case. However, the government responsible for their genocide is probably a recipient of foreign aid from a major power and international loans. Insofar as human rights sanctions attached to such aid are not enforced, these governments and transnational organizations are in complicity with the government of Amerinda, sanctioning the murder of the Agapé.

B. DESPOTIC GENOCIDE: CLEARING THE OPPOSITION

Scenario 2. The Bullwinders And Axehandler Tribes In Nutopia

Despotic genocides reappear in very disparate eras of historical development, in monolithic and predominantly homogenous societies and in plural societies. In the twentieth century, despotic
genocide is more likely to be the innovation of a leader of a new
state - we will call it "Nutopia" - composed of a mosaic of tribes
and ethnic groups without common myths or traditional political institutions which command loyalty. The state is viewed by its citizens as the creation of the Vanguard Party. The program of the
Vanguard may be based both on an idealization of a historic era in
the nation's past and/or a myth of a new revolutionary man for whom
the state exists. (New revolutionary women only exist to serve new
revolutionary man.) As is common in the newer states, this is a
one-party state. The leader's own cadres, his special security
squad and the paramilitary will be drawn from his own tribe (the
Bullwinders) so he can be assured of their loyalty. As partisan
conflict and group lines are apt to coincide in these states, the
opposition to the Vanguard will be disproportionately drawn from
another major tribe, the Axehandlers.

Members of Vanguard cadres vie for the leader's favor with
tales of conspiracy to prove their loyalty. Rumours are magnified so
that any unexpected event may be seen as a sign of a plot. Axehandler plots are plausible for the Axehandlers have proved to be
fierce fighters in the past; moreover, why should they tolerate a
leader of the Bullwinders whom they know the Bullwinders themselves
do not trust? The leader authorizes what he calls a "pre-emptive
attack" (or perhaps his foreign military advisors have suggested
that label) or a "token lesson" - the killing by his cadres of the
sixteen year-old Axehandler males gathered at a puberty initiation
rite or a religious study group or peasant cooperative in a remote
Axehandler village. The discovery of a cache of weapons and/or an
attack upon the military will be alleged if questions are raised by
other states or transnational organizations monitoring human rights
violations, but few questions are apt to be raised at home.

As rumours spread and more people have grounds for opposition,
these attacks will be renewed and the targets of massacre will be
broadened, for everyone is a potential enemy of the despot. Organizations of foreign students abroad, small groups of opponents in
exile, guerrillas in a neighboring state, and defecting diplomats
reinforce the insecurity of the despot. His insecurity (tending to
paranoia) triggers more massacres which lead toward self-fulfilling
prophecies; since all Axehandlers have been viewed as enemies to be
murdered, they view retaliation and vengeance as their best defense.
Potential victims flee from the country or to the countryside, para-
lyzing trade and negating the possibility of internal organization
against the despotism. But organization has been already negated by
the reign of terror which is internalized: each fears his neighbor

and organization means the possibility of infiltration by government spies.

Like all client states, Nutopia has patrons among the great powers which usually try to overlook these crimes as long as possible. Sometimes the patrons competing for favor may subsidize the crimes, arming the government and enabling them to kill more by supplying them with more sophisticated equipment: helicopters, anti-insurgency weapons and detection devices. Justification for "non-interference" include a theory of development which presumes lesser responsibility among some people than others, respect for absolute sovereignty in regard to internal affairs, the absence of other choices and the interest of other great power patrons in destabilizing the government. Trade patterns and occasional luxurious personal gifts to foreign ministers reinforce their aversion toward sanctions. Genocide and ideological massacres in Nutopia will go unchecked until a coup or invasion of a neighboring atate overthrows the despot.

C. RETRIBUTIVE GENOCIDE

Retributive genocide is a response to challenges to the structure of domination when two peoples (or more) - two nations, races, ethnic groups, tribes, religious collectives - are locked into an ethnically stratified order in a plural society. Their status may be formally denominated by law as unequal - colonial official and native subject - or domination may be de facto by effective exclusion of the other from democratic participation in the policy. Such orders arise from empire-building and colonization, war and conquest, slavery and decolonization; the latter case in which two nations are assimilated into one state and one nation/tribe/group becomes the governing class is the most common today. The ethnically dominant group is referred to herein as the governing class. The governing class does rule but I refrain from calling it a ruling class because of the Marxian connotation that its status arises from the economic order; the status of the governing class arises from its role in a political order.

Genocide is one alternative for a governing class which conceives itself to be threatened by a subject class. The latter may be eliminated by either expulsion or annihilation. Massacres or genocide may not be an alternative to expulsion but a trigger to impel flight.

There is always a latent threat of rebellion in polities based on group domination when the subject class is excluded from citizenship and participation in yielding power. Conflict is both a theoretical consequence and a practical problem. Both Parsons and conflict theorists have recognized that legitimacy is a function of solidarity; without solidarity between governing and subject classes, there can be no legitimacy (Parsons, 1967, p. 327; Allardt, 1964, p. 82). The threat is increased in the contemporary era when the universal ideology legitimating the state is national

self-determination, a credo celebrated in international organizations and human rights covenants. What grounds, then, can one
nation have to justify rule over another which can be "sold" to the
other and to third-parties?

The dynamic of class polarization and collective violence un-
folds repetitively in such situations. Where there is no solidarity
between the governing class and the governed, their coexistence is
likely to lead to greter enmity between them and increased "consciousness of kind" (Giddings, 1922) within each class, especially
exascerbated if/when the subject class rejects its place. "The common conscience is limited to one's own kind, members of one's class,
excluding the other from the universe of obligation - the people who
must be taken into account, to whom obligations are due, by whom we
can be held responsible for our action" (Fein 1977, p. 7). Challenges to the supremacy of the governing class, whether violent or
nonviolent, are likely to be seen as threats to all members of the
governing class and increase their class-consciousness evoked by
their perception of threat. While the governing class and the subject class may be viewed outside the system as topdogs and underdogs, this need not correspond to each class' self-perception. For
the governing class may view themselves as potential underdogs when
and if the presentday underdogs triumph, especially if they are a
numerical minority. For in a political order based on group domination, a zero-sum power game in which one's gain is the other's
loss, the governing class has everything to loose by the subject
class's empowerment. Thus both classes, dominant and subordinate,
aggressor and victim, may view and depict themselves as victims.
Further, there are ideological and tactical political reasons for
both to stress their powerlessness and vie to play the role of the
injured victim: playing the underdog enables the representatives of
each to appeal to bystanders and third parties in terms of universal
rights and norms. Also, the governing class may appeal to its own
constituency to unite as a beleaguered minority and underdog, enabling them to reinforce group solidarity on the basis of the need
for cohesion against enemies threatening their existence. How conflict increases group cohesion among parties who view themselves
surrounded by enemies (assuming there is an initial consensus that
the group "is a 'going concern'") has been remarked upon by Simmel,
Williams and other students of group process (Coser, 1956, pp.
87-93).

It is the threat from the subject class which is defined as
crime by the governing class (often regardless of whether the threat
is violent or nonviolent) which provokes their reprisal and the subject class counterreprisal; this is the basis of the social psychology of the crime-punishment-crime cycle often seen in colonial
situations and other plural societies. "In the eyes of the victimized class, each punishment (received) is a crime and each of their
crimes (committed) is a punishment (Fein 1977, pp. 12-13). Punishments are generalized frequently to all members or random members
of the subject class as they are held guilty collectively: "collective punishment assumes collective attribution of responsibility for
violations" Fein, 1979, p. 12). Pogroms, massacres and lynchings

are examples of such generalized or collective punishments which are ordinarily preceded by an accusation of a crime committed by the victims. Collective violence is not recognized as a crime by the class perpetrating it because it is viewed as punishment of an offense by a class outside the universe of obligation (Fein, 1979, pp. 12-14). Retributive genocide is both continuous with and discriminated from most collective violence by its conscious intent, scope and state organization: the state has taken over as the executive organ of the dominant class the function of collective punishment, the right to decide who shall live and who shall die. How the threat from the subject class is related to retributive genocide in plural societies is illustrated in the following scenarios.

Scenario 3. Ethnic Conflict, Separation, and Genocide in Amerindustan

Two ethnic groups separated by their location at the core and periphery coexist within Amerindustan, the dominant class dwelling in the rich highlands and the subject class at the periphery of the lowlands. A movement for local autonomy arises among the people of the lowlands and wins a local election. Their success provokes the state's military leaders to invade and take over the lowlands government. Attempting to incite solidarity, they first massacre the people of a religious minority among the lowlanders, trying to induce the others to join the attack. Although there is a long history of communal massacres and accusations of ritual provocations in the lowlands, this time the lowlanders do not join in the massacres. The highland troops begin to massacre entire villages, having already eliminated the educated class of both the majority and minority among the lowlanders.

The victims and potential victims flee in droves to the neighboring country which is composed of related ethnic groups. An international outcry for mediation and a ceasefire and/or the intervention of a peacekeeping force arises in response to the prompt broadcast of news by the neighboring state. The great powers repeat injunctions to that state to abstain from attacking its genocidal neighbor and kick in more or less generous contributions to the international refugee fund.

The refugees themselves have become a causus belli, a growing problem as hundreds of thousands continue to stream into the nation of asylum. They make clear that they will never return while the army rules. The welcoming nation of asylum sees provincial tension rise as the number of refugees increase (endangering public health) and cannot forsee any temporary or permanent solution such as resettlement. The great powers and other bystander-states continue to counsel patience. These pressures lead the nation of asylum to support an invasion by a guerrilla force recruited from the refugees, generously supported by its own military equipment and airforce. The invaders are victorious, the defending army flees and the refugees return, citizens of a new state.

*Scenario 4.   Dominant Minority Rule Leads to Terrorism and
Genocidal War in Traverstia*

Two major groups coexist within Traverstia, a state created by
colonial settlement.   The dominant group, a minority, has exclusive
control over the state machine of the core of the territory which
encompasses the industrialized area and extractive industries which
are the source of wealth in Traverstia.   The majority group are legally defined as aliens as they are citizens of hinterland ministates
created by the core state and regulated by passport and working
papers as are foreign workers. A widespread movement for nonviolent
change demanding equal rights for all inhabitants grows among the
majority group. This is legally repressed by the government of the
core of Traverstia which decrees the movement "a threat to order"
and representative of foreign ideologies, and incarcerates or exiles
the leadership.   Belief in nonviolence wanes among the next generation of political activists among the majority.   Their underground
organization which espouses selective terrorism to overthrow the
government is systematically infiltrated and broken.

The ruling minority, more than ever united by fear, begin to
train themselves for a confrontation. Universal military service becomes compulsory among their youth. Tactical alliances with neighboring states (in which groups related to the majority group in
Traverstia rule) ensures them effective control of the borders. Mass
action by the majority becomes less of a threat after a preemptory
and unplanned police shooting into an impatient crowd in front of a
police station becomes commemorated as the Crowville massacre.

Nonetheless, the minority's control over the majority is limited both by law and numbers. Opposition among the majority reemerges
in the next generation after the Crowville massacre as the economic
status of the underdogs improves because of the shortage of labor.
The sense of relative deprivation among majority workers holding
skilled jobs, still paid less than their minority peers in comparable jobs, increases even though their income grows. Mass movements
among the majority stress their unity and reject dependency upon the
minority or an appeal to them.

This is the background for the increasing use of urban terrorism by cadres of a self-rule movement among the underdog majority
which seeks equal rights in Traverstia.   No one is sure how the
movement is organized as all known leaders have been incarcerated,
interned or fled, but the incidents increase: bank holdups increase
their financial base and department-store bombings deter minority
customers causing the financial elite to advocate some accomodation
to the movement.   After militant newspaper editors among the governing class who defend the hard line taken by the regime are taken
hostage for ransom, critics within the governing class who advocate
concessions are stigmatized as disloyal.   Security is reinforced, the
government position hardens, and emigration among the minority increases. Everyday-life still goes on much as usual and the workers
of the underdog majority continue their daily work.

It is the bombing of a busload of minority school children
(later admitted by the underground movement to be a mistake) which
provokes collective reprisals from the government. Alleging that
they are reacting to tips as to the hideout of the terrorists'
leadership, the government bombs a densely populated township of the
majority repeatedly, causing tens of thousands of deaths and casualties. The majority begins to flee to the countryside where their
theoretical homelands are located. Both representatives of the majority and the minority allege genocide.

But many members of the majority still reside in the cities of
the core, especially domestic workers who often are allowed to sleep
in their employers' homes because commuting to their townships is
unsafe. Yet they are not safe in the core either, for if they go
shopping they are in danger of being stabbed by minority teenage
gangs. Rumours circulate that such victims and majority group
children who have been wounded are being denied blood systematically
because of the Minister of Health's decision to distribute blood
(now in short supply) on a priority schedule taking into account
group needs and the "compatibility of blood." This leads to an international outcry, including demands by transnational organizations
of physicians and health personnel and human rights organizations
for an investigation. A United Nations debate leads to the censure
of Traverstia.

The increasing insecurity of life leads the remainder among the
majority to flee their townships for their "homelands." Yet once
they are concentrated in these arid and now overcrowded areas, they
have neither employment nor food and they lack equipment and ferti-
lizer for more intensive farming. Appeals to the government of
Traverstia by relief organizations are rejected by that government
which demands that the guerrilla forces bordering the homelands-sur-
render and allow the army of Traverstia to check for hidden arms and
distribute the food. The majority is slowly but steadily reduced by
famine and malnutrition.

*Scenarios 5. The Deltas and Gammas - Neighboring Amazia and
Zenomia*

Two tribes in a caste-like relationship traditionally, the
Deltas - known as warriors - and the Gammas - known as sowers and
shepherds - coexist within two states created by decolonization with
reverse orders of domination. The Deltas have a myth that God
created them first out of marble and gold and made the Gamma out of
clay in order to serve them; indeed, the Gammas have traditionally
served and been protected by them in the past. But now there is formal equality and both go to school together and live in the same
villages. In Amazia, the Uhuru Party based on the Deltas (a minority in both states) is dominant over the Arawaki Party (based on
the Gamma majority) and there is nominal integration of the Gamma.
In Zenomia, the Arawaki Party is dominant and many among the Delta
minority have fled or been driven out of Zenomia (to Amazia) following massacres during their civil war which are described by some as
genocidal and by others as local pogroms.

There is a shift in power within the Uhuru Party in Amazia with a more radical faction emerging triumphant. Soon thereafter, a small cult-like guerrilla movement among the Gamma with some assistance from Zenomia attacks the borders of Amazia. Determined to put an end to the "Gamma problem," the ruling generals of the Uhuru Party expel the Gamma ministers from the government of Amazia, charging them with treason, and kill them along with all the Gamma civil servants, students and priests that they can find. The youth paramilitary organization of the Uhuru (along with the Army) rounds up the Gamma victims in trucks, drives them to the edge of the city, and then shoots the victims or bludgeons them to death in a more traditional fashion. The victims are shocked and bewildered. They have no ties with the Gamma guerrilla forces and have not heard of them, so they forsee no reason to flee. They have always been loyal to Amazia and expect that the state will be loyal to them. So they readily go along when they are rounded up by their executioners. However, many illiterate Gamma (who are not sought) do flee to the countryside.

Refugees and missionaries in Zenomia convey news of the selective genocide in Amazia to the press which broadcasts it around the world. The government of Amazia first denies that any massacres have occurred and then declares that they were acting in self-defense to thwart a conspiracy based in Zenomia. The foreign embassies with the greatest influence in Amazia (an uncommitted state) compete with each other in aid to help Amazia restore normalcy in the name of "state-building." International organizations send in assistance for refugee relief and for rehabilitation in Zenomia (often diverted by that government). To no one's great surprise, the massacres are resumed the next year.

Scenario 6. Altenuland Occupation and Rule Over the Bianu Leads to Rebellion, Massacre in Reprisal, and Resettlement

Altenuland is composed predominantly of the Altenu tribe and is their homeland. Among its citizens there are a minority of the Bianu tribe who are also indigenous to the land. Altenuland also rules over an adjacent territory almost wholly populated by the Bianus as a result of a war with Amit-Bianuran, a neighboring state composed predominantly of Bianus. The Bianus residing in the occupied territory are not citizens of Altenuland but may work there.

A political movement demanding independence of the territory grows among the Bianus there who fear annexation by Altenuland and incorporation. Both tribes - Altenus and Bianus - have myths justifying their sovereignty over the land and depicting the other tribe as more distant children of God; each claims it is their divine mission to colonize this land and/or keep the sacred fire lit there. Other reasons - economic expansion, national security - are alleged to be motives or justification for Altenu rule. The territory in dispute is progressively settled by the Altenus, reinforcing their claims.

To negate the threat of separatist movements in a plural society, the group defecting might either be assimilated, expelled, or
destroyed, assuming the dominant group will not coexist with them
on an equal basis. Both the myths of the Altenus and Bianus pros-
cribe assimilation by the other or of the other, narrowing their alternatives. If Altenuland were a military dictatorship or authoritarian state, the solution of the so-called "Bianu" problem would be
simpler. Some have proposed driving the Bianus out by reducing
their ability or desire to stay through expropriating their businesses and land, discrimination in employment, reducing services to
their townships, encouraging their students to leave and making it
more difficult for them to return, and by direct violence, all causing the Bianu to flee. This would allow more Altenu settlers to
take root, reducing the basis of claims of the Bianu for self-rule.
But Altenuland is a democracy in which free expression of public
opinion among the Altenus is virtually uninhibited and there is a
division of opinion among them about the "Bianu problem." Some
Altenus argue that chances for peace, the continued internal security of Altenuland, and democracy would be enhanced by excising the
conquered territory from Altenu rule and allowing the Bianus there
to determine their own form of government. Others of the dominant
party among the Altenus condemn these critics as being soft on the
Bianu question.

While there have been cycles of protest and mass disorder in
the territory before, a spontaneous rebellion erupts among the Bianu
cities after a spell of successful "pacification" in response to a
rumour of rape and torture of young Bianu women and the death of one
woman – in an Altenu prison. The Altenu authorities (themselves not
wholly certain what happened) issue a statement declaring that the
young women were agents of the Bianu Liberation Organization who
were smuggling explosives into the area on their bodies, and they
were not raped but submitted to a standard rectal search. The woman
who died was a victim of peritonitis, not police brutality; an
investigation is promised as to why she did not get medical aid
earlier.

The Bianu rioters, armed only with bricks and stones, drive out
the Altenu Army from the cities of the territory briefly. However,
there is no indication that the Bianus have any substantial amounts
of ammunition and they have no projectiles, tanks, or other veh-
icles. The Altenu authorities promise that all means necessary will
be taken to restore order with minimum force. But the interpretation of what is minimum force is left to the Altenu regional commanders. One, fearing that his troops will provoke further demonstrations that he cannot control, withdraws to the perimeter of a
Bianu city. Another, known as an advocate of a radical solution of
the "Bianu problem," orders carpet-bombing within the heavily populated area of another city, killing tens of thousands and destroying
the university which is the spearhead of Bianu opposition. Some
Bianu begin to flee toward the border with Amit-Bianuran. Bombings
are repeated in other cities under this regional commander's authority.

18

International protest leads the authorities of Altenuland to
intervene and offer the Bianus a truce: there will be a cease-fire
during which all who wish to leave will be guaranteed safe passage
to the border where they will be required to sign documents voluntarily renouncing their claims to their property or to repatriation.
Bianus who wish to remain will be resettled in government housing in
model villages encircled by Altenu army camps and settlements; deeds
of exchange of property in return for new housing will be required
for their transfer. Both the ruling Altenus and the fleeing Bianus
will explain that they have no choice, for were they to restore the
status quo ante, the other tribe would have committed genocide
against them.

Scenario 7. Retributive Genocide of Altenus in Abru-Bianu

Abru-Bianu is a state whose people are closely related ethnically to the Bianus of Amit-Bianuran. A section of these Bianus
live in Abru-Bianu which supports a training camp of the Bianu Liberation Organization. After the preceding events, a hostage minority
of Altenus in Abru-Bianu, 413 mostly elderly people living in a sequestered ghetto protected by the B.L.O., are rounded up one night
and murdered by the security squad of the government.

D. IDEOLOGICAL GENOCIDES

The first cause of ideological genocides and slaughters are the
hegemonic myths identifying the victims as outside the sanctioned
universe of obligation; myths based on religion exclude the victim
from the sanctified universe of salvation and obligation. Murder is
always a latent implication of totalitarian ideologies which elevate
the concept of the people or class(es) of the people ("workers and
peasants") and denigrate the ideal of the individual as anti-revolu-
tionary, a byproduct of the old decadent regime. Furthermore,
crises are endemic to revolutions: they may precede them and often
follow the totalitarian accession to power. Some see the sacrifice
of victims as inherent in the nature of such regimes:

> The step from totalism to victimization is easy; in fact,
> totalism requires victimization. The claim to ultimate
> virtue requires a contrasting image - and all too often
> an embodiment of absolute evil...Victimizers actually
> experience a threat to the life of their own group,
> around which they justify their actions...That sense of
> threat can be displaced onto those selected as victims
> (Lifton 1979, p. 302).

Scenario 8. The Utopia of Blood in Frankenriven and Sacrifice of the Ebrinu

Once upon a time there came to power in a defeated nation split
by religious, cultural and class differences, Frankenriven, a new

leader, Atlan, who held before them a dream of creating a new people, erasing social differences, guaranteeing security from womb to tomb, restoring the recently lost national territory and "reclaiming" lands which their ancestors had not ruled for generations, and sloughing off the obligations other states had imposed upon them as the price of peace.   There was a relatively small price to pay for this; the Ebrinu, a small group in their midst would have to be excluded from the promise and participation in the future.   They were aliens.   Later they would be decried as non-people and anti-people.   They had come to Frankenriven centuries ago as aliens, and had always been conceived of as aliens by the old religions and ideologies.   It was said that the Ebrinu were so ingenious that if they were thrust out of work and hungry, they could multiply loaves and fishes.   They always landed on their feet.

There were also other victims at first. The organized opponents of the new regime (and many innocent suspects) were seized and put into concentration camps if they did not flee.   In the beginning, some of the Ebrinu thought they might coexist with Atlan after the revolutionary stage was over.   Atlan's elite cemented its rule while tutoring the people in the ideal race they were going to create "of pure blood" which had to be distinguished from the blood they were wasting now.   No one had thought too much about blood before (except of course when they needed a transfusion), but, the people said, it proved that science also was on their side.   Atlan's teachers explained how the Ebrinu had polluted their blood, how blood couldn't mix, and that some hard choices had to be made.

Externally, the leaders of Frankenriven provoked challenges and crises throughout the continent and won most of them, expanding their reign.   The other states were anxious to avoid a new war and a body of public opinion abroad recognized the Frankish grounds for opposition to the old peace treaty and believed that some accomodations would prevent Frankish aggression.   As each accomodation evoked another new daring move from Frankenriven, leaders of other states became apprehensive and started talking about self-defense. Atlan then threatened the Ebrinu that if they started a war on the continent, they would perish.   Far from conspiring to threaten Frankenriven, the Ebrinu of that nation were trying to get as far away as they could from it.   Many of the Ebrinu in other states were busy about their own business, hoping their states wouldn't get involved and few conceived of challenging Frankenriven.   Many blamed the Ebrinu fleeing from Frankenriven for starting all this trouble. "There must be something wrong with them," they said, "or they wouldn't have got into all this trouble."

The war came precipitated by Frankenriven's invasion of a neighboring state.   When the decision was made to destroy the Ebrinu is a matter of controversy, but the social organization of the machinery of destruction is not.   The Ebrinus had already been defined, registered, separated from the non-Ebrinu, stripped of property, status and rights and segregated and labeled.   Using the same technology and social organization of the camps first used to get rid of internal opponents and the gas chambers used to purify the race by killing defective and sick children and adults, the couriers of Atlan destroyed the Ebrinu.

For their part, the executioners did not publicly admit what was going on but did not hesitate in praising it in closed councils as a glorious deed. The response of the bystanders varied greatly. The most powerful among them limited themselves to rhetorical denunciation. Where the bystanders aided the Ebrinu, most of them evaded capture.

The Utopia of Blood was ultimately defeated, but not before two out of every three Ebrinu on the continent had been killed and other peoples decimated by more selective genocide. Atlan had almost succeeded. The states which defeated Frankenriven tried and found guilty some of the better known organizers of the destruction of the Ebrinu; others found employment and sanctuary among the victors who were now preoccupied with a new threat.

Scenario 9. Upheaval in the Iron Empire and Disappearance of the Ebrinu

The Iron Empire was established by a revolutionary vanguard in the name of the people after a period of unremitting and unsuccessful war, strikes and famine which followed the erosion of the ruling authority's legitimacy among the intelligentsia and common people over several decades. The Empire spread after another war, extending its reign through concordat with its former enemy and the sweep of its army in self-defense over the territory its enemy overran when it turned against the alliance. The Iron Empire was constituted of a heterogeneous array of nominally independent states, federated states and conquered provinces in chronic rebellion.

The Iron Empire was known in its early decades for its widespread use of terror, including concentration and slave labor camps, and its secret police which have been emulated throughout the world. In recent decades it has diminished its reliance on violence although the basic totalitarian structure of the state has not changed and expressions of dissenting opinion may be severely repressed. Control of its client states is exercised by the local revolutionary party which modeled its control apparatus after that of the core state of the Empire; however, a number of states have plural centers of power or countervailing institutions (churches and unions) which have developed in them to everyone's surprise.

The Ebrinu are one of the many ethnic groups throughout the Empire. Most of them are located around the core although at one time they were spread throughout most of the Empire. The Ebrinu are not only renowned in the history of the Empire as the target of traditional hatreds during the pre-Ironist phase of the Empire, but they are members of an international collectivity found in many nations surrounding the Empire. Their homeland, Ebrianinu, has been labeled an enemy of the Iron Empire by its leaders who are now aligned with the enemies of Ebrianinu.

Prominent members of the Ebrinu used to be leaders of the Iron Empire in its revolutionary days and others were early supporters of the expansion of the Empire in its client states. So visible were they that it was easy for opponents of the Ebrinus to equate them with the party of the Empire; they charged that Ebrinus were really Ironists and vice versa. In times of crisis the real Ironists have projected blame and displaced accusations of opposition on to the Ebrinu, charging them with being enemies of the people and (more recently) agents of Ebrianinu. Faced with these charges and bars to their internal mobility within the Iron Empire, many of the Ebrinus have acted in a manner used to fulfill the latter charge, asking to be repatriated to their homeland, Ebrianinu. Because the Ebrinu are a highly visible people because of their location at the core of the Empire, their ties with other Ebrianinus, their literacy and ease of communication and their distribution abroad, their cause has attracted much sympathy in other powers with whom the Iron Empire is concerned with maintaining ties.

The crisis of the Iron Empire involved a chain of unforseen events which leaders of all sides would tell historians were just mishandled. It began not with a political movement but with a worker and consumer protest over potato shortages in a client state that was repressed by a standing force of Iron Empire soldiers and those of other client states. Several lynchings of soldiers from neighboring states and defections of a greater number threw the Iron Empire's alliance (as well as its forces) in disarray. News of the temporary defeat of the Ironist alliance precipitated widespread spontaneous (but unorganized) rebellions throughout the client states and a sympathy march of a few dissidents in the core of the Empire. Officials of the Empire ordered bans on civilian movements and communications, confiscation of radios and arrested leaders in the city (Polonis) from which the first wave of opposition stemmed.

The blue Alliance (a force made up of states opposed to the Empire) was by coincidence then engaged in war games in the state adjacent to Polonis and by miscalculation sent a reconnaissance plane over Polonis. Acting on standing orders, the Empire's bombers shot it down, leading to a war mobilization of both alliances. The rulers of the Iron Empire ordered all correspondents from the states of the Blue Alliance out, charging them with spreading hostile propaganda leading to war. They hoped that suspension of news broadcasts about the rebellion would lead toward their spontaneous demise, but general strikes had spread and pockets of urban guerrilla warfare now confronted them. The economies of several member states on which the Empire relied for food production were in disarray and the meager supplies had to go to the rebellious client states, further draining the Empire. A radical solution was clearly needed to pacify the rebellious states.

The announced discovery of a treasonous plot by the Blue Alliance to dismantle the Iron Empire from within by using the Ebrinu as agents is the signal for the secret police of the Empire to deport prominent members of the Ebrinu and opposition leaders throughout the client states to the arctic borders of the Empire,

Here they can construct slave labor camps and die slowly or be killed outright, depending on their usefulness as hostages. It is explained that the Ebrinus' diversion of food and exploitation of their positions accounts for the shortages. One cannot be one of the people - the Iron People - and an enemy of the people at the same time: the Ebrinus have always been enemies of the people. When the unrest continues, middle-ranking officers of the secret police enlarge the scope of the action, picking up more Ebrinus. As they have been all registered and enumerated previously, there is no problem locating them. Not by coincidence, the terror is escalated in the client states and more food is flown in, "proving" that as the Ebrinus' disappearance immediately improves provisions, they must have been responsible for hoarding them.

Meanwhile, leaders of the Blue Alliance are involved in intense negotiations to prevent a nuclear war from breaking out between the two alliances. The Blue negotiators fear that too persistent questions about the Ebrinu will fortify the fears of the Ironist leaders and be used to break off talks so they do not press inquiries. They are not at all clear as to what is happening within the Empire. Is this a standard crackdown on dissidents? Could all the rhetoric not be a cloak for a top-level coup? Clues and information are ambiguous and contradictory as usual. Within the Empire, confusion prevails and opposition becomes atomized as each person is unsure what their neighbor will do. Thus, law and order is restored by the usual methods.

CRITICAL RESPONSES TO GENOCIDE

The weary reader may respond with some irritation: how can we we be sure this or that scenario is a case of genocide? There are ambiguities about intent and central organization in the case of Traverstia and Altenuland especially. These are included to indicate the actual ambiguity of evidence and contexts in which genocide emerges and the range of prime facie evidence that may be presented. Further, the threat of genocide is confounded with the results of internal war in several instances and masked by the threat of global war in others. The question of priorities of goals of nations may well reoccur when they are confronted by a threat of war which will be borne by their civilian population and of genocide of distant victims to whom they owe no obligations of law or custom.

There are two principal strategies to aborting or reversing such deadly endings. One approach to genocide seldom considered is preventive or deterrent. Collective violence might be deterred by eliminating the structures which promote it: the domination of one group over another without participation or consent by the dominated. This pertains especially to preventing retributive genocides which are triggered by the threat from the dominated class which challenges its status. Eliminating structures of domination is not equivalent to eliminating all social inequality for some degree of inequality of rewards is related to difference in origins and func-

tions in all class systems, but it does demand restructuring social
systems based on exclusion from citizenship, or de facto disen-
franchisement, or collective denial of rights because of race, ethnicity, religion or another ascriptive barrier. Since violent challenges to the structure of domination regularly provoke retaliatory
collective violence, nonviolent strategies have a better chance of
achieving social change and minimizing the risk of genocide and
slaughter. While nonviolent challenges to the structure of ethnic
stratification in India, South Africa, the United States, and
Northern Ireland have not always led to success, major gains with
minimal bloodshed have been obtained in some campaigns which deserve
(as do the failures) further analysis. My own hypotheses is that
success depends not only on the solidarity of the class/group using
nonviolence, freedom of communications, but on the presence of a
third party or superordinate power on whom both classes in conflict
depend and to whom they can appeal.

Dismantling the totalitarian states and military dictatorships
that prevail throughout the world would also limit the ability of
such states to execute genocide. Thus, any strategy to defend human
rights which empowers individuals and associations and restricts the
state from exploiting its monopoly of force without internal checks
or external sanctions is a strategy to prevent genocide.

Another approach to deterrence focuses on strategic conditions
rather than radical restructuring of underlying causes. To deter is
to reverse the conditions which facilitate genocide. Facilitating
conditions include:

1) the lack of visibility of genocidal actions;
2) the inability by bystanders and third parties to apprehend
   the pattern of the crime;
3) the objective powerlessness of the victims and/or their
   stigmatization as not-so-innocent victims;
4) the inability of the victims to prosecute perpetrators under
   the Geneva Convention and the consensus within the U.N. on
   protecting the perpetrators rather than the victims of genocide (Fein, 1980, p. 255; Kuper 1981, p. 161);
5) the lack of sanctions by third parties and/or the lack of
   will of other states to use their sanctions against client
   states (Fein, 1980, p. 254) which makes genocide a low-cost
   option for the perpetrator; and finally,
6) there is the inability of the human rights movement to focus
   on victims of genocide and massacre as a priority and the
   movement's lack of a coherent analysis and strategy which
   would permit it to act effectively against human rights
   violators.

How could we heighten the visibility of the victim hypotheti-
cally, assuming a "we" with the will and power? Invisibility is related to 1) the isolation of the state in which the crime occurs; 2)
the elimination of observers from other states that is the norm in
times of war; 3) the distance the victims are from the core of the
state where there are more likely to be observers; 4) the timing and

strategy of eliminating the victim; 5) the absoluteness of state control over the media of communication. Avoiding war should be the first priority to those seeking to prevent genocide, for war both increases the motives and opportunities for genocide.

Another preventative approach is to make the prospective victims audible. The rights of minorities in peacetime and their ability to defend their lives in times of crisis could be enhanced by enabling minorities and especially isolated, tribal and indigenous peoples to communicate without dependence on their government, thus implementing the new information era in a novel way. International networks of sister communities corresponding across nations via shortwave radio might serve as an early warning system of famine, war, and genocide. By necessity, corresponding communities would have to be selected within the major global linguistic communities. This would imply linkage between the citizens of former colonies and of the colonizers and would probably be viewed by despotic, authoritarian and totalitarian regimes of the left and right as subversive of their control, undermining the state's absolute reign.

Past experience indicates that isolation is never perfect even in closed societies. Regardless of all attempts to conceal the design of the murderers, the raw first-hand reports of the victims of genocide are usually conveyed to others in a period of a few days to a few months. But the greater problem is to convince influential others of a pattern behind their personal experiences; the victims themselves usually do not have the information to indict a government of planning their destruction. It is not the inadequacy of the media as often as it is the inability of influential intermediaries and other governments to credit the imputation of a pattern. Let us focus on two twentieth century examples.

The massacre of the Armenians was announced in The New York Times as Turkish policy two weeks after it began and certified as such by Lord Bryce (nominal author of the British Foreign Office White Paper (1916) documenting their annihilation) only five months after its commencement.

The "Final Solution" was first reported to the west as official policy by a reliable German insider who contacted the World Jewish Congress in Geneva six months after the Wannsee conference of Jan. 20, 1942 (when it was communicated to the German bureaucracy), and thirteen months after it had begun with the Einsatzgruppen – mobile killing squads – following the invasion of the Soviet Union in June 1941. Reports about the mass murder of the Jews were broadcast by the BBC in July (largely due to the Polish-Government-in-Exile in cooperation with the Jewish Workers Bund in Poland), but the Allies did not publicly acknowledge and denounce the extermination of the Jews of Europe until December 17, 1942.

Difficulties inhere in the reluctance of governments to credit reports of genocide. Officials' reluctance can be attributed to the unwillingness of states (especially evidenced during the Holocaust) to incur any costs to save the victims and their consequent fear that acknowledgment that they are victims would instigate public demands for a response. There is always the evidential problem when confronted with reports of particular actions of explaining them as discrete atrocities, or labeling them "excesses" (as the British put it) rather than inferring a pattern and intent of genocide. Refugee reports, often the most frequent source of information, can be readily discredited as functions of the political animus causing the refugees to flee, disregarding how many refugees only became enemies of the regime because they were defined as such. Labeling a series of events is both an evidential and a political problem. Reports of multiple observers often contain discrepant elements, misperceptions and exaggerations.

The same problem confronts the human rights movement and intellectuals who are often the vanguard of the concerned public. Genocide labeling is, in effect, accusing a particular regime of a crime. Human rights organizations who maintain a "legitimist" approach to governments (Forsyth, 1978) are reluctant to label governments prematurely as this may annul their ability to get into the country for investigation, undermine their influence and cause embarassment if they have erred, threatening their reputation. Besides these fears of movement spokespeople, there is the reluctance of ideologues of the left and right to acknowledge reports of mass slaughter when this threatens their worldview.

The resistance to genocide labeling in the event of actual genocide and the inflated rhetoric about nonexistent genocides which are a product of ideological competition has deflated the worth of any charge of genocide not made with authority, seriousness, and responsibility. For all these reasons, an independent human rights data bank headed by scholars, journalists, lawyers and others who are used to weighing evidence and committed to making judgments about the risk, prevalence, and meaning of ongoing slaughters and committed not to a government or organization but to a single standard of judgment might be a valuable contribution. Their usefulness depends on their ability to take risks, balancing the risk of premature judgment against that of ignoring mounting deaths, and to generate publicity while adhering scrupulously to a nonpartisan role.

The objective powerlessness of the victim may be addressed in several ways. One might stop genocide by removing the victim (evacuation), by assisting the victim to resist (sending them arms and resources with which to defend themselves), or by blocking or removing the perpetrator. There is still debate whether the nineteenth century doctrine of humanitarian intervention could and should be used to remove or defend the victims of genocidal assault or whether it has been negated by the interdiction against aggression in the U.N. Charter (Lillich, 1973). In practice, both ideologies and justification seem derivations from the operational rule never stated in the charter which Leo Kuper (1981, p. 161) tells us, is that:

the sovereign territorial state claims, as an integral part of its sovereignty, the right to commit genocide, or engage in genocidal massacres against people under its rule, and that the United Nations, for all practical purposes, defends this right.

Genocides have not only been tolerated but assisted by great powers in their role as patrons since World War II (Fein, 1978). China was directly indicted in Tibet by the International Commission of Jurists (1960) and was directly involved with the Pol Pot regime in Kampuchea as a model and a patron. The United States continued giving aid to Paraguay and Indonesia despite substantive evidence of ongoing massacres in Paraguay in the '70's (Arens, 1976) and genocidal massacres in Indonesia during 1965-1967 (Crouch, 1978), and continued arming Pakistan which employed genocidal massacres in its war with East Pakistan in 1971 (ICJ, 1972) until the uproar from Congress caused the Administration to stop. France gave direct military assistance to the genocidal government of Burundi in 1972 and offered to replace any aid withdrawn by Belgium "thus removing all credibility from the threats of economic sanctions raised in Brussels," Lemarchand notes (1975, pp. 58-59).

For a state to take another policy towards genocide requires a change of basic assumptions, integrating human rights priorities as a basic element of foreign policy. The US commitment to human rights (began with Congress in 1975 attaching restrictions to foreign military aid) was elaborated by Pres. Carter and was then reversed by Pres. Reagan. Insofar as genocide and ideological slaughters are conceived of as self-defense by certain governments and those governments are conceived of as allies, genocide and slaughter are political questions to the officials and ideologues justifying "realpolitik" in foreign policy. Genocide and collective terror are also considered a political question by defenders of revolutionary ideologies and organizations. Double standards are held in common (or rather reversed) by the proponents and opponents of the status quo.

The lack of interest of most states to incur any obligation or costs on behalf of refugees of genocide (and other refugees) can be related to the costs they forsee, specific bonds (or negative repulsion) toward the victims, and bonds to the perpetrator of genocide who may be an ally, client, customer or supplier of theirs. Costs could be internationalized as they were during the Indochina crisis of 1979 through the office of the U.N. High Commissioner for Refugees. Joint international action by the north Atlantic states, Australia and Israel at Geneva in July 1979 and commitment to take in refugees from nations of first asylum caused the latter to halt threats of closing borders and sending boats back to sea. Informed public opinion in these states which increased their commitment seemed to play an influential role in pressing their governments to take in more Indochinese refugees.

The "conscience constituency" which is the forum to which the human rights movement speaks is a resource in the west. The orga-

nized sector of the movement is composed of human rights nongovernmental organizations (NGO's) boards and staff, which in turn may
call on networks of community leaders, intellectuals, and politicians, and other voluntary organization networks. They effectively
define the range of choices that enable us while "sorting through
the day's mail (to)...decide whether or not to express moral outrage
about political prisoners in Chile or in the Soviet Union, black or
Spanish-speaking victims of racial injustice in American cities, the
plight of farm laborers in California or that of whales in the Pacific Ocean" (Moore, 1978, p. 35).

It is ironic that the organized defenders of animals subjected
to mass slaughter are so much more daring, aggressive and inventive
than are the NGO's protecting people. Can we imagine nonviolent in-
tervenors using the same techniques employed to protect endangered
species protecting peoples: shaming, confronting the killers, moving
into the region where the kill takes place, and interposition.
There are several explanations of this, both structural and ideological.

Structurally, the NGO's are not a single movement but an array
of organizations and constituencies whose interest is particularistic, concerned with the continued protection or advancement of
their own people. Few NGO's focus on all minorities or "Fourth
World" victims as do the Minority Rights Group and Survival International. Amnesty International, the most universalistic NGO, does
not discriminate among violators, seldom judges the magnitude, prevalence, or direction of violations or discriminates between a crisis, a chronic, an emerging, and a deteriorating situation. The
slaughter of masses may receive the same attention as the arbitrary
imprisonment of individual dissenters.

An exhaustive study of NGO recognition of the autogenocide in
Kampuchea would be instructive. Kuper notes that Amnesty and the
International Commission of Jurists submitted statements presented
by the Sub-Commission on Prevention of Discrimination and Protection
of Minorities on 30 January 1979 (Kuper, 1981,p. 155). The AI report submitted in July 1978 stated "that fundamental human rights
had been violated" and observed there were grave allegations of
"summary execution of many people because of positions they held in
the former administration" (Amnesty International, 1979, p. 95).

Had the human rights movement the will and ability to unite to
deter genocide,they would be disabled in assessing the evidence (as
was AI in the case of Kampuchea) because of their assumptions and
methods. They usually assume the legitimacy of governments whose
policies are the object of examination and require their cooperation
to investigate. Legitimist organizations rely on or turn first toward the government for evidence and responses to allegation. But
cooperation by genocidal governments is unlikely and the pretenses
of cooperation may be a misleading blind; governments may establish
temporary "Potemkin villages" for international investigators, such
as the German disguise of Theresienstadt in 1944 for the benefit of
the Danish Red Cross, leaving their visitors with the unfortunate

impression that this was a stable residential community of senior citizens instead of a waystation to an extermination camp (Yahil, 1969, pp. 302-313). Relying on "legitimate" means of knowing and refusing to make inferences on the basis of first and second-hand sources who may be biased - refugees and families of victims - risks consigning the victims to death.

Dependence on a model of appeal to the violator and to the U.N. may restrict NGO's observing genocide to rely on ineffectual means as a principle. Adherents of the consensual approach assume a vision of world community based on common values which deny coercion and thus refuse to consider coercive means to achieve their ends. Yet genocidal governments do not base their rule on consensus but terror, for genocide premises a self-fulfilling prophecy: if their victims do not die today, they will be enemies tomorrow.

Were a human rights movement to emerge with changed assumptions and priorities, it would have to anticipate three stages in response toward putative genocides in order to make a difference:

1) Acknowledgment of genocide depends on evaluation, classification and labeling. Both time and reliability of assessment are important. The length of time people can endure partly depends on its numbers, dispersion, and the force and methods of the executioner. A genocide such as the Holocaust in which a potential target of nine million people were annihilated in four years is the exception, not the rule. Unobtrusive methods of gathering intelligence (which violate legitimist assumptions) need to be considered.

2) Prompt opening of borders and doors to refugees is imperative to save all people who can get out and to gather intelligence. Yet refugee relief must be seen in the context of the cause of the exodus and should not become a substitute for redressing the cause.

3) The movement needs a strategy, whether based on appeal, economic pressure, sanctions, or intervention, and a target. The latter may be the governments of the protestor, the government perpetrating genocide, adjacent states to the perpetrator, transnational organization and the victims themselves. A whole range of tactics have yet to be considered, including aggressive nonviolence (against the perpetrator by third parties). This is not to suggest that victims of genocide can extricate themselves without assistance: victims of the state need intervention from outside that state in the same way victims of the family - abused children, battered wives - need help from other organizations and influential others to protect or liberate them.

Despite the inherent problems in apprehending and labeling genocide, I believe the reasons why we have failed to deter or check it in the past is not the lack of warning or verifiability primarily, but firstly that there is no we - neither an organization, state(s), constituency, or community - with a commitment to do so. There is no we ready to rank commitment to life - regardless of nationality, race, religion, ethnicity, or politics - ahead of political, national or ideological interests. (Perhaps there is a "we" emerging to confront the threat of omnicide which is a universal, transcultural, pervasive, and devastating threat to all. Unlike the threat of nuclear incineration which is expected to occur once and envelop all, genocides and ideological slaughters occur irregularly in specific and often isolated places and do not threaten outsiders directly.) Such a commitment would require reexamination and perhaps radical alteration of our assumptions, strategy and tactics and might have implications for our other goals. Until the point such a we emerges, we here and now are part of the problem.

NOTES

1. Lemkin conceived genocide to include the destruction of national, racial and religious groups by physical, biological, and cultural decimation in his analysis, Axis Rule in Occupied Europe (Washington, D.C.: Carnegie Endowment for International Peace, 1944, pp. 82–89.) Prior to that, he had conceived the same acts as a crime, for he submitted a proposal to "declare the destruction of racial, religious, or social collectivities" to constitute the "crime of barbarity" to the International Conference on the Unification of Criminal Law in Madrid in 1933.

The General Assembly of the United Nations condemned genocide in 1946 and by implication included political groups as objects of genocide. However, the final version of the Convention passed in 1948 excludes political groups and what some have construed as "cultural genocide."

> In the present Convention, genocide means any of the following acts committed with intent to destroy, in whole or in part, a national, ethnical, racial or religious group as such:
>
> (a) Killing members of the group;
> (b) Causing serious bodily or mental harm to members of the group;
> (c) Deliberately inflicting on the group conditions of life calculated to bring about its physical destruction in whole or in part;
> (d) Imposing measures intended to prevent births within the group;
> (e) Forcibly transferring children of the group to another group.

From Human Rights: A Compilation of International Instruments of the United Nations. New York: United Nations, 1973, p. 41.
2. This is related to the controversy over explanation of the purportedly greater interracial integration and different effects resulting from slavery in Latin and North America. See Frank Tannenbaum, Slave and Citizen: The Negro in the Americas (New York: Knopf, 1946), the earliest statement of this thesis; Marvin Harris, Patterns of Race in the Americas (New York: Walker, 1964, pp. 16–17)

relates the Church's protection of natives to its material and in-
stitutional interests rather than values; and Carl Degler, <u>Neither
Black Nor White: Slavery and Race Relations in Brazil and the
United States</u> (New York: Macmillan, 1971, pp. 23-31) re-examining
Tannenbaum's thesis shows that slaves were defined as human beings
and protected in both the North American and Latin legal system.

REFERENCES

ALLARDT, Erik. A theory of solidarity and legitimacy conflicts. In
Erik Allkardt & Y. Littunen, <u>Cleavages, Ideologies and Party
Systems</u>. Helsinki: Academic Bookstore, 1964.

AMNESTY International. <u>Report 1979.</u> London: Amnesty International,
1979.

ARENS, Richard (Ed.), <u>Genocide In Paraguay</u>. Phila.: Temple University Press, 1976.

BRYCE, Viscount James. In Arnold J. Toynbee (Ed.), <u>The Treatment of
Armenians in the Ottoman Empire, 1915-1916</u>. London: HMSO, 1916.

CHARNY, Israel W. <u>How Can We Commit The Unthinkable?: Genocide,
The Human Cancer</u>. Boulder, Colorado: Westview Press, 1982.

COLLINS, Larry & LAPIERRE, Dominique. <u>Freedom at Midnight</u>. New
York: Simon & Schuster, 1975.

CONQUEST, Robert. <u>Kolyma: The Arctic Death Camps</u>. New York: Viking
1978.

COSER, Lewis. <u>The Functions of Social Conflict</u>. New York: Free
Press, 1956.

CROUCH, Harold A. <u>The Army and Politics in Indonesia</u>. Ithaca,
N.Y.: Cornell University Press, 1978.

DADRIAN, V. N. Genocide as a function of intergroup conflict - a
paradigm in macrosociology. Paper presented at the 70th annual
meeting of the American Sociological Association, San Francisco,
August 1975.

DUSTER, Troy. Conditions for guilt-free massacre. In Nevitt Sanford,
Craig Comstock, & associates (Eds.), <u>Sanctions for Evil</u>. San
Francisco: Jossey Bass, 1971, pp. 25-36.

ERIKSON, Erik H. <u>Life History and the Historical Moment</u>. New York:
Free Press, 1964.

FEIN, Helen. Crimes without punishment: genocide after the
Holocaust. In Jack L. Nelson & Vera M. Green (Eds.), <u>International
Human Rights: Contemporary Issues</u>. Stanfordville, N.Y: Human Rights
Publishing Group, 1980.

FEIN, Helen. <u>Accounting for Genocide: National Responses and Jewish
Victimization During the Holocaust</u>. New York: Free Press, 1979.

FEIN, Helen. <u>Imperial Crime and Punishment: The Massacre at
Jalliamwala Bagh and British Judgment, 1919-1920</u>. Honolulu:
University Press of Hawaii, 1977.

FEIN, Helen. Genocide in the post-Holocaust era: what has/can be
done? Paper presented at the 73rd annual meeting of the American
Sociological Association, San Fransisco, September 1978.

FORSYTHE, David P. <u>Humanitarian Politics: The International
Committee of the Red Cross</u>. Baltimore, Md.: Johns Hopkins University Press, 1978.

GIDDINGS, Franklin H.   Studies in the Theory of Human Society.   New York: Macmillan, 1922.

HOROWITZ, Irving Louis.   Genocide: State Power and Mass Murder. Brunswick, N.J.: Transaction Books, 1976.

INTERNATIONAL Commission of Jurists.   The Events in East Pakistan, 1971. Geneva: ICJ, 1972.

INTERNATIONAL Commission of Jurists.   Tibet and the Chinese People's Republic. Geneva: ICJ, 1960.

KELMAN, Herbert C. Violence without moral restraint: reflections on the dehumanization of victims and victimizers. Journal Social Issues 1973, 29, 25–61.

KUPER, Leo.   Genocide: Its Political Use in the Twentieth Century. New Haven: Yale University Press, 1981.

LEMARCHAND, Rene.   Ethnic genocide. Transaction, Jan.–Feb. 1975, 50–60.

LEMKIN, Raphael.   Axis Rule in Occupied Europe.   Washington D.C.: Carnegie Endowment for International Peace, 1944.

LIFTON, Robert.   The Broken Connection: On Death and the Continuity of Life. New York: Simon & Schuster, 1979.

LILLICH, Richard B. (Ed.), Humanitarian Intervention and the United Nations. Charlottesville, Va.: University Press of Virginia 1973.

MOORE, Barrington, Jr.   On moral outrage. New York Review of Books, Vol. XXV: 9 (June 1, 1978), 35–36.

PARSONS, Talcott.   Social Theory and Modern Society. New York: Free Press, 1967.

UNITED Nations.   Human Rights: A Compilation of International Instruments of the United Nations. New York: UN, 1973.

WEINART, Richard J.   Violence in pre-modern societies: rural Columbia. American Political Science Review, 1966, 60, 340–347.

YAHIL, Leni.   The Rescue of Danish Jewry: Test of a Democracy. Trans. Morris Gradel. Philadelphia: Jewish Publication Society of America, 1969.

HELEN FEIN, Ph.D., 33 Elting Ave, New Paltz, New York 12561, U.S.A.

2. Types of Genocide and Mass Murder*

Leo Kuper

During the course of many years work on comparative race and ethnic relations, I kept coming across charges of genocide, and complaints of the indifference of the outside world. I did not credit these charges and complaints, but when I finally came to investigate them I was overwhelmed to find that genocide was a continuing scourge, that the Genocide Convention of 1948 was virtually a dead letter, and that the performance of the United Nations was such as to deny the victims of genocide the protection of internationally available sanctions. This study is reported in my book, GENOCIDE. Since its completion, I have been working on the problem of the prevention of genocide, and I have been seeking to set up with colleagues an organization equipped to take preventive action, both within, and outside of, the United Nations.

A first distinction to be made is that between 'domestic' genocides, that is to say, genocides arising from internal divisions within a society, and genocides arising in the course of international warfare. The following types of 'domestic genocide' can be specified:

1. GENOCIDE AGAINST INDIGENOUS PEOPLES

In the course of conquest, or of later pacification, these genocides were all too frequent in the colonization of the Americas, Australia and frica. Now, it is mostly small surviving groups of hunters and gatherers who face the threat of extinction. These are the so-called 'victims of progress,' victims, that is to say, of predatory economic development. Two recent cases have aroused international 'concern.'

In March 1974, the International League for the Rights of Man, joined by the Inter-American Association for Democracy and Freedom, charged the government of Paraguay with complicity in genocide against the Ache (Guayaki) Indians. In a protest to the United Nations Secretary General, the organizations alleged the following violations, leading to the wholesale disappearance of the Guayaki (Ache) ethnic group, namely:

1. enslavement, torture and killing of the Guayaki Indians in reservations in eastern Paraguay;

---

* This chapter is excerpted from INTERNATIONAL ACTION AGAINST GENOCIDE, Report No. 53 of the Minority Rights Group, London (36 Craven Street, London WC2N 5N6) with their kind permission, and the kind permission also of Penguin publishers of my book, Genocide – Its Political Use in the Twentieth Century.

2. withholding of food and medicine from them resulting in their death by starvation and disease;
3. massacre of their members outside the reservations by hunters and slave traders with the toleration and even encouragement of members of the government and with the aid of armed forces;
4. splitting up of families and selling into slavery of children, in particular girls for prostitution; and
5. denial and destruction of Guayaki cultural traditions, including use of their language, traditional music, and religious practices.

This was followed by an attack in the United States Senate supported by intellectuals and churchmen in Paraguay. To these protestations, the Defense Minister replied quite simply that there was no intention to destroy the Guayaki, "Although there are victims and victimizer, there is not the third element necessary to establish the crime of genocide – that is 'intent.' Therefore, as there is no 'intent,' one cannot speak of 'genocide'" (Lewis, 1976, pp. 62-3).

A similar issue arose in relation to charges of genocide against Indians in the Amazon River region of Brazil, to which the Permanent Representative of Brazil replied that

...the crime committed against the Brazilian indigenous population cannot be characterized as genocide, since the criminal parties involved never eliminated the Indians as an ethnic or cultural group. Hence, there was lacking the special malice or motivation necessary to characterize the occurrence of genocide. The crimes in question were committed for exclusively economic reasons, the perpetrators having acted solely to take possession of the lands of their victims.[1]

In both cases, the defence raised was that of intent – its absence in the Paraguay case, and in the Brazilian case, the absence of the specific intent required to constitute the crime of genocide, a reliance, that is to say, on the ambiguity of the phrase as such in the Genocide Convention's definition of the crime as the commission of specified acts with the "intent to destroy in whole or in part, a national, ethnic, racial or religious group, as such." There is also the denial of governmental responsibility for the crime. We should note that in many cases, there may be a genocidal process involved, rather than a deliberate decision to annihilate.[2]

2. GENOCIDE FOLLOWING UPON DECOLONIZATION OF A TWO-TIER STRUCTURE OF DOMINATION

e.g., Tutsi domination over Hutu in the terrorities of Rwanda and Burundi under Belgian mandate.

The massacres of Hutu in Burundi were on a large scale and extended over some years. The Tutsi were a minority of some 14% in a population of perhaps three-and-a-half million. Their relationship to the Hutu was relatively fluid, in contrast to the situation in

Rwanda. There were divisions within both the Tutsi and Hutu groups, derived from regional differences, and differences in wealth, power and status, which offered many social bases, and the stimulus of varied interests for the transcending of ethnic exclusiveness. And initially, in the movement to decolonization, political division did not flow along ethnic lines. But very rapidly the society became ethnically paralyzed as Tutsi elite sought to eliminate their Hutu opponents by terrorism and assassination, and Hutu responded by counter-terrorism.

Within three years of independence, ethnic conflict had esca-lated to genocidal massacre. In 1965, on the failure of a Hutu at-tempted coup, and in reaction also to massacres of Tutsi in the countryside, the army, assisted by civilian defence groups, and the government acting through a Council of War, killed some 2,500 Hutu, virtually liquidating Hutu leadership. This was a precursor, as it were, to the genocide of 1972, which re-enacted, on a vastly des-tructive scale, the events of 1965. In the southern provinces of Burundi, Hutu rebels, with some assistance by rebels from Zaire, slaughtered and mutilated every Tutsi they could find and of what-ever age or sex, as well as the few Hutu who refused to join them. In the reprisals in which some 100,000 Hutu were slaughtered, the employed and educated and the semi-educated were the special targets for revenge, which was also directed indiscriminatley against Hutu. Nor did 1972 see the end of these massacres, which continued into 1973 with intermittent killings thereafter.

In Rwanda, the traditional lines of Tutsi domination over Hutu remained sharply defined under Belgian mandate. Following reforms introduced by the Belgian Government, including a progressive system of electoral representation, political parties consolidated on mainly ethnic lines. The society rapidly polarized, and in March 1962, some murders by Tutsi bands set off massacres, in which bet-ween 1,000 and 2,000 Tutsi men, women and children were massacred. In December of 1963, following a minor, but threatening invasion by Tutsi, over 5,000 Tutsi were massacred in one area, and perhaps an-other 5,000 to 9,000 in other areas. The massacres of Hutu in Burundi took many more casualties. Estimates range from well over 100,000 to 300,000.[3]

3. GENOCIDE IN THE PROCESS OF STRUGGLES FOR POWER BY ETHNIC OR RACIAL OR RELIGIOUS GROUPS, OR STRUGGLES FOR GREATER AUTONOMY OR FOR SECESSION, FOR EXAMPLE THE GENOCIDE IN BANGLADESH, IN 1971

Unity in the state of Pakistan, established in the partition of India was based on common religious faith and on fear of Hindu domi-nation. But the initial political and spiritual exhilaration of a new nationalism was beset from the earliest days by the divisive forces of ethnic pluralism. The main division was between the Bengali-speaking people of East Pakistan, and the Punjabi, Baluchi, Pathan and Sindhi populations of West Pakistan, with Urdu as their official language. Not only were the two sections separated by over 1,000 miles, but there were great differences between them in cul-ture, geography and economy. Moreover, the East included in its population of about 75,000,000 some 10,000,000 to 12,000,000 Hindus, as well as Urdu-speaking Muslims, immigrants, known as Biharis.

Long periods of military dictatorship and of martial law give some measure of the difficulties in arriving at a constitutional accomodation. Tensions were heightened by a relationship between the West and the East, which the Bengalis saw as colonialism, and which indeed bore many of the marks of colonial domination. Finally, in the course of the struggle for greater autonomy, and while negotiations were taking place, the West struck with devastating force against East Pakistan in March 1971, and engaged in large-scale massacres, directed against civilians, including women and children, political activists, students, professionals and business men, and against the Hindu population. The International Commission of Jurists expressed the view that there was a "a strong prima facie case that the crime of genocide was committed against the group comprising the Hindu population of East Bengal." It viewed the army atrocities as part of a deliberate policy by a disciplined force. As to the killing of non-Bengalis by Bengalis, the Commission found "it difficult to accept that spontaneous and frenzied mob violence against a particular section of the community from whom the mob senses danger and hostility is to be regarded as possessing the necessary element of conscious intent to constitute the crime of genocide" (International Commission Jurists, 1972).

There was mounting resistance by the Bengalis, and the civil war was finally ended in December 1971, as a result of the intervention of the Indian army. This sealed the successful secession of the now independent state of Bangladesh. Estimates of Bengalis killed vary greatly, with an upper limit of perhaps 3,000,000. In addition, some ten million had taken refuge in India.[4]

There have been other highly destructive conflicts of this type, though not genocidal; for example the civil war in Nigeria between the Federal Government and the Eastern Region, which was set off by massacres of Ibo in Northern Nigeria in 1966 (massacres which seem to me to fall within the U.N. definition of genocide). During the civil war itself, between 600,000 and 1,000,000 Easterners were killed in battle in the course of the war, or died of famine or disease. In the civil war in the Sudan between the dominant North (largely Muslim, peopled by Arabs and non-Arab Islamicized groups) and the subordinate South (Africans, mostly animist, but with appreciable numbers of Christians and a small number of Muslims), the deaths of Southerners as a result of warfare, massacres of civilians, reprisals against suspected collaborators, and famine and disease, are estimated at 500,000 or more (though these figures are controversial). In these three highly destructive conflicts, the crucial issue was one of self-determination.[5]

4. GENOCIDE AGAINST HOSTAGE OR SCAPEGOAT GROUPS

The major most recent cases of this form of genocide, prior to the Genocide Convention, are the Turkish genocide against the Armen-

ians in the Ottoman Empire and the German genocide against Jews and
Gypsies.

The twentieth century is sometimes viewed as initiating a new
process in genocide. Toynbee (1969, pp. 241-20) writes that its
distinguishing marks "are that it is committed in cold-blood by the
deliberate fiat of holders of despotic political power, and that the
perpetrators of genocide employ all the resources of present-day
technology and organization to make their planned massacres systematic and complete." He describes the massacres at the instigation of
the Sultan Abdul-Hamid II at the end of the nineteenth century as
amateurish and ineffective compared with the largely successful attempt to exterminate the Ottoman Armenians during the First World
War, and the latter in turn as less effective than the German genocide of the European Jews, "since the general level of technological
and organizational efficiency in Germany during the dozen years of
the Nazi regime was considerably higher than it had been in Turkey
during the ten years of the C.U.P. (Committee of Union and
Progress) regime." Arlen (1971) writes to similar effect that the
entire production of the Armenian genocide (of 1915) was based on
the imperfectly utilized but definitely perceived capacities of the
modern state for politically restructuring itself, which were made
possible by the engines of technology. In due course, "Hitler's
Germany was to perfect the process of railway deportation and to
develop the gas chamber and the crematoria, and Lenin's and Stalin's
Russia was to evolve further the institutions of the concentration
camp and secret surveillance...But in virtually every modern instance of mass murder, beginning, it appears, with the Armenians,
the key element...which has raised the numerical and psychic levels
of the deed above the classic terms of massacre - has been the alliance of technology and communications" (pp. 243-4).

The genocide by the Turks against the Armenians had been preceded by earlier conflicts, as Armenians protested against their
treatment in the Ottoman Empire and struggled for a measure of
greater autonomy. The massacres of between one hundred and two hundred thousand Armenians in 1895-1896 were a sort of ambassadorial
note by the Sultan to the European powers to refrain from intervention in the domestic affairs of Turkey, and a most bloody warning to
the Armenians themselves against seeking the intercession of these
powers on their behalf or aspiring to autonomy. The First World War
provided the opportunity, however, for a Final 'Solution' to the Armenian Question, as the Turks faced the threat of the dissolution of
their Empire, and as anxiety lest the Armenians revolt became the
conviction that they were disloyal, and the warrant for genocide.

The first step was to eliminate the possibility of effective
resistance. This was initiated by the disarming of Armenian soldiers serving in the Turkish army, and the disarming of the civilian
population. Armenian soldiers were reduced to road laborers, and
indeed to pack animals, or they were killed outright. The process
was completed by the arrest and deportation of Armenian leaders,
leaving the population a defenceless and easy prey for the next
stage. In some areas, this took the form of outright annihilation;

in others, the genocide proceeded under the guise of deportation. There were variations in the pattern of these deportations - in the treatment of the men, massacre or deportation, in the possibility, or denial, of conversion for the women, and in the fate reserved for the children. As for the deportations, they were death caravans, whether on foot or in cattle trucks; and the final destination was the desolate wasteland of the Syrian desert and the Mesopotamian valley, where the surviving remnant was subjected to the ultimate torment of slow death by exposure and starvation.

There is controversy over the number of deaths, but perhaps as many as one million or more - over half the Armenian population - died in the course of, and in the immediate aftermath, of the massacres and deportations.[6] Though the successor Turkish Government instituted trials of some of those responsible for the massacres, and found them guilty, its present position is a denial that the genocide took place, and it is assisted in this denial by some scholars, both inside and outside of Turkey. The evidence of eye-witness accounts, however, is overwhelmingly conclusive.

The German genocide against Jews in the Second World War reenacted many of the procedures of the centrally organized genocide against the Armenians, but on a much vaster scale, and with elaborate bureaucratic regulation and industrial efficiency. The genocide was world-wide in ultimate intention. It was directed not only against Jews in Germany and throughout Europe, but Nazi doctrine was exported to, or imported by, countries in other continents. Spearheaded by an anti-Christian Nazi movement, the genocide was nevertheless deeply rooted in the history of Christian antisemitism, reaching back to the pogroms during the Crusades. This ensured the active participation of other European peoples in the European genocides, though with most notable and courageous exceptions, and a complicity or indifference in the outside world, so that death seemed to guard all exits.

The bureaucracies of the State, of the Nazi party, of military and big business co-operated in the execution of the genocide. Hilberg, (1961) in a major work on The Destruction of the European Jews, writes that the civil service infused the other hierarchies with its sure-footed planning and bureaucratic thoroughness. From the army, the machinery of destruction acquired its military precision, discipline and callousness. Industry's influence was felt in the great emphasis upon accounting, penny-saving, and salvage, as well as in the factory-like efficiency of the killing centers. Finally, the party contributed to the entire apparatus an 'idealism,' a sense of 'mission,' and a notion of 'history-making.'

The major steps in the genocidal process included the definition of Jews and their identification by conspicous symbols, their expulsion from the civil service, the professions, responsible positions in business and industry, and the expropriation of their property. This expropriation extended ultimately to the last wretched possessions of the victims in the killing centers. But even in the

absence of the killing centers, Jews would have been annihilated by
the extreme exploitation of Jewish workers, with the minimum of
wages for the maximum of work, and by discrimination in food ration-
ing. Social and physical isolation of Jews accompanied the whole
process. They were subjected to the most vicious campaigns of vilification, they were excluded from community with their countrymen by
a series of laws and regulations, and they were relegated to a
pariah status. All these steps are so intimately related to the
final mass murders, that they appear in retrospect to have been part
of an initial overall plan for genocide. But the order for the annihilation of European Jewry was only given in about July, 1941, the
initial policy being to bring about a vast migration of Jews.[7]

The death camps were established after a brief period of exper-
imenting with mobile killing squads. Organized on the model of modern industrial plants, the killing centers processed their victims
for slaughter, as if on a conveyor belt; they eliminated waste; they
gathered in, with careful inventory, their few possessions, their
clothes, gold teeth, women's hair, and they regulated the distribution of these relics. And some of the killing centers were combined
with slave camps, in which the exploitation of labor was carried to
the extreme of expendability, with such leading German firms as I.
G. Farben and Krupp, for example, establishing branches in the vici-
nity of the gas chambers and crematoria of Auschwitz.

The killing centers served the whole of Europe, the level of
participation by other European Governments depending on a variety
of factors - the extent of German domination in the country concerned, the reactions of the local population and their rulers, the role
of the Churches, the structure of the Jewish communities, and the
course of the military campaigns (Fein, 1979). The Jewish dead are
estimated at about 6 million out of a total population of 8.3
million who remained in German-occupied Europe after 1939. Other
groups also suffered massacres on a vast scale. Perhaps as many as
26 million Poles and Russians were slaughtered in captivity, or
killed by starvation and exposure in the concentration and labor
camps. But the genocide against the Jews was pursued with a relentless determination and persistence. Initially, persecution of the
Jews had brought political gains in the support of an appealing doctrine, and material gains in the expropriation of Jewish possessions
and the evacuation of areas for German settlement in Poland. But in
the course of the destruction process, genocide became an overriding
end in itself, to which the economic priorities were sacrificed (as
in the slaughter of Jewish workers) and even military priorities (as
in the clogging of lines of retreat for the defeated German armies
by the deportations from Hungary in 1944). And the annihilation of
the Jews continued to the very last, in the frenzied slaughter of
Hungarian Jews, and the deportations from Italy, Greece and Slo-
vakia, and the last minute death marches. The annihilation of Jews
was a most complete realization of the annihilation of a people as
such.

The German genocide against the Gypsies shared this same quality of the intent to destroy a people as such. There were no mat-

erial advantages to be gained, no conceivable political or strategic gains. The massacres of the Gypsies seems to have been motivated by pure genocidal malevolence. Like the Jews, they were hostages to the fortunes of the host society, deemed expendable in time of crisis.

ANALYSIS

Reviewing these types of domestic genocide, one notes the following:

i In many cases there are differences of religion between the aggressors and the victims. This is not to suggest that these genocidal conflicts are about religious beliefs, but rather that differences in religion readily shape an alienation from, and a dehumanization of, the victims.

ii The catalyst is often a situation of change and of threat.

iii The crime is committed mostly by governments, though not exclusively by them.

iv It is a phenomenon of 'plural societies,' that is to say, societies characterized by deep and pervasive cleavages between ethnic, racial and/or religious groups.

v Many of the highly destructive conflicts involve struggles for greater autonomy or for secession, and arise from the denial of the right of self-determination.

I have drawn a distinction between domestic genocides and those arising in the course of international warfare. The line between the domestic and the international is not always clear. There is often, perhaps almost invariably, an international involvement in the domestic conflicts. This may take the form of training, and the provision of arms and advisers, for one of the combatants, or it may take the form of direct military engagement, as in the intervention by the U.S.A. in support of the Government of South Vietnam. The destruction inflicted by this army on the Vietnamese people and their country was so massive as to give rise to charges of genocide.[8]

In any event, international warfare, whether between 'tribal' groups or city states, or other sovereign states and nations, has been a perennial source of genocide. Indeed there were periods in which total genocide against the vanquished enemy, or the slaughter of the men, and the enslavement or other incorporation of women and children, were accepted practice.[9] Protection accorded to noncombatants under the Geneva Conventions should have served as a restraint on genocide in warfare, but this protection was denied in the Second World War by Nazi ideology, or by the invocation of military necessity in the pattern bombing of civilian populations engaged in war production, or resort to the doctrine of the lesser evil, as in the atomic destruction of Hiroshima and Nagasaki. With the present development of nuclear armament and other technology for mass destruction, and the precedents of the last war, it is difficult to know the current position regarding the rules for the regulation of international warfare.

MASS MURDER OF POLITICAL GROUPS

There remain the political mass murders. I am treating these as a special category, since they are now excluded by definition in the Genocide Convention. But logically and theoretically, they do not constitute a distinctive category. The ethnic and racial conflicts are for the most part political, and under certain conditions (e.g., communists in Indonesian villages, or political opponents in the labor camps in Kampuchea, or in Nazi Germany or in Stalinist Russia), political affiliation can be as distinctive and as immutable as ethnic or even racial origin. Moreover, political mass murder is often accompanied by massacres of ethnic or religious groups.

In Stalinist Russia, there were the deportations of whole national groups. Khrushchev, in his denunciation of Stalin at the Twentieth Congress of the Communist Party of the Soviet Union in February 1956, referred to mass deportations, "not dictated by any military considerations," in which whole nations were moved from their native lands - the Karachai in 1943; the entire population of the Autonomous Kalmyk Republic in the same year; the Chechen and Ingush peoples in March 1944, with liquidation of their autonomous republic; and all Balkars in April 1944, their name being expunged from the Kabardino-Balkar Autonomous Republic. "Not only a Marxist-Leninist," he declared, "but also no man of common sense can grasp how it is possible to make whole nations responsible for inimical activity, including women, children, old people, Communists and Komsomols, to use mass repression against them, and to expose them to misery and suffering for the hostile acts of individual persons or groups of persons." (Wolfe, 1967, pp. 190-192).

Solzhenitsyn (1974-8, Vol. I, pp. 24-5) described the third wave of deportations from 1944-1946, "when they dumped whole nations down the sewer pipes, not to mention millions and millions of others who (because of us!) had been prisoners of war, or carried off to Germany and subsequently repatriated." This wave extends over a longer period, going back to the 1930s, when 30,000 Czechs were sent off to the northern camps. It included the 'social prophylaxis' of occupied terrorites, the nationalities which had transgressed or had been designated as treacherous (Kalmyks, Chechens, Ingush, Karachai, Balkars, Kurds, Crimean Tatars and finally Caucasian Greeks). Solzhenitsyn's list of exiled nations is more extensive than that given by Krushchev. There were deportations too, for example the deportation of the Volga Germans in 1941-1942, and this quite apart from the liquidation of national leaders in the Baltic States and the Western Ukraine.

The deportations of the 'transgressing' nations were carried out under conditions reminiscent of the German deportations. Many of the exiles died even before arriving at their destinations, and the survivors were subjected, in terms of the United Nation's definition of genocide, to conditions of life calculated to bring about their physical destruction in whole or in part. Nekrich (1978) offers the following minimum estimates of losses to 1959 - Chechens

22%, Kalmyks 14.8%, Ingush 9%, Karachai 30% and Balkars 26.5%. This represents an average loss of over 20% or almost one quarter of a million people. Medvedev (1977) gives a higher estimate of as many as 40% of the deported Chechens, Ingush, Crimean Tatars, Kalmyks, Volga Germans and others perishing from hunger, cold and epidemics in the uninhabited places in the east to which they were shipped by the trainload. These peoples have now been politically rehabilitated, but the Crimean Tatars, Soviet Germans and Meskhetians are still not allowed to return to their former homes (Sheehy & Nahaylo, 1980).

These mass murders fall within the scope of the Genocide Convention, but in addition, there were the mass murders of economic strata and political groups. The liquidation of economic classes, the bourgeoisie to be sure, but also the kulaks, and the liquidation of political groups and opponents, were on an immeasurably greater scale. The kulaks (loosely defined to include the rich, middle and even poor peasants, and all those who opposed collectivization, or incurred the enmity of the local activists), were mercilessly uprooted and dispossessed, and condemned to lethal conditions of transportation and resettlement. Solzhenitsyn writes that whole families were uprooted, whole nests burnt out; "and they watched jealously to be sure that none of the children - fourteen, ten, even six year old - got away; to the last scrapings, all had to go down the same road, to the same common destruction" (Vol. I, p. 55). They were banished "to the haunt of wild beasts into the wilderness, to man's primitive condition...Only the peasants were deported so ferociously, to such desolate places, with such frankly murderous intent; no one had been exiled in this way before, and no one would be in the future" (Vol. III, pp. 362-9). Estimates of the numbers who perished range from five million to fifteen, and this is without taking into account the many millions of peasants who starved to death in the artificially induced man-made famine of 1932-1933. Then there were the continuous purges of political groups, with victims including also Communist Party and State cadres, and purges of all manner of political opponents, real or fancied, in the consolidation of despotic power. Medvedev (1971) in an attempt to convey some of the enormity of the Great Purge between 1936 and 1939, compared it to the murders of past tyrants. The scale of the Stalinist terror, however, was immeasurably greater. "In 1936-9, on the most cautious estimates, four to five million people were subjected to repression for political reasons. At least four to five hundred thousand of them - above all the high officials - were summarily shot; the rest were given long terms of confinement. In 1937-8 there were days when up to a thousand people were shot in Moscow alone. These were not streams, these were rivers of blood, the blood of honest Soviet people. The simple truth must be stated: not one of the tyrants and despots of the past persecuted and destroyed so many of his compatriots" (p. 269).

In Indonesia, it was the Communists who were massacred in large numbers, following an attempted coup in October 1965. There is controversy on the question of whether the Indonesian Communist Party was involved in the planning of the coup, and if so, in what measure. The events themselves had all the appearance of a revolt by middle-ranking officers against the military supreme command, that is to say, of an internal army conflict. In any event, the Indonesian Communist Party was compromised in a number of ways, and the army, in repressing the coup, imposed its own judgment of Communist Party guilt.

The background to the massacres was largely a struggle for power between the Communist Party and the army. There was also conflict between the Communists and a powerful religious group, religious and ideological opposition being interwoven with class conflict. The army engaged actively in the massacres of Communists, participating directly in them, or indirectly, by organizing and arming civilian killers. Communists were sufficiently stable and sufficiently identifiable to serve as the target for slaughter. They were readily identified from party lists of members and, particularly in the villages, by intimate knowledge of political affiliation. Of course, the massacres extended beyond known affiliation, and gave the opportunity to settle private scores, and to draw in other categories, as in the killing of Chinese merchants and their families in North Sumatra. Estimates of the number of Communists and affiliates slaughtered range from 200,000 to over one million. In addition there were great waves of arrest, and detention for many years without trial.[10]

In Cambodia (Democratic Kampuchea), the country had been devastated by many years of civil war, and by massive American bombing, designed to root out Vietcong bases. When the revolutionary forces of the Khmer Rouge finally prevailed in April 1975, they faced a desperate food crisis, and great uncertainty in the consolidation of their power; and they proceeded ruthlessly with the liquidation of selected social strata, and with a most radical restructuring of the society. They immediately evacuated the capital Phnom Penh, which had been swollen by refugees to perhaps as many as three million. Its inhabitants and those of other towns were driven out in a gigantic mass migration, and exposed, with much loss of life, to extreme hardship, accompanied by summary executions, in the journey to their new work sites.

Persons associated with the previous regime were special targets for liquidation. In many cases, the executions included wives and children. There were summary executions too of intellectuals, such as doctors, engineers, professors, teachers and students, leaving the country denuded of professional skills. Vietnamese in Cambodia, and Cambodians trained in Vietnam as revolutionaries, also came under attack.

The revolution itself was most radical in its objectives. On 2 November 1978 Izvestia, in a full-scale attack on Kampuchea, charged that a special course, aimed at the construction of an historically unprecedented society, had been proclaimed - a society without cities, without property, without commodity-money relations, without markets and without money, without families. Those who were dissatisfied with the new regime were being 'eradicated,' along with

their families, by disembowelment, by beating to death with hoes, by
hammering nails into the backs of their heads and by other cruel
means of economizing on bullets. Responsibility for this 'monstrous
situation,' according to Izvestia, and for a cultural revolution
which had destroyed the old intelligentsia and the student class,
eliminated doctors and technical specialists, and completely wrecked
the educational system, stemmed from the importation of the wild
ideas of Mao Tse-tung.[11]

The whole country had indeed been turned into an agricultural
work-site, in which the people labored ceaselessly on irrigation
works, on the cultivation of rice and on other agricultural pur-
suits. Here their rulers subjected them to what the Sub-Commission
on Prevention of Discrimination described as 'draconian discipline'
in both work and private life. Sentimental ties were dissolved in
the separation of families, the indoctrination of children, the continuous surveillance, and the ubiquitous presence of spies in a system of collectivized labor and communal living. Exhaustion from
the extremely arduous work, malnutrition from minimal diets, starvation and disease took a heavy toll of lives; and to this must be added the ravages of the revolutionary terror, with its purges of prescribed categories, and later its purges of party cadres, and with
the easy resort to executions, carried out most brutally, for slight
infringements of discipline, or for complaints or criticism. This
was a regimented setting in which it was nearly impossible to escape
the 'guilt' of social origins or past affiliations.

There are no reliable statistics of the deaths. Perhaps as
many as two million or more of a population of seven million may
have died as a result of starvation, disease and massacre during the
rule of the Khmer Rouge from 1975 to 1979, when the Government was
overthrown by invading Vietnamese and rebel Cambodian troops.[12]

In Uganda, a murderous regime was establishing itself at about
the same time as the massacres in Burundi. The killings started immediately after a successful coup by Amin in January 1917, but did
not become internationally notorious for a few years. The first
issue which evoked international involvement was the decision by
Amin, in August 1972, to expel the Ugandan Asians on 90 days'
notice. They numbered some 75,000, of whom a third were Ugandan
citizens. Some exemption was accorded the citizens, who might
choose between expulsion or banishment to remote and arid areas,
where they could occupy themselves as farmers. The expulsions took
their course, uninhibited by outside concern. The victims were
brutally treated, a few were killed, and they were systematically
stripped of their possessions, which were distributed to, or seized
as booty by soldiers and other supporters of the regime.

In the meantime, the slaughter of Ugandans by a military usurp-
er was becoming more widely known. It was carried out mainly in the
consolidation of despotic power, and it extended to almost every
conceivable category of victim - ethnic, as in the massacre of
Acholi and Lango soldiers in the Ugandan army, and as in the mass-

acres of the Karamajong; political, in the annihilation of the supporters of the ousted president, and of political opponents in general; the educated elite; religious leaders, and their followers
too, notably Catholic; and much indiscriminate killing, random,
whimsical, impulsive, with massacres also of entire villages. The
killers came from sections of the army, and from security forces,
consisting mostly of Southern Sudanese mercenaries, of members of
Amin's own ethnic group, the Kakwa, and generally of Nubians inside
Uganda. Godfrey Lule, who had been Minister of Justice under Amin,
described the Nubians and the newly recruited Sudanese as exercising
"a foreign tyranny more vicious than anything dreamed of by European
imperialists or modern white minority governments in Africa"
(Kyemba, 1977, p. 7). Amin's murderous regime continued until he
invaded Tanzania, and was overthrown in a counter-invasion.[13]

There are many other contemporary cases of massive murder and
torture as routine instruments of despotic power - e.g., Argentina,
Chile, and El Salvador, - but not falling within the scope of the
Genocide Convention. In Guatemala, however, the massacres of Indians by the Government have assumed genocidal dimensions.

It is a vast toll of human destruction, of genocidal and political massacres, most of which take a relatively uninhibited course,
unrestrained by international intervention.

NOTES

1. United Nations, Human Rights Communication, No.478, 29 September,
1969.
2. For discussion of genocide against indigenous groups, see Richard
Arens, Genocide in Paraguay, Philadelphia, Temple University Press,
1966; John H. Bodley, Victims of Progress, Menlo Park, Cummings
Publishing Co., 1975; Shelton H. Davis, Victims of the Miracle:
Development and the Indians in Brazil, Cambridge, Cambridge University Press, 1977; Hugh O'Shaughnessy & Stephen Corry, What Future
for the Amerindians of South America? London, Minority Rights
Group, 1977; Survival International Supplement (Paraguay), June
1978; Survival International Review, Spring 1979 and Autumn/Winter
1980.
3. For discussion of these two genocides and background see Rene
Lemarchand, Rwanda and Burundi, New York, Praeger, 1970; Lemarchand
& Martin, Selective Genocide in Burundi, London, Minority Rights
Group, 1974; Jeremy Greenland, "Ethnic Discrimination in Rwanda and
Burundi" in Foundation for the Study of Plural Societies, Case
Studies on Human Rights and Fundamental Freedoms: A World Survey,
The Hague, Martinus Nijhof, IV, 1975, pp. 97-133; Warren Weinstein
& Robert Shrire, Political Conflict and Ethnic Strategies: A Case
Study of Burundi, Syracuse, The Program of Eastern African Studies,
Syracuse University, 1976; and Leo Kuper, The Pity of It All,
London, Duckworth, 1977, pp. 87-107 and 197-208.
4. See Indian Ministry of External Affairs, Bangla Desh Documents,
Madras, B.N.K. Press, 1971; Albert E. Levak, "Provincial Conflict
and Nation-Building in Pakistan;" in Wendell Bell & Walter E.
Freeman, (Eds.), Ethnicity and National Building, London, Sage

publications, 1974, pp. 203-222; Anthony Mascarenhas, The Rape of Bangla Desh, Delhi, Vikas Publications, 1971; W. H. Morris-Jones, "Pakistan Post-Mortem and the Roots of Bangladesh," Political Quarterly, 43 (April 1972), pp. 187-200; J. E. Owen, "East Pakistan, 1947-1971," Contemporary Review, 221 (July 1972), pp. 23-8; and Ben Whitaker, The Biharis in Bangladesh, London, Minority Rights Group, 1972.
5. On the Nigerian conflict, see A. H. M. Kirk-Greene, Crisis and Conflict in Nigeria, London University Press, 1971; Colin Legum, "The Massacre of the Proud Ibos," Observer, 16 October 1966, p. 12; P.C. Lloyd, "The Ethnic Background to the Nigerian Crisis," in S. K. Panter-Brick (Ed.), Nigerian Politics and Military Rule: Prelude to the Civil War, London, Institute of Commonwealth Studies, The Athlone Press, 1970; and John de St. Jorre, The Brothers' War: Biafra and Nigeria, Boston, Houghton Mifflin Co., 1972. On the Sudan conflict, see Oliver Albino, The Sudan: A Southern Viewpoint, London, Oxford University Press, 1970; Mohammed Omer Beshir, The Southern Sudan's Background to Conflict, Khartoum University Press, 1970; Sondra Hale, "Sudan Civil War: Religion, Colonialism and the World System," in Political and Social Origins, Boulder, Westview Press, 1978; Nelson Kasfir, Still Keeping the Peace, American University Field Staff Reports, Northeast Africa Series, Vol. XXI, No. 4 (April 1976); Edgar O'Ballance, The Secret War in the Sudan 1955-1972, Hamden, Connecticut, Archon Books, 1977; and Joseph Oduho & William Deng, The Problems of the Southern Sudan, London, Oxford University Press, 1963.
6. See my discussion of the statistics in my book, Genocide, pp. 113-4. For further reference on the Turkish genocide against the Armenians, see Viscount J. Bryce & Arnold Toynbee, The Treatment of Armenians in the Ottoman Empire, 1915-1916, London, HMSO, 1916; Gerard Chaliand & Yves Ternon, Genocide des Armeniens, Brussels, Complexe, 1980; Richard G. Hovanissian, Armenia on the Road to Independence, Berkeley, University of California Press, 1967; and "The Critics' View: Beyond Revisionism," International Journal of Middle East Studies, (9 August, 1978), pp. 379-388; Johannes Lepsius, Le rapport secret du Johannes Lepsius...sur les massacres d'Armenie, Paris, Payout, 1918; Henry Morgenthau, Ambassador Morgenthau's Story, New York, Doubleday, 1918; Stanford J.Shaw & Ezel Kural Shaw, History of the Ottoman Empire and Modern Turkey, Cambridge, University Press, 1976-1977, and "The Authors Respond," International Journal of Middle East Studies 9(August 1978), pp. 388-400; and David Marshall Lang & Christopher Walker, The Armenians, London, Minority Rights Group, 1981.
7. There is controversy over the question whether the genocide was part of the original plan. See Helen Fein, Accounting for Genocide, New York, Free Press, pp. 23-24.
8. See for example, Jean-Paul Sartre, "On Genocide," Ramparts (February 1968), pp. 37-42 and Hugo Adam Bedau, "Genocide in Vietnam" in Virginia Held, Sidney Morgenbesser & Thomas Nagel, Philosophy, Morality and International Affairs, New York, Oxford University Press, 1974, pp. 5-46.
9. M. G. Smith has an interesting discussion of the different patterns of warfare of three Nguni segments, in which he emphasizes the role of structural factors in genocide ("Pluralism in Pre-Colonial

46

African Societies" in Leo Kuper & M. G. Smith, Pluralism in Africa, Berkeley, University of California Press, 1969, pp. 118-121).
10. For further discussion of the Indonesian massacres, see Benedict R. Anderson & Ruth I. McVey, A Preliminary Analysis of the October 1, 1965 Coup in Indonesia, Ithaca, Southeast Asia Program, Cornell University, 1971; Carmel Budiardjo, "The Abuse of Human Rights in Indonesia," in Foundation for the Study of Plural Societies, op. cit., Vol. III, pp. 209-41; Leslie Palmier, Communism in Indonesia, New York, Doubleday, 1973; and W. F. Wertheim, "Indonesia Before and After the Untung Coup," Pacific Affairs, Vol. 39, 1 and 2 (Spring-Summer 1966), pp. 115-127.
11. The Current Digest of the Soviet Press, Vol XXX, No. 34 (20 September 1978), p. 17 and No. 44 (29 November 1978), p. 12.
12. For discussion of the background to the conflict and the massacres, see Francois Debre, Cambodge: la revolution de la foret, Paris, Flammarion, 1976; Francois Ponchaud, Cambodia Year Zero, Harmondsworth, Penguin, 1978; John Barron & Anthony Paul, Peace with Horror, London, Hodder and Stoughton, 1977; George Hildebrand & Gareth Porter, Cambodia - Starvation and Revolution, New York, Monthly Review Press, 1976; William Shawcross, Sideshow: Kissinger, Nixon and the Destruction of Cambodia, New York, Simon and Schuster, 1979; "Cambodia: Nightmare Without End," Far Eastern Economic Review, 100 (14 April 1978), pp. 32-4. and "The Third Indochina War," New York Review of Books (6 April 1978), pp. 15-22; and Noam Chomsky & Edward S. Herman, After the Cataclysm: Postwar Indo-China and the Reconstruction of Imperial Ideology, Nottingham, Spokesman, 1979.
13. For discussion of Amin's rule, see International Commission of Jurists, Violations of Human Rights and the Rule of Law in Uganda, Geneva, 1974, and Uganda and Human Rights, Reports to the United Nations, Geneva, 1977; Amnesty International, The Human Rights Situation in Uganda, London, 1977; and David Martin, General Amin, London, Faber, 1974.

REFERENCES

ARLEN, Michael J. Passage to Ararat. New York: Farrar, Straus & Giroux, 1971.
FEIN, Helen. Accounting for Genocide. New York: The Free Press, 1979.
HILBERG, Raul. The Destruction of the European Jews. Chicago: Quadrangle Books, 1961.
INTERNATIONAL Commission of Jurists. The Events in East Pakistan, 1971. Geneva: 1972.
KUPER, Leo. Genocide. New Haven: Yale University Press, 1982, & London: Penguin Books, 1981.
KYEMBA, Henry. State of Blood, with a preface by Godfrey Lule. London: Transworld Publishers, 1977.
LEWIS, Norman. The Camp at Cecilio Baez. In Richard Arens, (Ed.), Genocide in Paraguay. Philadelphia: Temple University Press, 1976.
MEDVEDEV, Roy A. Let History Speak. New York: Alfred A. Knopf, 1971.

MEDVEDEV, Roy A. New Pages from the political biography of Stalin. In Robert C. Tucker (Ed.), Stalinism: Essays in Historical Interpretation. New York: Norton.

NEKRICH, Alexsandr M. The Punished Peoples: The Deportation and Fate of Soviet Minorities at the End of the Second World War. New York: Norton, 1978, p. 138.

SHEEHY Ann, & Nahaylo, Bohdan. The Crimean Tatars, Volga Germans, and Meskhetians. London: Minority Rights Group, 1980.

SOLZHENITSYN, Aleksander I. The Gulag Archipelago. New York: Harper and Row, 1974-8. Vols. I-III.

TOYNBEE, Arnold. Experiences London: Oxford University Press, 1969.

WOLFE, Bertram D. Khrushchev and Stalin's Ghost. New York: Praeger, 1967.

LEO KUPER, Ph.D., Dept. Sociology, University California, Los Angeles, California 90024, U.S.A.

Part II

Case Studies

3. Pol Pot's Cambodia: Was It Genocide?

David Hawk

David Hawk is a former Executive director of Amnesty International U.S.A. and a Consultant to Amnesty on U.S. ratification of the Genocide Convention and International Human Rights Covenants. Mr. Hawk was Director of the Khmer Program (Bangkok Thailand) for the World Conference on Religion and Peace. Currently Mr. Hawk is Adjunct Lecturer, Hunter College, CUNY and associate of the Center for the Study of Human Rights, Columbia University where he is conducting research on events in Cambodia during the Khmer Rouge regime. This paper is based on two field research trips to Cambodia and a version of this paper appeared in THE NEW REPUBLIC, Nov. 15, 1982.

It is well known that the Khmer Rouge reign in Cambodia constituted one of the most massive violations of human rights in the postwar world.[1] In three-and-a-half years, from mid-1975 to the end of 1978, an estimated one million (probably too low) to three million (probably too high) of approximately seven million Cambodians died from executions and combinations of induced starvation, preventable disease and exhaustion from forced marches and compulsory labor under draconian conditions.

Also known are the broad outlines of Khmer Rouge policy – the cruel urban evacuations, the execution of former government functionaires, army personnel and the intelligentsia, communalization of living and eating, the separation of families, forced marriages, the abolition of money, the destruction of religion, and so on.

However, although the gross facts are well known, the Pol Pot genocide has received scant attention except from relief and refugee workers and a handful of scholars and journalists who have seen for themselves the results.

The period of mass murders by Pol Pot's regime was somehow left shrouded in mystery and was allowed to be overshadowed by the Cambodian famine and refuge crisis of 1978-81, and the political conflict that followed the ouster of Pol Pot's Khmer Rouge by the Vietnamese and a dissident Khmer Rouge faction led by Heng Samrin.

There is very little documentation, interpretation or, most importantly, reaction to what was, arguably, in terms of magnitude and proportion the worst human destruction since the Holocaust.

The most informative and available materials on the human toll in Cambodia are based on 1975-76 refugees accounts gathered in the 1978 Submissions to the U.N. Human Rights Commission by the governments of Australia, Canada, Great Britain and the United States and the nongovernmental organizations, the International Commission of Jurists and Amnesty International.[2] But the Human Rights Commission managed to avoid a requested report based on these materials by the Chairman of its Subcommission, a body of experts that concluded that the situation in Cambodia was the "most serious that had occurred anywhere in the world since nazism" and was "nothing less than autogenocide."[3]

The Politicization and Denial of the Mass Murders

The Vietnamese-advised successor Khmer government in Phnom Penh tried and convicted in absentia Pol Pot and Ieng Sary for genocide. However the most valuable part of that effort, reportedly 900 pages of personal testimony and evidence, is not widely available and cannot be obtained in Phnom Penh.

The Vietnamese have submitted the tribunal's indictment and verdict against their former fraternal comrades to the U.N. Human Rights Commission.[4] Though thoroughly prepared, these documents have been largely dismissed. In fact the problem of genocide is now treated to the spectacle of human rights complaints being filed by Democratic Kampuchea, the Khmer Rouge, which is the ousted but still internationally recognized government for Cambodia. When the Khmer Rouge were in power they had promised to make "mincemeat" of the impudent affrontery and criminal maneuvers of the imperialist, partisan U.N. Human Rights Commission. The conflicting propaganda welter of charges and countercharges serve mostly to cancel each other out, and cynical politicization skews the debate.

The Soviet block which was not interested in U.N. consideration of the Cambodian situation while it was happening now has discovered how bloody it all was. On the other hand, some of the Western democracies which knew before what was happening now find it politically inconvenient to recall the mass murders. While enough information reached the outside world about the terrible human destruction while it was going on, the international community failed to believe and failed to respond. The United Nations having again 'risen above principle'[5] and ducked the issue, the Khmer people may face the same fate as the Armenians, unable to secure historical and international recognition that 'their' genocide even took place.

TRIP TO CAMBODIA

A recent trip to Cambodia, my second since 1979, afforded an opportunity for a first hand look at the aftermath. Inside Cambodia, as in the refugee camps in Thailand, the most direct way to find out about Pol Pot's policies is to talk to just about anybody. It is very difficult (and I did not) to find a Cambodian who did not lose family members or friends to Khmer Rouge policy and executioners. More systematic and extensive interviewing by a Japanese reporter with his own translator and by Khmer-speaking Cambodia scholars shows a surprisingly high proportion of people taken away for execution as opposed to deaths from malnutrition, sickness and exhaustion.

There are mass graves, fields of sunken or now emptied pits where variously hundreds to thousands of the executed were buried. A number of these mass graves have been opened, originally to count the skulls and multiply by the number of pits to estimate the number of dead at the site, now to collect and pile the skulls and bones into protected little (or not so little - one I saw had eight thousand skulls) enclosures where traditional Buddhist funeral rites are performed so as to allow the deceased spirits more peaceful passage into the Buddhist afterlife (no religious rites were allowed during the Khmer Rouge rule).

If these memorials survive the tropical elements and passage of time, it is also probably the only way this terrible era can be preserved to be remembered. Relief workers and foreign observers who saw the graves in the process of disinterment, as did I in 1981, were well advised to do so early in the morning before the midday tropical heat made the stench of human death unbearable.

I visited six of these mass grave sites in four provinces sometimes in areas so remote that armed escorts are provided (Khmer Rouge guerillas are trying to make a comeback) and passengers have to help push the cars over and around gulleys in the dirt roads. I was to have visited two other normally accessible grave sites, but early monsoon rains in Battambang province rendered the roads impassable except for jeeps and oxcarts.

In Phnom Penh there is presently no information about mass grave sites as to locations and estimates of numbers buried, when discovered or opened, etc., but provincial officials, relief workers, and office translators speak of numerous sites. The image of Pol Pot's Cambodia as a land of graveyards is a plausible one. Those so buried would not be the old, young and sick that died along the road during the forced evacuations and marches, or those who died of malnutrition, preventable or curable sickness, or from forced labor, but those deliberately executed. The Khmer Rouge boasted of "great victories thanks to our decision to track down and liquidate enemies in a systematic way," and as Ieng Sary "Democratic Kampuchea's" Foreign Minister explained, the situation was one of class struggle and proletarian dictatorship.

The Records of Deaths at Tuol Sleng

As would benefit a third world peasant country with one of the lowest per capita incomes in the world, most deliberate murder was anonymous and without record. Yet Cambodia was not without its Nazi-like bureaucracy of torture and death, its Asian equivalent of Auschwitz. At the Tuol Sleng, or "S21" prison-execution center in Phnom Penh, Khmer Rouge officials kept meticulous records of these murders, records which were left behind when the Vietnamese captured the city in 1979. There are documents on more than fourteen thousand persons, but the materials for June to December 1978 are missing, so it is estimated that perhaps fifteen to twenty thousand were processed to their deaths at Tuol Sleng.

"S21" was a former school with three four-storey buildings. A number of classrooms were used as common cells where usually forty to seventy, but occasionally up to one hundred persons, were kept in rows shackeled in leg irons. Other classrooms on separate floors were subdivided into tiny cinderblock cubicles, sixteen or eighteen to a room where important prisoners or those undergoing interrogation were isolated, also restrained by leg irons attached to chains cemented into the floor. "S21" held an average of one thousand to fifteen hundred prisoners at any one time.

Forty different categories of men, women, and children, including captured foreigners, workers, intellectuals, but mostly Khmer Rouge officials and cadre suspected of dissidence were brought to be photographed, interrogated and tortured into abjectly confessing to be agents for the CIA or KGB, naming their contacts, meeting places and accomplices, and then executed. It was the sort of place where former guards were, in turn, themselves, executed.

Officials of the successor Cambodian government in Phnom Penh have made the Tuol Sleng prison into a museum of the Cambodian nightmare, not without an overlay of the grotesque - in this case a huge wall map of Cambodia constructed of skulls wired together; superfluous after having walked through the interrogation and cell rooms and having seen the leg irons, torture implements and terribly haunting photographs of victims. Perhaps more suitably, there are plans and architects' drawing some day to convert adjacent land into a memorial park.

The former prison rooms on the upper floor of the central building now house the nearly one hundred thousand pages of handwritten confessions, typed summaries of the confessions, typed execution schedules and the mug shot photographs. Phnom Penh officials have allowed scholars access to these documents and hopefully forthcoming translations and analyses will afford a revealing, if partial, glimpse into the pathology of the Khmer Rouge regime. Cambodians come to search among the thousands of photographs, some of which line the ground floor walls, looking for missing relatives. Now a stop at Tuol Sleng is a regular part of any international visitors tour of Phnom Penh. And rightly so in the same sense that tourists to Israel ought not fail to visit Yad Vashem.

WERE THE MASS MURDERS IN CAMBODIA GENOCIDE?

Cambodia under Pol Pot was ruled by terror and racked by death. But was it genocide? The answer depends on words, numbers and law.

Genocide is an elastic concept - at its core it refers to the Final Solution; when stretched it includes many phenomena like the deaths of indigeneous peoples at the hands of colonialization or U.S. war policies in Vietnam; taken to its extreme it includes forced cultural assimilation. "Genocide" like "human" and "rights" gets blurred when philosophers and sociologists get a hold of it. "Genocide" is a recent word, coined by Raphael Lemkin whose bust now graces the   U.S. Mission to the United Nations. Its literal meaning is clear enough: the killing (Greek, <u>cide</u>) of a people/race/tribe (Latin, <u>genos</u>); its commonsense usage is most often that of very large scale massacres.

The international lawyers and diplomats who drafted the U.N. Genocide Convention, the first of the post World War II human rights measures preceding even that of the Universal Declaration of Human Rights, provided a flawed but necessary and unavoidable definition when they sought to make "this odious scourge" a criminal act under international law.   In the terms of Convention, the "Contracting Parties," now more than ninety nation-states that have ratified or acceded to the treaty, agree that what constitutes genocide are international acts that include killing, causing bodily harm, or deliberately inflicting conditions of life calculated to bring about the physical destruction in whole or in part of a national, ethnical racial or religious group.

The Genocide Convention is limited because the final text does not protect against genocidal acts against political, social, or economic groups, thus apparently allowing contracting nation-states to eliminate in whole or in part their political or class enemies. Obviously, a great deal of Khmer Rouge killing was precisely to this end.

However, in Cambodia there were also targets who are specifically enumerated and covered by the Convention who were the objects of executions, massacres and other acts calculated to bring about their destruction. Such was the case in regards to at least one major ethnic minority group, the Cham; and also the preeminent religious group in Cambodia, the Buddist monkhood.

The Cham

The Cham, an Islamic practicing non-Khmer minority group, originally from the historical kingdom of Champa, migrated to Cambodia during the 15th and 18th Centuries from the central coastal regfion of what is now Vietnam and settled mostly in the Cambodian provinces of Kompong Cham and Kandal.   Under Pol Pot there was a deliberate policy to "Khmerize" the Cham.   Formerly living together in their own villages and communities, the Chams were dispersed among the overall population.   Their community and religious leaders were executed, Islamic practices and the speaking of Arabic were rigorously and strictly prohibited. They were forced to eat pork as a test of loyalty, and their dead were buried "upside down," that is, not facing Mecca.   There are reports of entire villages being slaughtered, and only roughly two hundred thousand of a pre-1975 population generally estimated at four to five hundred thousand appear to have survived.

Generally corroborating stories of the destruction of the Cham are available from early 1975-76 refugee accounts, post-1979 refugee accounts, testimony presented at the 1979 Phnom Penh tribunal, and survivors in Cambodia interviewed by scholars and journalists.

The Buddhist Monkhood

Another case of a genocidal act, narrowly construed, is the destruction of the Buddhist monkhood. There was under the Khmer Rouge a general animus against religion, "reactionary" religion being prohibited in the Democratic Kampuchean constitution. The Catholic cathedral in Phnom Penh, apparently a symbol of French colonialism and Vietnamese colonization, was removed stone by stone from its former site on Monivong Avenue. Protestant churches and Muslim mosques were destroyed or converted into warehouses.

This animus fell most heavily on Buddhism, not only the former established state religion, but for centuries the focus of learning, transmitter of culture and center of village life in the countryside where most Cambodians lived before the U.S. bombing and Lon Nol-Khmer Rouge war drove people to the cities.

Buddha statues and holy objects were desecrated and destroyed as was most Buddhist literature. Buddhist temples were converted into warehouses or workshops, or more often destroyed – not so much in the cities from which people had been evacuated, but in the countryside. Worship, prayer, meditation and "merit making" were prohibited. The monkhood, which is to Therevada Buddhism what the priesthood is to Catholicism, was forcibly disrobed and decimated. Of an estimated pre-1975 population of sixty thousand monks, only eight hundred to one thousand survived and returned to their former monastery sites, where now bamboo and thatch temples arise on the foundations of the destroyed temples that once were a fixture of the Cambodian landscape. Conversations with surviving Monks inside Cambodia and in the refugee camps reveal regional variations but tell the same basic story: the most venerated monks were taken away for execution, others died of malnutrition, sickness and exhaustion, others were forced to marry, and many others were sent to their native villages or elsewhere and their fate is unknown – except that they did not return to rejoin the remnant monkhood.

Apart from the substantial destruction of groups clearly covered by the U.N. Genocide Convention, the overall situation in Cambodia needs to be seen on a continuum of repression – a scale that moves from miscarriage of justice at one end, to gross violations of human rights, to widespread or systematic political massacre or induced death that can reach such genocidal magnitude and proportion that the very existence of a substantial part of the nation is threatened.

Did the overall situation in Cambodia reach genocidal magnitude and proportions? The demographers and Khmer scholars need to develop the statistics more precisely. However, though it is not without academic criticism, the most sophisticated study available is Kampuchea: A Demographic Disaster by the U.S. National Foreign Assessment Center, in which the CIA estimates an absolute or gross population decline of 1.2 million to 1.8 million Cambodians during the three-and-one half years under Pol Pot.[6] In as much as there were births during these years, the number of deaths would be higher than these figures. The CIA range may also be low in that its calculations do not take into account that 1978 was an unusually bloody year even by Khmer Rouge standards.

Whether or not human destruction of this magnitude and proportion - one-seventh to two-sevenths of the Cambodian population (the Heng Samrin government's figures would be three-sevenths) - fits the Genocide Convention's provision vis-a-vis the partial destruction of a "national group" is something legalists can consider, as they will. However, as one legal scholar observes in regard to Cambodia, "This type of murder is precisely the type of crime the Convention was intended to prevent."[7] While it may be argued that the Genocide Convention refers to willful extermination by one people of another people, it can also be argued that there is no language in the Convention that rules out responsibility when mass murders are carried out by a nation's leaders against its own population.

ENFORCING THE GENOCIDE CONVENTION

Definitions aside, clearly the most important consideration has to be finding the will and means to deter and restrain recurring outbursts of large scale political massacre.

From this point of view it does not matter so much what the human destruction in Cambodia is called, so long as it is not swept under the international rug. Yet, the Genocide Convention remains particularly relevant to Cambodia, because unlike, for example, Uganda or Ruanda-Burundi, Cambodia - that is "Democratic Cambodia" is really a State or Contracting Party to the Genocide Convention. Unlike the subsequent international human rights treaties, the 1948 Genocide Convention, based on the revulsion against genocide of European Jewry and the Nuremberg experience, introduces the notion, if not the means, of punishment of those responsible for committing genocide "whether they are constitutionally responsible rulers, public officials, or private individuals." Yet Democratic Kampuchea remains the internationally recognized government for Cambodia and Ieng Sary, usually considered number two man in the Khmer Rouge comes to the U.N. to represent Cambodia while his brother-in-law, Pol Pot, remains the presumed head of the again clandestine Khmer Rouge Communist Party and proclaimed public commander of its guerilla army.

Surviving and exiled Khmer intellectuals and other Cambodian scholars may attempt to explicate the whys and wherefores in several ways. One explanation is that the policies of Cambodia's rulers can be explained as the work of fanatical utopians, educated in highly theoretical Parisian Marxism and influenced by Maoist theories of radical autarchy and cultural revolution, attempting to remold a social structure shattered by war from a system of feudalism to one of communism without the intervening stages of capitalism and socialism. Another is that the destruction stemmed from mundane attempts to solidify power after the 1975 takeover, by eliminating the social base of potential opposition, extending central domination to outlying areas, and maintaining control against insurgents and personal power struggles. As more information becomes available, sociologists and historians can examine the extent to which the violence of language (not that Asian Marxist rhetoric is prone to understatement) and dehumanizing categories, such as "Khmer bodies with Vietnamese minds" that seem to be common to genocidal situations fit the Cambodian experience.

However, the major and pressing lessons to be learned from examinations of the Cambodian genocide are not only, or primarily, for Cambodia nor are they for purposes of history or scholarship. Large scale political murder and genocide are terrible real life events that must be stopped, not just talked about or studied after the fact. Genocide is not synonymous with the Holocaust alone, or with other events of World War II. Genocides are major and severe problems of the world of the 1970s and the 1980s: Cambodia, East Timor, Uganda, East Pakistan, Paraguay, Burundi, Chile, Argentina, El Salvador, Guatemala, etc. The murders are in the millions.

The globe is a shrinking place, and as far as lip service goes, human rights are an increasingly accepted principle. In practice, however, the worst violations of human rights are not dealt with. Despite all of the post World War II human rights laws, policies and organizations, society is least able and willing to deal with or do anything effective about genocide. To an extent, this is to be expected. But that should not make it acceptable.

Cambodia, like some of the other worst case violations of the 1970's, also demonstrates the relationship of gross human rights violations to threats to the peace and international conflict. It took three years to get Cambodia even on the agenda of the U.N. and another year and scores of thousands of additional deaths for Cambodia to be considered. Surely this demonstrates the need for more systematic and comprehensive international monitoring of political assasination by governments and an early warning system to render some protection or at least protest on behalf of those whose lives are endangered.

That the perpetrators of mass murder and genocidal acts against the Cambodian people remain the internationally recognized and acceptable representatives for Cambodia demonstrates again the suspension - for political convenience - of the well-established principle in international law of governmental accountability for the murder of its citizens. It is difficult to see how murder by government can be retarded or halted as long as this is so.

Cambodia, like Uganda, shows that we need better ways of stopping the carnage and securing relief than through the armies of neighboring powers. For Cambodia, and the geopolitical conflict that now engulfs it, it remains to be explained how the issue of Cambodian self-determination and freedom from Vietnamese occupation can be constructively approached without first dealing with the unresolved problem of the Khmer Rouge genocide and preventing the return to power of those who committed it.

NOTES

1. See John Barron, & Anthony Paul, Murder in a Gentle Land, New York: Readers Digest Press, 1977; and Francois Ponchaud, Cambodia: Year Zero, New York: Holt Rinehart & Winston, 1978.
2. Australia, UN Doc. E/CN.4/Sub.2/414/Add.8 20 Sept. 1978
  Canada, UN Doc. E/CN.4/Sub.2/414/Add.1 14 August 1978 and E/CN.4/Sub.2/424/Add.7 8 Sept. 1978
  Great Britain, UN Doc. E/CN.4/Sub.2/414/Add.3 17 August 1978
  Norway, UN Doc. E/CN.4/Sub.2/414/Add.2 18 August 1978
  United States, UN Doc. E/CN.4/414/Add.4 14 August 1978
  Amnesty International, UN Doc. E/CN.4/414/Add.5 15 August 1978
  International Commission of Jurists, UN Doc. E/CN.4/Sub.2/414/Add.6
3. UN Document E/CN.4/SR.1510
4. UN Documents A/34/568; A/34/569; and A/C.3/34/1 Oct. 11 1979
5. Leo Kuper, Genocide, Middlesex, England: Penguin Books, 1981, p. 172.
6. Kampuchea: A Demographic Catastrophe. National Foreign Assessment Center, Director of Public Affairs, Central Intelligence Agency, Washington, D.C. 20505, GC 80 10019U, May 1980.
7. Professor David Weissbrodt, University of Minnesota Law School, letter to U.S. Sen. William Proxmire, April 19, 1979, p. 5.

DAVID HAWK, 251 W. 87 St., New York, N.Y. 10014, U.S.A.

4. The Soviet Gulag: Is It Genocidal?

Lyman H. Legters

Professor of Russian and East European Studies, School of International Studies, University of Washington, and Senior Fellow, William O. Douglas Institute, Seattle. A specialist in modern social thought, Legters has published widely on the history of Marxism and is currently working on a study of Marxism and Zionism. He has edited a conference volume, WESTERN SOCIETY AFTER THE HOLOCAUST, published in 1983 by Westview Press for the Douglas Institute (formerly the Institute for the Study of Contemporary Social Problems).

The deadliest society of the modern world, and by a considerable margin it would seem, has been the Soviet Union. It would have serious competition, of course, if the reckoning were done in per capita terms. But in sheer numbers over a comparatively short period of time, the country that was to show the way towards human emancipation has become instead the most life-threatening environment of the epoch.

Without entering into the controversies that surround all such estimates, some general magnitudes will suffice to make the point. Demographic evidence suggests that some 50 million unnatural deaths may have occurred in the Soviet Union between 1927 and 1958 (Dyadkin). This takes no account of the Revolution itself, which was despite its chaos not especially costly of human life, or of the Civil War, which was much more costly. It also leaves out the two more recent decades in which an essentially Stalinist penal system has continued to exact a heavy toll. And it takes no account of secondary effects in recent years when, according to more contemporary demographic study (Davis and Feshbach, 1980), rising infant morality and reduced life expectancy in virtually all age groups of the Soviet population may be ascribed to more "natural" causes such as alcoholism and poor medical care (Eberstadt, 1981).

For the three decades in question here, some 15 of the 50 million people may have perished, mostly in the countryside as a consequence of forced collectivization, between 1929 and 1936. Over four million lives were claimed during the so-called Great Purge of 1937-38; and in 1939-40, nearly two million more deaths occurred as a combined result of continued purge and the Winter War against Finland. (In the collectivization period, men and women suffered about equally, but at the height of the repression that followed, males were disproportionately affected and the reduced proportion of males in the total population is one of the bases for certain of the demographic estimates.)

The official figure for casualties, military and civilian, in World War II is 20 million persons killed by fighting or related deprivation, a figure that presumably includes the 1.5 million Soviet Jewish victims of the Nazi Holocaust as it was carried out on Russian soil. Demographic indicators suggest that another ten million died, mostly in the forced labor camps (the Gulag), in the same period. And another half million lives were lost to the Gulag by the time of Stalin's death in 1953. Solzhenitsyn (1973, 1975, 1978) asserts that a single forced labor camp claimed more victims in Stalin's era than did all of the Tsar's prisons in the nineteenth century. And Conquest (1978) concludes that Kolyma had more victims than Auschwitz.

Of lives lost through causes unrelated to military action during the period of Stalin's ascendancy, we are then probably talking about nearly 30 million victims of Soviet penology and repression, only a tiny fraction of whom could be considered ordinary or non-political criminals. In fairness it must be conceded, although it softens the verdict only slightly, that there is such a thing as death from natural causes and dying of old age in the Gulag, but in general it makes as little sense to speak of natural death in the camps as it does to speak of life there as natural; or as it does to regard a life of enslavement in the silver mines of Potosi or of confinement on a barren reservation as promoting "normal" life expectancy.

It matters very little for our purposes what proportion of victims actually perished in the labor camps. Even if the majority of the deaths occurred through random shootings of kulaks or the inability of portions of ethnic groups to survive the conditions surrounding sudden, forced migration, the Gulag remains, as Solzhenitsyn so well delineates, the centerpiece of Stalin's punitive system, the marriage of imprisonment and exile that was Russian before it was Soviet, a social institution deliberately fashioned to accomplish specifiable official purposes:

1. to punish at minimal social cost and with little embarrassing visibility those elements of Soviet society that opposed, or were presumed to oppose, that were out of step with, or thought to be so, the official party and governmental policies of the moment;

2. to accomodate large numbers and sizable groups, often discernibly ethnic or religious, that would overtax any prison system and that could be turned to marginally productive economic activity for which no available incentive would have been efficacious;

3. to terrorize, by means of the scale and capriciousness of penalization, the rest of the population into quiescence or passivity; and

4. to serve as a massive burial ground for society at large - in the sense that, notwithstanding completions of sentences, amnesties, and occasional rehabilitations, camp conditions were calculated to insure, as many besides Solzhenitsyn have testified, that death would usually foreclose a return to society.

In short, the Stalinist system was designed for slaughter and the Gulag, as the pivotal punitive institution, merely attenuated the appearance of massacre by prolonging the process sufficiently to extract a measure of productivity obtainable in no other way short of traditional enslavement. For a number of years, to be sure the primary aim of forced labor was economic, mainly extractive, under circumstances that only a species of slave labor would tolerate. But for most of Stalin's reign, the evidence is overwhelming that the principal product of the camp system was death, products such as gold and timber occupying a decidedly secondary rank.

But slaughter, regardless of scale, is not automatically genocide. The dilemma that arises at this point stems from the penumbral associations of the concept of genocide, which, from the time of Raphael Lemkin's campaign to make it an international crime, have sought to imply an offense of nearly unique barbarity. Some of the rhetorical impact of a charge of genocide would clearly be lost if a slaughter of Stalinist immensity and the penal system that was its primary instrument were found to fall entirely outside the meaning of genocide. It does not follow of course that any large-scale loss of life by natural calamity or military engagement or human accident must be termed genocide for that concept to retain its impact. But where deliberate action, by a government or an organized movement, leads to predictably mass loss of life - a notable instance of which would plainly be the Soviet Gulag - there is an understandable urge to include it within a category of especially heinous crime.

At the same time, from Lemkin's campaign forward, and including the final phrasing of the Genocide Convention, the crime in question was intended to be specific with respect to its incidence: genocide is a crime against identifiable groups - national, ethnic, religious - of sufficient scope and import as to threaten the survival of that group in recognizable form. (I take this to be the intended implication of the ambiguous "in whole or in part" of the Convention; the part - be it the political leadership of the Polish nation, the inhabitants of Hiroshima, or the intellectual elite of a national liberation struggle - must be numberous and crucial enough that its liquidation threatens the survival of the parent group). Thus, the eradication of large numbers of people randomly chosen or implicated would not count as genocide even if it far exceeded the numerical scope of a liquidation directed at a group of appropriate sort.

TENSION BETWEEN INCLUSIVENESS AND SPECIFICITY

The tension between inclusiveness and specificity calls to mind two other terms of current political discourse that are, in contrasting ways, fairly analogous. "Institutional racism" refers to a racism of outcome, one that does not depend, either for its demonstration or its very existence, on the identification of evil persons with villianous intentions as agents of the result. It is a term that purchases its definite meaning at the cost of rhetorical impact. Racism without identifiable villians is a comparatively mild-sounding transgression. Cutting in the opposite direction, "totalitarianism" entered our vocabulary as a way of classifying the singular horrors of Hitlerism and Stalinism, emphasizing the resemblances that, at least in certain respects, outweighed their ideological dissonances. By using that term promiscuously (as we commonly do) to include whatever we do not like, we have preserved its emotional impact at the price of precision. In all cases, including that of genocide, I would argue for the narrower and more precise construction.

For that reason, I would also side with the Soviet representatives, who in the debate on the Genocide Convention, struggled to exclude political groups from the official definition. Although I certainly do not endorse the companion premise of the Soviet brief, that genocide should be inseparably linked to fascism, and although I am quite aware of the widespread tendency to liquidate political opponents, the notion of political groups strikes me as too slippery for even the largely hortatory juridical practices of the United Nations. By the same token, while it is true, as Kuper (1982) maintains, that there are assorted ways of destroying the basis for a group's recognizable existence, cultural and territorial, for example, as well as biological, I am inclined, at least so long as the murderous forms of genocide are so much with us, to side with Horowitz (1982) in focusing on outright physical liquidation as the core of any viable concept of genocide. (I shall, on the other hand, argue presently on the basis of Soviet practice that the U.N. definition is seriously deficient on another count.)

Returning now to the Soviet Gulag and its surrounding punitive habits, it seems clear that we face at least one instance of genocide within the limits of the current U.N. definition. Samizdat literature requently refers to the high incidence, indeed striking over-representation, of Soviet nationalities and minorities in the Gulag. The Baltic peoples, ethnic groups from the Caucacus and the Crimea, Jews, Christians, and other identifiable groups are so conspiciously overrepresented in the camps, and therewith in the predictable outcome of Gulag existence, as to give rise to an inescapable presumption of threat to the very survival of those groups in recognizable form. Solzhenitsyn and Alexsandr Nekrich (1978) both document the dreadul measures - a combination of forced resettlement and Gulag sentences - taken against Koreans, Finns, Chechens, Crimean Tartars, Kalmyks, and others. Even though some groups, Germans and Greeks for example, survived and prospered after resettlement, the forced migrations were so murderous in their execution as to qualify as genocidal, and after Solzhenitsyn what more needs to be said of the Gulag where so many of them landed? The Jews, Solzhenitsyn believes, were next on Stalin's list as death overtook him.

As one European observer of Soviet nationality politics has noted, the first phase of the policy for constituent national groups - that of encouraging and facilitating cultural identity and aspirations - has been a grand success, whereas the second phase - that of submerging or assimilating all constituent groups into a Soviet supernationality - has failed dismally (Carrere d'Encausse, 1981). The coincidence of that failure with the implementation of measures amounting to genocidal assault is suggestive with respect to other aspects of wholesale victimization in Soviet history.

"GENOCIDAL" POLICY AND PRACTICES - AND STRICTER LEGAL DEFINITION OF GENOCIDE

The first direction in which the coincidence of policy frustration and draconian response points, so far as the Stalinist system was concerned, is toward a distinction between the nominative and adjectival usage. A genocide is a fait accompli, recognizable because it has already happened. "Genocidal" may refer simply to the policies and practices associated with that genocide. But the adjectival form may, alternatively, refer to a tendency that might issue in a genocide. There is, I think, no sense in which the virtual elimination of the Old Bolshevik leadership in the Great Purge could count as genocide, murderously effective though it was (Conquest, 1968). But it would not be absurd to describe the elimination of a fancied threat to Stalin's dictatorship as genocidal in the sense of manifesting a willingness to use the penal system for mass slaughter when the dictatorship deemed it necessary or desirable. Such an adjectival usage in 1938 might have functioned as a signal, a kind of early warning system, that similar measures would be taken against an ethnic or religious group regarded as a threat or a potential opposition to the regime's policies. A comprehensive early warning system (see the concept of a Genocide Early Warning System in Charny, 1982) would require much more than the intuitive reading of a single symptom, but it could well be built out of identifiable dispositions and capabilities such as the Great Purge that, however murderous, had not up to that point produced an actual genocide by the standard definition.

But the aforementioned coincidence also directs our attention to other aspects of massive victimization where, it seems to me, the U.N. definition of genocide reveals serious weakness. The original Marxian revolutionary project, which ostensibly sanctioned Bolshevik practices, was thoroughly unambiguous about the treatment of a counterrevolutionary class enemy. Proletarian revolution was expected to evoke violent resistance by the displaced ruling class, which was to be met in kind. So long as that displaced class posed a palpable threat of restoration, whether during the revolution itself or in an ensuing civil war, then the revolutionary regime must defeat the class enemy. Ascription of the cost in human life to the revolutionary process or to the restorationist impulse thus became merely the expression of a political preference. And, as the Czech theologian Lochman (1970) has acknowledged, to insist on revolutionary forebearance under such circumstances is to nullify the possibility of revolution.

Marxian theory provides no warrant, however, for the physical elimination of a quiescent or tractable class enemy. Absent violent resistance, the Marxian prescription is to eliminate the conditions that allow the enemy class to continue its existence as a class. And that brings us to the crucial but ambiguous case of the kulaks at the time of forced collectivization.

Different social orders have diverse ways of classifying their own populations. The Genocide Convention's enumeration of groups - "national, ethnical, racial, or religious" - is unexceptionable as far as it goes, also for the societies that call themselves socialist. But it fails to confront squarely the primary classificatory device of socialist systems. In the Soviet case, during the relaxation of strict socialist norms known as NEP, the emergence of a nonproletarian (officially: petty bourgeois) class known as kulaks was encouraged in the countryside. And then quite abruptly, as Stalin opted for forced collectivization, that group was identified as a class enemy and earmarked for elimination. Had elimination meant only the removal of conditions allowing such a class to persist, we would be talking about hardship to be sure but also about a legitimate revolutionary program. But when elimination proved to mean massive killing of kulaks and their families and wholesale deportation to the Gulag (also slaughter, but of a more protracted sort), then it seems to me that we are talking about measures that ought to count as genocide. Defined by their own social order as a class inimical to socialism and the proletariat, the kulaks (or simply wealthier peasants) were an identifiable sector of the population, a social and not a political group, targeted for physical destruction. To omit this slaughter of some 15 million peasants in the Soviet countryside, partly a massacre on the spot and partly a gradual destruction in forced labor camps, is to weaken and even trivialize the juridical concept of genocide.

CONCLUSION

My conclusion, then, is that genocide is a specific kind of crime, identifiable by its impact on existing social groups, that does not necessarily embrace all forms of mass murder. Random slaughter is no less horrible, but it need not count as genocide. To insist on an inclusive view of genocide - which is the tendency, it seems to me, of Charny's (1982) analysis as well as of Kuper's (1982) is to weaken the juridical precision of the term for the sake of rhetorical impact. At the same time, if the term is to be universal in its import, it must take account of other than ethnic and religious styles of classification. If an allegedly socialist society, whose primary form of classification is that of class, either targets or invents a class with extermination in prospect, that program must count as genocide lest the term lose its continuing pertinence for the contemporary world in all its variety.

REFERENCES

CARRERE d'Encausse, Helene. Decline of an Empire. New York: Harper & Row, 1981.
CHARNY, Israel W. How Can We Commit The Unthinkable?: Genocide, The Human Cancer. Boulder: Westview, 1982.
CONQUEST, Robert. The Great Terror. New York: Macmillan, 1968.
CONQUEST, Robert. Kolyma: The Arctic Death Camps. New York: Oxford, 1978.

66

DAVIS, Christopher, & Feshbach, Murray. Rising Infant Mortality in the USSR in the 1970s. Washington: U.S. Bureau of the Census, 1980.

DYADKIN, Iosif. Evaluation of Unnatural Deaths in the Population of the U.S.S.R. 1927-1958. Translation by L. Thorne, in mimeograph. (Utilized in Davis & Feshbach, and Horowitz)

EBERSTADT, Nick. The health crisis in the U.S.S.R. The New York Re- view of Books, 19 February 1981, 23-31.

HOROWITZ, Irving Louis. Taking Lives: Genocide and State Power. New Brunswick: Transaction, 1982.

KUPER, Leo. Genocide. New Haven: Yale, 1982.

LOCKMAN, Jan M. Church in a Marxist Society. New York: Harper & Row, 1970.

NEKRICH, Aleksander M. The Punished People. New York: Norton, 1978.

SOLZHENITSYN, Aleksandr I. The Gulag Archipelago, 3 vols. New York: Harper & Row, 1973/4, 1975, 1978.

LYMAN H. LEGTERS, Ph.D., University Washington, 501 Thompson Hall, Seattle, Washington 98195, U.S.A.

5. The Man-Made Famine of 1933 in the Soviet Ukraine: What Happened and Why?

James E. Mace

Born in 1952 in Muskogee, Oklahoma, Dr. Mace took a B.A. in history from Oklahoma State University in 1973, an M.A. in history from the University of Michigan in 1977, and a Ph.D. in history from the University of Michigan in 1981. Currently a post-doctoral fellow in the Ukrainian Research Institute of Harvard University, he has published a number of articles on Soviet Ukraine in the 1920s and 1930s. His first book, COMMUNISM AND THE DILEMMAS OF NATIONAL LIBERATION: NATIONAL COMMUNISM IN SOVIET UKRAINE, 1818-1933 is being published in the Harvard Series of Monographs in Ukrainian Studies by Harvard University Press. He is currently working on a book about the Ukrainian famine of 1933.

What Ukrainians call shtuchnyi holod (the man-made famine) or even the Ukrainian holocaust claimed an estimated five to seven million lives. Purely in terms of mortality, it was thus of the same order of magnitude as the Jewish Holocaust. It was, however, a very different kind of genocide in that it was neither motivated by any quest for racial purity, nor was it an attempt to physically murder every single Ukrainian. The purpose, insofar was we may discern it, was to destroy the Ukrainian nation as a political factor and social organism, a goal which could be attained far short of complete extermination.

A close parallel is offered by the events following the Communist seizure of power in Cambodia, when the new regime unleashed a reign of terror apparently designed to utterly destroy the nation as it had hitherto existed so that the regime might reshape it in its own image. In both Ukraine and Cambodia, genocide was committed by Communist regimes operating under an ideology which portrayed the nations they ruled as inundated by class enemies. In both cases, the regimes sought to destroy and to leave an amorphous mass which might then be restructured as the rulers saw fit.

To understand the Ukrainian famine, one must first look to the history of Russo-Ukrainian relations. Ukrainians have traditionally seen the history of Russian domination over a large part of their country as one long tale of oppression (Braichevskii, 1975), rather than the reunion of fraternal peoples which Stalinist and post-Stalinist historiography has attempted to portray (Tillett, 1969). Indeed, the Ukrainian nation can hardly be said to have prospered under Russian rule. Its autonomy was gradually abolished; its Orthodox Church was absorbed by the Muscovite; its economic growth was long stunted; its elites were assimilated. Like the Czechs after the 1620 Battle of White Mountain, Ukrainians gradually became a nation almost entirely consisting of priests and peasants, and they are one of the few nations on earth whose level of literacy actually declined from the seventeenth through the nineteenth centuries.

From 1876 to 1905, the Tsars even went so far as to ban the Ukrainian language from the printed page in an attempt to cut short the revival of national consciousness (Savchenko, 1970). When industries and mines were built in Ukraine late in the nineteenth century, the fact that Russian peasants from the central black soil region of Russia were poorer than their Ukrainian counterparts guaranteed that there would always be plenty of Russians to work the new establishments, and the belated development of their own country thus passed Ukrainians by (this was already recognized by Porsh, 1912). The xenophobia of the Black Hundreds found more fertile soil among Ukraine's Russians than in any other part of the empire. Even the liberal democratic Russian intelligentsia refused to support so much as token autonomy for the Ukrainians. By the time the Russian Empire disintegrated in 1917, Ukrainians possessed only a numerically small but extremely important national intelligentsia in the cities; the vast majority of them remained peasants who viewed the cities of their own land as alien entities inhabited by foreigners.

THE UKRAINIAN PROBLEM IN SOVIET POLITICS

Before 1917, Eastern and Central Europe were ruled by dynastic political structures which had little to do with ethnic boundaries. Even Germany ruled large Polish terrorities in the East. At the end of the war, Russia, Austria-Hungary, and Germany all disintegrated into national regimes which fought one another for national independence and terroritorial borders. Since the Russian Empire was largely reconstituted as the USSR, we easily forget that it was the first of the dynastic structures to crumble, but in 1917 a bewildering array of national governments appeared on its territory. Poland, Finland, and the Baltic states emerged as independent nation-states. Ukraine, with its territory the size of France and its people more numerous than the Poles, was the largest of those which did not, and the wars of the Russian Revolution ended with its partition between a Soviet regime in central and eastern Ukraine, while western Ukraine was ruled by the new Polish Republic until 1939.

The fact that Ukraine's cities were predominantly non-Ukrainian led both Russians and Poles to ignore the national aspirations of the Ukrainian countryside and to consider the country rightfully theirs. In the east this meant that two revolutions - one Russian and urban, the other Ukrainian and agrarian - came into conflict over the same territory (standard works on the Ukrainian Revolution are Reshetar, 1952; Hunczak, 1977). The struggle for Ukraine was especially fierce, and even the end of set-piece warfare in 1921 brought no peace, since widespread guerrilla warfare - dubbed kulak banditry in Soviet sources - dragged on for years thereafter (Kucher, 1971; "Protybol'shevyts'ki," 1932).

Early Bolshevik regimes in Ukraine were unabashedly Russian in their open hostility toward any manifestation of Ukrainian aspirations, and anti-peasant in their early predilection for forcing peasants into communes and taking their produce in the form of requisitions. The Russian Bolsheviks' inability to completely subjugate the society upon which they had imposed themselves led them to make a series of compromises upon which the regime was based until the Five Year Plan was put into effect at the end of the decade: they tolerated a private economy upon which peasants could sell their surplus produce, intellectual and cultural figures were allowed to express themselves more or less freely as long as their work was not openly disloyal, and the minimum demands of the colonies were met through a program of indigenization (see Mace, 1983, chapters 1, 2).

Ukrainianization, the Ukrainian variant of this latter policy, went farther in Ukraine than did its counterparts in any other part of the old empire. It offered the regime substantial benefits, but also held substantial dangers. On the one hand, it gave Soviet Ukraine a much needed aura of national legitimacy, persuading a number of prominent Ukrainian socialists to return from exile and stimulating pro-Soviet irredentism in Western Ukraine. On the other hand, it helped make possible an unprecedented flowering of Ukrainian intellectual and cultural creativity and legitimized a certain measure of Ukrainian national consciousness within the regime itself. In 1925, the Ukrainian Commissar of Education, Oleksander Shums'ki, demanded that the Ukrainian Soviet state and Communist Party be led by ethnic Ukrainians and that the Ukrainianization program be speeded up. The most popular Soviet Ukrainian writer, Mykola Khvyl'ovyi called for the cultural emancipation of Ukrainian literature through the rejection of Russian influence and adoption of European models. The official in charge of all political education in Soviet Ukraine, Mykhailo Volubuiev, published a study showing that Soviet Ukraine was being fiscally exploited under the Soviets no less than it had been under the Tsars, that its development was distorted by the legacy of tsarist colonialism, and he demanded that Ukraine be allowed to develop as a relatively autonomous economic entity. Moscow was shocked at such demands being voiced by Communists and demanded their condemnation (see Mace, 1983, chapters, 3-5).

Mykola Skrypnyk, an ethnic Ukrainian and Old Bolshevik sent to Ukraine by Lenin as his personal representative in 1917, helped condemn the so-called national deviationists. However, he was able to extract substantial concessions for supporting Stalin against Bukharin. According to the latter, Stalin "bought" the Ukrainians (i.e., Skrypnyk) by withdrawing his lieutenant, Kaganovich (and thereby leaving Skrypnyk as the political strongman of the Soviet Ukrainian state). Skrypnyk followed policies bound to win him popularity with the Ukrainians, and one might say that Soviet Ukraine became to the USSR of this period what Poland was to the Soviet bloc later on: it was that part of the larger entity most conscious of its national distinctiveness, most jealous of its prerogatives, and least willing to follow Moscow's lead in arranging its internal affairs (Mace, 1983, chapter 6).

Stalin almost immediately reneged on whatever deal he might have made with Skrypnyk. At the end of 1928, one of the latter's most important clients came under attack. Matvii Iavors'kyi, the "ideological watchdog" of Ukrainian historians was condemned as a deviationist by his Russian counterparts who soon made it apparent that all his ideological "errors" had stemmed from the fact that he treated the history of Ukraine as a process distinct from Russian history (Mace, 1982). The political implication was obvious and ominous: if Ukraine did not have a history of its own, it should no longer be considered a separate country and treated as such. Iavors'skyi's fall was a direct attack upon Skrypnyk and the regime he headed.

Attacking Skrypnyk was secondary to a grander design: even at this juncture Stalin appears to have been intent upon destroying that which had made a distinctively Ukrainian Soviet regime possible, the Ukrainian nation as a factor in Soviet politics.

Forced collectivization implied a war against the peasantry, and it made little political sense to placate the national aspirations of what was still predominantly a nation of peasants if one were engaged in an attack upon the peasantry as such. But attacking a nation is not the same thing as defeating it, and the attack on the social basis of Ukrainian aspirations was carried out in tandem with an attack upon its elites. Neither what happened in the cities nor in the countryside can be understood in isolation; both were part of a single policy designed to realize a common goal.

In the fall of 1929, the secret police "unmasked" a conspiracy dubbed the Union for the Liberation of Ukraine (SVU). So many members of the All-Ukraine Academy of Sciences (VUAN) were placed in the dock that whole institutions had to be closed. The Ukrainian Autocephalous Orthodox Church was also tied in to the alleged plot and forced to proclaim its own liquidation. When the trial took place in 1930, the defendants were accused not only of engaging in a terrorist plot to assassinate top Soviet leaders and lead a kulak uprising to establish an independent fascist state with capitalist support, but also with activities labeled "cultural wrecking," consisting in interpreting Ukrainian history as a national history, advocating the adoption of non-Russian terms in the Ukrainian language, or establishing an orthography with spelling rules different from Russian(Visti, February 28-March 9, 1930). In short, the flower of the national intelligentsia was brought low, and Ukrainian cultural self-assertion was identified with sabotage committed by class enemies. It would not be long before Skrypnyk himself would be accused of being in league with the alleged wreckers. The purge of the Ukrainian cultural elite became an ongoing process, such that by the end of the decade an estimated 80% of its members were silenced (Lawrynenko, 1959).

Skrypnyk was able to maintain his position, despite a number of ideological and bureaucratic moves to undermine his position, until the famine was at its height in 1933. In January of that year, Pavel Postyshev was sent by Moscow to become virtual dictator of the Ukrainian republic, push forward even more energetically the extraction of grain from the countryside, and defeat Skrypnyk. On March

1, Visti announced Skrypnyk's demotion to the Ukrainian Economic Planning Agency, and on June 10, Postyshev denounced him by name, accusing him of shielding nationalistic deviationists like those whom he held responsible for the regime's difficulties in procuring grain from the villages. Interestingly, the only specific charge made against Skrypnyk at this time was that his advocacy of the letter "g" in Ukrainian, a manifestation of Ukrainian cultural distinctiveness, had objectively aided the annexationist designs of the Polish landlords (Visti, June 22, 1933). Other members of the Ukrainian communist leadership vied with each other to expose further manifestations of this newly discovered "Skrypnykite deviation," and on July 6, 1933, Skrypnyk committed suicide.

THE COLLECTIVIZATION OF AGRICULTURE

Despite the progress achieved by Ukrainization, the vast majority of Ukrainians still worked the land in the 1930s. For them, the toleration for private farming under the NEP and Ukrainization were but two sides of the same coin, and both were in fact necessary in Ukraine to placate the same social group, the Ukrainian peasantry.

In the 1920s, the Party's main task in Ukraine was defined as winning over the "rural masses" in general and the village intelligentsia in particular. There is ample evidence to suggest that this approach enjoyed only limited success at best. Those connected to the regime, even in the most innocuous way as village newspaper correspondents, were shunned by their neighbors, as one of the leading figures in the regime frankly admitted (Zatons'kyi, 1926, p. 21).

Evidence of the regime's feeling of insecurity in the Ukrainian countryside is the fact that, while it abolished the kombedy (committees of the village poor) in Russia in 1920, it felt the need to retain them in only slightly altered form in the Ukrainian countryside as the komnezamy (committees of non-wealthy peasants) until 1933. Until 1925 they retained all the powers of the old kombedy, exercising state power without any elective village councils. During collectivization and in the early stages of the famine, they constituted the regime's main support in the village (Zahors'kyi & Stoian, 1960). The reason for their ultimate abolition may be discerned in the numerous accounts of survivors of the famine, who often note with barely suppressed glee how, after the komnezam members had helped extract foodstuff from the village, no special provision was made for them and they starved alongside their neighbors.

The regime also penetrated the villages during the 1920s by creating a dense network of secret collaborators (seksoty) with the political police. According to one account, OGPU residents in the raion level would have a cover which would allow them to travel to villages without arousing suspicion.

When visiting villages they merely observed, noted and selected possible candidates for the OGPU and notified the authorities. A man who was earmarked for work as a future seksot or agent

was called to the okrug department of the OGPU. There the
chief of the okrug department had a "talk" with him, while a
revolver lay on the table between them, and required him to
sign an obligation. From that moment on the seksot was in
touch with the district agent of the OGPU in the locality where
he lived. Numbers varied from place to place depending on the
size of the population, but everywhere the number of people
thus recruited constituted a considerable part of the population (Lutarewytch, 1956, p. 90).

The seksoty enabled the regime to identify real and potential
enemies, thus placing it in a far stronger position vis-a-vis the
peasantry than it had been in during the early years when the Bolsheviks confronted the village as foreigners who had no idea who was
who. Whenever the regime might decide the time was ripe to settle
the unfinished business left over from the civil war, it would thus
be ready.

The policy of the "liquidation of the kulaks as a class" and
total forced collectivization of agriculture was announced by Stalin
on December 29, 1929 and legalized by Central Committee resolutions
of January 5 and 30, 1930. How were these decisions carried out in
Ukraine? An outsider or group of outsiders - usually a plenipoten-
tiary or a non-Ukrainian worker recruited as a "thousander" - would
be sent into the village with the power to veto any action of the
local authorities or to remove them. A village meeting would be
called at which the new authority would try - often unsuccessfully -
to browbeat the peasants into joining the colective farm and approv-
ing dekulakization. The outsider would lead the local komnezam to
the farms of those who were slated for expropriation and either
carry off everything of value or throw the whole family out into the
snow. Those who were dekulakized were often shunned by their neighbors who had been threatened with the same fate if they ever helped
a kulak (see, for example, Harvard University Refugeee Interview
Project files; Black Deeds, 1955; Woropay, 1983). Simultaneously,
the local church was usually closed, the village priest and often
the local schoolteacher would either be arrested or run off
(Hryshko, 1963). Dekulakization thus meant the decapitation of the
village, the elimination of the best farmers and natural village
leaders - of anyone who might lead the village in fighting back.

Forced collectivization was carried out more vigorously in Ukraine than in Russia. At first the difference seems slight, but it
would grow more significant, as the following figures on the level
of collectivization in Ukraine and Russia show:

	Ukraine	Russia
Late 1929	8.6% of peasant farms	7.4% of peasant farms
Early 1930	65% of peasant farms	59% of peasant farms
Mid-1932	70% of peasant farms	59.3% of peasant farms

The trend continued until the private agricultural sector was
completely eliminated: by 1935 91.3% of all peasant farms in Ukraine
were collectivized, while Russia did not reach the 90% mark until

late 1937 (Hryshko, 1963). The higher level of collectivization in Ukraine is only partly explained by the higher priority given the most important grain producing regions; collectivization in Ukraine had a special task which the newspaper Proletars'ka Pravda summed upon January 22, 1930: "to destroy the social basis of Ukrainian nationalism - individual peasant agriculture."

The peasants responded by fighting back. Even Soviet sources make this clear. According to A. F. Chmyga, the number of "registered kulak terrorists acts" in Ukraine (and the regime dubbed practically every peasant it did not care for either a kulak or kulak henchman) grew fourfold from 1927 to 1929, with 1262 acts reported in 1929 (Chmyga, 1967; Chymga, 1974). During the first half of 1930, there were more reports of such "terrorism" than for the whole previous year - over 1500 (Krykunenko, 1970). Later figures are unavailable, perhaps because they became so numerous that officials could no longer keep count. Defectors who had worked in the village speak of finding colleagues with their bellies cut open and stuffed with ears of wheat (Kravchenko, 1946). There were also numerous cases when the women of the village, perhaps feeling that they were less likely to be arrested, took it upon themselves to expel the local administration, take what had been taken from them, and abolish the collective farm. These even became known as babs'ki bunty (revolts of the the babas) (Pravoberezhnyi, 1951).

Whatever expectations the regime might have had at the beginning of the campaign, the transition from individual farms to large collectives was extractive rather than productive; simply taking everyone's animals and implements to the center of the village and proclaiming them socialized did nothing to raise output. But harvesting collectively gave the regime much greater control over the farmers and their produce, because it was much easier for the state to take all it wanted from a single threshing room floor than to search individual farmsteads. And this is why, while agricultural productivity declined, the amount taken by the state ("marketed") rose: although the total Soviet grain harvest of 1932 was significantly below that of 1927, grain "marketings" from the harvest were two-and-one-half times those of 1927-1928 (Jasny, 1949).

As economic depression deepened in the West, agricultural prices dropped steeply in relation to those of manufactured goods. The USSR, whose entire plan of development was predicated on paying for imported capital goods with the proceeds from grain sales, found that a given machine cost far more grain than had previously been the case. This provided a motive for intensified exploitation of the peasantry (Holubnychy, 1958).

THE MAN-MADE FAMINE

Events in Kazakhstan in 1930 seem to have given Stalin the answer to the dilemma of how to obtain more produce and simultaneously deal with troublesome peasants. The Kazakhs, primarily herdsmen, had greeted collectivization by the wholesale slaughter of their livestock. So many starved in consequence that the 1939 census shows a drop of 21.9% in their numbers since 1926 (Kozlov, 1975). But resistance among them had ceased. The lesson that famine could be an effective weapon would be applied to the Ukrainians.

This was done by imposing grain procurement quotas on the Ukrainian Republic far out of proportion to its share of the total Soviet harvest. Although Moscow was aware of how collectivization had disorganized Ukraine's agriculture, it had to deliver 2.3 times the amount of grain marketed during the best pre-collectiveization year. In 1930, 7.7 million tons of grain were taken out of Ukraine, 33% of its 23 million ton harvest. Although Ukraine produced only 27% of all grain harvested in the USSR, it supplied 38% of all the grain procured. In 1931, despite a decline in sown area, Moscow kept the same quota even after it became apparent that the harvest was only 18.3 million tons and almost 30% of that was lost during the harvest. Already a conscious policy of leading the Ukrainian countryside to catastrophe can be discerned (Holubnychy, 1958).

It proved impossible to meet the 1931 quota, and only seven million tons could be collected in Ukraine. In May 1932, the grain delivery quotas were lowered for the Union as a whole, and as a result of the so-called May Reform, Ukraine's quota was lowered to 6.5 million tons, but even this was far beyond the republic's capability (Hyrshko, 1963). The 1932 wheat crop was less than two-thirds that of 1930, but still larger than it had been during the worst pre-collectivization year when there had been no famine (Ganzha, et. al., 1963). Moscow insisted the quotas be met. Frequent attacks on "opportunists" on the local level who "did not want to see the kulaks in their midst" (how could they when they had sent the "kulaks" to Siberia more than a year earlier?) left little to the imagination regarding the fate of those who failed to meet their quotas (see for example, Visti, August 16, 1932).

Draconian measures were taken against the farmers. On the Union level, the law on the inviolability of socialist property, adopted on August 7, 1932, provided for the execution - or in extenuating circumstances ten years sentence to the Gulag - of anyone who so much as gleaned an ear of grain or bit the root off a sugar beet. A second part of the decree provided for five to ten years in a concentration camp for collective farmers who attempted to force others to leave the kolkhoz. During 1932 fully 20% of all persons convicted in Soviet courts were sentenced under this decree, and Stalin himself called it "the basis of socialist legality at the present moment" (Conquest, 1968).

In Ukraine, a decree of December 6, 1932, singled out six villages which had allegedly sabotaged the grain deliveries. The "blacklist" established by this decree was soon extended in wholesale fashion. It meant the complete economic blockade of villages which had not delivered the required quantity of grain. It specifically provided for the immediate closing of state and cooperative stores and the removal of their goods from the village; a complete ban on all trade in the village concerned, including trade in essential consumer goods and foodstuffs, by kolkhozy, kolkhozniki,

and individual farmers; halting and immediately calling in all cre-
dits and advances; a thoroughgoing purge of the local cooperative
and state apparats; the purge of all "foreign elements" and
"wreckers" of the grain procurements from the kolkhoz which was at
the time equivalent to a sentence of death by starvation (Visti,
December 8, 1932).

Those who survived the famine do not describe the 1932 harvest
as being anything like a failure, but, at worst, mediocre and in
some parts even bountiful. When the first procurements campaign was
carried out in August, there were a number of areas where the overwhelming majority of peasant met their norms. In October a new levy
was imposed equal to half the earlier levy, and the "tow brigades"
went round searching and taking whatever they could find. At the
beginning of 1933, a third levy was announced, and whatever remained
in the villages from the earlier levies was taken. Neither food nor
seed was left (Pravoberezhnyi, 1951; also HURIP files).

There are so many accounts by survivors of the horrors of life
in the villages of Ukraine that it is impossible to present an adequate picture here. In some areas, people began to swell from hunger as early as the spring of 1932, but the most terrible time was
the winter of 1932-33. Survivors tell of mass death by starvation,
mass burials in pits, of whole villages depopulated, of homeless
waifs and adults flocking to the towns in search of food, of people
trying to sustain themselves with the leaves and branches of trees,
of railroad stations literally flooded with dying peasants who
begged lying down because they were too weak to stand (HURIP; Black
Deeds, 1955; Woropay, 1983). Such accounts are broadly confirmed by
a number of Western observers (Ammende, 1936; Muggeridge, 1934;
Chamberlin, 1934; as well as sources listed in Dalrymple, 1964-65;
Pidhaina, 1973). Many of the starving tried to get across the
border into ussia where bread was available. Iwan Majstrenko, a
former Soviet functionary and newspaper editor, recalled a case of
two villages on opposite sides of the river separating Ukraine and
Russia, where peasants from the Ukrainian side would swim across at
night in order to purchase bread the following morning, because
bread was obtainable only on the Russian side (Majstrenko, 1958).
In order to limit the famine to Ukraine, the political police established border checkpoints along the railroad lines to prevent the
starving from entering Russia and prevent anyone coming from Russia
from carrying food into Ukraine (Verbyts'kyi, 1951). This meant the
de facto "blacklisting," i.e., economic blockade of the entire
Soviet Ukraine.

Graphic portraits of the horrors of village life emerge from
the files of the Harvard University Refugee Interview Project, conducted during the early 1950s. It should be stressed that the in-
terviewers were not particularly interested in the famine and that
responses concerning the famine were made without prompting in the
course of life history interviews. One typical account (HURIP, case
128) is the following:

...there was the famine in the Ukraine in 1933. We saw people
die in the streets; it was terrible to see a dead man, when I
close my eyes I can still see him. We had in our village a
small church which was closed for services and in which we
played. And I remember a man who came in there; he lay down
with his eyes wide open at the ceiling and he died there! He
was an innocent victim of the Soviet regime and not even a
kulak. This hunger was the result of Soviet policy.

Other accounts are more graphic, as this one by a Great Russian
woman (HURIP, case 373):

Well, in 1933-1934 I was a member of a commission sent out to
inspect wells. We had to go to the country to see that the
shafts of the wells were correctly installed, and there I saw
such things as I had never seen before in my life. I saw villages that not only had no people, but not even any dogs and
cats, and I remember one particular incident: we came to one
village, and I don't think I will ever forget this. will always see this picture before me. We opened the door of this
miserable hut and there...the man was lying. The mother and
child already lay dead, and the father had taken the piece of
meat from between the legs of his son and had died just like
that...there were other such incidents on our trip...

Nor were such horrors confined to the countryside. Cannibalism was
known even in the cities, as a worker (HURIP, case 513) described in
the following account:

I remember a case in 1933. I was in Kiev. I was at that time
at a bazaar called the Besinabian market. I saw a woman with a
valise. She opened the valise and put her goods out for sale.
Her goods consisted of jellied meat, frozen jellied meat, which
she sold at fifty rubles a portion. I saw a man come over to
her - a man who bore all the marks of starvation - he bought
himself a portion and began eating. As he ate of his portion,
he noticed that a human finger was imbedded in the jelly. He
began shouting at the woman and began yelling at the top of his
voice. People came running, gathered around her, and then seeing what her food consisted of, took her to the militsia (police - JM). At the militsia, two members of the NKVD went over
to her and, instead of taking action against her, they burst
out laughing. "What, you killed a kulak? Good for you!" And
then they let her go.

The common folk were not the only ones to tell what they saw.
Famine was at the time a common topic of conversation within the
elite and among members of the foreign press, a few of whom reported
it. One account, no less valuable for coming to us second hand,
comes from Krushchev, who stated in his unofficial memoirs:

Mikoyan told me that Comrade Demchenko, who was the First Secretary of the Kiev Regional Committee, once came to see him in

Moscow. Here's what Demchenko said: "Anastan Ivanovich, does Comrade Stalin - for that matter, does anyone in the Politburo - know what's happening in the Ukraine? Well, if not, I'll give you some idea. A train recently pulled into Kiev loaded with the corpses of people who had starved to death. It picked up corpses all the way from Poltava to Kiev..."(Krushchev, 1970, pp. 73-74).

Of course, Stalin did know. In 1932 Terekhov, a secretary of the Ukrainian Central Committee reported to him on starvation in the Kharkiv region, and Stalin accused him of telling fairy tales (Medvedev, 1972). Later, the commanders of both the Black Sea Fleet and the Kiev Military District protested to Stalin and were also rebuffed (Plyushch, 1977).

According to the 1939 Soviet census, the number of Ukrainians in the USSR decreased by over three million or 9.9% since the last official census of 1926. Between 1897 and 1926, the Ukrainian population - despite the demographic catastrophes of World War I, revolution, civil war, and the 1921 famine - grew an average of 1.3% a year (Lewis, et. al., 1975). In 1958-59, the Ukrainian population of the USSR had a natural rate of population growth of 1.39% , although this slowed to 0.6% by 1969 (Naulko, 1965; Naulko, 1975). Official Soviet adminstrative estimates on the eve of collectivization show the natural rate of population growth for Soviet Ukraine declining slightly from 2.45% in 1924 to 2.15% in 1928, and even with a drastic decline in real living standards it was still 1.45% in 1931 when such figures stop (Naulko, 1965). And since Ukrainians were still concentrated in the countryside where the natural rate of population growth was always higher, one would expect their growth rate to be somewhat higher than these figures indicate.

The magnitude of the demographic catastrophe suffered by Ukrainians is brought most sharply into focus when we compare the 1926 and 1939 population figures for the three East Slavic nations and for the USSR as a whole (Kozlov, 1975):

	1926 population	1939 population	percent change
USSR	147,027,900	170,557,100	+ 15.7%
Russians	77,791,100	99,591,500	+ 28.0%
Belorussians	4,738,900	5,275,400	+ 11.3%
Ukrainians	31,195,000	28,111,000	- 9.9%

Comparison with the Belorussians is particularly important here. They had a lower birth rate than the Ukrainians, lower literacy, a relatively weaker tradition of national self-assertion: their natural rate of population growth would thus be lower and they would be more vulnerable to pressures to assimilate. Since their purely political fate was similar to that of the Ukrainians and the assimilatory pressures roughly the same, we would expect Ukrainians to increase more rapidly than Belorussians. The only difference between their fates in the period is that Soviet Ukraine suffered famine and Belorussia did not. Thus, the difference in their demographic fates is attributable solely to the famine. Given that Ukrainians should have increased <u>more</u> than the Belorussians had it not been for the famine, we may thus estimate on the basis of the 1939 census that the famine of 1933 cost the lives of five to seven million Ukrainians.

The figure may well have been higher. The census of 1937 was never released because those who prepared it were accused of trying to sabotage the dea of building socialism in one country by "deliberately undercounting" the Soviet population (Souvarine, 1939). Those who succeeded them were surely aware of the shortcomings found in their predecessors work, and it is reasonable to assume that they were eager to avoid any perception of similar shortcomings in their work. After all, no one wants to be shot.

Higher estimates of mortality also come from Westerners who claim to have been given figures by Soviet officials off the record. Adam Tawdul claimed that Skrypnyk told him eight million died in Ukraine and the heavily Ukrainian North Caucasus, and the famine had not yet run its course when Skrypnyk committed suicide. Other Soviet officials gave him a figure of eight to nine million dead for Ukraine and the North Caucasus, plus an additional million or more for other regions (Tawdul, 1935). William Horsley Gannt, a British psychologist who studied with Pavlov, stated that some said as many as fifteen million might have perished (Sawka, 1982). According to John Kolasky, a Ukrainian-Canadian ex-Communist who was selected to attend the Higher Party School of the Ukrainian Central Committee, a prominent Ukrainian poet disclosed that a secret report to the Ukrainian Central Committee had declared that ten million had perished in the famine (Kolasky, 1970).

Even Stalin once cited the same figure, although he did not exactly say that so many had died. Churchill recorded the following conversation with Stalin during the Second World War:

"Tell me," I asked," have the stresses of the war been so bad to you personally as carrying through the policy of the Collective Farms?"
This subject immediately aroused the Marshall.
"Oh, no," he said, "the Collective Farm policy was a terrible struggle."
"I thought you would have found it bad," I said, "because you were not dealing with a few score thousand aristocrats or big landowners, but with millions of small men."
"Ten millions," he said, holding up his hands (Churchill, 1950, p. 498).

Even if this estimate did circulate within the Soviet elite, they actually had no real way of keeping an accurate count. Regulations requiring registration of burials were promulgated, but by all accounts the peasants decided that the dead were not afraid even of the GPU and buried them without bothering about the legal formalities. All we can say for certain is that millions died, that the Ukrainian people lost at least 10% of its members, three million in dividuals, when it should have increased by an even greater number, and was thereby quite literally decimated.

FAMINE AS A TOOL OF NATIONAL POLICY

To be sure, all Soviet peasants faced hard times in 1933, and there was mass death from starvation not only in Ukraine but also in the North Caucasus and along the Volga. However, the North Caucasus was largely a non-Russian area inhabited by Ukrainians and the Kuban Cossacks who had supported Kaledin in 1917 and provided the initial bases for Denikin's anti-Communist Volunteer Army. The Volga contained the so-called Volga German communes. The Germans welcomed their countrymen during the 1918 occupation of Ukraine, and, in any case, mortality there seems to have been far lower there than in Ukraine and the North Caucasus. The point is that the areas affected by the man-made famine all contained groups which could plausibly be considered hindrances to the creation of the type of USSR Stalin created immediately after the famine, a politically homogeneous and Russentric successor to the tsarist empire. It did not strictly correspond with the main grain areas, as would be expected were it motivated primarily by economic concerns: there was no famine in Russia's Central Agricultural Region, while there was famine in the Ukrainian provinces of Volhyn and Podillia, hardly part of the basic grain producing area of the USSR.

Some Russian emigres have argued that the geography of the famine was essentially accidental and state that Russia suffered no famine because its population could live on potatoes. True, potatoes were more plentiful in Russia than in Ukraine, and they play a lesser role in the East Ukrainian diet than in the Russian or West Ukrainian diets. This might well have had some effect. Yet claims that this was a major factor seems dubious, for, had the regime's motive not been national, it would surely have allowed products with little economic value like potatoes to be brought into Ukraine, if only by "bagmen" on the trains, whereas in fact checkpoints on the Russo-Ukrainian border prevented even potatoes (and Ukrainians at this juncture considered even potato skins a rare delicacy) from entering Ukraine. The conclusion becomes inescapable that the entire Soviet Ukraine was placed on a de facto economic blacklist in order to teach the Ukrainians, as William Henry Chamberlin (1944, p. 96) put it, "a lesson by the grim method of starvation."

If we ask which groups were most likely to constitute a threat to the new Russocentric USSR Stalin was to create after the famine, we must conclude that it was the Ukrainians, second only to the Russians in number and who had succeeded in turning Ukrainization into a kind of surrogate independence under Skrypnyk; the Kuban Cossacks who had fought for Kaledin and Denikin; and the Germans, who could always be expected to welcome their countrymen in any future conflict. These were precisely the groups whose territories were affected by the man-made famine.

The indigenization program ends with the famine, and it was only shortly thereafter, in November, 1934, that a decree on the

teaching of history in Soviet schools condemned the hitherto dominate but "unpatriotic" schoool of M. N. Povrovskii and rehabilitated
Russian history, tsars and all, under the new rubric of the history
of the USSR. This fundamental change in the national ideology of
the USSR helps explain the famine, because only the famine, which
humbled the largest of the non-Russian nations of the USSR, could
have made it possible. It also helps explain why, in those territories affected by famine, Russians and non-Russians suffered
equally. Before Stalin had broken the non-Russians as political
factors it could still have caused political headaches had he ordered local officials to distinguish among different national groups
within a given territory in carrying out grain procurements, and
therefore the famine had to be created on a territorial basis by
means of excessive procurement quotas for those territories in which
the "suspect" nations lived. Within those territories all villagers
suffered equally, but in the final stages of the famine Russians
were sent into Ukraine to repopulate the most devastated villages
and were given special rations to prevent their dying alongside the
local population (Woropay, 1983).

One can find numerous unofficial statements connecting the need
to eliminate Ukrainian nationalism with the need to "overcome difficulties in procuring grain," the euphemism for creating famine. Indeed, in 1933 the official statements declared that it was necessary
to eliminate Ukrainian nationalism because "nationalistic wreckers"
were supposedly responsible for the difficulties in procuring grain
(Postyshev, 1933). Whether one consideration preceded the other in
the Bolshevik mind of the period does not really matter; they were
like the chicken and the egg: there is neither an answer nor need to
answer the question of which came first. As early as 1925, Stalin
wrote: "The nationality question is, by the essence of the matter a
problem of the peasantry" (Stalin, 1946, VII, p. 72). Given such a
view, crushing the peasants once and for all was the necessary condition for any final solution to the nationality question in the
oviet Union.

What was this solution? The Ukrainian elite were destroyed -
not only the officially sanctioned political leadership but also the
national intelligentsia: this meant the decapitation of the nation.
Ukrainization was ended, and Ukrainian language media and institutions shrank: this meant the gradual re-Russification of the cities
and the expulsion of Ukrainian nationality back to the village from
whence it came, the "pastoralization" of the Ukrainian nation. Famine decimated the village and taught it submission, while the internal passport system meant the legal attachment of the agricultural
population to the soil: this was little different from the old serfdom. Forced collectivization was a tragedy for the whole Soviet
peasantry, but for the Ukrainians it was a particular tragedy: with
the virtual destruction of their urban elites it meant their destruction as a social organism and political factor, their reduction
to the status of what the Germans used to call a Naturvolk.

REFERENCES

AMMENDE, Ewald. Human Life in Russia. London: Allen & Unwin, 1936.

The Black Deeds of the Kremlin: A White Book. Toronto & Detroit: DOBRUS, 1955.

BRAICHEVSKII, M. Iu. Prisoedinene ili vossoedinenie? Kriticheskie zamechanie po povodu odnoi kontseptsii. In Roman Kupchinsky (Ed.), Natsionalnyi vopros v SSSR: Sbornik dokumentov. Munich: Suchasnist', 1975, 62-125.

CHAMBERLIN, William Henry. Russia's Iron Age. Boston: Little, Brown, 1934.

CHAMBERLIN, William Henry. Ukraine: A Submerged Nation. New York: Macmillan, 1944.

CHMYGA, A. F. XV s"ezd VKP(b) o kollektivizatsil sel'skogo khoziaistva i nachalo osushchestvleniia ego reshenii no Ukraine. Vestnik Moskovskogo universitera, 1967, 6, 19-33.

CHMYGA, A. F. Kolkhoznoe dvizhenie na Ukraine. Moscow: Nauka, 1974.

CHURCHILL, Winston S. The Hinge of Fate. Boston: Houghton Mifflin, 1950.

CONQUEST, Robert (Ed.), Agricultural Workers in the USSR. London: Bodley Head, 1968.

DALRYMPLE, Dana. The Soviet Famine of 1932-34. Soviet Studies, 1964, 3, 250-284; 1965, 3, 471-474.

GANZHA, I. F., Slin'ko, I. I., Shostak, P. V. In V. P. Danilov (Ed.), Ukrainskoe selo na puti k sotsializmu. Ocherki istoril kollektivizatsii sel'skogo khoziaistva v Soiuznykh respublikakh. Moscow: AN SSSR, 1963.

HOLUBNYCHY, Vsevolod. Prychyny holodu 1932-1933 rr. Vpered: Ukrains'kyi robitnychyi chasopis, 1958, 10, 1, 5-6.

HYRSHKO, Vasyl'. Moskva sl'ozam ne viryt': Trahediia Ukrainy 1933 roku z perspektyvy 30 richchia. New York: DOBRUS, 1963.

HARVARD University Refugee Interview Project. Unpublished files in custody of the Russian Research Center, Harvard University.

HUNCZAK, Taras (Ed.), The Ukraine, 1917-1921: A Study in Revolution. Cambridge, Mass.: Harvard University Press, 1971.

JASNY, Naum. The Socialized Agriculture of the USSR: Plans and Performance. Stanford: Stanford University Press, 1949.

KHRUSHCHEV, Nikita. Krushchev Remembers. Boston & Toronto: Little, Brown, 1970.

KOLASKY, John. Two Years in Soviet Ukraine. Toronto: Peter Martin Associates, 1970.

KOZLOV, V. I. National'nosti SSSR: Etno-demograficheskii obzor. Moscow: Statistyka, 1975.

KRAVCHENKO, Victor. I Chose Freedom: The Personal and Political Life of a Soviet Official. New York: Garden City Publishing, 1946.

KRYKUNENKO, O. M. Borot'ba Komunistychnoi partii za dziisnennia lenins'koho kooperatyvnoho planu (1929-1931). L'viv: Vydavnytstvo L'vivs'koho universytetu, 1970.

KUCHER, O. O. Rozhrom zbroinoi vnutrishnoi knotrrevoliutsii na Ukraini u 1921-1923 rr. Kharkhiv: Vydavnytstvo Kharkhivs'koho universytetu, 1971.

LAWRYNENKO, Jurij (Ed.), Rozstriliane vidrodzhennia: Antolohiia, 1917-1933. Paris: Instytut Literacki, 1959.

82

LEWIS, Robert A.; Howland, Richard H.; & Clem, Ralph S. The Growth and Redistribution of the Ukrainian Population of Russian and the USSR: 1897-1970. In Peter Potychnyj (Ed.), Ukraine in the Seventies. Oakville, Ontario: Ukrainian Academic Press, 1975, 151-175.

LUTAREWYTCH, P. A resistance group in the Ukrainian underground, 1920-1926. Ukrainian Review, 1956, 1, 86-120.

MACE, James E. Politics and history in Soviet Ukraine, 1921-1933. Nationalities Papers, 1982, 1, 157-180.

MACE, James E. Communism and the Dilemmas of National Liberation: National Communism in Soviet Ukraine, 1918-1933. Cambridge, Mass.: Harvard University Press, 1983.

MAJSTRENKO, Iwan. Do 25-richchia holodu 1933 r. Vpered: Ukrains'kyi robitnychyi chasopys, 1958, 7, 1-2.

MEDVEDEV, Roy A. Let History Judge: The Origins and Consequences of Stalinism. New York: Knopf, 1972.

MUGGERIDGE, Malcolm. Winter in Moscow. Boston: Little, Brown, 1934.

NAULKO, V. I. Etnychnyi sklad naselennia Ukrains'koi RSR: Statystyko-kartohrafichne doslidzhennia. Kiev: Akademiia Nauk URSR, 1965.

NAULKO, V. I. Razvitie mezhetnicheskikh sviazei na Ukraine. Kiev: Naukova dumka, 1975.

PIDHAINA, Alexander. A bibliography of the Great Famine in Ukraine, 1932-1934. The New Review: A Journal of East-European History, 1973, 4, 32-68.

PLYUSHCH, Leonid. History's Carnival: A Dissident's Autobiography. New York & London: Harcourt, Brace, Jovanovich, 1977.

PORSH, Mykola. Vydnosyny Ukrainy do ynshykh raioniv Rossii na robitnychomu rynku na osnovi materialiv pershoho vseliuds'koho perepysu. Literaturno-naukovyi vistnyk, 1912.

POSTYSHEV, Pavel. Soviet Ukraine Today. New York: International Publishers, 1934.

PRAVOBEREZHYI, F. 8,000,000: 1933-i rik no Ukraini. Winnipeg: Nauka i osvita, 1951.

"PROTYBOL'SHEVYTS'KI povstannia na Ukraini v 1921," Litopys chervonoi kalyny. 1932, 6, 9.

RESHETAR, John. The Ukrainian Revolution: A Study in Nationalism. Princeton: Princeton University Press, 1952.

SAVCHENKO. Fedir. The Suppression of Ukrainian Activities. Munich: Harvard URI, 1970.

SAWKA, Jaroslaw. American psychiatrist: Fifteen million died in the hirties' Famine. Ukrainian Quarterly, 1982, 1, 61-67.

SOUVARINE, Boris. Stalin: A Critical Survey of Bolshevism. New York: Longman, Green, 1939.

STALIN, I. V. Sochineniia. Moscow: Gospolitizdat, 1946.

TAWDUL, Adam. Articles in The New York American, August 18-19, 1935.

TILLET, Lowell. The Great Friendship: Soviet Historian of the NonRussian Nationalities. Chapel Hill: University of North Carolina Press, 1969.

VERBYTS'KYI, M. (Ed.), Naibil'shyi zlochyn Kremlin: Stvorennyi soviets'koiu Moskoiu holod v Ukraini 1932-33 r. London: DOBPRUS, 1952.

VISTI VUTSVK. Kharkiv: daily organ of the Soviet Ukrainian state.
WOROPAY, Olexa. The Ninth Circle: In Commemoration of the Famine of 1933. Cambridge, Mass.: Ukrainian Studies Fund, 1983.
ZAHORS'KYI, P. S.,   Stoian, P. K.   Narysy istorii komitetiv nezamozhnykh selian. Kiev: Vydavnytstvo Akademii Nauk URSR, 1960.
ZATONS'KYI, Volodymyr. Leninovym shliakhom (Promova no poshyrenii naradi selkoriv hazety "Radians'ke selo." Kharkiv: Radians'ke selo, 1926.

JAMES. E. MACE, Ph.D., 1583 Massachussetts Ave. Cambridge,
Massachussetts 02138, U.S.A.

6. Genocide and Denial: The Armenian Case

Richard G. Hovannisian

The author is Professor of Armenian and Near Eastern History and
Acting Director of the Near Eastern Center at the University of
California, Los Angeles. His scholarship has focused on the history
of the Armenian question in the Ottoman Empire and on the short-
lived Armenian republic (1918-1920). He was drawn to the study of
the Armenian genocide by the continued and intensified denials and
rationalizations of this, the first genocide of the twentieth century. He has compiled and published a bibliography of relevant
works entitled, THE ARMENIAN HOLOCAUST: A BIBLIOGRAPHY RELATING TO
THE DEPORTATIONS, MASSACRES, AND DISPERSION OF THE ARMENIAN PEOPLE,
1915-1923 (Cambridge, Mass.: Armenian Heritage Press, 1980).

In ancient times, kings and despots often boasted in their in-
scriptions of the annihilation of entire peoples and nations who had
dared to resist or to challenge them. In modern times, however, admission of genocidal policies is a rarity, partly because of much
more complex standards of international relations and moral responsibility.

Even in post-Nazi Germany, which accepted the guilt of the old
regime and engaged in various compensatory acts, thousands of implicated individuals claimed innocence or ignorance in the face of the
incriminating evidence. Nonetheless, the German government, whether
of free will, necessity, or a combination of the two, extended reparations to the survivors, the families of the victims, and the state
of Israel. Discussion of the Holocaust has found a place in the educational curricula, literature, mass media productions, and scholarly forums of Germany.

The same cannot be said in the Armenian case. There has been
neither candid admission nor willing investigation, neither repara-
tion nor rehabilitation. On the contrary, state-sponsored attempts
to suppress discussion of the Armenian genocide have reached unprecedented proportions, with this very conference not being spared the
heavy shadow of intimidation. Presumably, the underlying cause for
the Turkish attitude is political, since there still exists an aggrieved party, however disorganized and scattered, which demands
some form of compensation. While many of the aggrieved would be
satisfied with a simple Turkish admission of wrongdoing and the end
to efforts to erase the historical record, there are others who insist upon financial and even territorial restitution, thus adding to
Turkish anxieties and attempts to obscure the past.

This political dimension raises at once the point that fundamental differences existed between the Armenian experience in World
War I and the Jewish experience in World War II. While comparative
studies rightly draw parallels between the two tragedies, occurring

in different places at different times, they cannot lose sight of the fact that the Armenians were still living in their historical homelands, had passed through cultural and political movements to the formulation of social, economic, and administrative reforms in the Ottoman Empire, and were perceived as a significant obstacle to the realization of ideals espoused by some members of the ruling Turkish Union and Progress party. This observation in no way diminishes responsibility for the genocide or mitigates its effects.

CONDEMNATION OF THE GENOCIDE

At the time of the deportations and massacres beginning in 1915, there was virtually universal condemnation of the operation and its perpetrators. The accounts of eyewitnesses and officials of many nationalities as well as the testimony of the survivors themselves were too detailed and corroborative to doubt the systematic nature of the operation. Being born into the targeted group was in and of itself sufficient to mark an individual for elimination.[1] United States Ambassador Henry Morgenthau testified that the deportations to the Syrian and Mesopotamian deserts were unquestionably meant to decimate the Armenian population:

> The Central Government now announced its intention of gathering the two million or more Armenians living in the several sections of the empire and transporting them to this desolate and inhospitable region. Had they undertaken such a deportation in good faith it would have represented the height of cruelty and injustice. As a matter of fact, the Turks never had the slightest idea of reestablishing the Armenians in this new country. They knew that the great majority would never reach their destination and that those who did would either die of thirst and starvation, or be murdered by the wild Mohammedan desert tribes. The real purpose of the deportations was robbery and destruction; it really represented a new method of massacre. When the Turkish authorities gave the orders for these deportations, they were merely giving the death warrant to a whole race; they understood this well, and, in their conversations with me, they made no particular attempt to conceal the fact (Morgenthau, 1918, p. 309).

Morgenthau concluded:

> I am confident that the whole of history of the human race contains no such horrible episode as this. The great massacres and persecutions of the past seem almost insignificant when compared to the sufferings of the Armenian race in 1915 (pp. 321-322).

The large corpus of evidence of genocide notwithstanding, the mechanism of denial and rationalization was put into motion as soon as the deportations had begun. During and immediately after World War I, with the evidence too fresh for total denial, the emphasis was placed on rationalization. Turkish publications and official declarations pointed to Armenian disloyalty, exploitation, and imminent general rebellion at a time when the fatherland was struggling for survival on several fronts.

The next phase, beginning with the international abandonment of the Armenian question and the founding of the Republic of Turkey in 1923, was characterized by the downplaying of the unpleasant past and concentration on a new image of a new Turkey, in which minorities enjoyed cultural and religious freedom. Apparently convinced that the Armenian problem would evaporate in due time, the Turkish government under Mustafa Kemal and his successors tried to deal with Armenian matters as quietly and expeditiously as possible through diplomatic channels.

But in 1965 the world-wide Armenian commemorations of the fiftieth anniversary of the genocide and the increasingly demonstrative and militant stance taken by many second and third generation Armenians of the dispersion ushered in a new phase in strategy. While continuing to capitalize upon the geopolitical, military, and economic importance of their country in efforts to pressure foreign governments to disregard Armenian manifestations, Turkish leaders also authorized an active campaign of counterpropaganda. The resulting books and brochures, usually sent out from Ankara in the month of April to detract from the annual Armenian commemorative programs marking the onset of the 1915 massacres, were addressed primarily to policy-makers and opinion-makers abroad, to members of legislatures and state and local governments, and to libraries, scholars, and teachers.

Only in the most recent phase, brought on by intensified Armenian violence against Turkish officials, has the strategy been directed toward public opinion in general. In newspaper advertisements, brochures and newsletters, and other popularly written literature, the heavily financed campaign aims at linking Armenian activism with an international conspiracy associated with the Soviet Union and the Palestine Liberation Organization. Giving special attention to Jewish leaders and Jewish opinion, the strategy attempts to dissociate the Jewish and Armenian experiences and to drive a broad wedge between the two peoples by expressing profound sympathy for the victims and survivors of the true Holocaust, while condemning the other as a hoax and "the greatest lie of the century." Enlisting the services of Turkish academics and a few non-Turkish writers, the architects of this strategy appeal to a Western sense of fair play in insisting that the "other side" of a grossly misrepresented situation be taken into consideration, and that the Armenian movement be exposed historically as a treacherous but abortive national rebellion and currently as a scheme to subvert Turkey and alienate it from its allies. That the repeated denials and refutations have achieved a degree of success is evidenced in the recent use by some Western reporters and commentators of qualifiers such as "alleged" and "asserted" in reference to the genocide.

DENIAL OF THE HOLOCAUST

The transformation of a historic genocidal operation into a
controversial issue causes anger and frustration among some, while
it leads others to ask if there might not be credibility in the Turkish version. It may also serve as a warning of things to come.
While there are antisemitic groups that have challenged the truth of
the Holocaust, they have by and large been discredited, and the
world remains strongly aware of the decimation of European Jewry.
Yet, I would suggest that, given conditions like those affecting
the Armenians, the Holocaust, too, would be challenged, not only by
prejudiced extremists and guilty governments but also by well-
intentioned individuals who believe that in a relativist world there
are always two sides to a story. To be more specific, let us ask how
the Holocaust might be regarded under the following ten conditions,
which approximate the Armenian situation:

1. The Jewish survivors of the Holocaust, left largely to
    their own devices, had scattered the world over as refugees.
2. The survivors, having no sovereign state or government to
    represent them, had to struggle for years merely to ensure
    physical and economic existence of their families, with
    their limited community resources concentrated on creating a
    new network of schools and temples to preserve the national-
    religious heritage as well as possible in diverse lands and
    circumstances.
3. No independent Jewish nation-state was created, and the
    Allied victors, despairing of assisting the survivors, aban-
    doned the Jewish question.
4. The Jewish communities were deprived of the leadership, in-
    spiration, and impetus provided by a Jewish nation-state.
5. In the absence of such a state, few resources were allocated
    for the founding of research institutes and other bodies for
    the gathering and analyses of materials relating to the
    Holocaust.
6. The number of Jewish survivors and expatriates was too small
    and lacking in sufficient political and financial influence
    to affect their host governments or to succeed in having the
    Holocaust dealt with in its many aspects in motion pictures
    and television productions and in educational and literary
    programs.
7. The survivors, nearly all with vivid memories and indelible
    details of the genocide, gradually passed from the scene,
    their children and grandchildren having become partially as-
    similated and unable to recount with preciseness the experi-
    ences of the survivors or to challenge deniers with personal
    eyewitness accounts.
8. The German government, defying the harsh terms initially im-
    posed by the Allies, succeeded in writing a new peace set-
    tlement that did not necessitate any form of compensation to
    the survivors or even formal acknowledgment of the genocidal
    operation, that government alternating thereafter between
    disclaimers of responsibility for any actions taken by pre-
    vious regimes and absolute denials that the Jews had been
    subjected to any conditions not also suffered by the German
    people themselves.

9. The strategic geopolitical, military, and economic value assigned to Germany in international relations was sufficiently compelling to incline foreign governments to disregard Jewish claims against Germany, and even to participate in the coverup by trying to satisfy German demands to prevent manifestations hostile to Germany and detrimental to its relations with allied countries.

10. A new generation of foreign students, scholars, and officials interested in German affairs espoused the goal of showing Germany in a new light as a progressive, democratic state and of revising its much-maligned image and unfair stereotypes such as those that presented an oversimplified picture of a victimizing Germany and a victimized Jewry.

It is not unlikely that in these circumstances the Jewish people would be facing the same general indifference and even annoyance that surround Armenians in their efforts to keep their case before world opinion, raising for them the question whether truth and justice can ever prevail in the absence of sheer political and military power.

THE SHIFTING CHARACTER OF THE DENIALS

With this broad overview of the problem, a look at the shifting character of the denials might prove instructive. In the first phase, during World War I, the Turkish authorities initially tried to hide the enactment of the deportations and massacres, but once the operations had gotten well under way shifted the blame for Armenian troubles to the Armenians themselves. In response to the discomfort of Turkey's wartime allies, the attempted intercession of neutral states, and the threatening behavior of the Entente powers who warned they would "hold all members of the Turkish Government, as well as all those officials who have participated in these massacres, personally responsible" (Hovannisian, 1967, pp. 51-52), the Young Turk rulers issued several publications incriminating the Armenians. With a selective compilation of hostile editorials from Armenian revolutionary societies, and photographs of Armenian bands and arms caches (many of them actually from the period of struggle against Sultan Abdul-Hamid II), the Turkish leaders attempted to convince the world of Armenian treachery.[2] Going even farther, Turkish diplomatic personnel such as Ambassador to Washington Ahmed Rustem Bey insisted that a government could not sacrifice its preservation to sentiments of humanity, especially as the laws of humanity were suspended in time of war (Rustem Bey, 1918). After the Russian imperial armies and Armenian volunteer units from the Caucasus had occupied most of the eastern provinces of Van, Bitlis, Erzerum, and Trebizond in 1916, the Turkish publications focused on the oppression of the Turkish and Kurdish population in the region, showing that the supposed Armenian lambs were quite capable of becoming merciless wolves.[3]

The Turkish wartime publications were roundly refuted in the West, and it seemed that with the Ottoman defeat in late 1918 the Allied Powers would now fulfill their pledges to punish Turkey and rehabilitate the Armenian survivors. Under these circumstances various Turkish groups and political figures who had opposed the Young Turk dictatorship surfaced with the goal of deflecting blame away from the Turkish people and holding territorial losses to a minimum. Acting under names such as the National Congress (Milli congre) of Turkey, they reiterated the charge that many Armenians had been subverted by Russian and revolutionary propaganda and had turned against their government by assisting the Allied armies and creating grave security problems. The Armenian deportations, therefore, could be justified by the "exigencies of war," but the same did not hold true for the "policy of extermination and robbery" enacted by the Young Turk leaders, who ranked "among the greatest criminals of humanity." Justice demanded that the Turkish people not be punished for the "criminal aberation" of an "unnatural government," which caused as much torment to Muslims as to Armenians.[4] Similar arguments were made by Grand Vizier Damad Ferid Pasha as he pled the Turkish case before the Paris Peace Conference in mid-1919. Admitting that there had occurred "misdeeds which are such as to make the conscience of mankind shudder forever," he shifted the blame to the German and Young Turk dictators and reminded the Allies of Armenian excesses as well. Armenians and Turks had lived together peaceably for centuries, and there was no validity in the view that the Armenians were the victims of innate Turkish racial or religious intolerance (US State Department, 1943, pp. 509-511).

Of the postwar Turkish writers, American-educated journalist Ahmed Emin (Yalman) was perhaps the most candid in admitting that genocidal acts had occurred. Ascribing these to an unfortunate past, Emin listed certain mitigating circumstances and pointed to the new, progressive role of Turkey in the 1930s. Without discarding the standard rationalizations about the Armenian threat to state security, he nonetheless wrote in a relativist manner that the action against the Armenians "was not commensurate with military necessity." Noting that the deportees, whom he identified as being mostly women and children, were subjected to the harshness of terrain and climate and the absence of basic facilities, he continued:

> In addition, as the event proved, the suffering of the deported were by no means confined to those which were unavoidable in view of strict military necessity or the existing general conditions. In the first place, the time allowed for leaving a town or village and for selling out all moveable goods was extremely short, being limited in some cases to a day or two. Second, the deported were not only left unprotected from attacks which were sure to come from marauders, but the "special organization" created with the help of two influential members of the Committee of Union and Progress was in some cases directly instrumental in bringing about attacks and massacres. Third, the area chosen as the home of the deported was in part a desert incapable of supporting the existence of a large mass of people who reached it from a cold mountain climate after endless hardships.

The deportations taken as a whole were meant to be only a temporary military measure. But for certain influential Turkish politicians they meant the extermination of the Armenian minority in Turkey with the idea of bringing about racial homogeneity in Asia Minor (Emin, 1930, pp. 217, 219-220).

Emin added that in 1917, because of the intensity of enemy propaganda and the pressure of officials opposed to the greatly extended scope of the deportations, a commission of inquiry looked into the reported excesses, but "those favoring the deportations being very influential in the Government, the whole thing amounted more to a demonstration rather than a sincere attempt to fix complete responsibility." Those who pushed for "the policy of extermination," Emin explained, knew that they would be universally condemned and believed that their personal sacrifice for the national cause might be recognized "only in a very distant future" (p. 221). Ironically, the prediction gradually came to pass, as the remains of Talaat Pasha have now been returned to a resting place of honor in Turkey, and there has been a general rehabilitation of persons widely regarded as the prime organizers of the genocide.

Not only did the opponents of the Young Turks attempt to lift the heavy onus of the massacres from the Turkish people in the postwar period, but members of the erstwhile Young Turk triumvirate themselves addressed the issue while they were fugitives under the sentence of death. Before his assassination in Berlin in 1921, Talaat Pasha, the former Minister of Interior and Grand Vizier, joined his own Turkish detractors in combining denials, disclaimers, and rationalizations. Insisting that the Ottoman Empire had been forcibly drawn into the war, he repeated charges against the Armenians, yet made partial admissions which went farther than subsequent Turkish governments and many revisionist historians were willing to go. The Armenians, he said, were deported from the eastern provinces but not upon a premeditated plan of annihilation. The responsibility for their fate, he wrote, fell foremost upon the Armenians themselves, although it was true that the deportations were not carried out lawfully everywhere, and that many innocent people suffered because some officials abused their authority.

Absolving himself of personal guilt, Talaat claimed that those involved were either common criminals and looters or simple, uneducated, zealous but sincere Turks who believed that the Armenians should be punished and that they were acting for the good of the country. While it would have been easy to deal with the first group, he explained, the second was strong and numerous and any punitive measures against it would have created great discontent among the masses. It was not possible to divide the country and create unrest in Anatolia when internal unity was essential for the war effort. Talaat concluded: "The preventive measures were taken in every country during the war, but while the regrettable results were passed over in silence in the other countries, the echo of our acts was heard the world over, because everybody's eyes were upon us" (Talaat, 1921, pp. 294-295).

Away from the capital during most of the war, Young Turk trium-virate member Ahmed Jemal Pasha commanded the Ottoman army in Syria at the time of the deportations and remains the most controversial of the triumvirate as regards his attitude towards the Armenians. While accused of complicity in the genocide, Jemal himself insisted that the decisions for the deportations had been made without his participation. "Just as I had nothing to do with the aforementioned negotiations about the deportations of the Armenians, I am equally innocent of ordering any massacres." Jemal indirectly admitted that the Armenian male population had been massacred by claiming that he had managed to save as many as 150,000 widows and orphans who made up the deportation caravans. He deplored "the crimes perpetrated during the deportations of 1915," but also called attention to the fact that the Armenians did not fall short in cruelty and treachery (Djemal, 1922, pp. 276-280).

Hence, in the postwar writings of both the Young Turks and their opponents, partial admissions of wrongdoing and even oblique references to wholesale massacres and advocates of extermination are mixed with charges of Armenian treachery and disclaimers of personal and collective responsibility for the Armenian tragedy.

In 1923 the international abandonment of the Armenians in the Lausanne treaties and the establishment of the Republic of Turkey initiated a new phase in the official Turkish attitude toward the Armenians. The Turkish authorities tried to play up the new image of Turkey as a secularist, modernizing state, while playing down the unpleasant past. There was little discussion of Armenians in Tur-kish publications, except for brief passages relating to sinister but unsuccessful Armenian and Greek imperialistic designs to in-fringe upon the nation's territorial integrity. In its response to continued though weakened Armenian efforts to influence world opi-nion, the Ankara government relied heavily on diplomatic channels in this period. Exemplary of this tactic was a case involving the pro-jected filming in Hollywood of Franz Werfel's celebrated novel, The Forty Days of Musa Dagh, the story of the desperate resistance of several Armenian settlements near Antioch during the deportations. Plans by Metro-Goldwyn-Mayer studios to begin production in 1934 evoked strong Turkish protests. In response to the State Depart-ment's active involvement in the issue, the studio offered to alter the script and even to allow the Turkish embassy to approve the re-vised version before filming commenced. The embassy continued to pressure the Department of State, which interceded with the presi-dent of the Motion Pictures Producers and Distributors of America, and was finally gratified with the news that plans to produce the film were being dropped. An attempt to revive the project in 1938 met with the repetition of Turkish protests, State Department inter-cession, and the shelving of the script.[5]

ACTIVE TURKISH EFFORTS TO REWRITE HISTORY

Efforts to make the Armenian genocide a nonissue had registered impressive gains by 1965, the year marking the fiftieth anniversary of the massacres. But then the unexpected occurred. The relatively

quiescent Armenian communities, though unable to sustain external
interest in their cause, burst forth with unprecedented fervid activity. With increasing frequency, municipal officials, legislators,
governors, and even prime ministers and presidents mentioned the Armenian tragedy when speaking about man's inhumanity to man.   Then,
in 1973, the first in a series of Armenian acts of political violence against Turkish diplomats brought the media to focus not only
on the violence but also on its background, the Armenian historical
experience, and the Turkish denials of genocide.   Nor were the attempts of the Turkish government to rely on diplomatic channels always successful. Pressure to prevent the erection of Armenian memorial monuments in Los Angeles and in Marseilles, for example, failed
despite sympathy in some quarters within the American and French
governments.

Under these circumstances the Turkish government came to the
conclusion that it could no longer simply dismiss or ignore the Armenian problem.   A campaign to counteract Armenian propaganda was
decided upon in the 1970s. In this phase of the denial process, the
pamphlets and brochures sent out from Ankara to foreign countries
were mostly photographic reprints of the Turkish publications issued
during and immediately after World War I with the intent to cast
blame on the Armenians and minimize Ottoman losses.[6] Evolving out
of this type of literature by the middle of the decade were new
tracts prepared by several Turkish historians and contemporary
writers.   These materials, which were intended to prove the base-
lessness of Armenian claims, included nothing new and were riddled
with contradiction, misquotation, and obvious distortion.   In his
essay entitled Armenian Question, for example, Enver Zia Karal asserted that, despite their treacherous behavior, the Armenians were
protected throughout Anatolia after the war. According to Karal,
Major General James G. Harbord, who headed an American military mission of inquiry to Asia Minor and Transcaucasia in 1919, admitted to
this when he supposedly reported:

> Meanwhile, the Armenian, unarmed at the time of deportations, a
> brave soldier who served in thousands in the armies of Russia,
> France and America is still unarmed and safe [italics mine] in
> a land where every man but himself need to carry a rifle
> (Karal, n.d., p. 22).

What Harbord actually wrote gives the opposite picture:

> Meanwhile, the Armenian, unarmed at the time of the deporta-
> tions and massacres [italics mine], a brave soldier by thou-
> sands in the armies of Russia, France, and America during the
> war, is still unarmed in a land where every man but himself
> carries a rifle (Harbord, 1920, p. 11).

Typical of the distortions in this genre of political pamphleteer-
ing, Karal put the words "and safe" into Harbord's mouth while removing the words "and massacres" in order to prove his point.
Harbord's real attitude about the genocide is public record:

Massacres and deportations were organized in the spring of 1915 under definite system, the soldiers going from town to town. The official reports of the Turkish Government show 1,100,000 as having been deported. Young men were first summoned to the government building in each village and then marched out and killed. The women, the old men, and children were, after a few days, deported to what Talaat Pasha called "agricultural colonies," from the high, cool, breeze-swept plateau of Armenia to the malarial flats of the Euphrates and the burning sands of Syria and Arabia...Multilation, violation, torture, and death have left their haunting memories in a hundred beautiful Armenian valleys, and the traveler in that region is seldom free from the evidence of this most colossal crime of all the ages (p. 7).

Efforts to defame the Armenians sometimes entered the realm of the ridiculous. In a pamphlet sent out from Ankara and entitled Truth about Armenians, Ahmet Vefa, aside from repeating the standard Turkish allegations against the Armenians, alerted the English-reading public to the existence of a letter in the Hoover Library at Stanford making it known that "the Armenians were not and never could be desirable citizens, that they would always be unscrupulous merchants." What may be of greater interest is Vefa's contention that when Adolf Hitler asked rhetorically in 1939, "Who after all speaks today of the annihilation of the Armenians?," he was making reference, not to the Turkish genocide of the Armenians but rather to the Armenian destruction of the pre-Armenian Urartuans in the seventh century B.C. (Vefa, 1975, pp. 7-8, 11).

Unable to make significant headway with this type of literature, Turkish officials encouraged friendly foreign scholars to present the "Turkish side" in the West and even afforded a few partisans access to some relevant archival files. But long before the unabashedly distorted writings of Stanford J. Shaw in the 1970s, the trend toward revisionism had already influenced a number of scholars interested in Turkish history and wishing to change the unfair stereotypes of the Turks. As the existence of the Republic of Turkey was seen as a good thing, it was not unnatural to be disposed to justify the events that led to that republic and its current boundaries. This disposition was reflected in the writings of Lewis V. Thomas, Bernard Lewis, Richard Robinson, Norman Itzkowitz, and a significant number of younger scholars.

The tenor of this revisionist approach was set already in the 1950s in the works of Thomas, who admitted that the Turks overreacted to a perceived Armenian threat and who regretted the fate of the Armenians but who nonetheless explained that the Turks had been desperate and concluded with the following rationalization:

By 1918, with the definitive excision of the total Armenian Christian population from Anatolia and the Straits area, except for a small and wholly insignificant enclave in Istanbul city, the hitherto largely peaceful process of Turkification and Moslemization had been advanced in one great surge by the use of force...Had Turkification and Moslemization not been accelerated there by the use of force, there certainly would not today exist a Turkish Republic, a Republic owing its strength and stability in no small measure to the homogeneity of its population, a state which is now a valued associate of the United States (Thomas and Frye, 1951, p. 61).

All previous levels of revisionism were transcended in the 1970s in the writings of Stanford Shaw, who not only repeated but also embellished the worn, unsubstantiated accusations against the Armenians under the guise of scholarly research. His treatment of the Armenian question in History of the Ottoman Empire and Modern Turkey includes gross errors of omission and commission and surpasses even the excuses of the Young Turk perpetrators themselves (Shaw, 1977). Setting a theme for subsequent Turkish propaganda, he contested sources showing that there were between two and three million Armenians in the Ottoman Empire, maintaining that there were actually no more than 1,300,000 and thereby minimizing the number that could have been deported or killed. Characterizing the Armenians as the invariable aggressors, the victimizers rather than the victims, the privileged rather than the oppressed, and the base fabricators of unfounded tales of massacre, Shaw has insisted that the Young Turk government took all possible measures to ensure the safety of those elements from the supposedly few districts affected by the deportation decrees, the availability of food and water and of medical attention while en route, and the suitability of new homes in prearranged relocation centers:

> Specific instructions were issued for the army to protect the Armenians against nomadic attacks and to provide them with sufficient food and other supplies to meet their needs during the march and after they were settled. Warnings were sent to the Ottoman military commanders to make certain that neither the Kurds nor any other Muslims used the situation to gain vengeance for the long years of Armenian terrorism. The Armenians were to be protected and cared for until they returned to their homes after the war. A supplementary law established a special commission to record the properties of some deportees and sell them at auction at fair prices, with the revenues being held in trust until their return. Muslims wishing to occupy abandoned buildings could do so only as renters, with the revenues paid to the trust funds, and with the understanding that they would have to leave when the original owners returned. The deportees and their possessions were to be guarded by the army while in transit as well as in Iraq and Syria, and the government would provide for their return once the crisis was over (p. 315).

In the face of the voluminous documentary evidence and eyewitness accounts to the contrary, Shaw would have the reader believe that the Armenians were removed only from a few strategic regions and this, with the utmost of concern for the safety of their persons and properties. In view of what actually happened to the Armenian population, the belaboring of this point seems ludicrous.

THE BATTLE FOR TRUTH IN THE UNITED NATIONS

The audacity of contemporary revisionists such as Shaw has been aided by the death of most foreign eyewitnesses to and survivors of the massacres and has been paralleled by renewed militancy within the Turkish government. Determined to prevent the Armenian question from ever again becoming a topic of international diplomacy, the Ankara government has engaged in strong political lobbying to expunge even passing references to the Armenians. Exemplary of this policy were the tactics used in relation to a United Nations subcomission Draft Report on the Prevention and Punishment of the Crime of Genocide. In 1973 the special rapporteur of the Subcomission on Prevention of Discrimination and Protection of Minorities wrote in paragraph 30 of the introductory historical section:

> Passing to the modern era, one may note the existence of relatively full documentation dealing with the massacres of Armenians, which have been described as the "first case of genocide in the twentieth century" (Kuper, 1981, p. 219).

The paragraph made no mention either of the Ottoman Empire or of Turks, yet the Turkish mission to the United Nations and the Turkish government regarded the sentence as menacing and immediately applied pressure on governments and delegations represented on the full Human Rights Commission. Yielding to this pressure, members of the commission followed their instructions to speak in favor of or maintain silence in adopting a recommendation that historic events preceding recent genocidal acts and the contemporary definition of genocide be omitted from the report. Matters that had been subject to "controversial explanations and evaluations in different publications" should be avoided. Hence paragraph 30 should be deleted (pp. 219-220).

When the issue was raised again in 1975, one delegate noted that the tragedy of 1915 was historical fact, "but in a civilized international community, consideration should also be given to the desire of a state not to be defamed on account of its past acts, which had been perpetrated by a previous generation and were probably regretted by the present generation." When the subcommission's rapporteur submitted the revised version of his report in 1978, the historical section began with the Nazi-perpetrated Holocaust. In the words of Leo Kuper, the Armenian genocide "had disappeared down the memory hole."

When the Turkish measures to erase even the memory of the Armenian victims in a draft report of a United Nations subcomission became known, the story spread swiftly throughout the Armenian communities. Armenian groups now mounted their own campaign, publicly invoking the human rights declarations of several member states of the UN Human Rights Commission. The subsequent lead of the United States in reversing its position during the Carter administration in 1979 was followed by several other countries, resulting in the request to the special rapporteur to take into account the various statements made in and to the commission about the Armenian tragedy.

Now, after a decade, the matter of whether to mention the Armenians
in the introductory historical section of the belabored report still
remains unresolved.[7]

CONCLUSION: DOES MIGHT MAKE RIGHT AFTER ALL?

The history of the denial of the Armenian genocide has passed
through several phases, each somewhat different in emphasis but all
characterized by efforts to avoid responsibility and the moral, material, and political consequences of admission. Only under the impact of the defeat of the Ottoman Empire and the flight of the Young
Turk leaders were there partial admissions, but this trend
was halted by the successful Turkish Nationalist defiance of the
Allies and the international abandonment of the Armenian question.
In the absence of external force, neither the perpetrators nor suc-
cessive Turkish governments have been willing to face the horrendous
skeleton in their closet. Rather, they have resorted to various
forms of avoidance, denial, repudiation, and vilification to keep
the door shut. In the meantime, Turkish writers and scholars have
been unable to deal with their national past honestly and have been
drawn wittingly or unwittingly into the wheels of rationalization
and falsification. Taking advantage of its strategic geopolitical
and military importance, the Republic of Turkey has repeatedly impressed on other governments and international bodies that dwelling
on a complex but no longer relevant past would be unproductive, dis-
ruptive, and unfriendly. Yet the problem has persisted and the tone
and tenor of the denials are now more strident than ever before.
This position severely obstructs investigation of the genocide, its
causes, effects, and implications, and the scholarly and humanitarian ends to which such studies could be directed.

In newspaper advertisements and a score of brochures and bulle-
tins, the Turkish government and its associated groups seek to link
Armenian demands for acknowledgment of the genocide with international terrorism and to create a breach between the Armenian and
Jewish communities by warning that acceptance of the Armenian "myth"
of genocide would dishonor the memory of the Holocaust victims and
mix the profane with the noble. When a Turkish terrorist attempted
to assassinate the Pope in 1981, the Turkish Ambassador to the
United States tried futilely to establish an Armenian connection.
The Ambassador's frequent declarations that claims about Armenian
massacres are "totally baseless" have been reiterated in a widely-
distributed brochure published in Washington, D.C. in 1982:

There was no genocide committed against the Armenians in the
Ottoman Empire before or during World War I. No genocide was
planned or ordered by the Ottoman government and no genocide
was carried out. Recent scholarly research has discovered that
the stories of massacres were in fact largely invented by Armenian nationalist leaders in Paris and London during World War
I and spread throughout the world through the British intelligence.[8]

As the number of persons who lived through the world war and who have direct knowledge of the events diminishes, the rationalizers and revisionists become all the more audacious, to the extent of transforming the victims into the victimizers. At the time of the deportations and massacres, no reputable newspaper or journal would have described the genocide as "alleged." The clouding of the past, however, and the years of Turkish denials, diplomatic, political, and military pressures, and programs of image building have had their impact on some publishers, correspondents, scholars, and public officials. In an increasingly skeptical world, the survivors and the descendants of the victims have been thrust into defensive positions from which they are required to prove repeatedly that they have truly been wronged, individually and collectively. It may be no wonder that they should look upon Holocaust victims with envy for not having to face an unrepentant and uncompromising German government and a high-powered political, diplomatic, and public informational campaign of denial to persuade reporters, announcers, educators, and national and international officials that a state-organized plan of annihilation was in fact not enacted. They may rightly ask despairingly whether there are any effective alternatives to the old adage, "Might Makes Right."

NOTES

1. For listings of archival materials and published works in Western languages pertaining to the Armenian genocide, see Richard G. Hovannisian, The Armenian Holocaust: A Bibliography Relating to the Deportations, Massacres, and Dispersion of the Armenian People, 1915-1923 (Cambridge, Mass.: Armenian Heritage Press, 1980).
2. See, for example, Verite sur le mouvement revolutionnaire armenien et les mesures gouvernementales (Constantinople: n.p., 1916); and Aspirations et agissements revolutionnaires des comites armeniens avant et apres la proclamation de la constitution ottomane (Constantinople: n.p., 1917).
3. See, for example, Documents sur les atrocites armeno-russes (Constantinople: Societe Anonyme de Papeterie et d'Imprimerie, 1917).
4. National Congress of Turkey, The Turco-Armenian Question: The Turkish Point of View (Constantinople: Societe Anonyme de Papeterie et d'Imprimerie, 1919), esp. pp. 74-92. See also Memorandum of the Sublime Porte Communicated to the American, French, and Italian High Commissioners on the 12th February 1919 (Constantinople: Zellich Brothers, 1919).
5. See the Musa Dagh file in United States National Archives, Record Group 59, General Records of the Department of State, Decimal File 811.4061.
6. See, for example, Documents sur les atrocites armeno-russes and The Turco-Armenian Question, cited above, and Documents relatifs aux atrocites commises par les Armeniens sur la population musulmane (Constantinople: Societe Anonyme de Papeterie et d'Imprimerie, 1919) War Journal of the Second Russian Fotress Artillery Regiment of Erzeroum and Notes of Superior Russian Officer on the Atrocities at Erzeroum (Constantinople: n.p., 1919).

98

7. In March, 1983, the U.N. Commission on Human Rights, meeting in Geneva, requested the Subcommission on Prevention of Discrimination and Protection of Minorities to appoint a new special rapporteur to revise and update the study on the Question of the Prevention and Punishment of the Crime of Genocide. Several members recommended that the report simply be updated rather than revised. In August the subcommission appointed Benjamin Whitaker of the United Kingdom as the rapporteur.

8. Assembly of Turkish-American Associations. Setting the Record Straight on Armenian Propaganda against Turkey (Washington, D.C.: n.p., 1982), p. 4. For other recent Turkish publications broadly disseminated in Europe and America and reflecting the degree of state resources committed to the campaign of denial and accusation, see, for example, The Armenian Issue in Nine Questions and Answers (Ankara: Foreign Policy Institute, 1982); Prime Ministry, Documents (Ankara: Directorate General of Press and Information, 1982).

REFERENCES

ASSEMBLY of Turkish-American Associations. Setting the Record Straight on Armenian Propaganda against Turkey. Washington, D.C.: n.p., 1982.

DJEMAL Pasha. Memories of a Turkish Statesman, 1913-1919. New York: George H. Doran Co., 1922.

EMIN (Yalman), Ahmed, Turkey in the World War. New Haven & London: Yale University Press, 1930.

HARBORD, Major General James G. Conditions in the Near East: Report of the American Military Mission to Armenia. Senate Document 266, 66th Cong., 2d. sess. Washington D.C.: Government Printing Office, 1920.

HOVANNISIAN, Richard G. Armenia on the Road to Independence, 1918. Berkeley & Los Angeles: University California Press, 1967.

KARAL, Enver Ziya. Armenian Question (1878-1923). N.p., n.d.

KUPER, Leo. Genocide: Its Political Use in the Twentieth Century. New Haven & London: Yale University Press, 1981.

MORGENTHAU, Henry. Ambassador Morgenthau's Story. Garden City, N.Y.: Doubleday, Page & Co., 1918.

RUSTEM Bey, Ahmed. La guerre mondiale et la question turco-armenienne. Berne: Imprimerie Staemfli, 1918.

SHAW, Stanford J. History of the Ottoman Empire and Modern Turkey. Vol. II (coauthored with Ezel Kural Shaw), Reform, Revolution and Republic: The Rise of Modern Turkey, 1808-1975. Cambridge, London, New York, Melbourne: Cambridge University Press, 1977.

TALAAT Pasha. Posthumous memoirs of Talaat Pasha. Current History, 1921, 15, 287-295.

THOMAS, Lewis V., & Frye N. Richard. The United States and Turkey and Iran. Cambridge, Mass.: Harvard University Press, 1951.

UNITED States of America. Department of State. Papers Relating to the Foreign Relations of the United States, 1919: The Paris Peace

Conference. Vol.IV. Washington, D.C.: Government Printing Office, 1943.

VEFA, Ahmet. Truth about Armenians. Ankara: n.p., 1975.

RICHARD G. HOVANNISIAN, Ph.D., Department of History, University of California, Los Angeles, California 90024, U.S.A.

7. What Genocide? What Holocaust?
News From Turkey, 1915–23: A Case Study

Marjorie Housepian-Dobkin

Marjorie Housepian-Dobkin (author, dean and professor of English at Barnard College), two of whose sons are half Jewish, was stunned by the parallels between the Armenian genocide and the Holocaust when she began, in 1965, to "find out what really happened" in the first instance. Precedents, she says, must be recognized if we are to avoid the next stage and final stage in the fatal progression from World War I and genocide, World War II and Holocaust, to World War III and omnicide. With her husband and three sons, she is actively involved in the nuclear disarmament movement.

During the annihilation of the Turkish Armenians in 1915–16, an act now called genocide, the United States media (periodicals as well as newspapers) gave extensive coverage to what was then called the Armenian "extermination." In that age before broadcasting, almost every literate American learned from these sources that the Turkish government was systematically liquidating every Armenian man, woman and child in the land, outside the cities of Smyrna and Constantinople which had large foreign communities.

The media also predicted Turkish leaders would pay dearly after the war for what were called "unprecedented crimes" and "crimes against humanity." Powerful testimony also came from German eyewitnesses, some so upset that they left Turkey and even Germany. Johannes Lepsius, a German clergyman, after going to Turkey to investigate, returned so shaken that he published and secretly distributed all he had seen before his government learned what he had done.[1] Word of his testimony leaked out, however. Protestant missionaries in Turkey, virtually all American, were also eyewitnesses whose reports made the news regularly. The American missions had some 551 elementary and high schools, 8 colleges and countless dispensaries[2] serving Armenians and some Greeks. They had gone to Turkey in the 1830s and quickly discovered that under Koranic law conversion from Islam meant death. Yet they stayed, convinced as one of their historians wrote, that Armenian Christians converted to a more evangelical denomination would ultimately be their best missionaries "because native to the soil."[3] In the years before World War I, joining the Foreign Service either for God or Flag was the fashionable thing to do after graduating from the trend-setting Ivy League schools. This meant great interest in the news about missionaries, and hence about Armenians.

PRIMARY SOURCES

I have studied closely The New York Times and its monthly magazine Current Events, very popular at the time. I have also looked through enough reports from other newspapers (The New York Herald Tribune, The Boston Herald, The Chicago Tribune, and such magazines as the Literary Digest, The Atlantic Monthly, The Nation, The Outlook) to note that the Times coverage was not exceptional.

The genocide began with the arrest of all Armenian community leaders in Constantinople on the night of April 24, 1915. By December, the Times alone had published over 100 articles in increasingly vivid detail. The majority were featured in the first six pages, about half on the first three.

Reading these articles shows the extent to which they tell the story and constitute a primary source of the genocide. They began tentatively in late April, 1915. Armenian deaths were news, but not a novelty. The massacre of about 300,000 in 1895-96 had been well reported though without anyone in Turkey (besides the Armenians) suffering any consequences.

March, April and May headlines on "Renewed Massacres of Armenians"[4] vied with news of sporadic resistance and a pitifully few, isolated and unsuccessful attempts at retaliation. But from August to the end of the year the reports became increasingly ominous. "Armenian Horrors Grow - Massacres Greater than under Abdul Hamidi!" (August 6);[5] "Armenians sent to Perish in the Desert" (August 18) with subhead: "Turks Accused of Plan to Exterminate Whole Population."[6] On August 27 was the headline "Turks Depopulate Towns of Armenia, Traveller Reports," and subhead "Traveller Reports Christians of Great Territory Have Been Driven From Homes."[7] On September 5: "1,500,000 Armenians Starve."[8] A smaller piece on September 3 had indicated that the Turks had massacred all the Armenians of Ismid.[9] As the Times observed, Ismid is 56 miles from Constantinople, and nowhere near the Russian frontier where Turkey claimed Armenians were aiding and abetting the enemy and thus provoking the "deportations" - the euphemism for genocide. (It is true that Armenians who were residents of Russia were fighting with the Russian army against Turkey. This is a distinction Turkey has never made - then, or now).

The Germans were of course allied with the Turks and the United States was still officially neutral; thus American missionaries, many of them, were staying on in Turkey. The official German view was quoted in the Times when the German ambassador in Washington said that the reports were "pure inventions," on September 28,[10] and on the next day said that the Armenians had brought the reprisals on themselves by stirring up rebellion.[11] All the same, the Ambassador added, the reports about extermination were "greatly exaggerated." However, a front page article a week later (October 4) reported that a Committee of eminent Americans had, after thoroughly checking out every eyewitness story, found that the "Turkish record was outdone," that the atrocities had been "unequaled in a thousand years" and that "a policy of extermination was in effect against a helpless people." These phrases were headlined on page one, as well as expanded in the piece. The text, in part, reads as follows:

The Committee on Armenian Atrocities, a body of eminent Americans which for weeks has been investigating the situation in

Turkish Armenia issued, yesterday, a detailed report of that investigation...The report tells of children under 15 years of age thrown into the Euphrates to be drowned, of women forced to desert infants in arms and to leave them by the roadside to die, of young women and girls appropriated by the Turks, of men murdered and tortured. Everything an Armenian possesses, even to the clothes on his back are stolen by his persecutors.

The signatories of this report - a compendium of church leaders, businessmen and financiers - include Oscar Straus, former secretary of commerce and labor and ex-Ambassador to Turkey, Cleveland Dodge, the Reverend Dr. Stephen H. Wise, the Right Reverend David H. Greer, Protestant Episcopal Bishop of New York, George Plimpton, and several leaders of the missionary movement including the Reverend Dr. James Barton, Secretary of the American Board of Commissioners of Foreign Missions and John R. Mott of the International Committee of the YMCA. I mention these names because, despite the many testimonies they collected and presented confirming the Armenian genocide, those named except for Rabbi Wise and the Episcopal Bishop were among those who, after the War, lost little time in exonerating the Turks and thus, in effect, repudiating their own earlier testimonies for reasons I shall presently touch on.

First, let me document a little more of the news treatment:

"Germany says she cannot Stop the Turks" (October 23)[12] "Americans' Deaths Laid to the Turks: Five Missionaries Succumb to Shock of Armenian Horrors, says Report of the Board of Commissioners for Foreign Missions" (November 3)[13]

"Million Armenians Killed or in Exile: American Committee on Relief says Victims of Turks are steadily Increasing. Policy of Extermination. More Atrocities detailed in Support of Charge that Turkey is acting Deliberately" (Dec. 15)[14]

"Saw Armenians Go Starving to Exile (Feb. 6)[15]

"Tells of Great Plain Black with Refugees" (Feb. 7)[16]

On November 27, 1915, Viscount Bryce, in London, had made public[17]the details of horrors which, he says in a letter accompanying his Report, "surpass in horror, if that were possible, all that has been published already." He is quoted as saying, further, that "these atrocities were not produced by imagination. Many are vouched for by several coincident testimonies. They are all in keeping and the evidence is most complete and most terrible. At the present phase of events the civilized world is powerless to intervene but we must bear these unspeakable crimes in constant memory against the day of reckoning..."

Against that day Lord Bryce collected the evidence and published it in a Blue Book, hiring as the Editor of this compilation a young Professor of Byzantine History named Arnold Toynbee.[18] Unfortunately for history Lord Bryce died in 1922.

In the November 1916 issue of <u>Current History</u> magazine date-
lined Aleppo, there appears an impassioned letter of protest to the
German authorities written by a group of German teachers:[19]

We feel it our duty to call attention to the fact that our
school work, the formation of a basis of a civilization and the
instilling of a respect in the natives will be henceforth impossible if the German government is not in a position to put
an end to the brutalities inflicted here on the exiled wives
and children of murdered Armenians.*

How can we possibly read the stories of Snow White and the
Seven Dwarfs with our Armenian children; how can we bring ourselves to decline and conjugate when in the courtyards opposite
and next to our school buildings death is reaping a harvest
among their starving compatriots? Girls, boys and women, all
practically naked, lie on the ground breathing their last sighs
amid the dying and among the coffins put out ready for them.

Forty to fifty people reduced to skeletons are all that is left
of the two to three thousand healthy peasant women driven down
here from upper Armenia. The good looking ones are decimated
by the vice of their jailers and the ugly ones are beaten, left
hungry and thirsty. Even those lying at the water's edge are
not allowed to drink. Europeans are forbidden from distribut-
ing bread among them.

The fifty skeletons lying heaped in our yard are practically
insane. They utter low groans and await death. Ta-a-lim el
Alman (the cult of the Germans) is responsible for this, the
natives here declare. It will always remain a terrible stain
on Germany's honor among the generations to come.

One of the signers of this letter, a Dr. Graetner, signed a
separate letter as well, which <u>Current History</u> also published in the
same article:

This time the question was not one of the traditional massacres
but of nothing more nor less than the complete extermination of
the Armenian people in Turkey. This fact Talaat's officials
cynically admitted with some embarrassment to the German consul. The government made out at first that they only wanted to
clear the war zone and assign new dwellings to the emigrants...

As one example - out of 18,000 people driven out of Kharput and
Sivas only 350 reached Aleppo, only 11 out of 1,900 from

---

*It is noteworthy, and should be pointed out, that the able- bodied
men, having been drafted into the Turkish army, had then been
separated into "labor battalions," taken aside and killed, some
after torture but still relatively mercifully when one considers
what happened to the women and children then herded away.

Erzerum. Once at Aleppo those who did not die here (the ceme-
teries are full) were driven by night to the Syrian steppes toward the Zor on the Euphrates. Here a very small percentage
drag out their existence, starving. I state this as an eyewitness.

Again in Current History, this in November 1917, a former German army officer and war correspondent in Turkey, who had left that
country and gone to Switzerland when his Swiss wife pleaded that she
could no longer live in Constantinople after witnessing the brutalities against the Armenians[20] has written, in part: In spite of
the pretty official speeches I often heard at the German Embassy,

the diplomats at bottom had little interest in saving this
people. I was often at the Embassy when the Armenian patriarch, after some particularly terrible attack on his people,
came in with tears in his eyes and begged for help. I could
discern nothing in the excited hurrying hither and thither of
our diplomats except anxiety to preserve German prestige and
vanity - never a worry for the Armenian people...There were
even cases, I am ashamed to say, when German officers in a village or two fired on women and children when no Turks were
found to do so; they did it to show their skill in artillery
practice. When an instance of this criminal interference by
military persons was brought to the attention of the Ambassador, Count Wolff-Metternich and he reported the matter to Germany, this crime which he reported was made the pretext for his
dismissal...[Actually, he had become persona non grata with the
Turks for concerning himself about Armenians].

Germany will never live down the shame that the refinedly
cruel extermination of a civilized people coincided with the
period of Germany's hegemony in Turkey.[21]

"Refinedly cruel" was an apt phrase, if one follows the testimony of American Ambassador Morgenthau. In November 1918, precisely
at the time of the armistice, he wrote, in an issue of The World's
Work, a leading missionary publication:

There is no phase of the Armenian question which has aroused
more interest than this: had the Germans any part of it? Did
they favor it? Did they merely acquiesce or did they oppose
the persecutions?...

For centuries the Turks have ill treated their Armenians with
inconceivable barbarity. Yet their methods have always been
crude, clumsy and unscientific. They excelled in beating out
an Armenian's brains with a club - and this unpleasant illustration is a perfect indication of the primitive methods they
applied. They have understood murder, but not murder as an
art.

But the Armenian proceedings of 1915 and 1916 evidenced an entirely new concept - the concept of deportation....

In a conference held in Berlin some time ago Paul Rohrbach recommended that Armenia should be evacuated and the Armenians dispersed in the direction of Mesopotamia and their places taken by the Turks...Mesopotamia might be provided thus with farmers which it now lacked...Germany was building the [Berlin to Baghdad] railway across the Mesopotamian desert from Hamburg to the Persian Gulf. But this railroad could never succeed unless there should develop a thrifty and industrous population to feed it...The Armenians were made of just the kind of stuff this enterprise needed. The mere fact that they were being sent to a hot, barren desert evidently furnished no impediment in Pan-German eyes. I found that Germany had been sowing these ideas for several years; I even found that German savants had been lecturing on this subject in the East.[22]

In July 1919 the front page of the New York Times carried the news that the new Government (of a new Sultan) in Turkey had sentenced Enver, Talaat and Djemal, the ruling triumverate of the Young Turks, to death in absentia for their crimes against the Armenians. The article noted that "Henry Morgenthau American Ambassador at Constantinople, and Sir Louis Mallet, the British Ambassador at the same place, have left no doubt in their dispatches, books, articles and inteviews of the guilt of the Young Turk leaders which has just been proclaimed with sentences pronounced by a Turkish court-martial ordered by the new Grand Vizier..."

Nobody, it seemed, knew, or admitted to knowing, where these former leaders were, however.

THE ASSASSINATION OF TALAAT IN BERLIN AND THE ACQUITTAL OF THE ASSASSIN

The assassination of Talaat in broad daylight on a Berlin street less than two years after the verdict referred to above, made only page 3 of The New York Times interestingly enough. Much had happened in the interim to turn official U.S. policy, and its reflection in the American press, towards Turkey. Public opinion, however, lagged behind.

The German press mourned Talaat as a friend, according to another Times story a few days latter[23] (the story added that Talaat had a 10,000,000 mark fortune in a Berlin bank and a wife who was "in favor of women's emancipation"). The assassin, a young student named Telirian, had witnessed his brother's head being split open with an axe, and his mother's and sisters' rapes and deaths by sword. He had been left for dead after being struck unconscious. Berlin's most famous criminal and international lawyers defended him. According to the Times, "The damning German angle to the Turkish war atrocities was obvious to all present."[24] Johannes Lepsius, the pastor who had gone into Turkey and secretly published his evidence was among those who testified on the youth's behalf. The assassin was acquitted. Official Turkish documents produced at the trial and reproduced in the newspapers in America and London "proved beyond question," Current History magazine stated, that

Talaat and other officials "had ordered the wholesale extermination of the Armenians including little orphan children."[25]

> One of the documents published in Current History follows:
> We hear from certain orphanages which have been opened that they have received also the children of the Armenians. Whether this is done through ignorance of our purpose or through contempt of it, the Government regards the feeding of such children or any attempt to prolong their lives an act entirely opposed to its purpose since it considered the survival of these children detrimental. S/Minister of the Interior Talaat

SUDDENLY THE TURKISH POSITION GAINS IN THE PRESS

One year later (in Sept. 1922), Current History along with the Literary Digest and in fact any magazines still concerned enough to run articles on Armenians were giving equal time to the Turkish view. The following is from an article by a retired U.S. Admiral, William Colby Chester. Chester declares that the Turks were falsely maligned during the World War, that their policy toward the minorities had been one of the utmost benevolence:

> The Armenians in 1915 were moved from the inhospitable regions where they were not welcome and could not actually prosper to the most delightful and fertile parts of Syria...where the climate is as benign as in Florida and California whither New York millionaires journey every year for health and recreation. All this was done at great expense of money and effort.[26]

What in the world happened to provoke such a shift? A shift, I need not add, that has remained to this day, granting that Chester's view is rather extreme - even the Turks have not dared go quite so far, as yet. He, and others like him, had powerful motives, however: Chester was on his way to Turkey to claim some rights which the German Kaiser had promised him (exclusive rights, he mistakenly thought) to exploit the oil fields of Mosul, then belonging to Turkey and called "the greatest oil find in history." He was not alone in his longing to reach this treasure: the new technology that began to boom after the war demanded quantities of this liquid gold. Henri Berenger in a letter to Clemenceau expressed the universal attitude in just nine words: "He who owns the oil shall rule the world."

For a more complete answer to "What Happened," I researched for six years, looking into the United States archives of the Dept. of State and the Navy Dept., the Library of Congress, the papers of the Board of Commissioners for Foreign Missions, read exhaustively in primary and secondary sources, and wrote a book which focuses on the burning of the city of Smyrna by the Turks in 1922 after their massacre of the entire Armenian and much of the Greek population.[27]

Those who underestimate the power of commerce in the history of the Middle East cannot have studied the postwar situation in Turkey between 1918 and 1923 when the peace treaty with Turkey was finally

signed at Lausanne. There were, of course, other <u>political</u> factors
which proved disastrous for the Armenians, the Russian revolution
high among them, but the systematic effort (chiefly by the Harding
administration) to turn American public opinion toward Turkey was
purely and simply motivated by the desire to beat the allied powers
to what were thought of as the vast, untapped resources of that
country, and chiefly the oil. Needless to say, it was not possible
to bring about the desired change in public opinion without deni-
grating what the Armenians had suffered. A close look at American
foreign policy toward Turkey in the years 1920-23 (and since) shows
an unrelenting effort to maintain Turkey's friendship by maintaining
a favorable image of that country in the American press by every
possible means, including outright censorship and falsification.

During the War, the American press, as had been pointed out,
convinced the American public that the Turks had committed what was
then considered the most barbarous and unforgiveable act of extermination known to man. In setting out to change this opinion, the
Harding administration had a cast of characters well suited to the
task. Charles Evans Hughes, the Secretary of State, had been an official of Standard Oil and was untroubled by conflict of interest.
The official history of the Standard Oil Company of New Jersey
covering those years boasts that the company flourished as never before when Hughes was in office.[28]

Allen Dulles, later to be head of the CIA, had been chief of
staff to the American High Commissioner in Constantinople after the
armistice and under Hughes was put in charge of the State Department's Near East desk. And the High Commissioner himself, Admiral
Mark L. Bristol, was a positive gift to the Turks. A virulent antisemite, he equally abhorred Armenians and Greeks ("If you shake them
up in a bag you wouldn't know which one will come up first," he
wrote in his diary and in letters to his friends, referring to Armenians, Syrians, Jews, Greeks and Turks, "but the Turk is the best
of the lot"). And "The Armenians are like the Jews - they have no
national feeling and poor moral character."[29]

Bristol was, in his own words, "a pitiless publicist" and he
set out to change the hearts and minds, first, of business and financial leaders and industrialists by a vast letter-writing campaign
in which he pointed out the enormous opportunities that lay ahead
for them in Turkey if they would just realize that "when it comes to
violence all these people out here are all the same," and make
friends with the Turks.

Bristol also cultivated the missionary leaders and leaders of
the Near East Relief (the original Armenian and Syrian Relief Committee) urging them to get together with the business community for
the sake of their common interests.[30] In short, if they wanted
to continue to work in Turkey, they had to forget the Armenians and
get friendly with the Turks. It was obvious that Kemal was going to
be the new leader of Turkey, that he was going to secularize the
State, dissolve the Caliphate and finally open the way for the

108

missionaries to do what they had wanted to do all along, i.e., convert Moslems.

The papers of the Board of Commissioners in the Houghton Library at Harvard University show that there was a good deal of
breastbeating among the missionaries and that a good many left the
movement in disgust. The leaders, however, went along with
Bristol's suggestion, and thus the same people who had certified to
the authenticity of the genocide: Cleveland Dodge, George Plimpton,
and others, were now lending their names to articles insisting that
the excesses of the Turks had been "greatly exaggerated."[31]

Bristol himself exercised strict censorship over the news coming out of Turkey,[32] and when the Turks renewed their death
marches in Cilicia, killing thousands upon thousands of Greeks and
Armenians who had escaped the massacres and returned to their homes
without the slightest doubt that they would henceforth be safe, he
kept the news under wraps.

It is instructive to note that in his reply to Bristol's pleas
for stricter censorship in the U.S., Allen Dulles wrote: "...Confi-
dentially the State Department is in a bind. Our task would be
simple if the reports of the atrocities could be declared untrue or
even exaggerated but the evidence, alas, is irrefutable and the Secretary of State wants to avoid giving the impression that while the
United States is willing to intervene actively to protect its commercial interests, it is not willing to move on behalf of the
Christian minorities." Dulles bemoaned the agitation on behalf of
the Greeks, the Armenians and the Palestine Jews, and added, "I've
been kept busy trying to ward off congressional resolutions of sympathy for these groups."[33]

By now, the Near East Relief officials were cooperating to the
extent of making their workers sign pledges of silence about anything they witnessed (the excuse was that speaking out would be detrimental and create more victims).[34] In 1922, after two men
named Ward and Yowell published the stories in London (the American
press would not touch them,[35] having also been convinced that
the Near East Relief was keeping quiet on behalf of the victims, or
future victims), Bristol simply denied the stories publicly and
called them "Yowell's yowl."

During these years the press offered a very schizophrenic vision of the news from Turkey. Although many newspapers, including
the Times continued for several years to support the Armenians, and
the Armenian cause, articles giving "both sides" often ran side by
side, each contradicting the other. This was particularly pronounced (and confusing) immediately after the burning of Smyrna in Sept.
1922 when eyewitness accounts describing the Turks in uniform pouring kerosene over buildings and setting them to the torch, vied with
articles implying that the Armenians and Greeks had set fire to
their own homes, and that the Turks were "doing everything possible
to restore order."[36]

A year later Turkey carried the day at the peace conference at
Lausanne. There was no reference in the treaty to Armenians or to
past promises of a free Armenia. The conferees agreed that there
should be an "exchange of populations" between Greece and Turkey;
in all, over 1,300,000 Greeks were exchanged for about 400,000 Turks
- this was deemed "an admirable solution." One reads heart-rending
accounts in the British press, and in the Toronto Star by Ernest
Hemingway who was then its correspondent in Turkey,[37] of the
mass exodus of Greeks through the knee-deep mud of Thrace, but
little was made of this tragic drama in American papers. Americans
were by now thoroughly confused and sick to death of violence and of
Armenians, now referred to as "starving Armenians." Gradually such
news petered out, and by 1927 even the new publisher of the once
pro-Armenian New York Times was thoroughly sold on Turkey and the
idea of bygones being bygones, especially when there were, after
all, "two sides to every story."

ARE THERE REALLY TWO SIDES TO EVERYTHING - INCLUDING GENOCIDE?

At a well-reported four day Institute of Politics at Williams
College in the summer of 1928, Halide Edib, Kemal's chief propagan-
dist and the first emancipated woman out of Turkey (she had a degree
from the American-run Constantinople women's college) led a round
table discussion on Turkey and "won the hearts and minds of 200 experts,"[38] according to the Times reporter. There things pretty
much remain. Before she had won them over, the fiction of the 50/50
theory of "two sides to everything, with the truth somewhere in between" had been superceded by the "plague on both your houses" school
of history, as reflected in the press. After Edib won hearts and
minds, the Turkish view that terrible things happened but the Armenians brought it on themselves prevailed. This of course was the
identical justification the same media had repudiated, with documentation, during the genocide.

The Turks are now rewriting history, and our media is accepting
the "new improved" version based on "new improved" census figures
quite suddenly discovered in Turkish archives. In this version
"some 200,000 Armenians died (in 1915-1916) of the same causes of
war, disease and hunger that took the lives of over a million
Turks."[39]

Some years ago, A. M. Rosenthal of the New York Times published
an article titled "No News at Auschwitz." This powerful, understat-
ed piece unforgettably made the point that such horrors must not be
forgotten, must continually be written about, lest they be repeated.
Yet in a recent advertisement in The Times, a group of Turkish "associations" repeated this "new improved" version of 200,000 Armenians and 2 million Turks. The Times is among a vast number of important papers which treat news from Turkey as if that area is
sacrosant - news is presented as inoffensively as if it had been
dictated by the U.S. State Department's Turkish desk.

The treatment of the Armenian genocide in the press after World War I shows that when the media collaborates, <u>eventually</u> the public can be convinced (even within the same generation) that they had previously held the wrong view. This should be a lesson to those who feel that <u>their</u> case is different, that "it couldn't happen again." If it <u>once</u> did, the chances are all too certain that it <u>will</u> happen again. Indeed, to an extent it already did happen when, in the early forties, war crimes in Germany were reported almost apologetically, all too tentatively, in the back pages of the <u>New York Times</u> and other papers, as though, having been "fooled" by propaganda (as they now thought it) in the previous war, they were not going to risk being "taken" again. One wonders how many lives might have been saved had the Armenian horrors and exterminations <u>not</u> been repudiated and forgotten by all but the perpetrators of the renewed horrors.

The help of a supposedly free press in exonerating and ultimately denying the crime of genocide is all it takes to bring about the Orwellian nightmare of laundered history, which of course can only encourage and indeed <u>insure</u> the repetition of genocide on a more horrible scale - as happened. It bears repeating that Germany was implicated in 1915-16, that the world not only forgot this soon enough but the Turkish deeds as well.

The day could come when - if the world survives - all but a handful of Jews will find the revision outside of Israel complete:

<u>Holocaust? What Holocaust?</u>

NOTES

1. Johannes Lepsius, <u>Le Rapport Secret sur les Massacres d'Armenie</u>, Paris 1918.
2. Joseph Grabill, <u>Protestant Diplomacy and the Near East</u>, Minnea polis 1971, p. 27
3. Julius Richter, <u>A History of Protestant Missions in the Near East</u>, London 1910, p. 72.
4. <u>The New York Times</u>, March 22, 1915, p. 4:3; April 26, p. 3:2; May 1, p. 1:7; May 17, 3:2; May 25, 3:3.
5. <u>Ibid</u> Aug. 6, p. 6:6.
6. <u>Ibid</u> Aug. 18, p. 5:7.
7. <u>Ibid</u> Aug. 27, p. 3:3.
8. <u>Ibid</u> Sept. 5, II p. 3:6.
9. <u>Ibid</u> Sept. 3, p. 1:2.
10. <u>Ibid</u> Sept. 28, p. 2:4.
11. <u>Ibid</u> Sept. 29, p. 1:2 ("Armenians' Own Fault Bernstoff Now Says")
12. <u>Ibid</u> Oct. 23, p. 3:2.
13. <u>Ibid</u> Nov. 3, p. 9:1.
14. <u>Ibid</u> Dec. 15, p. 3:5.
15. <u>Ibid</u> Feb. 6, 1916, II p. 9:3.
16. <u>Ibid</u> Feb. 7, p. 3:7.
17. <u>Ibid</u> Nov. 27, p. 4:4.

18. Having been overwhelmed by the evidence in the course of his work, Toynbee developed and advertised his virulent dislike of Turks. Later, he would visit a Turkish hospital in the course of reporting for the Manchester Guardian on the Greco-Turkish War (in 1921). Thus his first sight of Turks was as victims of Christian violence. This, according to his own admission in a published interview with his son Philip in (A Dialogue Across a Generation), made him remorseful enough to reverse his stand in such a way as to repudiate the testimony in the Blue Book - even though he later protested that he stood by the truth of that testimony.

19. Current History Magazine, "Protest of German Teachers against Armenian Massacres," Nov. 1916, pp. 335-6.

20. Yet it was in Constantinople (and Smyrna) that the Armenians were relatively well off, simply because foreign eyewitnesses were so plentiful.

21. H. Sturmer, "Germany and the Armenian Atrocities, Current History Magazine, Nov. 1917, pp. 336-9.

22. H. Morgenthau, "Ambassador Morgenthau's Story," The World's Work, pp. 92-116, 221-236, 294-304.

23. The New York Times, March 18, 1921, p. 3:2.

24. Ibid, June 3, 1921, p. 1:4.

25. Current History Magazine, "Why Talaat's Assassin Was Acquitted," July, 1921, pp. 551-5.

26. Ibid, "Turkey Reinterpreted," Admiral Colby Chester, pp. 939-47.

27. Smyrna, 1922, The Destruction of a City, Faber and Faber (London), 1972. The American edition titled The Smyrna Affair and published in 1971 by Harcourt Brace Jovanovich is unfortunately flawed by excessive typographical errors and improper annotation. The book centers on the burning of Smyrna in 1922, but it deals concisely and, I believe, thoroughly, with the bizarre and Byzantine situation that developed after World War I in Turkey.

28. George S. Gibb, & Evelyn H. Knowlton, History of the Standard Oil Company (N.J.). Vol. II. The Resurgent Years 1911-1917, New York 1956, p. 277.

29. Letter to Admiral W. S. Sims, May 18, 1919, The Bristol Papers, The Library of Congress, Washington, D.C.
Also, Diary, May 25, 1919, Bristol Papers.
Also, Letter to Frank Polk, U.S. Embassy, Paris, Dec. 4, 1919, The Naval Records.
Also, Letter to Admiral W. S. Sims May 5, 1920, The Naval Records, U.S. National Washington, D.C. Subject File WT Record Group 45.

30. See, for example, Letter to Admiral W. S. Benson, June 3, 1919. Letter to Dr. C. F. Gates, Pres. of Robert College, Dec. 13, 1919. Letter to L. I. Thomas of the Standard Oil Company, N.J., July 24, 1922 (all in the Bristol Papers).

31. General Committee of American Institutions and Associations in Favor of Ratification of the Treaty with Turkey (compilation of articles), The Treaty With Turkey, New York, 1926.

32. See, for example, Bristol Diary, Sept. 5, 1922, The Bristol Papers.

33. Letter Dulles to Bristol, April 21, 1922, Bristol Papers. 34. See Clayton Report in the U.S. National Archives 867.40.6/618, Chicago Daily Tribune, May 19, 1922, and letter, Bristol to Allen Dulles, May 24, 1922, Bristol Papers.

35. See Housepian, _Smyrna, 1922_, p. 95 and its Notes (p. 255) for sources.
36. See, for example, dispatches about the fire of Smyrna in _The New York Times_ from Sept. 10-27, 1922.
37. Hemingway's dispatches from Thrace have been compiled in _The Wild Years_, edited by Gene Z. Hanrahan, Bantam (paperback, date missing from library copy).
38. _The New York Times_, Aug. 4, 1928, p. 3:1.
39. Stanford Shaw, & Ezel Kural Shaw, _History of the Ottoman Empire and Modern Turkey_, Vol. II, Cambridge Univer. Press, New York, 1977, p. 316.

MARJORIE HOUSEPIAN DOBKIN, M.A., Litt.D., Barnard College, Columbia University, New York, N.Y. 10027, U.S.A.

8. Gypsies and Jews: Chosen People

Leita Kaldi

Leita Kaldi has been researching, working with, and writing about Gypsies for several years. She has taught courses and lectured at Tufts University, Harvard, Wellesley College, Cambridge Center for Adult Education, University of South Florida in Tampa, Denison University in Ohio, and at the Southeast Memorial Holocaust Center. She is a former employee of the United Nations, and is affiliated with the World Romani Union in Geneva, the International Federation of Gypsy Women in Belgium, Rom Und Cinti Union in Hamburg, and Romania of Massachusetts, Inc., in Boston. Her participation in the International Conference on the Holocaust and Genocide was funded by the Robbins Foundation in New York.

There are few people in this world who would appreciate being associated with Gypsies. Yet, the similiarities in the history and traditions of Gypsies and Jews make comparison irresistible. Their diaspora from an eastern land, their legacy of prejudice and persecution, their preservation of an ancient culture and a universal language, their exclusivity and survival through centuries of changing times in unhospitable lands, all bear striking parallels.

On the other hand, there are many dissimilarities between Gypsies and Jews. Perhaps the most striking is the Gypsies' high rate of illiteracy, compared to the Jews' generally advanced levels of education and the tradition of aspiring toward knowledge. Also, unlike the Jews, Gypsies place little value on economic security and spend the money they earn immediately in a nomadic style, with no thought for the next day, while Jews strive to attain comfortable and stable standards of living. While Jews have gained respect and power in most western countries, Gypsies still exist in the shadows of our societies.

The Gypsies have lessons to teach us, however, which some may not want to hear. For they are, in many ways, "the last grasshoppers in a world of ants."

Gypsies migrated from northwest India more than a thousand years ago. In periodic waves, the nomadic tribes of Rom, Sinti and Cale Gypsies washed through the Middle East, eastern Europe and Russia, across North Africa into Iberia. They first appeared in Europe as early as the fifteenth century. Caravans of brightly painted wagons trailed horses, dogs and children; dark men with smouldering eyes led tawny women who wore all the tribe's wealth in gold on their dusky bodies.

They found Jews already settled in communities all over Europe. The Jews had migrated from the Middle East into Europe long before the Gypsies arrived there, and were already settled in shtetls or ghettos in each nation.

113

The Gypsies spoke a mysterious language - Romanes - an ancient Sanskrit dialect overlaid with words absorbed from countries through which they had wandered. The old women told fortunes, while the mean dealt with horses and other animals, or were skilled metal crafters and artisans. Their children begged, barefoot and audacious, in the town streets. The unbridled vivacity of the Gypsies was anathema to cultures steeped in social conformity and discipline.

The Jews spoke their Biblical language, which also fell foreign on European ears. The women and children were protected in the midst of their closed communities, while the men practiced farming, or were merchants or scholars. Gaiety was generally expressed in private celebrations, while the image they presented the European was one of mysterious reserve.

Jews and Gypsies, with ther exclusivity, their dark foreign looks and strange tongues, have fanned flames of fear and hatred among Europeans. Everywhere. and for centuries, both peoples have left a wake of wonder and suspicion that still warps perceptions of them. Both peoples' histories have been forged in crucibles of so much persecution that, paradoxically, tend to reinforce the belief that they are indeed the "chosen peoples."

Gypsies, along with Jews, immigrated to the colonial countries as early as the 17th century. The majority streamed into the Americas at the turn of the 20th century, however, with the flood of citizens of many European countries. Both Gypsies and Jews brought with them atavistic memories of persecution. Gypsies had been enslaved upon their arrival in eastern Europe, to be emancipated only after nearly 300 years or at the end of the 18th century.

Signs at village gates depicting a Gypsy under a gallows were common warnings to them to stay out. They were driven into the mountains and remote regions where their reputation as brigands were further reinforced. They were subjected to laws in every land which condoned their annihilation, which forbade them to associate with non-Gypsies, which forced them into bondage to noblemen. Children were torn from their parents, fathers were forced into ship gallies and mothers into workhouses, where they languished, not only for their families, but for that freedom of open spaces so essential to the Gypsy soul. Jews also were legally prosecuted by many of the same laws that tormented Gypsies - laws that laid the base for the Third Reich's genocidal policies.

Carrying such legacies, Gypsies arrived in the new world, still nomadic, not interested in settling in communities, but seeking the anonymity of vast spaces. Their wagons wound through the new lands as they had through Europe and Asia for centuries past. On the other hand, Jews sought the cities, for the most part, where their inherent thirst for education would be slaked and commerce with other people indulged.

During the Great Economic Depression, Gypsies underwent a transition that changed their way of life irrevocably. Unclaimed camping grounds became scarce. Their traditional occupations became obsolete; horse dealing was outmoded by the automobile; fortune tellers were an unaffordable luxury; and new technologies made metal smithing an undemanded skill. So the Gypsies were forced into the cities, to seek a livelihood doing auto body repair, roof and facade restoration, or road repair. Women still tell fortunes as "readers and advisors" with Americanized names. Children do not attend school but shine shoes and learn "street ways" while girls tell fortunes or beg.

Jews also suffered during the Depression. Many lost the tenuous foothold they were groping for and drowned in economic and cultural whirlpools. Others, however, survived this bitter period and rose during the post-Depression economic boom to positions of power and wealth.

Jewish intellectuals and artists have poignantly portrayed the story of their people for many generations. Gypsies, however, have not been able to publicize their plight for many reasons. They have always jealously guarded their ancient culture against western education, thus remaining illiterate, for the most part, and they consciously keep a low profile, for fear of further persecution.

However, many politically-oriented Gypsy organizations have sprung up recently, especially in Europe. Among the goals of these organizations are the preservation of Gypsy culture; provision of educational opportunities adapted to their life style; economic assistance; the right to maintain nomadism and have access to camping areas where, ironically, Gypsies are prohibited. (The irony is that Gypsies have given us the notion of camping, and even the very word came from Romanes.) Legal protection against bigotry and prejudice, and compensation of Gypsies by the West German Government for losses suffered during World War II are strong aims of Gypsy organizers.

In their book, The Destiny of Europe's Gypsies. authors Donald Kenrick and Grattan Puxon (1972, pp. 183-4) painstakingly collected documentation of Gypsies during World War II and report figures which, since their publication, have been found to be conservative, but give an indication of the relative numbers of Gypsies murdered during the War.

Below we give a table of deaths during the war period. It should be remembered that these figures do not represent the full measure of Gypsy suffering during the Nazi period. Of those not killed thousands were interned in camps and prisons or suffered other restrictions on their liberty. Many had mental breakdowns as a result of this confinement, worse perhaps for nomadic Gypsies than for sedentary citizens. Others were engaged in forced labor on the land, in mines and factories. Many survivors still bore the marks of experiments carried out on them and others were unable to bear children after irreversible sterilization operations. The birth rate dropped not only through direct interference but also through the separation of young men from their families.

COUNTRY	POPULATION IN 1939	DEATHS	SOURCE FOR DEATHS FIGURE
Austria	11,200	6,500	Steinmetz
Belgium	600	500	Estimate
Bohemia	13,000	6,500	Horvathova
Croatia	28,500	28,000	Uhlik
Estonia	1,000	1,000	Estimate
France	40,000	15,000	Droit et Liberte
Germany	20,000	15,000	Estimate (See Sippel, Spiegel
Holland	500	500	Estimate
Hungary	100,000	28,000	Nacizmus Uldozotteinen Bizottsaga
Italy	25,000	1,000	Estimate
Latvia	5,000	2,500	Kochanowski (1946)
Lithuania	1,000	1,000	Estimate
Luxembourg	200	200	Estimate
Poland	50,000	35,000	Estimate
Romania	300,000	36,000	Romanian War Crimes Commission
Serbia	60,000	12,000*	Estimate
Slovakia	80,000	1,000	Estimate
USSR	200,000	30,000	Estimate
	Total	219,700	

* These figures may prove to be much higher when further documentation is available.

At the Third World Romani Congress held in Gottingen in May 1981, about 350 Gypsies from all over the world gathered to make public their desires and demands. Much publicity was given the Congress locally, but no representatives of the West German Government attended. At the Congress, days were spent in "bearing witness" to stories told by Gypsies from all over Europe of their suffering during the war. One of many notable figures in the Congress was Simon Wiesenthal, who delivered a moving address in which he stated, inter alia:

I have concerned myself with the investigations of Nazi crimes since my liberation from the concentration camps, thirty-six years ago. In the course of these activities, I have also tried to obtain justice for the crimes committed against Gypsies. So, in 1965 I sent a dossier with documents about the persecution of the Gypsies in 1939 to the West German Central Persecutor's Office in Ludwigsburg; among these papers were also the correspondence between Eichmann and his collaborator Nebe about a decision always to add to the transport of Jews to the East a few wagons with Gypsies.

Until 1947, the Gypsies returning from the concentration camps risked in several West German federal provinces to be arrested and sent to a labor camp. This went back to a law of 1926, decreeing that Gypsies who could produce no proof of employment would fall under the authority of the police. This discriminating law had been overlooked by the Allies and was only repealed in 1947.

But then again since 1954, the Bavarian criminal authorities have had a special office for the registration of Gypsies, which is even conected to Interpol.

Contrary to the Jews, who shortly after their liberation started to write down the history of their persecution, the Gypsies largely failed to do the same, and only much later was the world informed of this people's tragedy.

In December 1943, Hitler issued his fateful order that all Gypsies, including those of mixed blood, were to be brought to Auschwitz. There they came into the so-called family camp in Birkenau, where they fell into the hands of the notorious Dr. Joseph Mengele, who sent them to the gas chambers. Of special interest to Mengele were Gypsy twins, who he used for his pseudo-scientific tests, which always ended with death of the children.

The persecution of the Gypsies and their oppression and the intolerance and contempt they are faced with have not ended with the fall of the Third Reich.

I have heard a Gypsy proverb - Every Fire Leaves Behind Some Live Coal in the Ashes. The danger is that the live coal in the ashes of a funeral pyre can set it ablaze again; and the continuing persecution of the Gypsies is such a live coal after the conflagration of the Holocaust. All decent people must therefore strive to extinguish the glowing fire and to enable the Gypsies to live among the rest of us as equal citizens.

While Jews have become assimilated citizens, for the most part, of most countries, and made important contributions to their education, science and culture, Gypsies have not assimiliated. They resist temptations of power, pretensions of patriotism, fanaticisms of religions and ideologies. They have never subscribed to war, or persecuted others; they do not perpetuate pollution, for they have always been an outdoor people and natural ecologists.

Gypsies live in the shadows of our societies, shrouded in fear, suspicion and secrecy. But they are emerging from those shadows now and, as they come into the light, we must open our eyes and our hearts to the lessons they have for us about a different, perhaps deeper human existence.

REFERENCES

KENRICK, Donald, & Puxon, Grattan.   The Destiny of Europe's Gypsies.
London: Cox & Wyman, 1972

LEITA KALDI, 801 NE 17 Avenue, Fort Lauderdale,
Florida 33304, U.S.A.

9. Tibet: A Case of Eradication of Religion Leading to Genocide

Phuntsog Wangyal

Born and brought up in Tibet, Phuntsog Wangyal went into exile in India in 1959 where he continued his studies, gaining an M.Phil. in Political Science and International Relations, and later teaching at Jawaharlal Nehru University, Delhi. He was Assistant Director of the Library of Tibetan Works and Archives in Dharmsala, India in 1974, and taught Tibetan at the School of Oriental and African Studies in the University of London in 1976. In 1980 he spent three months in Tibet as a member of the Dalai Lama's second fact-finding delegation. Currently, he directs the Office of the Dalai Lama in London. It is on account of the tragedy of the Tibetan people that Phuntsog Wangyal has a great interest in making some contribution towards finding solutions to the genocidal process.

I would like to begin by expressing my gratitude for this opportunity to present the facts of the great human tragedy of the Tibetan people - especially here in Israel, whose people have suffered so much - as the Tibetans are suffering now.

Much of what I shall be saying to you today will be based on my own experience of present-day Tibet from my visit in 1980 as part of the second delegation sent by His Holiness the Dalai Lama.

A few words are needed to briefly put the Tibetan genocide into its historical setting. As you may know, throughout its history, Tibet existed as an independent nation, with its own particular customs, language and traditions. The development of Tibet since the seventh century A.D. is the history of the development of Buddhism. The Tibetan people adopted and "transported to Tibetan soil the whole active Indian Buddhist culture, developing it energetically until it permeated every sphere of Tibetan social life and became the psychological mainstay of every individual Tibetan" (Snellgrove & Richardson, 1980, p. 159). Remote and unaffected by any other cultural influence, over thirteen hundred years of Tibetan history saw the whole thrust of Tibetan civilization directed towards the development of Buddhist practice and thought. Tibet's unique culture became inseparable from its Buddhist faith, which completely saturated and inspired all areas of life.

In the words of Hugh Richardson, the most eminent western historian of Tibet, and representative of the British and Indian governments in Tibet for a number of years, when speaking on the destruction of Tibetan culture:

The Tibetans have a civilization that had developed for 1300 years...they had an immense literature...and they had developed a very special and very important practice of Buddhism...They are a unique people; they have their own language and their own civilization. Surely it is a tragedy to see any civilization

119

dying, even if it is not so long established, so literate and so polished as the Tibetans' (Richardson, 1982, p. 159).

The Communist Chinese began to make serious inroads into Tibet from 1949 onwards, in the name of ideology and "liberation from imperialist forces." The main anxiety of the Tibetan people focused on the future of Buddhism, knowing full well the rigorously anti-religious nature of communism. Any organized resistance on the part of the Tibetans was doomed to failure, since centuries steeped in the non-violent principle of Buddhism had equipped them with no military experience or resources. The Dalai Lama eventually had no alternative but to accept, in 1951, a treaty with the Chinese, the so-called "Seventeen Point Agreement," which guaranteed the continuity of the existing political and social fabric of Tibet, and above all declared that "the religious beliefs, customs and habits of the Tibetan people shall be respected" (International Commission Jurists, 1960, p. 215).

All through the next nine years, China consolidated her military strength in Tibet, and carefully laid, as it was to be revealed later, the foundations for the destruction to come. This period was euphemistically characterized by Tien Pao , Vice Chairman of the Revolutionary Committee of Tibet Autonomous Region, as one of "building roads and united front work with the People's Liberation Army" (Pao, 1977). The Chinese flagrantly broke their 1951 treaty by suppressing Tibetan customs and religion, to the extent that the Tibetans were no longer able to tolerate it. There was widespread resistance, culminating in the National Uprising of 1959, which was suppressed by the Chinese with the utmost severity. It was then that H.H. the Dalai Lama, spiritual and temporal leader of the Tibetan people, fled to India, accompanied by approximately 100,000 refugees. There they have devoted themselves to speaking on behalf of the Tibetans inside Tibet, and to ensuring the survival of Tibetan culture outside Tibet.

THE "REFORM" OF TIBET

From 1959 onwards, the Chinese displayed their true intentions and launched their program of earnest "reform," namely the full-scale destruction of Tibetan culture - and therefore Buddhism - and the oppression of the Tibetan people. This continues today. It has resulted in the following:

- The destruction of all traces of religious life and belief. Along with this went the destruction of all religious institutions. Of the estimated 4,000 monasteries, nunneries and temples that existed in Tibet, parts of only 13 survive today.
- The execution of large numbers of Tibetans, both lay people and religious.
- The imprisonment, torture and starvation of many others.
- The eradicating of Tibetan culture and language, and the denial and destruction of any Tibetan way of life.

- The forced indoctrination with Chinese propaganda, and compulsory learning of Chinese language - all of which is passed off as education.
- The creation of a nationwide atmosphere of terror, with constant surveillance by the secret police - "the Public Security Bureau," the ubiquitous presence of spies, and threat of notorious 'thamzing' "struggle" sessions.
- The deportation of Tibetans and absorption of the Tibetan population in a mass influx and settlement of Chinese.
- The discrimination against Tibetans in favor of Chinese in housing, education, work, the supply of food, etc.

One of the predominant motivating forces of the Chinese regime is a feeling of national superiority, the famous "great Han Chauvinism." "From time immemorial, the Chinese have considered themselves as superior to all other peoples, and have called all others 'barbarians'..." (Sinha, 1975, p. 60). It is recognized by the Chinese themselves; no less a person than Mao Tse Tung himself warned about the dangers of "great Han Chauvinism" in his writings (e.g., Mao Tse -Tung, 1957, p. 22).

Chinese contempt for other races, in which one might see some similarities with the Nazi attitude to non-Aryans, is most clearly demonstrated in their treatment and sinicization of the so-called "minority peoples," amongst whom they place the Tibetans. Of the deeply-rooted nature of this phenomenon, a British journalist has recently commented: "The assumption behind sinicization is that of a superior culture, so deeply embedded in Chinese consciousness that their paternalism, verging on racialism, is mostly unconscious and therefore all the more resistant to reform." (Gittings, 1981). In Tibet, this has manifested in the annihilation of all manifestations of Tibetan culture and traditional ways of life, as well as religion. Today it continues as a cynical and total discrimination against anything or anyone Tibetan in all spheres of life.

The principle objective of Chinese policy throughout has been to eradicate religion. The authority for this lies in the Chinese Constitution, which gives people the right (1) to practise religion, (2) not to practise religion, or (3) to propagate against religion. It does not permit people to propagate religion, and hence legitimizes the suppression of any kind of activity which can be deemed to cause the furthering of religion.

The Chinese authorities in Tibet feel the need to continue restating the official party line on religion for the benefit of their followers, in a series of booklets and documents. For example in the "Basic Study Guide No. 55," produced in 1980 for members of the Communist Party and Youth League, it states quite adamantly:"We have to stop religion in that it is blind faith, against the law, and counter-revolutionary..." It adds: "Although our constitution allows people to have the right to religion, it should be abundantly clear that Communist Party and Youth Organization members do not have the right to practise religion" (Wangyal, 1980, pp. 22-24). A more recent broadsheet, of February this year, for party members,

underlines a number of destructive or unconstitutional acts incompatible with modern revolutionary socialism, such as public religious gatherings and "poisoning" the younger generation with "religious and superstitious beliefs."[1]

The picture that emerges is that even communist party members,
Tibetans, have been slipping back into religious beliefs, as is further demonstrated in a broadcast on Radio Lhasa in March of this
year. It was reported that some party members had taken part in
religious activities, and reminded them that: "Communists never
conceal their political viewpoints and openly declare their belief
in materialism and atheism and not in any god or saviour," also
"they must all become ardent atheists," and "partymen have the
responsibility to propagate materialism and atheism by all means
possible."[2]

The basic fact underlying the need for the Chinese to issue
such statements in 1982 is that the Tibetan people are still so dedicated to Buddhism that they would rather chose death than give up
their faith. Just as it would be difficult to disassociate the Jewish people from Judaism, in the same way to be a 'Tibetan' means to
be a Buddhist. Since the Chinese aim is the destruction of religion, they must therefore destroy the Tibetan race. Here we have
the origin of the process of genocide, of killings on a scale that
may even match those of Pol Pot's regime in Kampuchea.

GENOCIDE IN TIBET

Daljit Sen Adel of the International Secretariat, Asian Buddhist Conference for Peace, estimates that during the last three decades, about four million Buddhists have been killed in Kampuchea
and Tibet. It should be pointed out, of course, that in Tibet the
Chinese faced the problem of not simply removing religious figures
but all who would not give up their Buddhist faith.

The first attribution of genocide to the events in Tibet came
from the Legal Inquiry Committee on Tibet of the International Commission of Jurists, who found that: "Acts of genocide had been committed in Tibet in an attempt to destroy the Tibetans as a religious
group, and that such acts are acts of genocide, independently of any
conventional obligation" (International Commission Jurists, 1960, p.
215). They highlighted four principal facts:

a) that the Chinese will not permit adherence to and practice
   of Buddhism in Tibet;
b) that they have systematically set out to eradicate this religious belief in Tibet;
c) that in pursuit of this design they have killed religious
   figures because their religious belief and practice was an
   encouragement and example to others;
d) that they have forcibly transferred large numbers of Tibetan
   children to a Chinese materialist environment in order to
   prevent them from having a religious upbringing.

It is clear that the Chinese have contravened Article II of the United Nations Genocide Convention. As an example of systematic and ruthless genocide, it perhaps bears closest resemblance to the genocide of the Armenians at the hands of the Turks.

The formidable success of the genocidal policy in Tibet can be seen in the severe decline of the Tibetan population over the last three decades. This can be attributed to a number of factors:

- Executions and mass murder
- Imprisonment and subsequent death
- Famine due to Chinese agricultural mismanagement
- Deportation to parts of China and Inner Mongolia
- Mass conscription into the PLA and subsequent heavy casualties among Tibetans, for example, in the Sino-Vietnamese war.

It should be noted that, although there is no shortage of eye-witness accounts of all of these, it has often proved extremely difficult to arrive at exact figures with supporting evidence on account of the nature of the situation and the fact that the genocidal process still continues.

However, some detailed figures are available. For example, it was announced on Radio Lhasa on October 1st 1960 that in the first year following the 1959 uprising, 87,000 Tibetans were executed in Central Tibet. A pooled eye-witness report confirms that in and around Lhasa, within seventeen days in 1966, 69,000 were executed. According to the Indian Statesman Shashi Bhushan (1976), in 1972 in Kongpo Tramo, in Central Tibet, 500 Tibetan youths demonstrating in the name of Tibetan freedom, were executed. And from fifty-four documents presented to the three delegations to Tibet sent by H.H. the Dalai Lama in 1979-80, it emerged that 23,419 Tibetans had been killed either by execution or by being worked to death in two labor camps - the Gansu railway construction and Qinghai borax mines.

The typical pattern can be seen in figures for the six districts of Golok in Kham, E. Tibet. In 1957, the population of Golok was 120,000. Between 1958 and 1962, 21,000 local Tibetans were killed fighting the People's Liberation Army. 20,000 were executed in local prisons, and a further 20,000 died of starvation as a result of famine. 53,000 were deported in 1962 and "disappeared." Of the original population, only 6,000 remained, and between 1963 and 1979 these were reduced to 4,700. New settlers were brought in, to swell the population in 1979 to 10,000, these being composed of 2,500 Chinese and 2,500 "non-Chinese." The PLA garrison in October 1979 numbered about 6,000. The total number of monasteries and nunneries in the area in 1957 was 150; in 1979 none remained. Even despite this, an underground religious movement is struggling to secretly print Buddhist texts.

The most common method of eliminating Tibetans is their removal to prisons or labor camps reminiscent of the concentration camps of Stalin's Russia, where they subsequently "disappear." Untold numbers of Tibetans have died by being worked to death in such camps, especially in the 1960s. Sentence to a labor camp, administered, needless to say, without trial or vestige of human rights, is tantamount to a death sentence. Prisoners are kept alive in famine conditions calculated to drive out all human instincts. At the same time they are subjected to violent political indoctrination sessions. The majority die from: exhaustion from the extremely arduous work, malnutrition from minimal diets, and disease and exposure. Over 10,000 died between 1960 and 1965 in Drapchi prison in Lhasa.

In 1979, Time magazine (1979) reported on a "vast prison system" existing in Qinghai, formerly Amdo, an Eastern province of Tibet. An American imprisoned there for two-and-a-half years believes that half the provinces' estimated four million people are either prisoners or "forced employees" forbidden to leave the area. Three large "labor reform camps" along with scores, even hundreds of smaller prison camps, make up what the former prisoner maintains is only one of a number of Chinese prison systems. A 1979 estimate put the number of Tibetans still in prison at 80,000 (Tibetan Bulletin, 1979).

A special contribution of the Chinese to methods of totalitarian oppression and torture is the "thamzing" or struggle session. This particularly dehumanizing and ingenious torture goes hand in hand with interrogation. It involves the accusation of anyone in an unfavorable category, i.e., on any charge at all, and enforced beating or torture by his fellows, relatives or peers. The majority of the accused die from these thamzing sessions, but a slow death is ensured by reviving them, where possible, after each session. The result is widespread intimidation and creation of a climate of fear amongst the people, and the invention of a false "class" system between beaters and beaten. The thamzing sanctions oppression with the pretence of mass participation, and the simple fear of it has been the result of large numbers of suicides.

Finally, the surviving population of Tibet has been swamped by Chinese settlers, especially in the warmer and more temperate regions. Some Tibetan areas, for example in Yünnan, are now completely populated by Chinese. In addition, there is an enormous concentration of Chinese troops in Tibet, particularly along the border area with India. An estimate of February this year put the numbers of PLA troops in the Central Tibetan area alone at 500,000.

The disappearance of the written language is almost accomplished, and in some places, people can no longer understand correctly spoken Tibetan. This is among the more disturbing testimonies to the efficiency of the Chinese destruction of Tibetan culture. There can be little hope for the young people in Tibet, with no culture of their own, with absolutely no educational opportunities, dicriminated against at every turn, and condemned to forever being second-class citizens in their own country.

It is clear that the Tibetan people will not give up their Buddhist faith. They have formed underground movements to practise religion and take monastic vows, and have started, against great opposition, to renovate parts of certain monasteries. Even young people and children born after the Chinese invasion display a fervent desire for Buddhism. Consequently, the Chinese will be obliged to continue their oppression and genocide. In January of this year Radio Lhasa attributed unrest to those "actively engaged in the propagation of religion." No other outcome suggests itself other than the continuation of the genocidal process, through which the Tibetans will finally vanish as an ethnic unit.

THE LIMITED MACHINERY OF WORLD RESPONSE

The United Nations passed three resolutions, in 1959, 1961 and 1965, calling for human rights and freedoms to be restored in Tibet. They had no effect on the Chinese authorities, and were not able to be enforced. Other governments and non-governmental organizations have taken no action at all, even on the level of human rights. They could, of course, be excused on the grounds that they were unaware of the extent of atrocities in such a remote country as Tibet.

Yet if allowed to continue, what has happened in Tibet could only serve as an encouragement and invitation to other totalitarian regimes. The principle at stake is that a small nation should not be crushed and exterminated by a greater power. Therefore what is happening in Tibet must be brought to the attention of the world - even though it is a remote country with a small population. The Tibetan genocide should receive public exposure and pressure be exerted for it to be documented as fully as possible, with supporting evidence. Only then can public opinion be mobilized, to press for some kind of action or humanitarian intervention. And only then can people have the information to alert themselves to prevent similar atrocities in the future, at the hands of the same or different oppressors.

It is an established fact the the United Nations is handicapped in initiating any action against genocide, especially where an oppressive government can portray it as an internal problem. There is an urgent need both for a forum where victims of ongoing genocide can have a voice to present their case, and for the setting up of effective machinery for taking action against genocide itself.

Here lies the importance of such meetings as this. The Tibetan people, now undergoing genocide, would like to hope that their suffering could contribute, through the medium of this conference and others like it, to the prevention of similar human suffering in the future.

NOTES

1. Chinese Communist Party and State Council's Approved and Published Document No. 6, February 1982.
2. Radio Lhasa, March 24, 1982.

126

REFERENCES

BHUSAN, Shashi. China: the myth of a super-power. New Delhi: Progressive People's Sector Publications, 1976.

GITTINGS, John. 'Tibetans' Struggle for Identity. The Guardian, September 9, 1981.

INTERNATIONAL Commission of Jurists, Geneva, 1960. Point 7 of the 17-point Agreement of May 23, 1951, quoted in "Tibet and the Chinese People's Republic."

PAO, Tien. Quoted in David S. Broder, Tibet under Peking's control - the gulf between the rulers and the ruled! Washington Post, October 16, 1977.

RICHARDSON, H. In "The World About Us" - "Tibet," two BBC-TV documentary films produced by Simon Normanton, and shown in April, 1982.

SINHA, Nirmal C. An Introduction to the History and Religion of Tibet. Calcutta: 1975, p. 60.

SNELLGROVE & Richardson. A Cultural History of Tibet. London: George, Wiedenfield & Nicholson, 1968; & Boulder: Prajna Press, 1980.

TIBETAN BULLETIN, Dharamsala, India, Vol. xi, No. 4, Oct./Dec. 1979.

TIME. The gulag that Mao built: the West gets its first glimpse of a vast prison system. November 26, 1979.

TSE-TUNG, Mao. On the correct handling of contradictions among the people (1957). Foreign Language Press, 1964, p. 22.

WANGYAL, Phuntsog. Translation of Basic Study Guide No. 55 ('Lobjung Che Zhi'), Information Office, Chamdo, Tibet, April 1980. Translated in "Tibet and the Tibetans." Tibet News Review, Vol. 1, Nos. 3/4, London, Winter 1980/1.

OTHER SOURCES

CHOEDON, Dhondup. Life in the Red Flag People's Commune. Information Office of H.H. the Dalai Lama, Dharamsala, India, 1978.

GASHI, Tsering Dorje. New Tibet. Information Office of H.H. the Dalai Lama, Dharamsala, India, 1980.

GLIMPSES of Tibet Today - an Anthology. Information Office of H.H. the Dalai Lama, Dharamsala, India, 1978.

NORBU, Jamyang. Horseman in the Snow. Information Office of H.H. the Dalai Lama, Dharamsala, India, 1979.

PALJOR, Kunsang. Tibet: the Undying Flame. Information Office of H. H. the Dalai Lama, Dharamsala, India, 1977.

PHUNTSOG WANGYAL, Office of His Holiness the Dalai Lama, 3 Heatherock Court, Strand, London WC2R, OPA, England

Part III

Dynamics of Genocide

10. From Holocaust to Genocides

Monty N. Penkower

Monty N. Penkower's extended study of the Holocaust is rooted in a personal belief that "the cancer of bestiality is the concern of us all, and the infinite preciousness of life requires daily affirmation." Currently Professor and Chairman of the History department at Touro College, his numerous publications on American history and modern Jewish history include THE FEDERAL WRITER'S PROJECT: A STUDY IN GOVERNMENT PATRONAGE OF THE ARTS (1977), and THE JEWS WERE EXPENDABLE: FREE WORLD DIPLOMACY AND THE HOLOCAUST (1983) - an account of the free world's tragic failure to respond decisively to the Holocaust. A member of the Academic Council of the American Jewish Historical Society and a consultant to the U.S. Holocaust Memorial Council, Professor Penkower is completing research for a volume on Anglo-American foreign relations regarding Palestine during World War II.

THE KINGDOM OF DEATH

Six centuries after Dante Alighieri penned his tortured portrait of hell, Adolf Hitler resolved to translate this vision of the Divine Comedy into reality. With regard to European Jewry, the German Fuehrer succeeded fully. His mechanized kingdom of death actually created hell on earth in ways surpassing at times even the Florentine poet's fevered imagination. "Evil, more than good, suggests infinity," concluded the survivor Elie Wiesel after numbly leafing through photograph albums devoted to the Holocaust (Wiesel, 1970, pp. 46-47). Once the Third Reich posited the quintessence of its Weltanschauung on a unique, murderous hatred of all "non-Aryans" - read Jews - the Nazi progression into the inhuman knew no limits. As a consequence, all earlier boundaries between reality and fantasy blurred for the Jewish centers of Europe, which vanished along with six million innocent human beings in the ashes of Ponary, Chelmno, Janowska, Auschwitz-Birkenau.

Obscuring History

Paradoxically, the very incredibleness of the Holocaust during World War II, which often led Jew and Gentile within and beyond Hitler's Europe to misjudge its dimensions, has since threatened to deprive that historical event of its true significance. Some well-intentioned writers resort to allegory and metaphor (Auschwitz is "another planet," for example) in describing the destruction of Europe's Jews. On the opposite extreme, neo-Nazi literature denies the Holocaust outright, while Soviet-bloc publications and opponents of the State of Israel even dare to propose that Zionists aided the Third Reich in butchering the Jewish masses. Revisionist historians attempt to de-demonize Hitler, and ignore entirely his primary victims. Some academicians unwittingly consign these dead to oblivion by burying them beneath a morass of documents, comparable to all

129

130

other objects of scientific inquiry. Still others obscure the particularity of this Jewish tragedy by glibly universalizing it, much
as the Allies did throughout World War II, to include all who perished under the swastika and to signify man's inhumanity to man
(Bauer, 1978, pp. 38-49).

A Unique Phenomenon

Yet the Holocaust was a specific and concentrated effort by the
Third Reich to murder the Jewish people. The Nazi dictatorship, a
purely German manifestation, deemed its accomplishment essential in
the pseudo-religious quest to assure the existence of the racially
pure herrenvolk. SS Reichsfuehrer Heinrich Himmler logically received the order to oversee both the "Final Solution" of the "Jewish
question" and the Reich Commission for the Strengthening of German-
dom; the first directive of the latter in October 1939 began with
the expressed need to expel about 550,000 Jews from Danzig and Posen
into the Polish government-general (Koehl, 1957). The commanders of
Belzec, Sobibor, and Treblinka, as well as many members of the SS
assigned to work in the gas chambers and crematoria had first been
schooled in euphemistically labeled "euthanasia centers," intended
according to their designers for the "destruction of lives unworthy
of life."

Nazi Genocide

A number of different national communities fell victim to Nazi
"genocide," the term coined by Polish-Jewish refugee Raphael Lemkin
in 1943 to mean calculated elimination of a nationality by oppression and murder; millions died, Russians and Poles suffering the
heaviest losses. And the campaign of racial biopolitics was projected for the future Thousand-Year Reich as well: when the forces
of the Red Army overran the camps in Poland, they found enough Zyk-
lon B to gas 20 million people. Yet, National Socialist ideology
portrayed the Jews alone as a satanic and parasitic power, locked in
unconditional struggle with the "Aryan" Germanic race for control of
the world. Gypsies, of whom the Nazis murdered at least 200,000 of
the over 700,000 living in Europe in 1939, were regarded as an anti-
social element; Gypsy soldiers and city dwellers received protection
on occasion. The Jews, however, were viewed as the "mortal enemy"
(Todfeind was Hitler's word). Following the Wehrmacht invasion of
the Soviet Union, they had to be destroyed at any cost (Dawidowicz,
1981, pp. 9-14).

The closest parallel might be the annihilation of over one million Armenians during World War I, yet not all Armenians - seen by
Turkey as a local menace to nationalist aspirations - were then
marked for slaughter (Bauer, 1978, pp. 36-37). Emmanuel Ringelblum
noted the stark reality in the pages of his Warsaw diary after
grasping Hitler's fanatical plan for the Jews: "History does not repeat itself, especially now, now that we stand at the crossroads,
witnessing the death pangs of an old world and the birth pangs of a
new" (Ringelblum, 1974, p. 300). Now birth itself constituted the
most heinous crime of all, expiated only by death. Abetted by cen-

turies of Christian antisemitism, by modern technology, and by the unsurpassed callousness of the so-called free world, the Nazi state and its citizens systematically killed with impunity a helpless people on the soil of "Enlightened" Europe.

The West Dehumanized the Jewish Plight

The West, which alone could have checked the tempo of the Final Solution, dehumanized in a different fashion the one people targeted for murderous annihilation in World War II. London and Washington consistently denied Jewry the sense of communal distinction which had accounted for its mysterious survival these past 4000 years. The unique Jewish plight was either concealed under "Poles," "Belgians," etc., or refused sympathy because Jews were classified as "enemy aliens" when found in countries loyal to the Axis. Rarely did Allied statements refer to the persecution of Europe's Jews; the Bermuda Conference on Refugees, the U.S. War Refugee Board, and like organizations all omitted mention in their titles of the one group for which each had been principally created. Even at the war's end, not a word of the infamous SS death marches appeared in supreme Allied headquarters directives or in the Western press (Penkower, 1983).

Discrimination of Allies' Response

The Anglo-American Alliance discriminated in its response. Greeks obtained relief to avert famine, and Poles and Czechs arms for resistance, but not Jews. Tens of thousands of Yugoslavs and Greeks received a cordial welcome in Middle East camps, yet those most needing their national - and accessible - homeland found the doors to Palestine bolted. While more than 400,000 enemy prisoners were ferried to the United States, only 918 Jewish refugees were allowed on those shores by means of an executive order. Members of the French resistance and the 1944 Polish uprising in Warsaw got airborne support, but the crematoria and the railroad lines leading to them never became major targets. Definite rescue proposals to aid Jews were peremptorily ruled out time and again. These officially designated nonpersons did not fare better, ultimately, with self-professed guardians of humanitarianism and morality like the International Red Cross and the Vatican, or with the neutral governments. Moscow ignored the entire matter. Such spectators avoided the moral imperative not to postpone attempts to save blameless human lives, including one-and-a-half million Jewish children who were forever enveloped in the darkness of the long night. Through their silence, a decay of conscience already evident before September 1, 1939, those who stood aside became accomplices to history's most monstrous crime (Penkower, 1983).

A few courageous souls attempted to shatter the Allied conspiracy of silence, as well as the prevailing illusion that nothing could be done. Some who responded to the cry of conscience have been rightly acknowledged in Yad Vashem's "Avenue of the Righteous" - an impressive grove of trees, hardly a forest. The Babylonian Talmud prescribes their reward: "Whosoever saves a single Jew,

Scripture ascribes it to him as though he had saved an entire world" (Sanhedrin: 37a). Yet these individuals' valiant race against mass-production death wrested but limited successes. Killers and indifferent bystanders, by depersonalizing the Jews of Europe, marked these persons for doom. Hitler, Himmler, Adolf Eichmann, Rumania's Antonescu, Hungary's Horthy, and others of their ilk believed with apocalyptic certainty that a demonic international Jewry controlled Germany's opponents; the West, in whose councils the stateless Jews commanded no political leverage, consigned the Nazis' major adversary to one category: expendable (Penkower, 1983).

Lessons for Jewry

The Holocaust shocked world Jewry and its friends into recognizing the fundamental truth jotted down by Yitschak Katznelson in his Vittel diary, a few months before the poet of "The Song of the Murdered Jewish People" met a ghastly end in history's greatest slaughterhouse at Auschwitz: "A nation of Jobs" became easy prey for the murderous Third Reich, no one desiring the Jews of Europe in their "utter powerlessness" (Katznelson, 1964, pp. 140, 36-38). Hence the overriding necessity, emphasized foremost by the survivors themselves after V-E day, to end the curse of anonymity and enter history once again with autonomous sovereignty in reborn Eretz Yisrael. Understandably, too, the vast majority of Jews today view the State of Israel as inspiring their faith in the continuity of the Jewish people, with attacks on that small land hugging the eastern Mediterranean correctly regarded a threat to Jews everywhere.

A MORE OMINOUS LEGACY

The destruction of European Jewry during World War II bequeathed another, more ominous, legacy to the century deservedly known as the Terrible Twentieth. In an amoral world where the reality of power transcended justice and reason, the Holocaust first demonstrated that the blood of an entire people could be shed at will. Few in the democracies had shared Edgar Snow's publicly articulated vision in October 1944, grasped after his inspecting Majdanek, of the diabolic system which "for the first time made a totalitarian industry out of the reduction of the human being from an ambulatory animal to a kilogram of grey ashes" (Snow, 1944, p. 19). Now the hitherto unthinkable lies within the realm of distinct possibility.

Modern-Day Genocides

And mankind has forgotten too soon. Notwithstanding numerous signatures to the U.N. General Assembly's Genocide Convention of December 9, 1948, a treaty conceived in the cinders of the Holocaust and making genocide an international crime, continued depersonalization of the powerless has resulted in a plague of genocides in our own post-Hitler age. The Chinese sought throughout the 1950s to destroy the Tibetans as a religious group, the Pakistani government systematically slaughtered Hindus in East Pakistan during 1971. Selective genocide was carried out against liberated Hutus in Burundi by that African government a year later and renewed in 1973. With the complicity of Paraguay from 1971 onwards, the local Ache Indians have been killed, trapped in reservations, sold for slave labor and prostitution, and stripped of their cultural identity. (A scenario similar to that of East Pakistan might have been enacted in Nigeria, where an estimated 50,000 Biafrans died from hunger after the war ended with the secessionist Ibo-dominated eastern region, if not for Biafran ability to repel the Nigerian federal government while making their individual plight visible to the West). Comparable mass-acres and atrocities occured, for example, in Mozambique, the Sudan, Syria, Uganda and Cambodia (Fein, 1973).

Power Politics

These newest martyrs to dehumanization are victims of a world that seems to have learned little from Auschwitz, an obtuse world that persists in disregarding the warning signals that came from the smokestacks of the crematoria. With a silence that is deafening, power-politics-as-usual tolerates such genocides and mass murders. The U.S. Senate has yet to ratify the Genocide Convention, a step which would affirm the American Founding Fathers' passionate concern for individual liberty, and which would immeasurably aid in fashion-ing a structure of international law based on principles of human dignity (Korey, 1981). Rather, Washington "tilted" towards Pakistan and continued to aid Paraguay. On the other hand, France was in lea-gue with Burundi, while the Soviet Union consistently voted with China in 1959. At the U.N. Commission on Human Rights, the U.S.S.R. steered clear of the Aché Indians' travail in return for U.S. non-intervention concerning human rights violations among Soviet Satellite countries. Chile, South Africa, and Israel - quarantined isolates - alone have been subject to censure. For various reasons, even nongovernmental organizations have reacted only belatedly and failed to aid genocidal victims, who usually do not reach the legal "prisoner" stage (Fein, 1980). It is well to recall, in the latter connection, the intractable acceptance during World War II by the International Red Cross' Geneva headquarters of the Nazi distinction between protected "civilian internees" and defenseless Jews, then classified as "detained civilians." (Penkower, 1983).

Despair and Hope

"I should like to believe that they are exaggerated," wrote Arthur Ruppin upon hearing eye-witness reports in September 1940 of the Nazi persecution of Polish Jews a year earlier: "Otherwise one would have to despair of humanity and its 'civilization'" (Ruppin, 1971, p. 305). Given his anxiety, the father of Zionist settlement was indeed fortunate not to have lived much longer to witness what unequivocally was the greatest challenge to the values of the En-lightenment and the vaunted beneficence of modernity. But what hope can we maintain in the wake of the Holocaust, subsequent genocides, and today's madness of an escalating arms race which casts a lengthening shadow of omnicide - the transformation of this globe into a universal, nuclear crematorium?

Confronting Evil

To fulfill what is best in ourselves, we must also understand the capacity of men for evil. The deadliest nihilism ever to envelop mankind's landscape, the abyss which ultimately claimed a third of word Jewry during the years 1939-1945, must be confronted in our other search for meaning. Recalling the Holocaust helps to defeat the passionate effort of the Nazis then, as well as their strident and passive accomplices now, to hurl a whole people down an eerie memory hole. Remembrance instructs us, too, that Auschwitz, subsequent synonym for absolute evil, occured because "it was far away in the back of beyond." Not merely fifty miles west of Crakow on the River Sola in Poland, as commandant Rudolf Hoess wrote in the opening line of his autobiographical memoir (Hoess, 1978, p. 33), but also in the minds of those who alone could have wiped out that scourge from the face of the globe. Members of the death camp Sonderkommando, like many other foresaken Jews across occupied Europe, refused, however, to yield to Western Civilization in abandoning a sense of moral dignity. Some fragmentary testimonies and a revolt which defied all reason represented their heroic counterforce against a world which achieved the gassing of 2000 individuals in less than half an hour at the cost of one-half cent per body, until Hoess ordered that Hungarian Jewish children be thrown alive in Birkenau's burning pits to economize on Zyklon-B insecticide (Penkower, 1983).

Relentless Dehumanization

The fires of the crematoria illumine, as no other phenomenon could, dark recesses of human behavior in evidence after the Third Reich's Gotterdammerung. The Nazis' degenerate ideology made inroads even in Western circles. How far removed is the judgment of U.S. Assistant Secretary of War John McCloy that Hitler's "mass extermination of the Jews was only one of a number of military measures" employed by the Nazis to execute their operations in a "most economic matter" (Smith, 1981, p. 94), an estimate privately delivered in December 1944, from Col. Paul Tibbet's description of his dropping the Atomic bomb on Hiroshima (New York Times, sec. II, May 16, 1982) as a "routine" and "unexciting" mission? Currently, "powerless Jews" may be translated into Kurds, Bahais, Falashas (itself a derogative term denoting "stranger"), and who knows which other threatened victims in a troubled tomorrow. On the broader scale, relentless dehumanization, whether in a society of terror or one of computerized comfort, enables the two superpowers to speak in casual, bloodless fashion of neat "surgical strikes," "bearable war," "margins of superiority," and "overkill."

TRANSCENDING THE HOLOCAUST

To transcend the Holocaust it is necessary to take up the gage of battle against barbarism. In a world which continues to treat people like objects and ciphers, we must affirm the sacredness of individuality. Escape into abstract thought and polarization is easy, but it masks truth, concealing the variegated richness of life while multiplying dangerous stereotypes. At an international meeting in Geneva, in 1979, the then Vice President of the United States underscored this legacy acknowledging that the world had failed at the 1938 Evian Conference on Refugees to respond properly to Jewry's plight, Walter Mondale announced that his government would admit 250,000 "boat people" from a torn Asia; those other nations present followed with a commitment which came, all told, to 2,000,000.

No one is Expendable

None, the Holocaust tells us, should be deemed expendable. Rather, the limited vision of bureaucrats and politicians requires that transnational constituencies be created to represent the powerless and to challenge technological obscenity which progresses from mounds of shoes to mushroom clouds. With silence itself a statement, active compassion that flows from mutual need has to replace the crime of indifference.

The Infinite Preciousness of Life

World War I, by applying industrial methods to warfare, first aroused man's sensibilities to mass carnage and the terrible cheapness of life. One Jewish soldier, whose czarist company had been ordered in early September 1914 to charge the forces of von Hindenberg and Ludendorf in hand-to-hand combat at the Battle of Tannenberg, advanced an alternative. "Please sir, show me my man!," he cried to his commanding officer. "Perhaps I can come to an understanding with him." (Wisse, 1971, p. 6). Absurd, one is tempted to say, but beneath the absurdity lies the only possible response if a decent world is still to arise after the Holocaust. Ours is the mandate of conscience. We had better begin to act as human beings now.

REFERENCES

BAUER, Yehuda. The Holocaust in Historical Perspective. Seattle: Univ. Washington Press, 1978.
DAWIDOWICZ, Lucy S. The Holocaust and the Historians. Cambridge: Harvard University Press, 1981.
FEIN, Helen. Tolerance of genocide. Patterns of Prejudice, 1973, 7, (Sept.-Oct.), 22-28.
FEIN, Helen. On preventing genocide. Worldview, 1980, 1, (Jan.-Feb.), 42-45.
HOESS. Rudolf. Autobiography. In Jadwiga Bezwinska, & Danuta Czech (Eds.), KL Auschwitz Seen by the SS. Krakow: Panstwowe Muzeum W, Oswiecimiu, 1978.
KATZNELSON, Yitschak. Vittel Diary. Tel Aviv: Bet Lochamei HaGetaot, 1964. Trans. Myer Cohen.
KOEHL, Robert L. RKFDV: German Resettlement and Population Policy 1939-1945. Cambridge: Harvard University Press, 1957.
KOREY, William. America's shame: the unratified genocide treaty. Midstream, 1981, 27, (Mar.), 7-13.

136

PENKOWER, Monty Noam. The Jews Were Expendable: Free World
Diplomacy and the Holocaust. Champaign-Urbana: University Illinois
Press, 1983.
RINGELBLUM, Emmanuel. Notes From the Warsaw Ghetto: The Journal of
Emmanuel Ringelblum. New York: Schocken, 1974, Trans. and ed. John
Sloan.
RUPPIN, Arthur. Memoirs, Diaries, Letters. New York: Herzl Press,
1971, Ed. Alex Bein, Trans. Karen Gershon.
SMITH, Bradley, F. The Road to Nuremberg. New York: Basic Books,
1981.
SNOW, Edgar. How the Nazi butchers wasted nothing. Saturday Evening
Post, 217, (Oct. 28, 1944), 18-19, 96.
WIESEL, Elie. One Generation After. New York: Random House, 1970.
WISSE, Ruth. The Schlemiel as Modern Hero. Chicago: Univ. of
Chicago Press, 1971.

MONTY N. PENKOWER, Ph.D., Touro College, 30 W. 44 St. New York,
N.Y. 10036, U.S.A.

11. Societal Madness: Impotence, Power and Genocide

Ronald Aronson

Ronald Aronson is Professor of Humanities in the College of Lifelong Learning, Wayne State University, Detroit. His books include THE DIALECTICS OF DISASTER: A PREFACE TO HOPE (NLB-Verso), and the forthcoming SARTRE'S SECOND CRITIQUE (University of Chicago Press). He received his Ph.D. in The History of Ideas from Brandeis University. In exploring the basis of hope today, he was drawn, inevitably, to the Holocaust and other instances of mass murder in our century. As historian, philosopher and political activist, his main concern is to disentangle the twin prospects made increasingly possible by human energy, inventiveness and struggle - to combat the threat of total destruction and to realize peace.

The Holocaust stands out as the most horrible mass murder in a century of mass murder. As we delineate its barbarism, its madness, its evil, we do so symbolically surrounded by the century's one hundred million other victims - Indonesians, Armenians, Poles, Russians, Kampucheans, Congolese, Vietnamese, Chinese, Japanese and others. They have all been targets of systematic and calculating efforts to use human ingenuity, organization and resources - to kill en masse.

Our century of technological innovation and revolutionary change is also...a century of mass murder. We must of course - to preserve the moral and intellectual distinctions if for no other reason - distinguish war from mass murder, mass murder from genocide, genocide from the Holocaust. But we must also see, in this ominous late twentieth century, that each shades into each, that at this very moment the targets of nuclear weapons are we noncombatants held hostage everywhere in the world, that crazed dictators with racist ideologies will not set them aloft but apparently sane, sophisticated leaders selected through normal procedures in normal times. When it happens it may be on a day, like today, when people like ourselves are attending a conference on the world's problems. At the blinding flash, many of us will turn to each other in shock, some exclaiming words like "Damn," or "It happened" as our last words, the earth's last words.

The next holocaust, in short, may be rather different from the last. Are there possible similarities from which we may learn? Do other examples from this century of death, when studied alongside the Holocaust, yield parallels, similarities, understandings which help us to confront today's threat of nuclear war?

I have studied three vastly different instances of mass murder in our century - the Holocaust, "liquidation of the kulaks" and the Great Terror in the Soviet Union in the 1930s, and the American War in Vietnam.[1] Indeed so different are they that I am sure some of

you will disagree that they belong together in the same discussion.
Opinions will differ over the scope, the nature, and even the fact
of mass murder in the three cases. Let us begin with the facts:

THE HOLOCAUST, STALIN'S MASS MURDERS, AND AMERICAN KILLINGS IN
VIETNAM.

The Germans, we know, killed approximately six million Jews in
nearly three-and-one-half years through shooting, gassing, starvation, and disease - during a war, we must not forget, which saw
forty million people die, half of them Russians. The Jews were
singled out not merely for genocide in Lemkin's original sense -
national destruction - but for extermination. They were murdered
not in order to control or administer a territory, or for other
political, military or economic purposes. Their elimination itself
became a major German purpose.

Under Stalin two great waves of death occurred, "the liquidation of the kulaks as a class" from late 1929 to 1933, and the
"Great Purge" from 1936 to early 1939. In addition to the over
three million peasants who were shot, more than five million starved
to death in the countryside due to deliberate government policy, and
still others died in forced labor camps. From 1936 to 1939 another
million were executed and over six million died in camps. The total
toll for the Stalin years (1930-1953) was perhaps twenty million
dead, one in every eight Soviet citizens, with an equal number surviving the camps. In the atmosphere prevailing in the Soviet Union
in the 1930s, this meant that virtually everyone lived in fear of
death. And yet this was one of the great periods of construction in
modern history: during these years the Soviet Union became a modern
industrial society overnight to become strong enough to beat back
the German armies at the gates of Leningrad, Moscow and Stalingrad.

My third example seems, strange to say, modest by comparison:
largely between 1965 and 1972, the United States, waging war in
Vietnam, devasted Indochina. Twice as many bombs were dropped on
South Vietnam, the country the U.S. claimed to be defending (an area
slightly larger than England and Wales) than the Allies dropped in
all of World War II. A policy of laying waste the countryside was
adopted in eary 1965 which intentionally created six million refugees (40% of the population) - and caused many of over one million
deaths the U.S. estimates as the toll of its intervention. Large
parts of South Vietnam - and Laos, Cambodia and North Vietnam - became "free fire zones," meaning that anyone living there, as well as
any dwelling, could be bombed. Herbicides destroyed one-seventh of
the country's agricultural lands, 35% of its hardwood forest and
half of its coastal mangrove forest. Bomb craters alone - and one
500-lb bomb was dropped for every second man, woman and child in
South Vietnam - left eight million unusable, unfillable, malarial
holes in the earth 30 feet in diameter by 15 feet deep - destroying
at least 200,000 acres of land. Whatever the numbers, the U.S. intervention was genocidal according to both the definition of genocide as systematic mass murder and as the destruction of a national
group.

Taking place in the one case under fascism, in another under communism, and the third under bourgeois democracy, these are considered, deliberate practices of mass murder. But what kind of a society is it that intends to systematically murder its own members; a religious or ethnic group, members of which indeed may be citizens of the society and play a vital role in it; or a national group halfway around the world? I would argue that these instances of mass murder reflect not what we might call rational societies in the pursuit of appropriate political goals, but rather reveal forms of social madness. I want to renew this problematic and obsolescent term, madness, as a social-psychological and moral-political category – that is, to revive, in our secularized, technically sophisticated world a way of simultaneously describing and judging human acts which seek intentionally, violently and systematically to rupture with reality.

SOCIAL MADNESS

Fully perceiving one's own and the world's reality (yes, this obsolescent term, reality, remains decisive too), and fully gearing one's activities to it, may still be considered tokens of complete sanity – to be fully "in touch," so to speak. At the other pole, complete madness, we would expect to find individuals totally out of touch with reality. Neither, of course, is even conceivable; if Freud is right, for example, civilized life itself imposes a series of ruptures with our own psychic and biological reality; and at the other pole complete rupture would make survival itself impossible. Madness and sanity, then, must be relative terms to which "more" or "less" are always applicable and which will always be measured in degrees. Even within these limits we can identify madness: a systematic rupture with decisive dimensions of external or internal reality, usually suggesting their replacement by fantasy. This further suggests living according to fantasy, and in its violent form, attempting to impose the fantasy beyond oneself.

Judgments of sanity and madness are difficult, except in the most obvious cases, given not only psychological and ideological distortion but also the reality of a shifting, subtle world where even accurate perception or effective action are achievements. Still, when we hear Hitler rail about the Jews, or Stalin about the "Trotskyite-rightist-capitalist-imperialist-fascist" plot, or Lyndon Johnson about the Vietnamese Communist "threat" to America and American "help" to Vietnam, we know we are in the presence of both perception and policy that are deeply out of touch with reality. Each ruler showed tactical as well as strategic brilliance – a grasp of goals and the most effective use of means to achieve those goals. Yet, in decisive areas each systematically broke with reality and sought both to transform reality according to a fantastic vision and to destroy it: madness.

The current publicity about the Hinkley trial in the United States reminds me that the notion of madness I am developing does not rule out responsibility. Indeed, I have emphasized the inten-

tionality of each instance of genocide. Societies, like individuals, choose their madness, right down to the most insignificant
details of behavior. To quote Jean-Paul Sartre, "mental illness (is)
the way out which the free organism, in its total unity, invents in
order to be able to live an unlivable situation." As Sartre's
thought evolves, he comes to mean freedom not in the sense of some
unmotivated and absolute choice, but rather the act of making oneself from what has been made of one. To act is always to go beyond
the given, to project and intend some goal, to seek to achieve it.
A mad act would be one which intentionally breaks with reality when
other exits seem blocked.

Hitler's vision of the Jews cast them as parasites, as the
source of pollution of German Society - both as subhumans and as
superhumans. We must note the obvious, that to perceive human beings this way is so systematic a distortion of their humanity as to
be mad; that it is even madder to treat them this way by withdrawing
from them the rights and privileges accorded to all human beings;
and even madder to seek to transform them into living subhumans and
then, as parasites, to exterminate them. This is the ultimate violent transformation of reality according to fantasy: madness. How
mad? Surely in the Spring and Summer of 1944, with D-Day imminent
and then present, with the Soviets pushing the Germans across the
Carpathians - surely the Germans could have desperately used the 150
trains that bore the Hungarian Jewish community to Auschwitz, the
fuel, the railroad crews. Extermination indeed had become a goal of
the Nazi empire that transcended survival itself.

In the Soviet example, less widely known, tens of millions of
peasants resisting collectivization became - by the fact of this resistance - kulaks (wealthy peasants who employed and exploited
others). This was clearly more and other than cynical manipulation:
it was widely believed that these people were "enemies of the
people," just as this was believed of the millions who suffered
later. The spring of both was the transformation of the Soviet
Union during the early 1930s, undertaken to break out of the situation in which the Bolsheviks found themselves by the late 1920s. It
was madness to collectivize and madness to industrialize because the
Soviet Union was far too backward for either. In an act of will,
governed by fantasy, Stalin and his subordinates drove the people
into collective farms, into industrial cities and into work camps.
This violent, tranformative rupture with Soviet society and Soviet
possibilities sought the impossible: to build industrial socialism,
virtually overnight, in a single isolated and backward country. It
was accompanied by and intimately connected with brutal attacks on
tens of millions of fantasy-enemies, attacks which wrought havoc
upon Soviet agriculture, crippled industrial growth, and decimated
the military on the eve of war. These acts allowed the creation of
"socialism in one country" as an amalgam of genuine achievement,
forced labor camps, death, and madness.

To turn to the third example, Vietnam, our first question is
whether the very category of madness applies: we see behind the U.S.
war no crazed dictator, but mostly the rather typical originally

lower-middle class politicians and generals who became American presidents: Truman, Eisenhower, Johnson, Nixon. We see no severe social upheaval, such as the German sequence of war, defeat, revolution, partial restoration, inflation, depression; or the Russian sequence of war, two revolutions and civil war. And no dead ends,
such as the position of the German lower-middle class after 1918 or
the Bolsheviks by 1929. There seems, in the unprecedently rich and
powerful postwar America, no deep systemic abnormality pushing towards a mad "solution," no impulsion to genocide. Rather, the war
in Vietnam seems primarily to be a specific, limited policy, a
single horrible adventure of a well-functioning, successful society.
Moreover, as we study the war we find in it no startling break such
as "dekulakization" or the "Great Change" in the Soviet Union, or
indeed the very accession of an evil force such as the Nazis to
power in Germany. Rather we see a small series of distortions,
overreachings, irrationalities accumulating in the phenomenon - per-
ceptually, intellectually and morally more elusive than Stalinism or
Nazism - of normal man in normal times in a normal society pursuing
a war which happens to become genocidal.

In describing their actions as mad, am I merely imposing a
rather fascinating thesis on a situation it scarcely fits, or am I
finding in the situation behavior, however elusive and puzzling,
that warrants such description? I ask this question not at all rhetorically. One cannot help but be bemused by the seeming normality
of the American war and its planners, tempted by the ease with which
Vietnam can be called a mistake based on the "containment" policy or
a result of the logic of imperialism. Yet madness-become-policy -
because it is policy - takes on a solidity, a reality, a place in
the logic of events even if it drastically and decisively breaks
with rationality. In Vietnam we return again and again to a presence
so violent, so self-defeatingly destructive, so blind, so adamant,
that the notion of a systematic rupture with reality is inescapable.
The same is true of attempting violently to transform the society in
keeping with a fantasy imposed on it from outside and of, ultimately, seeking to obliterate it. Perhaps the genocidal madness of
the American presence there is best expressed in the officer's famous description of an action at the village of Ben Tre during the
Tet offensive of 1968: "We had to destroy it in order to save it."

Speaking about the whole American presence over the course of
two decades one might say that the "it" - the Republic of (South)
Vietnam - never had a reality of its own, but was, beginnning to
end scarcely more than an American fantasy-construction using native forces that had no roots, no organization but the colonial army
and bureaucracy, no authority or legitimacy. Its purpose was to
"save" the South from the Viet Minh - the only national social force
of any significance. As it failed to "take," this construction, the
RVN, resorted to ever-greater violence, provoked widespread opposition and - after the fall of Diem - revealed its only base to be the
army.

The U.S. response to impending defeat in 1964-5 was to insist
on victory in the face of facts. The "escalation" is the closest we

come in Vietnam to a dramatic and massive rupture with reality. The decision was threefold: to bomb North Vietnam (primarily undertaken to boost the morale of the disintegrating RVN) which no serious observer, even in Washington, thought was giving decisive aid to the insurgents; to land massive numbers of Americans to take over fighting the war; and to destroy the rural-based Southern insurgency by destroying the society that nurtured it ("forced urbanization," as it was called by its advocates).

The bombing of the north was, to put it most simply, for show; having no tangible goals, it took on a deranged punitive quality. The massive intervention confirmed that "South Vietnam" had not "taken," and only deepened the dependency of those weak, corrupt, purposeless elements the U.S. had brought into its employ. The obliteration of the countryside was, very simply, a choice of genocide to stave off defeat - to destroy what could not be otherwise saved. The results: over one million dead, four countries bombed to bits, millions homeless, the creation of a grotesque parasite "society" in the southern cities wholly dependent on the U.S. presence and - which, left to itself, collapsed only fifty-five days after the first sustained offensive. I put "society" in quotation marks because it produced no leaders (that were not chosen by the Americans), no organizational forms (but the Army), and no purpose but the profit and survival of individuals.

The U.S. war in Vietnam like the other forms of genocide was appropriate to its society and its historical situation. I would argue that each instance comes from the depths of a society, rather than being the somehow autonomous decision of a ruler, or the result of disastrous policy choices. "Societal madness" suggests that these genocidal undertakings have their source in fundamental social problems whose actual resolution evades the comprehension, desire or capacity of the ruling forces - and whose mad and genocidal fantasy-resolution becomes social policy. As I said earlier, they are an intentional break with reality chosen when other exits seem blocked.

I am thus speaking of the impotence of ruling groups to achieve ends to which their rule has become bound - in Germany, first the dead end with which the lower-middle class found itself after 1918, leading to the impossible amalgam of "national socialism" and the desire to return to earlier times; in the Soviet Union the impossible construction of "socialism in a single country"; in the U.S. the impossible creation of an "independent non-Communist South Vietnam" as part of an equally impossible "free world" imperium controlled by the U.S.

THE UTTER IRRATIONALITY OF THE END

In each case we must note the utter irrationality of the end. In each case this may be expressed in class and social-structural terms: Nazism expresses the enraged fantasies of a German lower-middle class which managed to contend for political power because of a constitutional standoff caused by the political weakness or obsolescence of more appropriate candidates for social power. Stalinism expresses the Bolshevik determination - and absolute survival need - to construct a modern socialist society out of backward, rural, illiterate Russians. The war in Vietnam expresses the drive for total domination - to create a world in their image - by the rulers of the most powerful country the world has ever seen. Hatched from great social crises in the first two cases and great social success in the third, the movements or goals sprang from the depths of each society, on the one hand, and ran into a fundamental obstacle - reality - on the other.

In each case the irrational goal reflected an irrational starting point - a Germany in which the modern world had not triumphed sufficiently to place a fit ruling class in political and ideological dominance after 1918; a Russia whose rulers may have had the most advanced outlook in Europe but presided over one of its most backward societies; an America whose rulers, for a whole series of reasons, including the country's legendary productivity, anti-Communism, overwhelming technical strength and a successful history of racial oppression, sought and had too much power. In each case the irrationality of the starting point need not have led to human disaster were the rulers not bound to the reasons for which they achieved power and the social forces that brought them there. In a sense the starting points already implied ruptures with reality; pursuing such goals in the real world led them up against major obstacles. The result was a kind of impotence.

But if one hardly thinks of any of these ruling forces as impotent, it is not only because their own outlooks blindly emphasized their power - in the case of the dictatorships to the point of omnipotence - but also because of their control of the twentieth century state apparatus. Both the Nazis and the "pragmatic" American rulers had their own versions of the Stalinist motto: "There are no fortresses which the Bolsheviks cannot storm." Challenged, the formulator of this phrase would have referred, no doubt, to the Bolshevik's scientific outlook and political organization as making possible even the overnight industrialization of Russia. His American and German equivalents would have emphasized technical "knowhow," capitalism and democracy triumphing everywhere on the one hand, and the genius of the Aryan volk ruling lesser peoples on the other. In each case impotence in power generated a deranged sense of omnipotence.

What happened when the dominant social forces, beginning from an irrational starting point and having postulated goals out of touch with reality, reached the inevitable limits of their effective power to control and transform?

The logic of each situation seems to rule out a calculation of means and their relationship to ends - confronting the attainability of the goals given the available means, etc. After all, such calculations are based on a sense of reality, of an awareness of limits. Rationality, technique, science, were all employed extensively, but not to correct goals - rather as method in the service of madness.

144

Nazism in its very essence - especially in its antisemitism, Bolshevism in its vision of overnight collectivization and industrialization, and U.S. policy in Vietnam - all were premised on a denial of reality.

Reality is, ultimately, the human beings who make it up. Denying actual social conflicts taking place in Germany from the outset, the Nazi saw Germany's crisis in mad pseudobiological terms and ascribed it to the Jews. Denial may be an epistemological and a psychological fact; in the hands of those seeking power it can also become politics. In power, denial can be murder, mass murder. Denial of Russia's crippling backwardness meant not only changing it - the constructive side of the Stalinist project - but also assaulting it, violating it, destroying Russia's backward people, its peasants. Later denial became also the denial of any other socialism than that one, and was carried out as the murder and imprisonment of most of those who had the memory of a different socialism - under the label of "Trotskyism." In Vietnam denial became expecially lethal when directed, first, against North Vietnam: as if to make true the myth of a northern invasion of the South. After all, wasn't this the reason, the only possible reason, for sending B-52s to bomb the North? Denied also was the real South Vietnam, the rural society which had supported the Viet Minh and in which the NLF insurgency was reborn - physically "denied" by four million tons of bombs.

Genocide is, then, a kind of ultimate denial of reality: a madness of those in power who are impotent to use that power effectively to change reality, and who, lost in visions of omnipotence, instead seek to destroy it. We have seen the destruction accompanied by the creation of fantasy-states, amalgams of madness and reality - Stalin's socialism, the Holocaust kingdom and America's Vietnam. In each case genocide becomes the denial-solution of an otherwise insoluble situation.

There is, I am arguing, a logic startlingly similar to each genocide I have discussed. Filling out my suggestions would take a volume, a volume which would have to, as I indicated at the outset, pay full attention to the vast differences between the three cases.

The absolute evil of the "Final Solution of the Jewish Problem" certainly differentiates it from genocidal efforts to build a new society on the one hand or win an unwinnable war on the other, even though each project was itself a violation of sense.

With regard to the Soviet Union, we must recall Stalin's prophetic words, voiced in 1929 and then again two years later: "We are 50 to 100 years behind the industrial countries: we must catch up in ten years or we are lost." For all the destructive fury accompanying and generated by the Stalinist project of catching up, we can only imagine with a shudder the consequences to all of humanity if Russia had not caught up in the military and industrial sectors that mattered most.

Most remarkable in the case of Vietnam is the U.S. withdrawal from the war, under the pressure of a mass democratic movement, without ever having chosen fully to utilize its destructive power. It was achieved at a tremendous cost to them, amounting to a defeat in victory, but the irreducible fact is that the Vietnamese, not the Americans, won the war.

The point is, as I suggested earlier, that each instance has its own characteristics rooted in its own history and social situation. But the very idea of similar logics takes us beyond national particularities and forces us to ask about salient features of social life in the twentieth century. The reason for looking at our century rather, say, than at the pursuit of power through the ages, is because this may throw light on the most important question of all, namely how to prevent future genocides. With the threat of nuclear omnicide staring us in the face, and discussing these issues in the lap of the most explosive region in the world, our purpose in studying this history must be to prevent any and all forms of repetition.

It seems to me that the relevant tension has to do with the dynamics of development and underdevelopment. Reading the Communist Manifesto lately I was struck by how optimistic were Marx and Engels, as well as how positive towards bourgeois society. The bourgeoisie would modernize and industrialize chiefly in Western Europe, and would create the preconditions for socialism. They would, in the process, modernize the entire world. At some moment of economic, social and political maturity, the struggles of the international proletariat would reach the point - presumably everywhere - of overthrowing bourgeois society. Marx and Engels did not see that nonsynchronous contradictions, in Ernst Bloch's phrase, might shape our history - that the fact that social groups live at different levels of historical development might become decisive.[2] The German lower-middle class belonged in an earlier time and wanted, however madly, to return to it;[3] the Bolsheviks were obsessed with the future yet crippled by a rural society which had barely emerged from serfdom. We can see in our world today the violent rejection of the present, the flight into the past - by social forces whose very existence may be threatened by modernization. We can also see a headlong urge towards the future, the brutal break with the past and all those who represent it. Genocidal ruptures with reality seem built into the dynamics of uneven development within contemporary societies.

And between them as well: a sense of omnipotence seems a common stance of the developed towards the less developed, a sense that "our" objectives can and should be imposed on "them." At its most modern and alienated - and mad - this stance merges with technicism. Since World War II especially, U.S. leaders have believed in the fantasy that social problems - problems of human relationships with other humans - (and recently of human relationships to the planet and its fragile ecology) could be converted into technological problems and solved on that plane. Perhaps this is one meaning of overdevelopment: to seek to bypass human relations and conflicts

146

with technological wizardry. Inasmuch as it transcends conflict and creates consensus, it is a device of rulers. The repressed returns, grotesquely distorted. The conflicts find their way into the technology, thereby achieving a haunting autonomy while threatening the human race. I refer, of course, to nuclear weapons - the ultimate mad fruits of impotence/omnipotence in power. A significant variant of the logic we have been discussing, the nuclear threat has at its core a violent rupture with reality - the conversion of struggle, which is ultimately political, into annihilation.

Let me conclude by stressing the utter - and utterly terrifying - normality of this madness. I have suggested from the beginning a link between violence and irrationality, genocide and madness. I have focused on Vietnam to emphasize its occurrence under bourgeois-democratic conditions - of freedom, democracy, full public view, moderation. If a "sickness" created the war in Vietnam, it was the kind we are accustomed to reading in the newspapers and watching on television daily. It is our sickness. I do not think that the next "final solution" will be directed against we who are Jews. It may, but it is no less possible that our catastrophic history has placed us in the political position, and frame of mind, to instigate it. In any case, I fervently hope not, but we waste our time looking for the past to repeat itself in recognizable forms when we should be looking instead for the dynamics of potential catastrophe. We need to see, for example, that kind of madness, however normal, that insists on threatening atomic holocaust as a contribution to peace. In this discussion I have not discussed the corruption of language that becomes such a necessary part of genocidal societies. Normal men, yes, but those who make wars for peace - as Richard Nixon declared in his phase of the war in Vietnam - are mad. We must not allow them to govern us, for when they have destroyed us it will be too late.

NOTES

1. This paper summarizes conclusions of the author's The Dialectics of Disaster: A Preface to Hope, NLB-Verso, London, 1984. A full study of each of the examples will be found there.
2. Jean-Paul Sartre, Foreword to R. D. Laing and D. G. Cooper, Reason and Violence, Tavistock Publications, London, 1964, p. 7.
3. Ernst Bloch, Nonsynchronism and the obligation to its dialectics, New German Critique, Spring 1977, No. 11, p. 35.

RONALD ARONSON, Ph.D., Wayne State University, College of Lifelong Learning, Detroit, Michigan 48202, U.S.A.

12. Nuclear Insanity and Multiple Genocide

Ronald E. Santoni

Ronald E. Santoni is Maria Teresa Barney Professor of Philosophy at Denison University. He is co-editor of SOCIAL AND POLITICAL PHILO-SOPHY, contributing author to CURRENT PHILOSOPHICAL ISSUES, and editor and contributor to RELIGIOUS LANGUAGE AND THE PROBLEM OF RELIGIOUS KNOWLEDGE, among other works. Long active in civil rights, anti-war and peace activities, he is, at present, Vice-President of the Union of American and Japanese Professionals Against Nuclear Omnicide (American Division), a member of the board of Concerned Philosophers for Peace (formerly PANDORA).

Andrew Kopkind, a prominent American social critic, scolds "most advocates of disarmament" for consigning the arms race to "irrationality and insanity." The persistence of the arms race is maddening," he affirms, "but it is not madness." He goes on to argue that "militarism is not a mere malfunction of government but the very basis of governmental power." "Those who wield that power" he contends, "deploy their weapons, mass their armies and invest their treasure in ways they believe will advance and protect their interests (Kopkind, 1981, p. 280).

Although - to be sure - I agree with Kopkind's view that governments and their military power-brokers do what they do in the belief that they are advancing their self-interests and self-protection, I take issue with his contention that the continuation of the arms race is only maddening, not insane, irrational or mad. I want to contend that, according to both ordinary usage and dictionary meaning of words such as "insane" and "mad," the arms race is, indeed, insane and mad. Because power (and militarism) is at the basis of governments, and because governments proceed according to what they believe to be their self-interest and self-protection, it does not follow that these beliefs are neither irrational nor insane.

To put it another way, because governments can be understood according to a "logic" (in the everyday sense) of self-interest or acquisition of power, it does not follow that the beliefs that they hold or the deeds that they perform, on the basis of that "logic," are either sane or rational. By pointing out the militaristic roots of government and the political, self-interested motives of governmental power, Kopkind has failed to show that the arms race is not madness.

Both according to ordinary usage and dictionary definitions (see e.g., the unabridged Random House Dictionary of the English Language), the words "insane" and "mad" connote, among other meanings, the sense of "extremely foolish or unwise," "not being of sound mind"; and have as synonyms such words as "irrational," "senseless," "deranged," and even "maniacal." I understand that

147

professional application of these terms connotes that the person described as insane is not grasping "external reality" lucidly, and that his thinking is "disarranged," "disordered," or "deranged." Being "mad" or "insane" is a sickness which involves, among other features, a psychic break from "reality." A diagnostic manual of the American Psychiatric Association partially describes psychosis as involving "a serious distortion of (the) capacity to recognize reality" (Diagnostic and Statistical Manual of Mental Disorders -II).

THE ARMS RACE IS MAD

Given these connotations, I do not think that we need to fuss too much about whether we can appropriately refer, or continue to refer, to the intensification of the arms race as "insane or "mad." Whether one is appealing to the dominant ordinary-language and dictionary uses of these terms, on the one hand, or to a more specific use of these words in pathology, on the other, I think that one has a compelling case for calling the nuclear arms race - with its unparalleled preoccupation with unparalleled destruction - "extremely foolish and unwise," "irrational," "insane," "mad" or even "deranged."

Let me offer just a few illustrations that give warrant to my continuing to call the nuclear arms race "mad or "insane." Although it is widely recognized that the United States has enough nuclear weapons to overkill (i.e., the capacity to use nuclear weapons beyond "mutually assured destruction") the Soviet population 40 times, and the Soviet Union has enough to overkill the American population 20 times, the United States (and perhaps the U.S.S.R.) continues to produce 3 hydrogen bombs a day. Even though any two of the present American arsenal of 43 Polaris and Poseidon submarines, or any one Trident submarine, has the combined missile and nuclear warhead power to destroy all the major population centers of the U.S.S.R. (or the Western Hemisphere), the United States Navy is intent on building 25 more Trident submarines.

We go on increasing our arsenals of nuclear extermination even as we calculate that the 50,000 U.S. and Soviet nuclear warheads possess a combined explosive yield of 20 billion tons of TNT, or one million, six hundred thousand times the yield of that dropped on Hiroshima. This senseless addiction to excess in destructive power, by both superpowers, is surely mad.

It is as though the dead could go on killing the dead, as though increase in the quantity of nuclear weaponry were divorced from the likelihood - and unspeakable horrors - of nuclear war, as though escalating the number of nuclear carriers and the amount of potential nuclear fire power had little or nothing to do with accelerating the probability of a nuclear Armageddon, or of ending the sentient world.

There are other examples. I contend that it is mad when in the name of stability and national security the President of the U.S.

proposes, and the Senate approves, the largest military budget in history - 239 billion dollars for 1983 alone; that it is mad when their authorizations project military expenditures of 1.7 trillion dollars between 1984 and 1988, including $30 billion for the homeless MX and $40 billion for the B-1. These programs will most surely destabilize further the U.S. military and political relationship with the Soviet Union and introduce increasing insecurity in a gravely threatened planet. By nourishing both the capacity (e.g., MX, Trident II, Pershing II missiles) and fear of "first strike," they will doubtless make nuclear war more "thinkable" and likely. In a thermonuclear age, to pretend to reduce world tensions by both preparing and threatening to use weapons that will initiate the universal and final holocaust reflects precisely the kind of psychic break from reality that characterizes pathological irrationality.

Consider, too, the Pentagon's attraction to the "Launch on Warning" defense system. In spite of hundreds of errors by the electronic early warning system (about 150 false warnings are reported to have occurred in the 18 months period prior to October 1980 alone), the Pentagon - as part of its "counterforce" strategy - seems prepared to deploy a system that, on the basis of computer indication alone of a Soviet missile attack, would automatically launch its devastating missiles of holocaust. Conversely, the U.S.S.R. is also ready to deploy such a system. Given the marked history of computer fallibility, the possible use of this system strikes one intuitively as so irrational and dehumanizing that one has no difficulty understanding the scientist Nigel Calder's reference to it as a form of "electronic roulette." This is selfdestructive madness couched in the language of electronic "national defense" and technological "security."

It is mad - even by the "logic" of war - when a nation invests, with outrageous extravagance, in weapons like the MX, which it does not know how to deploy; mad, when nuclear strategists bring into being weapons (e.g., Pershing II and Cruise missiles) whose potential "overaccuracy" becomes a basis for military alarm and consternation; mad, when in a universe in which human beings are creators and articulators of meaning, military "defenders" of "peace, "honor" and "humanity" decide to deploy an "enhanced radiation weapon" (the neutron bomb) strategically designed to obliterate human beings while preserving human artifacts and environments. If, as the philosopher Berdyaev contends, war is the "most extreme form and the utmost limit of anti-personalism" (Berdyaev, 1944, p. 156), surely the neutron bomb symbolizes the demonic depths of the depersonalization involved in arms race technology. Only a "deranged mind" - numb to nuclear reality - or one that has internalized the "logic" of nuclear madness and national superiority, would suggest that we must annihilate a large segment of the human race in order to preserve the human species.

PRE-ATOMIC BEHAVIORS ARE MAD

I wish to invoke further the use of "mad" in the pathological sense. Given the unprecedented context of possible omnicide, i.e., the possibility of exterminating irreversibly all forms of life on this planet, it is neither unfair nor extreme to suggest that the superpowers' nuclear preparations for a nuclear war - whether offensive, "preemptive" or retaliatory - also are mad. The nuclear gamesmanship and brinkmanship, the nuclear threat and counter-threat, the appeal to irrational patriotism, the feverish race to have the biggest and best arsenals of nuclear weaponry, are all testimony to the stubborn fact that leaders of nations are still perceiving war from a pre-Atomic perspective.

In proceeding according to the attitudes and "rules" of a pre-Atomic age; in talking and acting as though we lived at a time in which we did not have to confront the nightmarish dimensions and horrendous consequences of hydrogen and thermonuclear weaponry; in continuing to behave - in spite of all the studied counter-predictions - as though a nuclear war, like a conventional war, could be limited or won; in consistently refusing to sign a mutual agreement with the Soviets to renounce "first use" of nuclear weapons in any military encounter[1] (consider the three offers made by the Warsaw Pact nations in the last five years and the most recent proposals against "first use" made by the Soviet Union at the United Nations General Assembly); in rejecting - on the refutable grounds that the United States has not yet attained "nuclear parity" with the U.S.S.R. - the Soviet offer of a bi-lateral nuclear freeze; in drawing up strategies for fighting "protracted" nuclear wars; in considering and allocating funds and resources to useless, preposterous "civil defense" or "Crisis Relocation" programs - in all these cases, United States officials and policy makers seem to manifest a profound incapacity to grasp the realities of the nuclear age. They appear to be "stagnating" the world according to their own wishes; substituting fantasies for authentic confrontation with the real problems of today's imperiled nuclear world. They are systematically "rupturing" with present reality and the whole of civilization (Aronson, 1982).

This incapacity of recognition takes the form of a pathological "psychic numbing" (Lifton, 1967, 1983), and seeming denial of the fact that the start of nuclear "war" would likely lead to multiple genocide, ecocide, or omnicide. So grisly is this possibility that we must invent new words to refer to it. It is the epitome of irrationality and, I think, an indication of a schizoid break with reality when a government, in the name of "national interests," "freedom," "human rights," or "the essential values of Western civilization,"[2] takes <u>any</u> ideological or political difference with "our enemy" - always distortedly conceived - as worth the nuclear incineration of our planet.

George Kennan is right: In continuing the arms race "we are like the children of Hamlin marching blindly along behind their Pied Piper" (Kennan, 1981, p. 14). We systematically dehumanize and monotonously misrepresent the leadership, intentions, and capabilities of another great people (this is a preequisite common to wars and genocides); we continue to succumb to the "temptations and [sick] compulsions of a 'first strike' mentality" (Kennan, 1982, p. 10);

we drunkenly ignore the decaying, debilitating, consequences of the arms race for our economy, our cities, our morale as a people, and - most importantly - our humanity. We are sick in mind and at heart and our sickness relates to our nation's blind, apocalyptic preoccupation with nuclear supremacy.

FROM GENOCIDE TO OMNICIDE

It is time to call a spade a spade. Preoccupation with nuclear war, with utter destruction, is an illness, a form of extreme irrationality. In a nuclear age, with its unprecedented capacity for universal devastation, the continuation and escalation of the arms race is a course of insanity chosen by people who seem devoid of nuclear imagination and oblivious to the likely consequences of their nuclear initiatives. It will eventually lead to multiple genocide or - its logical extension - omnicide

It is clear that, by both the original U.N. General Assembly Resolution on Genocide (96-1) and the 1951 Genocide Convention now in force,[3] the superpowerful architects of nuclear war mutually intend "genocide," no matter what "noble" reasons they may invoke. In preparing for nuclear war, the superpowers are preparing to destroy the existence of each other as nations - hence to deny each other's "right of existence" as an "entire human group" (Robinson, 1960, p. 121).[4] The "genocidal intent"[5] is transparent in the "facts" of these preparations and "it is necessarily premeditated" (Sartre, 1968, p. 78).[6] It is equally clear that these architects of annihilation - perhaps because of the psychically anaesthetizing demands of their work - fail to see that, in a world of nuclear intimidation and overkill, nuclear genocide also spells nuclear suicide. The upshot is evident: the insanity that permits nuclear first-use on a grand scale will inevitably result in multiple genocide. Only added time and megatonnage stand between massive extermination of peoples (multiple genocide) and the end of our planet (omnicide). As JeanPaul Sartre foresaw, the whole human community is now hostage to genocidal (I would say omnicidal) blackmail "piled on top of atomic blackmail" (Sartre, 1968, p. 84).

If our planet is to survive, we must face lucidly our own complicity with madness, correct our infantile distortions of the world, and insist that our leaders abandon their suicidal game of nuclear superiority and one-upmanship. In resisting nuclear distortions we must reorient our governments to nuclear reality. We must learn to ripen our spirit more quickly than nuclear strategists spawn more deadly types of ICBM's. We must act freely and with unparalleled haste: for, as Camus put it, in the omnicidal context, "we have nothing to lose except everything" (Camus, 1960, p. 188).

Andrew Kopkind says that we let our leaders and military strategists "off the hook of history when we define them as pathological rather than political" (Kopkind, 1982, p. 280). I say that, in specified senses, our leaders are both political and pathological, but that we get them on the hook of history and reality when we insist that they face the madness of their present ways and join in

humanity's imperative common task - both recuperative and creative -
of "keeping the world from destroying itself (Camus, 1965, p. 1073).
To many, the project of disarmament seems naively disarming: yet it
is the only course - within human capability - that insures the continuation of that human project called "history."

In the last of his collective appeals against nuclear weaponry,
Einstein said: "Remember your humanity and forget the rest."[7]

NOTES

1. George Kennan has recently said that "the insistence on this option of first use has corrupted and vitiated our entire policy on
nuclear matters ever since these weapons were first developed" ("On
Nuclear War," New York Review of Books, Vol. XXVIII, Jan. 21, 1982,
p. 8). See, also, his Einstein Peace Prize address published in
Disarmament Times (June 1981) and elsewhere (e.g., N.Y. Review of
Books, Vol. XXVII, July 16, 1981, pp. 14-16), in which he makes a
similar point. One should note that as recently as April 6, 1982,
Secretary of State Alexander Haig announced, once more, U.S. opposition to a "no first use" policy, on the grounds that acceptance of
this policy would threaten both our ability to sustain nuclear deterrence and "to protect the essential values of Western Civilization." Neither reason is acceptable. A 'first use' policy appears
fatally contradictory to "mutual deterrence," for it allows precisely that which deterrence is supposed to deter. Far from preserving the "essential values of Western Civilization," first use of
nuclear weapons would expedite the annihilation of Western Civiliza-
zation and all of humanity.
2. See note 1.
3. See the text of the Genocide Convention as published in the Department of State Bulletin, XIX (1948), Article II esp.; also the
U.N. General Assembly Resolution 96, reprinted in e.g., N.
Robinson, The Genocide Convention (New York: Institute of Jewish
Affairs, 1960).
4. Article II of the original U.N. General Assembly Resolution 96-1
makes clear, it seems to me, that preparing for nuclear obliteration
of another nation or people qualifies as genocidal in intent. My
judgment is supported by Leo Kuper's statement that "technological
developments, and nuclear armament, represent preparedness for carefully calculated genocides on a vast scale" (International Action
Against Genocide, Report 52, London: Minority Rights Group, 1982),
p. 3. In this regard, I wish also to point out that the text of the
Genocide Convention published in the Department of State Bulletin,
XIX (see note 3) classifies acts as "genocide" if they have "the intent to destroy, in whole or in part, a national, ethnical, racial
or religious group, as such" (p. 756).
5. For an important discussion of "genocidal intent" as it relates
to Sartre's usage and others', see Hugo Adam Bedau, "Genocide in
Vietnam?" in Held, Virginia et al, Philosophy, Morality and International Affairs (New York: Oxford, 1974).
6. Although Sartre says this in respect to the U.S. Government's involvement in the Vietnam War, it applies, with even less ambiguity,

to the superpowers' preparations for an unspeakable nuclear "exchange."
7. This is quoted in Kennan, 1981, p. 16.

REFERENCES

ARONSON, Ronald. Technological Madness. Unpublished Manuscript, 1982.
BERDYAEV, Nikolai. Slavery and Freedom. New York: Charles Scribner's, 1944.
CAMUS, Albert. The wages of our generation. In Resistance, Rebellion and Death, New York: Alfred Knopf, 1960.
CAMUS, Albert. Essais. Textes etablis et annotes par R. Quilliot et L. Faucon. Paris: Gallimard, 1965.
HELD, Virginia, et al. Philosophy, Morality and International Affairs. New York: Oxford, 1974.
KENNAN, George. A modest proposal. The New York Review of Books, 1981, 28, Nos. 12, 14-16.
KENNAN, George. On Nuclear War. The New York Review of Books, 1982, 28, Nos. 21-22, 8-12.
KOPKIND, Andrew. Maddening not madness. A review of Ruth L. Sivard's World and Social Expenditures 1980. The Nation, 1982, 232, 277, 280.
KUPER, Leo. International Action Against Genocide. London: Minority Rights Group, 1982.
LIFTON, Robert Jay. Death in Life: Survivors of Hiroshima. New York: Random House, 1967.
LIFTON, Robert Jay, & Falk, Richard. Indefensible Weapons: The Political and Psychological Case Against Nuclearism. New York: Basic Books, 1983.
ROBINSON, Nehemiah. The Genocide Convention. New York: Institute of Jewish Affairs, 1960.
SARTRE, Jean-Paul. On Genocide. Boston: Beacon, 1968.

RONALD E. SANTONI, Ph.D., Denison University, Granville, Ohio 43023, U.S.A.

13. Genocide and Mass Destruction: A Missing Dimension in Psychopathology

Israel W. Charny

Israel Charny is the Executive Director, Institute of the International Conference on the Holocaust and Genocide (POB 50006, Tel-Aviv, Israel), and was the Chairperson of the 1st International Conference on the Holocaust and Genocide in 1982. He is Assoc. Professor of Psychology at the School of Social Work at Tel-Aviv University. He is the author of HOW CAN WE COMMIT THE UNTHINKABLE?: GENOCIDE, THE HUMAN CANCER (Westview Press, Boulder, Colorado, 1982; Paperback by Wm. Morrow (Hearst Books), New York, 1983).

The Holocaust has shattered once and for all existing psychological concepts of normality and abnormality. For according to accepted psychiatric definitions, it was largely normal people who were the leaders and followers who executed the most systematic evil in the history of humankind. Yet it is inconceivable that we reconcile ourselves to mental health concepts that do not define, in some intelligent way, the leaders and followers who execute mass murder as disturbed and abnormal.

Psychology and psychiatry lose much of their commonsense credibility so long as there is no way of defining execution and participation in mass murder and genocide as pathological.

It is my strong conviction that we must expand the standard classification system in psychopathology to include abuses and destruction of people. We must revise the theory base of psychopathology to define persons who terminate the lives of others to prove their own pseudomastery of vulnerability and death as disturbed.

We have known this intuitively. It does not matter even that the majority of human beings, including potentially ourselves, can be drawn to this disturbance under sufficiently inciting conditions. Men of good will have always known that wanton destruction of life is an act of madness - even if an entire group and society of people are mad at the same time. But up until now we have failed to create the language-concepts to express this truth and work with it in our traditional discipline of psychopathology.

One reason for the existing absurdity is that most psychopathological concepts of disturbance emphasize weakness and self-renunciation of one's power, and thus account best for evil acts based on despair. Most of our language of psychopathology refers to various incompetence and giving up one's powers, but in genocide, and many lesser abuses of human rights, we are dealing with madmen who are altogether too competent in taking power over others. The greatest evils arise in this world not from incompetence so much as from too-competent exercises of power at the expense of others, and espe-

cially when such power is achieved and consolidated through align-
ment of oneself with a collective group to whom one surrenders one's
judgment and responsibility.

I am going to suggest, first of all, a new way of looking at
the evil of mass destruction of human life as the other side of the
coin of our traditional definitions of psychopathology.

For the most part, existing psychiatric disturbances are what I
shall call Disorders of Incompetence, Vulnerability, and Personal
Weakness where life's anxiety is solved through exaggeration of
weakness and disavowals of potential competence, strength and
mastery to the point where the "patient" is "sick," uncomfortable or
unable to function in society.

I am going to suggest that the opposite side of the coin is the
same range of disturbances exercised not on oneself but on other
human beings, so that the disturbance is visited on or delivered to
the well-being of others. I will refer to these conditions as Disorders of Pseudocompetence, Invulnerability, and Doing Harm to
Others. Here the solution of life's anxiety on the part of a person
who brings about a state of incompetence in others is a disavowal of
their own incompetence, weakness and vulnerability.

A second reason for the failure of existing concepts of psychopathology to include genociders and their numerous accomplices and
bystanders is that there are relatively few psychopathological concepts which concern the important issue of abandoning one's identity
to a group or collectivity.

It hardly makes sense that our concepts of abnormal psychology
do not also systematically include ways in which individuals surrender their identity and values to a larger group identity or ideology, especially when the collective with which one identifies commits itself to actually embarking on mass destruction of life.

I am going to suggest that we also add to our traditional concepts of psychopathology definitions of the extent to which persons
abandon their individual identity and self to any collective process
or ideology.

One of the significant developments in the last two decades of
family therapy has been to identify the myriad of serious disturbances that are generated not simply by a symbiotic dyad, e.g.,
mother and child, but by the patterning of the entire family group
in a "pseudomutual" or "enmeshed" pattern (Wynne et al, 1958;
Bowen, 1966; Dicks,1967; Minuchin, 1974; Sprenkle & Olson, 1978).
The host disturbance is the state of undifferentiation or blending
or fusion which does not permit individuals to grow for themselves,
and then a variety of serious psychiatric symptomatology (including
psychosis, severe learning disorders, severe psychosomatic conditions) and family breakdowns are visited on one or more family members as consequences of this original condition for which traditional psychopathology, to date, has had no name.

I am going to suggest that states of enmeshment and surrender of one's identity and autonomy to others - family, group, or any collective or ideology - should be identified as disturbances long before any behavioral symptoms may appear, and I will refer to these conditions as <u>Disorders of Surrender of Identity and Autonomy</u>.

Note that <u>both</u> disorders of incompetence and pseudocompetence are seriously influenced by and often are actually set in motion by people giving up their real selves in their relationships with groups - whether they surrender and disown their individuality in their family group, or bury themselves in a collective group or ideology, or blindly accept a charismatic leader with little reservation or retention of personal judgment.

Participation in groups that are committed to destroying life should qualify as psychopathological on the counts of both proposed principles: first, adopting a commitment to do serious harm to others, and second, abandoning oneself and one's values to a collective ideology which is taken to justify everything, including destruction of innocent lives.

THE "NORMALITY" OF MASS MURDERERS

Before we develop these concepts further, I want to emphasize that it is still absolutely essential for us to hold on to our hard-won knowledge that the mass killers of humankind are largely everyday people or what we call <u>normal</u> people according to presently accepted definitions of our mental health profession.

Following the Holocaust, we wanted to believe that the leader of the German people, his major followers, and the bulk of the executors were insane, and then it became a first important task to grasp the terrible truth that most of the genociders were not insane by the current concepts and standards of mental health.

Moreover, it has become clear that <u>the potential for being genociders and accomplices is in all of us</u>. The potential for compliance and participation in the execution of mass murder lies in the hearts and minds of all human beings and societies, though of course there are real differences in how different people and societies deal with this potential. It is very important that if we now work towards relabeling genociders as mentally ill, we not allow our redefinition to throw us back to denying the potential cruelty and destructiveness in the human condition that is in all of us.

I have previously summarized the evidence of the normality of the mass murderers in the chapter "Normal Man as Genocider" in my book <u>How Can We Commit the Unthinkable?</u> (Charny, 1982). I do not at all mean now to abandon my earlier position that the potential for genocide is in "nearly all of us" and that most genocide is the work of <u>normal</u> people, but I am looking for a better way to describe what is clearly an entirely common and near-universal condition of humankind at this stage of civilization.

The profession of psychology is duty-bound not only to describe what is normal equals statistically normative or usual, but also, and more important what is normal equals desirable and healthy.

If we turn to metaphors of illness, there have been many illnesses in the history of humankind to which huge numbers of people succumbed until a way was found to contain, treat and prevent the deadly illness. The fact that even a majority of people succumb to whatever plague does not mean that being sick is "normal," or that being the exceptional survivor who does not die of the plague is "abnormal." The first crisis for psychology following the Holocaust was to recognize that genocide is not the work of a relatively few madmen. But we also cannot leave it that genocide is the doing of normal people and be left with a semantic that implies that genocide is in any way normal, acceptable or inevitable.

Moreover, just as the guiding criterion for defining health in medical thought must be all that preserves life, so the guiding value for psychological health must be what human beings do to support life and the quality of life experience. Mass murder and genocide clearly do neither.

Psychologist Hans Askenasy (1978) devoted a book-length treatment to the subject under the title, Are We All Nazis?

Most men and women, including those who start wars, and commit murder, mass murder, and genocide, have been and are considered "normal." And of course their behavior is also considered "legal"...

Askenasy saw no alternative but to propose a new definition that would take precedence over existing concepts.

Behavior is criminal if it is destructive without justification - regardless of local laws. The criteria I have used are common decency and commonsense (pp.103-4).

Gustave Gilbert (1950) was the psychologist who studied the Nazi war criminals at the Nuremberg trials. He concluded unambiguously that although psychopathic personalities played an important role in the revoluntionary nucleus of the Nazi movement,

Without the support of normal and respectable leaders in that society, without a considerable following among the masses of the people, and without the facilitated action of certain cultural trends, it would hardly have been possible for the Nazi leaders to precipitate as great a social catastrophe as they did (p. 287).

Douglas Kelly (1961, p. 171) otherwise known for developing the Rorschach Method with Bruno Klopfer, was the psychiatrist who studied the Nuremberg prisoners, and he too concluded quite clearly, "The Nazi leaders were not spectacular types, not personalities that appear only once in a century. They simply had three quite unremarkable characteristics...overwhelming ambition, no ethical standards, a strongly developed nationalism..."

British psychiatrist Henry Dicks (1972) went back to study imprisoned Nazi war criminals and also concluded that they were essentially normal:

> The SS killers were not "insane" or uncontrollable people, in any generally understood clinical sense...There clearly exists in many people a burned, split-off "enclave of deadly ruthlessness"...round which relatively healthy parts of the personality based on the likewise "good object-relations" can develop (pp. 230,246).

I have elsewhere presented the fascinating findings of the Israeli husband/wife team of psychiatrist and psychologist, Shlomo and Shoshana Kulcsar (1978) who together examined Adolf Eichman before his execution, and who essentially concluded that this was a man who would not encounter the aggression in his personality or experience himself as an individual; he was a cog in a machine who insisted that all other people be cogs in a machine, and could not see people as people.*

Most students of psychopathology basically have ignored the issue raised by the fact that the mass killers were largely "normal."

For the most part, the professional world of mental health goes on till today blithely teaching about mental illness that there are crazy people who hear voices, are unable to get along with others, cannot work, are sexually incompetent, get drunk, write bad checks, accuse their neighbors of plotting against them, and so on, but little is said about deeply prejudiced people who deny the validity of other people's existence, and actually nothing is said of people who put on uniforms and kill others en masse, as if these were not psychopathological issues.

My own feeling is that this ignorance in psychology is not mainly because we don't care. On the contrary, I believe that a high percentage of mental health professionals are among the vanguard who care very much, but that we have been trapped by the existing definitional system of psychopathology.

---

*Supposedly only one psychological test identified Eichman in his own right as a vicious killer. This was the interpretation of the Szondi protocol which was sent for blind analysis to Szondi himself. However, I have never been able to get any other objective verification that this protocol in another Szondi analyist's hands would have yielded the same interpretation, and all the above psychological tests showed the picture described above of disconnection from aggression and from people.

Understandably our diagnostic system developed out of a medical model for understanding sickness and inability to function in the individual, and by definition this way of thinking did not relate that much to what individuals do to make others incompetent.

There is at least one other instance where people do frightful harm to others, namely child battering, where traditional mental health thinking is stymied by the fact that most child batterers are largely "normal." Yet any sane individual knows that it cannot be "normal" to batter one's children and even cause their death.

Some teachers of psychopathology have at least confronted the problem squarely and acknowledged that, in their opinion, they had no choice but to conclude that being a mass killer is normal if you are living in a society which calls for it. Thus Leonard Ullman and Leonard Krasner (1975) have the courage to state the unbearable conclusion directly:

A critical example is whether an obedient Nazi concentration-camp commander would be considered normal or abnormal. To the extent that he was responding accurately and successfully to his environment and not breaking its rules, much less coming to the attention of professional psychiatrists, he would not be labeled abnormal...Although such a person may be held responsible for his acts - as Nazi war criminals were - the concept of abnormality as a special entity does not seem necessary or justified. If it is, the problem arises as to who selects the values that apply to others. This situation of one group's values being dominant over others is the fascistic background from which the Nazi camp commander sprang (p. 16).

On the other hand, James Coleman and his associates (1980), who also refer to the above from Ullman and Krasner and cannot reconcile themselves to a definition that leaves mass destructiveness outside of the boundaries of psychological disturbance, propose a further criterion for normality.

The best criterion for determining the normality of behavior is not whether society accepts it but rather whether it fosters the well-being of the individual and, ultimately, of the group. ...Unless we value the survival and actualization of the human race, there seems little point in trying to identify abnormal behavior or do anything about it (pp. 14,15).

For all of their good intentions, however, Coleman and his associates can only superimpose this criterion on the existing system of classification of psychopathology, since they are unable to provide a conceptual framework which systematically ties together disturbing and destroying the well-being of others with disturbances in oneself. Nor do they find a conceptual stratagem to attack the problem that Ullman and Krasner posed that a person cannot be called abnormal if he conforms to the dictates of his society, albeit a killing society.

The "Rationality" of the Holocaust

It is important also to see that the Holocaust was, in fact, a "rational event."

Sociologist Helen Fein (1979) defines the rationality of the Holocaust as the ability of the persecutors to get away with their intentions without being stopped in terms of costs to them.

Theologian Franklin Littell (1981) concludes that the Holocaust cannot be understood in normal psychological-ethical terms, but rather involves some incredible press in the human spirit towards doing anything and everything which is apparently normal to the human condition.

> The Holocaust cannot be explained in the traditional language of human wrong-doing - "sadism," "brutality," "cruelty," - qualities that describe human emotions and passions. The awesomeness of the event is related to its rationality. The fatal curiosity, the Faustian passion by which whatever can be done will be done - regardless of ethics, morality, or human life itself - led readily to Dr. Mengele's experiments upon helpless victims, Freisler's hanging courts, and the technical skill of engineers and psychiatrists and chemists who built and staffed the Death Camps. The awfulness of the engine of destruction is not its pathology but its normalcy (pp. 371-2).

Obviously neither of the above authors intends to justify the Holocaust when they describe the rational and normal processes that determined the gruesome mass murders. Fein and Littell are deeply devoted scholars of the Holocaust whose outrage at the events of destruction is evident in all of their work. Yet they have the scientific and philosophical courage to label the Holocaust as acts of rational human beings.

On the other hand, social philosopher Ronald Aronson (1981) cautions that in the course of our studies of the Holocaust we may add an undue quality of rationality to its existence:

> It achieves a solidity, a thereness, that incorporates it easily into the rationality of human history. In seeking its causes and meanings, we inevitably endow it with an aura of legitimacy, even necessity. When historians try to bracket out their outrage, horror and shock that such a thing happened, the last step is taken towards making it a rational project of human energy and intentions (pp. 68-69).

SUMMING UP THE CHALLENGE TO PSYCHOLOGY AND PSYCHOPATHOLOGY

I am convinced that we must stand up to the challenge of this issue if we are to keep the science of psychology, and the speciality of psychopathology, at all credible.

For it makes no sense at all to have a discipline that purports to study the nature of man and his behaviors that does not take into account the most incredible behaviors of all, mass destruction - the single most frequent cause of unnatural loss of life that exceeds the toll of any dread illness (see Pilisuk & Ober, 1976, on torture and genocide as "public health problems"). At the same time, it makes no sense whatsoever to have a psychology of normal men that does not include a clearcut acknowledgment of the potential of all human beings to participate, support or allow genocide.

It seems to me that both very real sides of the truth need to be integrated into a psychology which makes it clear that genocide is, tragically, a very common and widespread expression of the human condition, but that it is a distinctly unhealthy and abnormal expression of psychological man - the individual as well as the collective process.

The challenge to psychology must be to project a picture of the normal human being as he might be in his more mature development - in any of a variety of senses such as Kohlberg's (1966) concept of arriving at a higher stage of ethical thought, Erikson's (1975) unfolding to greater maturity and responsibility, or Maslow's (1971) movement toward self actualization. Psychology must provide normal well-intentioned people with new tools to help them avoid being drawn into prevailing trends of violence towards others.

If making other people's lives miserable, persecuting and tormenting them and actually killing cannot be linked with existing definitions of abnormality, the profession of psychology has a serious problem of credibility. Some major revision is inescapable if we are to retain a sense of "sanity" about the field of psychopathology.

At the same time we must be sure when we build new concepts into our theory of abnormality that they link up with and extend existing definitions of what is "sick" and "insane" and "mad," and not impose on us a language that would require an abrupt revision of all the accepted language and tradition of mental health.

Historian George Kren and psychologist Leon Rappoport (1980) insist correctly that the Holocaust is the major historical crisis of the 20th century which imposes on virtually all existing institutions - law, religion, education, all professions - a funda- mental reevaluation of basic concepts, for the awesome facts of the Holocaust render all the existing models and values of virtually all disciplines near meaningless.

The Holocaust will never be assimilated - given substantial meaning - in terms of the familiar normative thought structures provided by Western culture... To call it a nightmare quality is inadequate; by all accounts it was another world in which everything previously considered human and meaningful was turned upside down...

DISORDERS OF INCOMPETENCE, VULNERABILITY AND PERSONAL WEAKNESS	DISORDERS OF PSEUDOCOMPETENCE, INVULNERABILITY AND DOING HARM TO OTHERS
Traditional Categorization of Disturbance in the Individual:	*Expanded to Include Disturbances to Wellbeing of Others:*
Solutions of anxiety through exaggerated disavowals of competence, mastery and strength	*Solutions of anxiety through exaggerated disavowals of incompetence, vulnerability and weakness*

NEUROSIS | NEUROSIS

INABILITY TO ENJOY ONESELF AND LIFE
. RENUNCIATION OF SELF

. EXCESSIVE DEMANDS SELF

DISTURBING OTHERS' ENJOYMENT OF THEMSELVES AND THEIR LIVES
. DENIAL OF WEAKNESS AND VULNERABILITY
. CLAIMING POWER OVER OTHERS

PERSONALITY DISORDERS | PERSONALITY DISORDERS

CHARACTEROLOGICAL RESTRICTION OR EXAGGERATION IN STYLE EXPERIENCING

. DEMEANING OF SELF
. NARCISSISTIC OVERCONCERN WITH SELF

CHARACTEROLOGICAL STYLE OF RELATING TO OTHERS THAT IS REPEATEDLY DISAPPOINTING, INTRUSIVE OR UPSETTING
. DEMEANING OF OTHERS
. PREJUDICE, DEHUMANIZATION AND
. EXPLOITING OTHERS

BEHAVIOR DISORDERS | BEHAVIOR DISORDERS

DISTURBANCE IN ABILITY TO DELAY NEEDS; REPEATED SELF-DESTRUCTIVE BEHAVIORS
. ABUSES OF ONESELF AND SELF-PUNISHMENT
. DAMAGING SERIOUSLY ONE'S LIFE OPPORTUNITY

EXPLOITATION AND HURTING OTHERS

. ABUSES OF OTHERS AND CRUELTY
. DAMAGING SERIOUSLY OTHERS LIFE OPPORTUNITY

PSYCHOSIS | PSYCHOSIS

BREAKDOWN OF ABILITY TO FUNCTION IN THE ORDINARY EVERYDAY REAL WORLD

. DESTROYING ONE'S BASIC ABILITY TO FUNCTION
. IRREVERSIBLE SELF-DESTRUC-TION IN TERMINATION OF LIFE

TAKING AWAY OTHERS' RIGHTS OR ABILITY TO FUNCTION IN THE ORDINARY EVERYDAY REAL WORLD

. DESTROYING OTHERS' BASIC ABILITY TO FUNCTION
. IRREVERSIBLE DESTRUCTION OTHERS IN ACTUAL TERMINATION OF LIVES

Figure 1. EXPANDING THE TRADITIONAL DEFINITIONS OF PSYCHOPATHOLOGY IN THE INDIVIDUAL TO INCLUDE PARALLEL ACTS OF DOING HARM TO OTHERS

Since the Holocaust was possible, prior cultural values supposed to make it impossible were manifestly false, and a moral crisis was imposed upon the whole fabric of the culture (pp. 12,3,131).

TWO MISSING PRINCIPLES IN PSYCHOLOGY: DISORDERS OF PSEUDOCOMPETENCE AND DOING HARM TO OTHERS, AND DISORDERS OF SURRENDER OF IDENTITY AND AUTONOMY

My proposal for resolving the problem that we have been unable to label mass murderers abnormal is based on adding two new principles to our classification of abnormal behavior.

The first expands definitions of abnormality to include not only weakness and harm to oneself, but inducing weakness and doing harm to others.

The second expands definitions of abnormality to include not only failures to make relationships with other people, but also instances when people create relationships to others in which they abandon their individual identity and integrity, be it to their family, a group, or any collective.

As stated earlier, my goal is not to tamper with the existing knowledge base and definitional system in psychopathology, but to add to it. Figures 1 and 2 describe how these definitions relate to existing psychopathological theory.

1. Traditional definitions of psychiatric disturbance largely describe states of incompetence, vulnerability and personal weakness in the individual. The proposal I am now making adds states of pseudocompe- tence, invulnerability and doing harm to others by taking the traditional range of disturbances and turning them on their axis so to speak. In the traditional definitions, one is disturbed mainly when and because one causes harm to oneself. In this extended definition, delivering or inducing the same disturbances in the life experience and functioning of the other is also abnormal.

2. Traditional definitions of psychiatric disturbances are based largely on the problems individuals show in their individual functioning, very much including their interpersonal relationships, but it is increasingly clear that many problems are based on and derive from overconnection, enmeshment, blind obedience and surrender of autonomy and integrity to a group process - whether one's family group, an outside community group, or a larger societal collective or ideology. In the traditional definitions, one is disturbed when one begins to act disturbed. In this extended definition, disturbance is identified already on the basic of exaggerated closeness, unseparatedness, fusion and loss of

164

DISORDERS OF SURRENDER OF AUTONOMY

*Disorders of incompetence & pseudocompetence
develop and intensify through overidentifi-
cation of self and surrender of autonomy to
any collective process*

OVERCONNECTION AND OVER-
IDENTIFICATION SELF WITH OTHER

Undifferentiated in family
of origin or current family
Living through group identity
Conforming to authority or
ideology

RENUNCIATION OF OWN IDEAS AND VALUES
Failure to separate from family
to extent of renouncing personal
goals, e.g., marriage, career
Enmeshed family
Acquiescing to clearly wrong facts (e.g., Asch)
Acting on otherwise unacceptable values
(e.g., Milgram)

FUSION OF SELF WITH OTHERS;
SURRENDER OF SELF TO "MINDLESS BEHAVIOR"
Symbiotic family relationship, e.g.,
mother-child
Folie a deux and more
Participation in cults and other
orgiastic groups (e.g., Jonestown)
Mass hysteria
Collective psychosis

PARTICIPATION IN GROUP PERSECUTION
& DESTRUCTION OF HUMAN LIFE
Bystander to group persecution
Participant in group destruction
including "following orders"
Mass suicide
Pogroms - smaller scale or "spontaneous" events
of destruction of others
Genocide - systematic murder and
extermination of a target group

Figure 2. A PSYCHOLOGICAL SCALE OF SURRENDER OF
SELF TO OTHERS CULMINATING IN PARTICIPATION IN
CULTS OF DEATH AND MASS MURDER

self in relationships with others - even before disturbed symptomatic behaviors are necessarily evidenced.

Neither the principle of disorders of pseudocompetence and doing harm to others, nor the extension of individual diagnosis to include the relationship of the individual to the collective require any changes in existing basic definitions of psychopathology. I am adding to existing theory without proposing any changes in the present classification of abnormality.

Disturbances to <u>others</u> are defined along the same continuum of severity as traditional definitions of disturbances to oneself, from neurosis to personality disorders to behavior disorders to psychosis. The extent to which one causes harm or brings about a state of incompetence in the life of any human being defines the extent of the pathology; in the first case, such incompetence is located in oneself, and in the second case the incompetence is vested in others.

The addition of this dimension is accomplished by a "simple" structural device of rotating existing definitions of disturbances to oneself on their axis towards their counterparts in the same degree of disturbance a person induces or forces on others. It is a change that seems to make simple good sense, and the situation is not unlike other theoretical advances in science where an existing known principle has proved to yield hidden extended meanings when turned over or reversed.

Similarly, evaluating an individual's definition of himself in relation to others allows for a definition of psychopathology based solely on the surrender or overalignment of one's identity to other, long before clearcut symptoms or pathology, whether incompetence or pseudocompetence, have emerged in behavioral terms.

DISORDERS OF PSEUDOCOMPETENCE

Disorders of pseudocompetence represent solutions of the same universal anxiety about life and death through disavowals of one's weakness and proof of one's pseudomastery of existence at the expense of other people. The dread of normal human weakness and needs is answered by various degrees of overstriving, an inflated sense of oneself, claims of power over others, exploitation and manipulation of others, denial of others' human rights and lives, abuses, cruelty and actual destruction. (See Metscherlich, & Metscherlich, 1975, and Hartman, 1982 for perspectives of the German people in this regard.)

Disorders of pseudocompetence are denials of one's vulnerability and mortality, ultimately one's humanity, and include both everyday and more serious evils that people do to their fellow human beings. This definition can include a family group that drives a child crazy, industrialists who are willing to pollute waters that endanger human lives, militarists and arms manufacturers who are eager or willing to expand their power at the expense of other people, and concentration camp guards - whether they are "just following orders" and escaping anxiety and responsibility by not being themselves, or fully into the excitement of their occupation.

Exactly like disorders of incompetence, disorders of pseudocompetence also represent a failure to balance and integrate the two sides of strength and weakness that are intrinsic to the human condition, and which derive from the ultimate human conditions of life and death. The traditional conditions of psychopathology have involved, for the most part, disavowal and renunciation of strength and life; the definitions I propose to add now of causing other people to be unable to function involve disavowals and renunciations of one's own weakness and death vulnerability.

At the end of How Can We Commit The Unthinkable? (Charny, 1982), I conclude:

Evil and psychopathology, in effect, are two sides of the same coin of denying either power or vulnerability. Both represent a failure to balance and integrate the two sides of strength and weakness that are intrinsic to the human condition...I think that seeing genocide as the ultimate expression of a disturbed balance between strength and weakness - an extreme form of pseudostrength that is as psychotic as the maddest form of mental weakness and incompetence - may open the door to a solution to the conceptual dilemma in psychology that we have not known how to call this very abnormal (evil) and antilife act what it really is, profoundly abnormal (p. 341).

DISORDERS OF SURRENDER OF AUTONOMY

The problem of maintaining a firm sense of one's identity is an issue in its own right long before we get to the problem of memberships in groups which are openly committed to destroying others. The problem begins much earlier whenever one assigns too much of one's identity-maintenance and loyalty to one's family or any group.

Acquiescing to clearly wrong facts under group pressure (e.g., the classic Asch experiment where a short line is judged longer than a long line under group pressure), acting on otherwise clearly unacceptable values (e.g., the Milgram experiment), blind participation in cults and orgiastic groups (e.g., Jonestown) are all cardinal expressions of disturbances.

Submerging oneself in any group process at the expense of one's individual autonomy or conforming blindly to any ideology or authority are personality processes which set off and combine with other psychopathology: whether the loss of individual identity in one's family that has been implicated in many cases of schizophrenia; mass hysteria, mass suicide or collective psychoses - which also have been included in traditional psychiatric disturbances; or standing by as silent bystanders when neighbors or colleagues are marched off to unknown fates, and joining willfully in pograms or blind obedience to orders to massacre people in concentration camps.

A lifetime of avid rooting for the Yankees or a lifetime of passionate activity in the Zionist movement can also be at considerable expense to one's own identity, and would also qualify as over-identification of self with a group depending on the extent to which one gives oneself to these causes and at what cost to other aspects of life. However, both cases would be defined as far lesser disturbances than membership in a group or cause whose announced intentions are to actually injure and destroy other persons or groups. In the latter, the psychopathology is unreservedly greater because there not only is surrender of self to a group but the surrender is to joining in activities intended to destroy life.

If we look, for example, at Hitler's followers in terms of their identification with the Nazi movement long before Krystall-nacht and full-scale overt attacks against Jews, there are many Germans who submerged their identities in the Nazi ideology-movement. They included not only those who actually donned the uniforms of the SA and SS, but also the many more who joined full-heartedly in the orgiastic mass meetings of the Nazi party where a charismatic Hitler proclaimed the superiority of the German race and spewed his antisemitic venom. The very abandonment of oneself to the mass process would already be indicative of a state of psychopathology in our proposed schema. There were some Germans during this period who disavowed the rhetoric or "exaggerations" of antisemitic "propaganda" but still applauded the party's stand for a newly strong Germany. They would be less implicated for giving themselves over to the new cult, and later the question would be whether they remain loyal to the party when the actual persecutions of Jews begin and intensify.

As in any diagnostic scheme, there is always a matter of de-gree. I propose that identification of oneself with a collective group at the expense of one's identity be defined as a first level of disturbance. Going beyond identification to a degree of giving up one's ability to think for oneself and one's judgment in the face of group pressures should be defined as a further level of disturbance. This includes going along with instructions of authorities to believe in things which normally are unacceptable to the individual. Surrendering oneself to orgiastic group behaviors "mindlessly," especially with little regard for the safety and welfare of people, is a still more advanced stage of loss of self. The cult process that existed in Jonestown long before the culminating events of murder and mass suicide is a powerful example.

The highest level of disturbance would be asquiescing to and participating in actual group programs of mass murder or persecution and execution of other people. There is of course no end to ex-amples including Jonestown; the Manson killer group; torture and death chambers in Uganda, Phnom Pen, and wherever; antisemitic pogroms through the centuries; the incredibly well-organized death factories of Auschwitz and the other extermination centers; and atomic and other more terrible forms of mass killing, or what John Somerville and Shingo Shibata (1982) call "ecocide and omnicide - the new faces of genocide."

Hitler himself presents an interesting illustration of our proposed redefinition of psychopathology. From what we know of biographical studies of Hitler, there is a strain of latent and disguised psychopathological symptoms in Hitler's personal life over the years, but for a long time he functions only too powerfully in the real world. During all the time this monster functions at the height of his pseudocompetence, it is difficult to define him as abnormal in the traditional diagnostic system unless one sees him as suffering from a rare condition of paranoia - a not unreasonable possibility, but even if true still very hard to define in the early years of his rise to leadership and consolidation of power. However, using the proposed model, we can label Hitler as disturbed from early years onfor two reasons: first, the extent to which he calls for doing harm to others; second, the extent to which Hitler himself lives through the cult of the collective process he develops around him. It is of great interest that, later, when his power system breaks down, this monstrous human being also begins to show increasing signs of traditional madness - some say exposing the truth of what lay behind his maniacal and paranoiac strivings for power all along. The advantage of our new proposal is that it removes all ambiguities and any need to search for a "real truth" inside of Hitler all through the earlier years of his visibly "superior" functioning.

"DISORDERS OF PSEUDOCOMPETENCE" AND "DISORDERS OF SURRENDER OF AUTONOMY" ALSO SOLVE OTHER EXISTING PROBLEMS IN PSYCHOLOGY

Although it was not at all the original purpose of this essay to solve any other problems in the field of psychopathology beyond the glaring fact that the mass murderers were escaping our standard definitions of abnormality, the proposed extensions of our standard classification of abnormality may very well prove to be helpful in unraveling several other nasty problems in psychopathology:

1. The so-called behavior disorders (sometimes "conduct disorders" or "personality disorders") have always been difficult to integrate conceptually along with standard neuroses and psychoses, because these involve a different psychological mechanism where instead of harming oneself, the patient indulges in acting out and causing harm to others.

The dramatic dilemma in One Flew Over the Cuckoo's Nest (Kesey, 1962) is a case in point. Here the protagonist "Mac" causes so much trouble to others that a place has to be found for him in the pychiatric definitional system in order to justify holding him. The difficulty is that traditional diagnoses don't fit very well

people who get along with themselves spiritedly, so that the psychiatric establishment in effect has to beat "Mac" into suffering a
degree of personal incompetence that will qualify him as a bonafide
patient.

The problem with the behavioral disorders is that instead of
becoming incompetent under the pressure of anxiety, people "suffering" these conditions often "enjoy" one or another form of pseudocompetence and superiority through which they manage for some time
not to suffer anxiety or vulnerability. In the process they can and
do make life such a crazy mess for their families and for others
around them that the mental health profession has to work hard to
find ways of defining them as bonafide "patients" during all the
time they don't complain about themselves. Most of these "patients"
in fact don't allow mental health practitioners to work on them very
readily until the trouble and discomfort they cause to others turn
around and bring on them personal forms of breakdown; only at this
point are the mental health professions able, as it were, to breathe
a sigh of relief for having the "proof" that the person was in fact
"sick" underneath all along.

The present proposal says much more clearly that anxiety is a
universal experience which has to be dealt with authentically, and
that either incompetence or power at the expense of others are disturbances. Disorders of incompetence and pseudocompetence can alternate and change places with one another. The early stages of many
serious mental health problems can be expressed in symptoms of isolation, self-doubt, and self-hurt but then move into attempts to
transmit these distressing experiences to others by causing them
harm. Likewise, there can be early symptoms of mental problems of
disturbing the lives of others, such as antagonizing neighbors, emotional abuse of family and friends, drinking, gambling, and so on,
all largely at the expense of others, and at a later stage there may
follow a full breakdown of the individual self. If we redefine disorders of pseudocompetence as full-fledged alternatives to disorders
of incompetence, and especially if we accept that there is no contradiction whatsoever in patients alternating or combining both
sides of disorders, we achieve a much more comfortable way of defining the troublesome behavior disorders along with the traditional
neuroses and psychoses.

2. Family therapy has underscored the fact that, in many instances, there are family members directly contributing to
   or inducing disturbances in the obviously incompetent or
   traditionally sick mental patient through their pseudocompetence and other subtly powerful ways of projecting disturbance and doing damage to the personality of the identified
   patient.

If there is any clearcut theoretical advance in the innovat-
tions of family therapy, it is precisely that there are many disturbed people who may not look or act disturbed for a long while because their hidden disturbance is based on scapegoating someone else
in the family to feel powerless, incompetent or "crazy." It has of-

ten been observed that it is the "good ones" who end up being the patients in the mental health clinics and hospitals and the "bad ones" stay adequate while tormenting the hapless good ones. Family therapy has insisted correctly that bringing psychic damage to others is no less an aspect of psychopathology than being unable to function oneself (Framo, 1982). There have also been many observations that when the manifest patient gets better, or when the power and scapegoating of the pseduocompetent members of the family are interfered with, traditional mental disturbances may manifest themselves in the latter. The present clarification solves the problem of being able to assign a definition of emotional disturbance from the very outset to the pseudocompetents in families who invite and trigger mental disturbances in others.

3. Family therapy has also shown us that there are many seemingly normal and even outstandingly superior-seeming people who are headed for breakdowns because they are too emotionally "enmeshed" in their families.

Blending into a family (Minuchin, 1974), over-reliance on a mate, being part of a "pseudomutual" family where differences are swept under a rug of continuous unanimity and forced joyousness all prove to be powerful harbingers of very high risks of emotional disturbances, including sudden irreversible flights from relationships, serious psychosomatic diseases, major learning problems in children, and even psychoses (Dicks, 1967). Traditional psychopathology never diagnoses disturbances in the "healthy" members of families until and if actual symptoms are apparent in their functioning, whereas the present proposal makes it possible to diagnose disturbances long before symptoms of inability to function are evident on the basis of an over-attachment or blending into one's family at the expense of one's personal identity.

4. There are glaring instances of damage to human lives that previously have not qualified for diagnoses of abnormality.

I referred earlier to the remarkably widespread situations of serious child abuse that turn out, in most cases, not to be the acts of "disturbed" parents but of "normal" people (Gil, 1974). Similarly there are many insoluble arguments over whether criminals living off exploitation and injury to others are psychiatrically disturbed. The present proposal would have it that child batterers and criminals and all others who harm their fellow human beings are disturbed by virtue of and to the extent that they bring serious harm to others, let alone because of the harm they also may do themselves and whatever other personal problems may be discovered in their personalities. The proper treatment of child-battering parents may wisely include a large dose of understanding and helping them to recognize when they may be in danger of erupting so that they can gain prior control of themselves, but this does not mean they are not disturbed. Similarly, the proper treatment of criminals may be through agencies of law rather than clinics and treatment centers, but this also does not mean they are not psychologically disturbed by virtue of their permitting themselves to do damage to others.

5. Traditional psychopathology allows for many absurd situations where giving over all of one's being to a collective process or ideology is not diagnosed as disturbed until it is too late and being part of the group has turned into doing obviously crazy things.

.Giving up all of one's earthly possessions to the Moon cult and finding refuge in a new life identity as a member of the church collective does not in itself command a definition of psychopathology - unless perhaps one's family can afford to hire psychiatrists to prove the choice to join the Moonies was a result of "brainwashing."
.Belonging to a Charlie Manson group to which one gives all of oneself is not considered abnormal until the point where one participates in the Charlie Manson orgy of killing.
.Relocating with one's family to Jonestown in Guiana and pledging allegiance to the Reverend Jones is not considered pathological until the day one is part of the group that murders a U.S. Congressman and then enforces the Reverend Jones' command for mass suicide.
.A young man who devotes his entire self to a passionately antisemitic group which distributes The Protocols of the Elders of Zion is considered exercising a personal ideological or political choice until and if the antisemitic statements are more blatantly irrational - unless, of course, this young man happens to seize political power along the way and becomes the designated leader of a whole nation that murders millions of Jews, so that now even mass murder is accepted as "rational" governmental policy and not madness.

The present proposal is that any time a person turns the keys to his mind or being over to any group process or ideology, a psychological disturbance is operating.

Needless to say, defining identification with any group process or ideology as disturbed opens a Pandora's box of problems. So many of society's most accepted and vaunted institutions also are based on commitment and positive participation by constituents and believers: nothing is more characteristic of the serious religious orders of all faiths than abandonment of oneself to the divine calling; giving all of oneself to study a beloved profession such as music or medicine at the expense of other personal needs and the needs of family is generally highly valued; and intense devotion to a political humanistic cause or movement for human rights such as Martin Luther King's crusade for nonviolence commands the enthusiastic respect of most of us.

Where does the line get drawn? In all these instances the individual goes about his everyday life as a member of a powerful, captivating ideological group, and the connection with this group is the center of his experience through which he wards off encountering a great deal of anxiety, choice and personal responsibility.

My opinion is that the solution to the problem begins with an honest test of the degree of loss of self, and an acknowledgment that whenever one gives "all of oneself" to any cause, even those that are culturally valued, it is right to think in terms of some degree of emotional problem. Of course, it also makes a difference what the cause is to which one surrenders oneself, and here reference to both principles of disorders of doing harm to others and disorders of autonomy gives us our strongest conceptual leverage. A young adult woman who gives up her independence to stay forever devoted to her parents is at one stage of disturbance. If she goes on to attempt to take her life, we obviously define a more serious disturbance. If she gives herself over to a cult or potential group which destroys many human lives (their own - e.g., a suicide cult, or others - e.g., terrorists bombing in civilian settings), the disturbance is still more blatant and serious. Destroying one's own ability to function culminating in actual termination of one's life, and destroying others' ability to function culminating in actual termination of other people's lives are, both, the ultimate psychopathologies.

CONCLUSION

Thomas Merton (1967), the beloved Trappist monk, wrote some years ago as the world was just beginning to emerge from the shock of the Holocaust and Hiroshima:

We rely on the sane people of the world to preserve it from barbarism, madness, destruction. And now it begins to dawn on us that it is precisely the same ones who are the most dangerous. It is the sane ones, the well-adapted ones, who can without qualms and without nausea aim the missiles and press the buttons that will initiate the great festival of destruction... The whole concept of sanity in a society where spiritual values have lost their meaning is itself meaningless...In a society like ours, the worst insanity is to be totally without anxiety, totally "Sane" (pp. 21-23).

I hope that we can now embark on a road towards a redefinition of sanity and insanity that will make more sense, first for humanity's sake so that the world hears the science of human behavior state, unambiguously, that destroying other people is mad; and second for the science of psychology itself so that it does not become foolish for calling the most insane people in the world sane.

REFERENCES

ARONSON, Ronald. Why? Towards a theory of the Holocaust. Socialist Review, 1981, 11, (4, No. 58), 63-81.
ASCH, Solomon E. Studies of independence and conformity: I. A minority of one against a unanimous majority. Psychological Monographs, 1956, 70 (9), No. 416.

ASKENASY, Hans. Are We All Nazis? Secaucus, N.J.: Lyle Stuart, 1978.

BOWEN, Murray. The use of family theory in clinical practice. Comprehensive Psychiatry, 1966, 7, 345-374.

CHARNY, Israel W. In collaboration with Chanan Rapaport, Foreword by Elie Wiesel. How Can We Commit The Unthinkable? Genocide: The Human Cancer. Boulder, Colorado: Westview, 1982.

CHARNY, ISRAEL W., & Davidson, Shamai (Eds.), The Book of the International Conference on the Holocaust and Genocide. Book One: The Conference Program and Crisis.Tel Aviv: Institute of the International Conference on the Holocaust and Genocide, 1983.

COLEMAN, James C.; Butcher, James N.; & Carson, Robert C. Abnormal Psychology and Modern Life. 6th ed. Glenview, Illinois: Scott, Foresman, 1980.

DARLEY, John M., & Latane, Bibb. When will people help in a crisis? Psychology Today, 1968, 2, 54-57, 70-71.

DICKS, Henry V. Marital Tensions. New York: Basic Books, 1967.

DICKS, Henry V. Licensed Mass Murder: A Socio-Psychological Study of Some SS Killlers. London, Heinemann, 1972.

ERIKSON, Erik H. Insight and Responsibility. New York: Norton, 1964.

FEIN, Helen. Accounting for Genocide: National Responses and Jewish Victimization During the Holocaust. New York: Free Press, 1979.

FRAMO, James L. Explorations in Marital and Family Therapy. New York: Springer, 1982.

GIL, David. A conceptual model of child abuse and its implications for social policy. In Suzanne K. Steinmetz & Murray A. Strauss (Eds.), Violence in the Family, New York: Dodd, Mead, 1974, pp. 205-212.

GILBERT, G. M. The Psychology of Dictatorship: Based on the Examination of the Leaders of Nazi Germany. New York: Ronald, 1950.

HARTMAN, Dieter. Compliance and oblivion: The absence of sympathy in Germany for the victims of the Holocaust. Paper presented at the International Conference on the Holocaust and Genocide, Tel Aviv, June, 1982.

KELLEY, Douglas M. 22 Cells In Nuremberg. New York: MacFadden, 1961 (original publication 1947).

KESEY, Ken. One Flew Over the Cuckoo's Nest. New York: New American Library, 1962.

KOHLBERG, Laurence. Moral education in the schools: a developmental review. School Review, 1966, 74, 1-30.

KREN, George, & Rappoport, Leon. The Holocaust and the Crisis of Human Behavior. New York: Holmes & Meier, 1980.

KULSCAR, I. Shlomo. De Sade and Eichman. In Israel W. Charny (Ed.), Strategies Against Violence: Design for Nonviolent Change. Boulder, Colorado: Westview, 1978, pp. 19-33.

LITTELL, Franklin H. Lessons of the Holocaust and church struggle: 1970-1980. Journal Ecumencial Studies, 1981, 18 (2), 369-373.

MASLOW, Abraham H. The Farther Reaches of Human Nature. New York: Viking, 1971.

MERTON, Thomas N. A devout meditation in memory of Adolf Eichman. Reprinted in Reflections (Merck, Sharp and Dohme), 1967, 2 (3), 21-23.

174

MILGRAM, Stanley. Obedience to Authority. New York: Harper & Row, 1974.

MINUCHIN, Salvador. Families and Family Therapy. Cambridge, Mass: Harvard University Press, 1974.

MITSCHERLICH, Alexander, & Mitscherlich, Margarette. The Inability to Mourn: Principles of Collective Behavior. New York: Grove, 1975.

PILISUK, Marc, & Ober, Lyn. Torture and genocide as public health problems. American Journal Orthospychiatry, 1976, 46 (3) 388-392.

SOMERVILLE, John, & Shibata, Shingo. Ecocide and omnicide, the new faces of genocide. Workshop at the International Conference on the Holocaust and Genocide, Tel Aviv, June, 1982.

SPRENKLE, Douglas H., & Olson, David H.L. Circumplex model of marital systems: an empirical study of clinic and non-clinic couples. Journal Marriage & Family Counseling, 1978, 4 (2), 59-74.

TAMARIN, Georges R. Studies in Psychopathology. Ramat Aviv, Israel: Turtledove Press, 1980.

ULLMAN, Leonard P., & Krasner, Leonard. Psychological Approach to Abnormal Behavior (2nd ed.). Englewood Cliffs, N.J.: Prentice Hall, 1975.

WYNNE, Lyman L.; Ryckoff, Irving M,; Day, Juliana; & Hirsch, Stanley I. Pseudomutuality in the family relationships of schizophrenics. Psychiatry, 1958, 21, 205-270.

ZIMBARDO P. G.; Haney, C.; Banks, W.C.; & Jaffe D. The psychology of imprisonment: privation, power, and pathology. In David Rosenhan & Perry London (Eds.), Theory and Research in Abnormal Psychology (2nd ed.). New York: Holt, Rinehart & Winston, 1975, pp. 270-287.

ISRAEL W. CHARNY, Ph.D., Institute of the International Conference on the Holocaust and Genocide, POB 5006, Tel Aviv, Israel 61500

14. Genocidal Mentality: Nuclear Weapons on Civilian Populations

Gerard A. Vanderhaar

Dr. Gerard Vanderhaar is Professor of Religion and Peace Studies at Christian Brothers College, Memphis, Tennessee, U.S.A. He is a member of the editorial board of DISARMAMENT CAMPAIGNS, the international magazine on actions against the arms race published in the Hague. He chairs the National Council of Pax Christi USA, and is on the board of the Mid-South Peace and Justice Center in Memphis. After participating in the International Conference on the Holocaust and Genocide, he led two local conferences on the subject, believing that a widespread awareness of the past will help prevent such horrors in whatever form they might threaten in the future.

The United States and the Soviet Union have thousands of nuclear warheads targeted on each other's cities. They also have weapons aimed at other targets - military, industrial, logistical, but the heart of the deterrence theory on which the defense of the two superpowers rests is the ability - and willingness - to kill large numbers of people simply because they are citizens of the enemy country.

The first part of this paper will explore the striking similarities between the mentality of those who are prepared to use nuclear weapons on civilian populations today, and the mentality of those who perpetrated the Nazi Holocaust 40 years ago. The second part will suggest some ways of dealing with the current problem on the basis of what we have learned.

What is at issue here is the policy - conditional though it is - of using nuclear weapons on civilian populations and, more exactly, the mentality of those who are prepared to carry out that policy.

That this policy bears examining in the context of the Nazi Holocaust is clear from more than just the numbers involved, although the numbers themselves are impressive. Six million Jews perished in the Nazi Holocaust, and close to 50 million in the Second World War which surrounded it. A substantial nuclear attack on the population centers of the United States and the Soviet Union would involve well over 100 million deaths, some say as high as 200 million. One United States Secretary of Defense estimated that only 400 hydrogen bombs on Soviet cities would kill 74 million people in those cities. The Soviet capacity is equally enormous.

More important than the numbers is the recognition that the millions of people targeted for nuclear destruction are innocent of crimes against the attacker. They, as were the Jews in Europe, will be killed precisely because they are people having a certain identity - in the nuclear case citizens of a particular country.

175

If we understand genocide in its dictionary definition as "the deliberate and systematic destruction of a racial, political or cultural group" of people, the nuclear holocaust would be genocide because its intention, as stated clearly by at least one planning nation, is to damage "the aggressor to the point that his society would be simply no longer viable in twentieth-century terms," (Mcnamara, 1968, p. 53). A society is no longer viable when most of its people are permanently out of commission, that is, dead.

The nuclear holocaust has not yet happened. But plans for it are in place, and the mentality to perpetrate it is already set in those who would carry the plans out.

When - if - the nuclear holocaust happens, the levels of involvement by a variety of people will be similar to the Nazi Holocaust. Top government officials will order the release of nuclear weapons. Military officials will receive the orders and convey them through a chain of command that has been previously readied. Other military personnel will carry out the orders and perform the physical tasks that send the weapons on their way.

Here we note one major difference. In the Nazi holocaust the killing was done at close range - by shooting the victims directly, as millions were killed in Eastern Europe by the einsatzgruppen, the mobile death squads, or by herding them into gas chambers in the large death camps, a job in which even other camp inmates sometimes assisted under the direction of the SS. The nuclear killing will be done at a distance, out of sight of the victims, by missile crews in control centers deep in the earth thousands of miles away, or in submarines under the sea, or by airmen six miles up in the sky.

Essential in both holocausts are those people who design, manufacture, and maintain the instruments of destruction. And finally neither holocaust would be possible without the support of the vast majority of the people of the countries involved, who contribute to a climate of opinion that in the very least tolerates, and in most cases actively agrees with, if not the killing itself, at least the ideology behind it, an ideology that we will take up later.

THE MIND-SET OF DESTRUCTION

Now, the mentality of the people at these various stages of involvement. By mentality I mean the way of thinking, the mind-set, the combination of ideas and feelings that readies a person to take part in mass murder.

For a relatively few people the dominant force will be a pathological hatred, or sadistic cruelty. Hitler's hatred of the Jews was certainly pathological. Probably some military personnel and civilians in Germany and the occupied countries were infected with a pathological antisemitism. There were undoubtedly torturers in the camps who took sadistic delight in the pain they inflicted. But the pathological hatred and sadistic cruelty in a relatively small num-

ber of people were in no way responsible for the Nazi Holocaust.
The vast majority of those who perpetrated it were clinically normal, "good" Germans - and Poles and Belgians and Rumanians and
Austrians. Adolf Eichmann was certified as normal by the team of
psychiatrists who examined him in Jerusalem. Special care was taken
by the military authorities to spot signs of pathological behavior
in the military personnel in the einsatzgruppen, the mobile death
squads, and weed them out of the units.

Comparably, in those preparing the nuclear holocaust there may
be some pathological hatred - of Russians by Americans, and of capi-
talist-imperalists by people in the Soviet Union. But the vast majority of those involved in the nuclear threat are normal, "good"
Americans and Russians. Special care is taken by American military
authorities - and no doubt by the Soviets also - to spot signs of
pathological behavior in those Air Force and Navy personnel responsible for launching nuclear missiles. They must be clinicaly
"normal" to do the job entrusted to them. As in the Nazi Holocaust,
the dominant mentality responsible for mass killings is something
different, something that a so-called normal person can develop.

I would suggest that the two key elements in this mentality
are: dehumanization of the victims, and desensitization of the
self.

By dehumanization of the victims I mean the tendency to view
those who are to be killed as though they do not quite belong to the
human race, and to deny them some of the characteristics considered
most human. This may be done by portraying them as sub-human, as
super-human, or as bad-human (Group Advancement Psychiatry, 1964, p.
345).

Nazi propaganda often portrayed Jews as sub-human. They were
described as "vermin." In Soviet propaganda Americans have been
pictured as degraded monsters. The Soviet Union is sometimes symbo-
lized in the United States as a crude and dangerous bear. Sub-
humanizing also happens when victims are considered to be simply
statistics, not people.

Dehumanization may also be done by portraying the victims as
super-human. In Nazi Germany Jews were sometimes seen as agents of
Satan, diabolical forces bent on weakening the master race. It is
possible today to hear Russians described as fiendishly clever, mil-
itarily superior, able to conquer the world if the restraining force
were relaxed even slightly. Americans are seen on the other side as
technological wizards, controlling puppet governments in the Third
World, fomenting unrest in Eastern Europe.

The third way of dehumanizing is to view the victims as bad-
human, deserving of their harsh t guilt and shame in inflicting pain
death on them. Russians are seen as cruel and insensitive; Americans are depraved.

The second key element in the genocidal mentality is the desensitization of the self. It is possible to build defenses in oneself against a whole cluster of feelings - fear, compassion, guilt and shame - that would normally arise when inflicting suffering on other human beings.

We have to be careful here. There are times when a degree of densensitization is necessary for personal balance and professional productivity. To be constantly and sensitively aware of all the misery and injustice in the world would drive a person insane. A medical doctor, a social worker, a lawyer, has to have the kind of control over emotions that allows helping skills to function effectively. It's not always clear where such control stops being ego-supportive and becomes psychologically and sociologically maladaptive.

But it is an established fact that desensitization was a key element in the mentality of those who participated, at whatever level, in the mass murder of the Nazi Holocaust, and it will be in those who perpetrate the nuclear holocaust.

One can block feelings of compassion and guilt by refusing to think about - or even denying - one's role in the action. Missile crews may choose to believe that they are aiming at purely military targets. Or they may suppress thoughts about the target at all, and concentrate on the technical skill necessary to launch the missile. They may block their sense or responsibility, as many Germans did, by telling themselves that they are only acting under orders, that their superiors must know what they are doing, that they have no other choice but to obey.

 Another factor contributing to the desensitization is the separation of functions in effecting the final result. The people who design the death machines are not the ones who use them. Those who organize the logistics do not make the overall policies. The result, in Richard Barnet's term, (1972, p. 14) is the "bureaucratization of homicide" or, as he said, "Those who plan do not kill, and those who kill do not plan." This bureaucratization, according to Barnet, contributes greatly "to absence of passion, and the efficiency of mass-produced death."

The distancing of executioner from victim also aids the desensitization process. It's much easier to be insensitive to the pain and suffering one is causing when one is hundreds or thousands of miles away, neither hearing nor seeing the tragic human effects of one's actions.

Self-desensitization was more difficult in the Nazi Holocaust, but it was still done. One of the techniques developed by Heinrich Himmler in the training of the military death squads and the camp personnel was to shift the focus of the suffering from the victim to the executioner. Instead of saying, "What horrible things I did to people!," the murderers were able to say, "What horrible things I had to watch in the pursuance of my duties, how heavily the task weighed upon my shoulders!" (Arendt, 1965, p. 106).

Desensitization is assisted greatly by the words that are used in referring to aspects of the killing. The Nazi developed what they called "Language Rules." The official code name for extermination was "Final Solution." Instead of liquidation or killing, all official correspondence was to use the phrase "special treatment." Deportation was called "resettlement," or "labor in the East."

In the preparations for the nuclear holocaust we find the same kind of language manipulation. Bombs are called "thermonuclear devices." The neutron bomb is called an "enhanced radiation instrument." Citizens are referred to as a country's "values." Killing them is called a "counter-value attack." Plans to kill them are called "providing for national security." Deployment of the weapons to kill them is called "defense." One recent Secretary of Defense (Rumsfeld, 1977, p. 17) described U.S. policy of using nuclear weapons on population centers as "retaliate with devastating force against an enemy's basic economic and political assets." Flesh and blood human beings become "political assets."

What Hannah Arendt, (1965, p. 85) pointed out about the Nazis is equally applicable to the nuclear system: this kind of language use, she said, "proved of enormous help in the maintenance of order and sanity in the various widely diversifed services whose cooperation was essential in this matter."

The net result of the dehumanization and desensitization, aided by the linguistic euphemisms, is a powerful social climate where what is wrong in normal life becomes right, where what was illegal became legal, and where otherwise normal people, sometimes even the best and the brightest, support mass murder without any visible qualms.

The ideology behind the mass murder is critical. As Yehuda Bauer pointed out in a recent article, any adequate understanding of the Nazi Holocaust must take account not only of the "planned total annihilation of a national or ethnic group," but also the "ideology that motivated the murder" (Bauer, 1980, p. 45). Both the nuclear and Nazi holocausts involve the same first element, the planned destruction of a group of people. The second element, the ideology, is different. In the Nazi Holocaust the ideology was antisemitism. In the nuclear holocaust the ideology is the "Enemy."

The nuclear holocaust will not be the result of prejudice against Jews, but of prejudice against enemies.

Much can be learned about prejudice against enemies from a study of antisemitism. We see in both the tendency to project on to another group characteristics one is unwilling to face in oneself. In both antisemitism and the Enemy we find stereotyping - attributing to all members of a group the unpleasant qualities of a few.

Both prejudices thrive on misinformation, derived, often, from government propaganda. We also see efforts to find religious underpinnings for the prejudice: Jews were God-killers; Russians are God-deniers and atheists.

PREVENTING A NUCLEAR HOLOCAUST

The Nazi Holocaust happened when technological proficiency and social organization made possible the effective carrying out of the genocidal mentality motivated by antisemitism. If the nuclear holocaust happens, it will also be because the technological proficiency which has produced these awesome weapons, and the social organization which has readied their use, join with the mentality on the part of government leaders, military personnel and accepting civilians to perpetrate genocide on the Enemy.

But the nuclear holocaust hasn't happened yet.

Perhaps it hasn't happened - and this is the conventional wisdom - because those who would launch it face the certainty of the self-destruction of their own society in the process. Nuclear holocaust is also nuclear suicide. (This ultimately was true of the Nazi Holocaust too - it brought on the complete destruction of the Nazi regime in the Second World War.)

Or perhaps the nuclear holocaust hasn't happened yet because of the relatively small but determined and persistent moral protest against it - from the post-war repentance of Robert Oppenheimer, Father of the Atomic Bomb, who said, "The physicists have known sin," through the Ban-the-Bomb movement of the 50s, the awakening of the Churches in the 60s and 70s (Vatican Council II affirmed that an attack on a population center would be "a crime against God and humanity, deserving complete and unequivocal condemnation"), and the broadening grassroots movements of the 80s - as we saw 3/4 million people march in New York in 1982.

Before we dismiss this possiblity too quickly, we should note that where the Nazis met determined protest, as in Norway and in France after early efforts, they did not pursue the deportation of Jews from those countries. We should not overlook either the Nazi abandonment of their euthanasia project, in which mentally crippled people were gassed to death, after public protest particularly by the churches.

But whatever the actual reasons are, we have not (yet) had the nuclear holocaust. It can happen at any time. All the elements are in place. A sober assessment of the situation almost invariably leads to a pessimistic prognosis.

Because it has not yet happened, there is still time in which to work to prevent it from happening. I want to suggest some specific directions that work should take.

1. First, we must pay careful attention to the Nazi Holocaust. The reality of that horrible experience, the single greatest evil in the history of the human race, must not be allowed to fade from our consciousness. We know from the physical reality of the Nazi Holocaust that it is really possible systematically to kill millions of innocent human beings in a fairly short time. We know from the psychological reality of the Nazi Holocaust that human beings can work themselves into the frame of mind to carry out the slaughter. And we know from the social reality of the Nazi Holocaust that people tend to go along with their governments, and to accept as morally right what the government defines as legal.

To me the most enlightening aspect of the social process of the Nazi Holocaust was not that the leaders of a country were criminal or crazy, but that tens of millions of people followed them in their crazy criminality. The lesson I have learned from that is: always question your government, always subject its procedures to moral scrutiny. This may lead to considerable discomfort in daily life, but it is an absolute necessity if future holocausts - of whatever kind - are to be prevented.

2. Secondly, it is important to learn more about this phenomenon of the "enemy." An enemy is defined as one who has committed, or threatens to commit, a hostile action against me or my group. The hostility on the part of the enemy needs to be examined. Is it real, or only imagined? Or perhaps is it provoked? If it's real, then it has to be dealt with. But if it's only imagined, or if it's provoked, then the enmity becomes my problem.

3. But if it's real, it has to be dealt with. That leads to the third area of special importance: an exploration of nonviolent ways to resolve real conflicts. Steps are being taken in the United States government to set up a National Peace Academy in which nonviolent techniques of negotiation, bargaining, and arbitration will be studied, and out of which, hopefully, a corps of professional peacemakers will take their place alongside the already large corps of professional warmakers my country maintains to deal with international tensions.

4. But just as the Nazi Holocaust was not perpetrated only by the German government, so the nuclear holocaust will not be the responsiblity of only a government either. The cooperation of the people is essential in both holocausts. The surest way of preventing the Nazi Holocaust would have been the elimination of antisemitic prejudice in the millions of people who cooperated with the Nazis, and the presence instead of a genuine human appreciation of all other peoples.

The surest way of preventing a nuclear holocaust is to eliminate the enemy prejudice in people in nuclear nations today, and the building up instead of a genuine nonviolent approach to all conflicts - not just international, but also social and personal.

5. The above are long-term projects. But there may not be enough time to see them through. The last area I will mention that is of special importance in preventing a nuclear holocaust is immediate and vital. It is active protest, organized opposition, public demonstration of the resolve to preserve our earth, not destroy its people. As has already been mentioned, the Nazis stopped their genocide efforts in those countries where they were confronted with determined, public, nonviolent protest. Government leaders of nuclear nations today must be confronted with similar courageous, continued protest. It may serve to forestall the horrible event long enough for the long-term efforts to counteract the enemy ideology to take effect.

And if it does, then when we visit the indispensable monuments of Dachau and Auschwitz, we can say with full meaning the words inscribed on the memorial centotaph at Hiroshima: "Let the souls here rest in peace, for we shall not repeat the evil."

REFERENCES

ARENDT, Hannah. Eichmann in Jerusalem: A Report on the Banality of Evil. New York: Viking Press, 1965.
BARNET, Richard J. Roots of War. Baltimore: Penguin Books, 1972.
BAUER, Yehuda. Whose Holocaust? Midstream, November, 1980 (Vol. 26, No. 9), 42-46.
GROUP for the Advancement of Psychiatry. Psychiatric Aspects of the Prevention of Nuclear War. New York: Report No. 57, 1964.
McNAMARA, Robert S. The Essence of Security. New York: Harper & Row, 1968.
RUMSFELD, Donald. Annual Defence Department Report, FY 1977. Washington, D.C.: Government Printing Office.

GERARD A. VANDERHAAR, S.T.D., Christian Brothers College, 3554 Boxdale, Memphis, Tennessee 38118, U.S.A.

15. Power and Powerlessness: The Jewish Experience

Alice L. Eckardt

Alice L. Eckardt has taught the Holocaust, its history and theological impact, at Lehigh University since 1975. She has published articles on the churche's responses to the ENDLOSUNG, Christian observances of Yom HaShoah, biomedical issues, and post-Holocaust theology; and coauthored LONG NIGHT'S JOURNEY INTO DAY: LIFE AND FAITH AFTER THE HOLOCAUST (Detroit: Wayne State University Press, 1982). She was Special Consultant to the President's Commission on the Holocaust; is Special Advisor to the United States Holocaust Memorial Council; on the Executive Board of Zachor: Holocaust Resource Center; and the Board of Directors of the National Institute on the Holocaust.

Political power involves the right and responsibility of a group to administer its internal and external affairs. The purpose of power at the national level is to make somebody "do something or not do something or stop doing something" (Schelling, 1973). The aim is usually to influence behavior, though at times national power may be directed at influencing ideals and mental constructs as well. Power at the international level is fundamentally "the capacity of a political unit to impose its will on other political units" (Aron, 1968, p. 57), or conversely, the ability of a political unit to resist other political units' efforts to impose their will on itself.

The opposite of power is impotence - the inability to affect the course of events, that is, history. It may even involve the conscious withdrawal from an attempt to influence history, at least political and temporal history, in favor of a nontemporal, apolitical mission as numerous religious groups and societies have done. An impotent political unit is unable to determine its own fate or ensure the wellbeing of its citizens. A powerless individual or minority is subject to the will or mood of the majority and its government.

Since the individual's strength is not sufficient to maintain existence, collective power is necessary. Thus, the original meaning of Jewish power and its legitimacy is to be found not in some abstract "spirit of Judaism," but "in a collective will and existence," argues Abba Lessing (1976, p. 55), just as for all peoples and national communities. Because collective power was essential to existence, neither biblical nor rabbinic sources grant an individual the right to separate himself from the nation's decision to commit itself to warfare.[1]

Because Judaism has emphasized the responsibility of the community to concern itself with the total wellbeing of all its members, in all aspects of life, it has not had (or at least did not originally have) a negative attitude towards power per se. For Jewish thought accepts power as at once natural (it was one of the ten media by which the world was created and continues to be created) and also necessary (in order to enable people to live in some kind of harmony) Lamm, 1971). Rabbi Hanania said, "Pray for the welfare of the government, since but for fear thereof men would swallow each other." (Ethics of the Fathers, 3.2). Israeli scholar Ephraim Urbach (1977, p. 110) comments, "It is the peace of the kingdom which justifies its authority. The fear of the government...is needed to preserve life."[2]

Of course the prophets and sages recognized the need to control power by limiting it. Even the Creator had set a limit to divine power by stopping creation at a finite universe, and giving human- kind responsibility for cooperating with the Holy One to perfect the unfinished, imperfect world.[3] Therefore, for every power, there must be a counter-power, a check and balance of opposing forces. This balance forms the covenant of society in Judaism. "Counter- power is the charter for man living in peace with his power." "In- telligent, restrained, and moral use of counterpower is the only method by which we can neutralize evil," Maurice Lamm affirms. In addition, power has to be refined - by mitzvot, by legislation, and by constitutions - in order that it be used for the wellbeing of the community (Lamm, 1971, pp. 425, 427).[4] The achievement of justice, as nearly as possible, became the goal of Jewish Halakhah and Aggadah (as well as of modern liberal Judaism).

WHAT HAS BEEN THE JEWISH EXPERIENCE WITH POWER AND POWERLESSNESS?

If power is "the ability to initiate movement or change," it was only when Jews became a collective unit that they could "take their own identity and fate into their own hands." For Lessing then the accession of power first occurred when Israel left Egypt: Sinai is "a drama in which God commits [divine] power to the power of a newly collective power." Reaccessions of power occurred with the return from Babylon, the overthrow of the Seleucid overlords, and the establishing in our time of the State of Israel. In all these situations a Jewish national will could emerge, and reemerge, and the entire people could mobilize their energies to respond actively in history instead of being forced into an inactive role on the sidelines, or withdrawing from history (Lessing, 1976, pp. 54, 55, and Hartmann, 1982)[5]

Lessing clearly reflects the view of Jewish history especially dominant since at least the nineteenth century, a view that in the long centuries of statelessness Jewry was totally powerless, impo- tent, perhaps even lacking in political sagacity. Ismar Schorsch rejects this view, arguing that medieval Jewry had a genuine, if unique, political history based on its legal status and group co- hesiveness, which, he suggests, gave it power of a sort. Moreover, the leadership demonstrated considerable political astuteness in order for the communities to have survived at all in their precar- ious situation (Schorsch, 1977).

Collective power and national will can also be defeated and cause great tragedies, as the rebellions against Rome in the first and second centuries of the Common Era demonstrated all too vividly. For that very reason, the rabbis set out deliberately to suppress the example of Maccabean military prowess and the ferment of messianic expectations that had contributed to the nationalistic uprisings, and to secure Jewish survival through submission to the empires that must, they felt, somehow represent God's will. This latter point of view - that God's judgment was at work in historical events - persisted from the biblical period despite the efforts of the Pharisees and the rabbis to free the Covenant People from events of history, that is at least from too close a linkage of catastrophe and divine judgment. They sought to avoid the very sort of conclusion which in our own age some ultra-Orthodox Jews have drawn: that an event such as the Holocaust was divine punishment. Rather, recognizing the obvious imbalance of righteousness and justice in the world, the Pharisees sought to transfer the "locus of Providence" essentially to "the world to come" (Gellman, 1980).

With the loss of their nation state, the long Jewish age of powerlessness began (though for some centuries Jews not only waited expectantly but acted along whatever lines were feasible to accomplish a resumption of national existence as after the first exile). From the first or second centuries through most of the eighteenth century, and even beyond, their historical experiences increasingly fostered ambivalent attitudes towards the powers that ruled them. Though a good deal of internal autonomy was frequently granted to Jewish communities, it was always vulnerable to arbitrary cancelation. Suspicion, fear, lack of respect, and resentment toward the authorities oppressing them were mingled with a neccessary reliance upon the power of rulers who were their only source of legal status and of protection against hostile mobs.

There was almost always a positive aspect to Jews' relationship to their countries of residence. As early as the Babylonian exile, Jeremiah had set the pattern by advising his people to live by the law of the land, to pray for the peace and wellbeing of the kingdom in which they lived, to establish homes and raise children. At the same time they were told to look forward to an eventual return to the Land of Israel, i.e., to a resumption of power. We can say that Jeremiah gave us a foretaste of Emil Fackenheim's (1972, 1975, 1978) prophetic counsel today: to survive, to survive as Jews, to raise Jewish children, to "return to history" through the reborn national community, and to live in the hope that God is still - in spite of the Holocaust - a redeeming God.

Without national power, the only available means of resistance to threats to their communal integrity and to their spiritual and ethnic autonomy were of an internal and essentially quietist or accommodative kind. This required demonstrating the utility of Jews to the ruling powers. In place of a genuinely political existence in dispersion,[6] Jews were forced to assume a "symbolic life." Perseverance and endurance rooted in a deep faith were the only available instruments of Jewish collective survival.[7] Under such conditions the effort to survive was sustained by Jewish communal institutions that enabled the individual and the community to preserve some sense of collectivity as the covenanted people, and to sustain the values which all deemed central to a meaningful existence. These institutions rested entirely upon freely-given consent, since any Jew could opt out of the community by embracing the majority religion (Avineri, 1975).

Powerlessness As Virtue

A major consequence of the Jewish situation was that powerlessness had to become, so to speak, a Jewish virtue, through "surrendering, sacrificing, even dying in front of one's enemies" (though, to be sure, martyrdom was never to be sought). Spiritual authenticity had to become a substitute for political self-determination and national decision-making. All this resulted in power itself becoming suspect, a "corruption of the soul," a distraction from the life of study and prayer - quite in contrast to the earlier point of view regarding power. Powerlessness was more and more interpreted as God's way with his people, as his way of introducing the dimension of nonpower into the world (Lessing, 1976, p. 56; and Berkovits, 1973).

STRATEGIES DURING POWERLESSNESS

An important historiographical question is: Did Jews at some period in their history deliberately substitute martyrdom for actual self-defense? And have they only in the last century reverted to active resistance instead? Did the rabbis turn this world into "an antechamber of the world to come" so successfully that self-preservation all but abandoned?

The contemporary scholar Emanuel Rackman, (1977, p. 119) gives a categorical "no" to these very questions. "Jews have always engaged in every type of defense that was possible." However, he is forced to admit that the difficulties of physical resistance were usually so numerous and so severe that the defense measures failed (though not for want of trying). Israel Abrahams, (1969, p. 253) in his study of Jewish life in the Middle Ages emphasizes "the martial spirit of the Jews of Spain," who fought under both the Cross and the Crescent, who insisted on their right to bear arms, and who made the Spanish mobs pay for their attacks on the Jewish quarters (though of course the mobs prevailed). He also refers to the "courage and proficiency in self-help" which Jews elsewhere in Europe and the East "occasionally displayed..."

However, courage alone, or lack of courage, is not the crucial issue: what is crucial is the residual powerlessness of the communities despite their courage.

Abba Lessing would answer our questions by saying a categorical "yes" - Jews did substitute martyrdom for self-defense.

It is true that long before the twentieth century Judaism taught that one must not submit to evil but must resist it ("eradicate the evil from your midst"). Self-defense was an obligation for both the individual and the nation: no "lofty withdrawal from the world" was to be coveted. Jews were <u>not</u> to "stand idly by the blood" of their fellow men but were <u>obligated</u>, even at risk of their own life, to come to that person's defense (though in these situations too restrictions were introduced to try to prevent killing when a lesser action would suffice). War was permitted and even commanded under certain circumstances, not only for self-defense but to rescue those suffering under oppression (Gendler, 1978).[8]

Nevertheless, a nation at war was obligated to avoid unnecessary violence and to do everything possible to preserve humaneness. Within Torah and the rabbinic tradition, restrictions upon the conduct of war, as well as on action to stop a murderous pursuer, served as reminders of the brutalizing effects of violence upon all parties. It is true that "one must do what one must do in order to stay alive" - but nothing beyond that. Above all, there must be no rejoicing in killing, not even a wicked enemy (Brown, 1975; Urbach, 1977). The well-known midrash wherein God rebuked the angels for singing while or because the Egyptians were drowning is often cited to make this point. Significantly, that midrash is included in the manual of the Israel Defense Forces.[9]

Given the positive halakhic stance on self-defense and defense of others, and given the readiness of Jews to defend themselves when it was feasible, how and why did martyrdom come to have such a dominant place in Jewish history and tradition?

Martyrdom in order to sanctify God's name - kiddush haShem - is not presented as a <u>mitzvah</u> in the Written Law, nor was it ever "a <u>mitzvah</u> of the first order," Emmanuel Rackman, (1977, p. 118) asserts. For the rabbis it was "a much greater <u>mitzvah</u> to save one's life..."

There were, however, three situations, according to talmudic literature, where submission to being killed came to be expected: first, if one were told to murder another person; second, if ordered to commit illicit sexual intercourse; third, if commanded to commit idolatry. But because martyrdom was to be avoided if at all possible, a number of rabbis tried to limit the conditions under which martyrdom would be necessary. According to the formulations enunciated in the second century of the Common Era, the mass suicide at Masada was <u>not</u> halakhically justified since none of the three obligatory conditions was present, and suicide in place of capture did not and does not sanctify God's name. Yet those on Masada were not alone in their time; in that same war whole communities committed suicide as the culmination of their lost battle (Encyclopedia Judaica, 10:982). The non-halakhic nature of such suicides and the rabbis' emphasis on preserving life is the reason that Masada was "expunged from the collective memory" by the rabbis of the second and third centuries (Schorsch, 1977, p. 10).

Nevertheless, kiddush haShem through martyrdom was implicit in Jewish life and faith even before the medieval period, and especially during the Hellenistic period. Moreover, when Judaism itself was endangered with extinction through the enemy's demands and actions, then martyrdom to preserve even the least commandment was deemed necessary.

Martyrdom was appropriated by the people themselves so that they could confront terrifying situations and not give way to threats or torture, could preserve their individuality and national identity, and could struggle for the right to profess their religious faith. It was frequently the only means of demonstrating courage; and it offered suicide (though under a different name) as an alternative to submission and slavery. It helped them escape spiritual degradation during the long centuries of galut, and ironically perhaps, kept their courage and the spirit of resistance alive.[10]

As we look back at the various Jewish strategies for living without real power in generally hostile situations - such strategies as submission, reliance on charters of rights and protection, usefulness to the ruling powers, martyrdom when faced with unacceptable choices, separation from the majority culture - we wonder whether we should attribute Jewish survival to these policies. Lessing, (1976, p. 57) goes so far as to say that we cannot even speak about "survival": Judaism as a system of thought may have survived, but "Jews have not survived. They have been murdered by the millions...for thousands of years...over and over again."

In any case, the late twentieth century is not that of any of the earlier centuries. We live in the century when an estimated 100 million (or perhaps even 200 million) human beings have been killed by other human beings; in an age when mass murder has been demonstrated not only as politically and technologically possible but as an accomplished fact.

During the Nazi era, Jewish powerlessness and its consequences reached its apogee, despite the presumed radical alteration in Jewish status which in the modern era made Jews equal members of the national societies where they lived. Accordingly, the responses to this most desperate and helpless situation and the conclusions that were drawn from it in the final years of the Shoah after people realized the actual situation, and in the years since are of great import. To the extent that these conclusions are generally appropriated by the world Jewish community, they must be seen as the present counterpart to the conclusions of Rabbi Yohanan ben Zakkai and his colleagues after 70 C.E. which became normative for so many centuries.

CONCLUSIONS TO BE DRAWN FROM THE SHOAH

Initially, in the first years of the Nazi period, and even in the beginning of the "Final Solution," there was a continuation of what had become the dominant patterns of Jewish existence. At first some post-Emancipation tactics such as protestations of loyalty to the nation, appeals to facts, and rational denials of the lies were attempted. But very quickly there was, and in many cases had to be, a reversion to the older techniques of survival: trying to accomo-

date to the new conditions (even when this meant going beyond the
more traditional accomodations); buying the right to emigrate; brib-
ing officials; and attempting to outlast the enemy. For the religiously Orthodox: waiting for Messiah to lead them to Eretz Israel;
accepting the present Haman as Heaven's instrument of punishment, as
the Lubavitcher rebbe insisted during the Warsaw Ghetto uprising
(Wells, 1977); trusting in the continued existence of the Jewish
people despite the present catastrophe (which was seen as but one of
Jewry's many holocausts, and not even its largest - since Rabbi
Mandel held that half of the entire people was killed at the time of
the Temple's destruction (Wells, 1977); rejecting armed resistance
religiously as a form of opposition to God's will or pragmatically
as endangering the lives of other Jews (Schneiderman, 1978); and remaining halakhically observant in spite of the difficulties,
dangers, and health hazards involved.

1. Degradation Through Powerlessness

Despite following the time-honored strategies for survival, the
first "lesson" that the Shoah made ruthlessly clear was the degradation that powerlessness brought: total vulnerability, absolute help-
lessness, and complete isolation (even from human sympathy).

If "neither God nor his people is intended to be powerless,"
argues Abba Lessing, (1976, pp. 55, 56), then the "first concern of
the Jewish people today must...be public power...existence precedes
ethics and power is of the essence when we dare to exist." Though
the prophets preached peace, they denounced those who "cry 'peace'
when there is no peace." Moreover, peace or even coexistence is a
two-way, not a one-way, street. A contemporary Israeli peace advocate Amos Kenan (Fackenheim, 1972, pp. 91-2) put it bluntly but
poignantly after the 1967 war:

I want peace peace peace, peace peace peace.
...
[But] Until you agree to have peace, I shall give back nothing.
And if you force me to become a conqueror, I shall become a
conqueror. And if you force me to become an oppressor, I shall
become oppressor. And if you force me into the same camp with
all forces of darkness in the world, there I shall be.

2. The Relation of Powerlessness, Resistance, and Evil

Lack of collective status and recognition, together with the
inability to act on behalf of one's people can lead to desperate
acts of violence as a way of breaking out of one's helpless state.
The various ghetto and death camp uprisings were undertaken without
any hope of victory, even without the hope of individual survival.
Rather, they were attempts to break the circle of impotence: "We
shall not go like sheep to the slaughter!" was the call for resistance by Abba Kovner in December 1941 in Vilna. (However, that call
was turned down by the majority until they could no longer escape
the realization that death was everyone's destiny).

The resisters recognized that there was radical evil in the world, a radical evil to which Rabbi Marc Gellman claims rabbinic Judaism had become blind. By and large, resistance to this evil was led almost entirely by Jewish secularists and radicals. Gellman, (1980) insists that the Fourth Commonwealth of Judaism must never again delude itself about the real and ominous evil in this world. We have here a challenging reversal of the traditional Jewish and Christian positions on evil, with Jews now taking evil more seriously than Christians.

3. Resistance as a Moral Obligation and Rejection of Martyrdom

In the midst of the Nazi campaign of total annihilation, the Jewish community gradually came to recognize its absolute impotence in the face of those who fitted no traditional category of enemy. The acknowledgment of the unique plight of the whole people led a few rabbis (a very few as far as we can tell) to call for an alteration in the community's response. In the very first ghetto established, on October 28, 1939 - Piotrkov - Rabbi Yitzhak Finkler immediately saw the German trap (both physical and moral). When the Germans called for work volunteers and promised benefits in return, Rabbi Finkler (Fackenheim, 1978, p.191) told his people, "Let no one go voluntarily! Do anything, everything. Disappear, hide, lie down, anything - but don't volunteer. Two Warsaw rabbis finally came to recognize the face of the new Amalek. Rabbi Yizhak Nissenbaum (Zimmels, 1977, pp. 64,159n) reminded the Ghetto inmates how during the Middle Ages the mitzvah required martyrdom because the enemy wanted to conquer the souls of Jews by converting them to Christianity. But since "Hitler and his cohorts" want to destroy the Jewish body, the mitzvah of kiddush haShem now requires that the enemy be frustrated by Jewish survival. "Jews should do everything...to live." "This is the hour of kiddush ha hayyim [sanctification through life]...the enemy demands the physical Jew, and it is incumbent upon every Jew to defend...his own life."

At last it was realized that in such "a time of general extermination" it was no longer possible to try to save part of the community by a partial acquiescence with the ruling authority. In mid-January 1943, at a meeting of the new communal leaders who had replaced the Jewish Council, of the Warsaw Ghetto. Rabbi Menahem Ziemba, Gaon of Praga (Zimmels, 1977, pp. 63-4), concluded:

We must resist the enemy on all fronts. We shall no longer heed his instructions...we must refuse to wend our way to the Umschlagplatz...on the road to mass annihilation...we have no choice but to resist. We are prohibited by Jewish law from betraying others, nor may we deliver ourselves into the hands of our archenemy...In the past during religious persecutions, we were required by the law 'to give up our lives even for the least essential practice.' In the present, however, when we are faced by an arch foe, whose...ruthlessness and total annihilation purposes know no bounds, Halachah demands that we fight and resist to the very end with unequalled determination and valour for the sake of sanctification of the Divine Name.

One rabbi reportedly concluded that <u>active resistance</u> to the Germans was essential on the ground that the Covenant would be abrogated unless a portion of the Jewish people survived. Since God apparently was not going to take the necessary action to prevent this possibility, Jews must assume the responsibility of saving the Covenant (Chernick, 1977).

Though the resistance in the ghettos and the uprisings in several camps appears to be the traditional response of martyrdom, since it was undertaken with the expectation of death, it was in fact a step in the direction of a Jewish resumption of power. A conviction that some Jewish life would survive the Nazi enemy's defeat was the motivation for the doomed fighters to establish a new response to evil as a model for future generations.[11]

4. Political Sovereignty and the "Suffering Servant"

As we reread the saga of Jewish vulnerability and torment, culminating as it did in Hitler's "Final Solution," what is to be said about the tradition that upholds Israel as a "holy nation," as God's "suffering servant?" How long must this one people be the vicarious victim for God's long-suffering with the evil-doers of the world? Is there no alternative to either the ongoing suffering of the people of the Covenant or to the destruction of the world and human history if divine justice were enacted?

Neither Zionism nor the State of Israel can be equated with messianism for they do not promise redemption. But they do constitute a renunciation of the "suffering servant" model[12] which the people of Israel accepted for so many centuries, a model that neither saved Jewish lives nor influenced the world to emulate such self-sacrifice. The Jewish state enables Jews to fight for their lives; it is as simple, and as complicated, and as painful as that. In fighting for the nation's right to exist, Jews are saying, in effect, "'We are here to live. We are going to defend our right to do so, if necessary by fighting for our lives. And if we have to die, we are going to die in battle, not in crematoria.'" (Peli, 1971, p. 13). For many people (and I include non-Jews), Israel is so far "the only serious attempt to challenge...the possible eventuality" of a second Holocaust (Peli, 1971, p. 15). For it is the only restitution of power- the ability to determine one's fate, at least to some degree - in an effective form.

This is anything but a glorification of war or aggression. For the most part such an attitude has been absent in most of Israel's history as it has always been in Judaism. But Judaism and Jewish history both attest to the fact that <u>not</u> resisting evil can lead to tacitly accepting evil, to pretending evil is not as serious as it actually is, to succumbing to it, or even to condoning evil (especially if one is not the victim). Judaism's commitment to life, and to life in this world, must lead it to emphasize that problems cannot be solved by either opting out of society or history, or yielding to the evildoer.

5. The Search for Peace Versus Pacifism

A "passion for peace" must not be confused with pacifism. The greatest desire for peace cannot by itself avert war. It is the passion for peace that has been, and continues to be. the thrust of mainstream Judaism and of the State of Israel, as against pacifism or a counsel to "resist not evil." Maurice Lamm (1971, p. 419) asserts that pacifism is rejected by Judaism because, among other reasons, it absolutizes a concept (nothing is worth fighting for) and thereby creates an idol (peace) in place of the living God. As such, it can demolish justice, freedom, equality, liberty, religion, homeland; it becomes "an insatiable, satanic idol."

Furthermore, pacifism misreads political reality and the human condition. It affirms perfection as presently achievable; it treats an ideal as if it were a practical procedure. It applies an uncompromising ethic where compromise is essential, and it does so with tragic consequences. Just as involuntary powerlessness encourages the aggressor, so does pacifism which is voluntarily-assumed powerlessness. Further, Judaism insists that the reality of evil must be faced and combatted through an ethic of power and mercy, or "sweetness and strength" (Lamm, 1971, pp. 419-20, 423).

If civilization is to be protected, confrontation at the international level must be maintained in place of one-sided sacrifices, concessions, or capitulations, no matter how tempting such a way out of tension may appear (Aron, 1968). To follow the path of pacifism in the face of evil is to abnegate the co-responsibility which God bestowed on humanity We can never forget that only the military defeat of Nazi Germany and its allies made possible the survival of any of its intended victims, as Jews struggling to stay alive well knew.

Dare we even suggest after the Holocaust that the Jewish people must be "holy," "a nation of priests," the suffering servant of the Lord, who should renounce their political and military power, or forego its use? Any such renunciation of power, which only a collective entity can provide, would make each person in the nation dependent on the good will of those who had not abandoned power. To be dependent on others' good will has been shown over and over again to be a dangerous risk. The risk may be immediate, at the moment of submission, or it may arise at some later time, for generations yet unborn.

Martin Buber, (1939, p. 29) wrote to Gandhi in 1939: I do not want force, but "if there is no other way of preventing the evil from destroying the good, I...shall use force, and give myself into God's hands." On another occasion he said, "I do not believe that violence must always be answered with nonviolence."[13]

6. Power and Hope

Colin Morris, a Methodist clergyman in England, has observed that the commandment to hope requires first of all survival. He believes that Christian despair in this world can be overcome by witnessing the act of faith which the Jewish people have been living out since the Shoah by reaffirming their Jewishness and raising Jewish children.

What is the basis of hope? If it is not to be mere wishful thinking, escape from reality, or other-worldly spiritualism, it must be commanded, argues Emil Fackenheim (1975). Hope is commanded - commanded by the silence of Auschwitz.

Yet the silence of Auschwitz underlines the fact that hope without power is not a hopeful position in a world where power dominates, in a world that has seen all too clearly the price of powerlessness. It was this existential realization that made survivors of the Shoah such a crucial factor in bringing to an end two millennia of Jewish powerlessness (Bauer, 1979). Zionism (Jewish liberation movement) and its end product reflect the "courage of a people who dared to embody 2,000 years of hope in the fragile vessel of a state" (Hartmann, 1982, p. 8). And the State is a "testimony to the ability, spiritual as well as physical, to perform the deed and live with its results" (Fackenheim, 1979, p. xiv).

The Jewish history of powerlessness culminating in the Shoah, and the positive views of Jewish tradition with regard to power combine to produce for all of us important conclusions about the problems of power and powerlessness.

Those conclusions which most Jews have reached, along with some Christians who have understood the absolute challenge which the Holocaust continues to represent, include: an insistence that the end of Jewish statelessness (which the State of Israel represents) is a responsible religious and political commitment; that forces of death and destruction - radical evil - must be resisted on behalf of life and a community's existence, even if force and power are required for that resistance; that martyrdom can no longer be either the ideal religious or the responsible political method of responding to tyranny or other forms of evil; that peace and community must be the continual goal of our strivings, but not at the expense of a "sacrificial offering" of some one nation or people. It is time for the Jewish "return into history" with all the responsibilities and ambiguities - and mistakes - of power and decision-making which that entails, and all the courage which it requires.

NOTES

1. In a "permissive" or "discretionary" war (milhemet reshut), though numerous categories of men were exempted from conscription on the basis of Halakhah, an individual "conscientious objection" to war as such or to a particular war was not one of the factors to be

considered. For such a war to take place, there had to be a joint decision of the "king," the Sanhedrin of seventy-one, and the high priest through the Urim and Thumim. Its purpose could not be conquest per se or plunder or destruction, but only the protection of Israel and the sanctification of the Name of God. However, expansion of the borders as part of the strategy of protecting Israel appear permissible (Gendler, 1978).

2. In both these observations, separated by centuries, we have a recognition of the need for governmental power to secure or work for peace and to preserve life. But Rabbi Hanania was attempting to quell nationalist aspirations on the part of Jews in the wake of the disastrous wars against Rome, whereas Urbach speaks in the context of a revivified Jewish sovereignty, though also in the name of seeking peace in place of unnecessary military ventures or excessive land claims.

3. "...The heavens are the heavens of the Lord; but the earth He has handed over to the children of men" (Psalm 115:16). Ephraim Urbach insists that "the guiding principle in using force or defense, both for the individual and the state, remains the absolute value of human life, for it is made in the image of God" (1977, p. 110). This is a fundamental criterion by which the use of power is to be restrained.

4. The balance of power arrangement is essentially democratic; the people play a significant role in establishing customs, observances, beliefs, etc. The rabbis decreed that no court can or should set up a ruling that would not be accepted by the majority of the people.

5. Hartmann argues that the movement for Jewish political independence (Zionism) "initiated a greater Jewish involvement with the world [and] implies a movement toward greater interhuman dependence" (1982, p. 8).

6. I considered using "sovereign existence" here in place of "political existence" since both Avineri and Ismar Schorsch argue so cogently for the political nature of the disaspora communities through the medevial period and right up until the Emancipation era. However, I believe political is still a legitimate and the more accurate term since we are talking about a diaspora people whose political (legal) rights were extremely tentative and who were not permitted to share in any of the decision-making processes.

7. When the faith weakened, the will to persist also weakened, as in fourteenth to sixteenth century Spain.

8. In June 1982, the Chief Rabbinate of Israel ruled that Operation Peace for the Galilee was, in all its stages, a milhemet mitzvah (mandatory war) based on Maimonides' definition that such a war is one in which Jews are delivered from an enemy. The Rabbinate went on to cite the "moral" aspect of this military undertaking, especially the restraint with which soldiers used their arms in order to avoid harming innocent civilians (The Jerusalem Post, July 1, 1982).

Some rabbinic scholars argue that "no war today can be regarded as either [milhemet] hovah or mitzvah [obligatory or mandatory]...," that "all wars today are at best reshut [discretionary] and therefore must be morally evaluated very carefully." Among the rabbinic limitations on discretionary war, the purpose is critical: it must

not be conquest or plunder or destruction, but only protection of
Israel and sanctification of God's Name.
Over the centuries rabbis increasingly stressed the need to fear
killing, even in the midst of combat, regardless of the type of war
involved (Gendler, 1978).
9. In the days of tension prior to the 1967 Six Day War, many
Israeli commanders issued to their units S. Yizhar's short story
"The Prisoner." The author of that story unflinchingly deals with
the brutalizing effects of war and violence through a tale of inhuman treatment meted out to an Arab prisoner by an Israeli patrol.
Neverthless, despite Yizhar's views on war, he was a Member of the
Knesset. He recognizes the inescapable need of his people - and
other peoples - to possess and exercise power and saovereignty.
10. Nevertheless the killing of children and especially of infants
in order to prevent their being forced into apostasy was condemned
by at least one rabbinic authority. At a time when there was a decree of forcible conversion, one rabbi slaughtered many infants for
this very reason. Another rabbi called him a murderer. Subsequently the decree of forcible conversion was annulled, and the
children would have been spared from both conversion and death
(Rosenbaum, 1976).
11. Rabbi Pinhas Peli of Israel goes so far as to say that "Israel
was actually established in the Warsaw Ghetto when Jews picked up
arms and fought back literally to the last drop of blood" (1974, p.
13).
12. A modification of this statement is required: There is some retention of the biblical ideal in the Israel Defense Forces' "morality of arms use" policy which voluntarily accepts more casualties
for itself in the effort to harm as few civilians as possible "on
the other side."
13. Mahatma Gandhi advised German Jewry to commit collective suicide
at one given moment in order to shock the conscience of the world.
When Rabbi Leo Baeck received this advice, he did not pass it on.
He said, "We Jews know that God commands us to live." (Friedlander,
1978, pp. 13-14).

REFERENCES

ABRAHAMS, Israel. Jewish Life in the Middle Ages. New York:
Atheneum, 1969.
ARON, Raymond. Peace and War. London: Weidenfeld & Nicolson, 1967.
Citations from review by Howard, Michael. Encounter (London), 1968,
30, 55-59.
AVINERI, Shlomo. Power and powerlessness: a Jewish perspective.
WCC & IJCIC Study Encounter, 1975, 4, 8-10.
BAUER, Yehuda. The Jewish Emergence from Powerlessness. Buffalo &
Toronto: University Toronto Press, 1979.
BERKOVITS, Eliezer. Faith After the Holocaust. New York: Ktav,
1973.
BROWN, Michael. Is there a Jewish way to fight? Judaism, 1975, 24,
466-475.
BUBER, Martin. Brief an Gandhi. Zurich: Verlag die Gestaltung
Zurich, 1939.

CHERNICK, Michael.   Unpublished conversation and correspondence, May and October, 1977.
ENCYCLOPEDIA JUDAICA. Kiddush haShem. 10: 977-986.
FACKENHEIM, Emil. God's Presence in History. New York: Harper Torchbook, 1972.
FACKENHEIM, Emil. Commanded to hope. In Ryan, Michael D. (Ed.), The Contemporary Explosion of Theology.   Metuchen, N.J.: Scarecrow Press, 1975, pp. 155-162.
FACKENHEIM, Emil. Jewish Return Into History. New York: Schocken, 1978.
FACKENHEIM, Emil. Foreword. In Yehuda. Bauer, The Jewish Emergence From Powerlessness. Buffalo & Toronto: University of Toronto Press, 1979, pp.vii-xiv.
FRIEDLANDER, Albert. Stations along the way: Christian and Jewish post Holocaust theology. Common Ground (London), 1978, 6-15.
GELLMAN, Marc. The Fourth Commonwealth. Unpublished paper presented to the Israel Study Group, Greenwich, Conn., October 4, 1980.
GENDLER, Eric. War and the Jewish tradition.   In Menachem Marc Kellner (Ed.), Contemporary Jewish Ethics. New York: Sanhedrin Press, 1978, pp. 189-210.
HARTMANN, David. The moral challenge of Israel. Jerusalem Post, June 20, 1982, 8.
LAMM, Maurice. After the war - another look at pacifism and SCO. Judaism, 1971, 20, 416-430.
LESSING, Abba. Jewish impotence and power. Midstream, 1976, 22, 52-58.
PELI, Pinhas. The future of Israel. Proceedings of the Rabbinical Assembly 74th Annual Convention, 1974, 8-19.
RACKMAN, Emanuel. Violence and the value of life: the Halakhic view. In Salo Baron, & George S. Wise (Eds.), Violence and Defense in the Jewish Experience. Philadelphia: Jewish Publication Society, 1977, pp. 113-141.
ROSENBAUM, Irving. Holocaust and Halakhah. New York: Ktav, 1976.
SCHELLING, Thomas. Introduction. In Gene Sharp. The Politics of Nonviolent Action. Boston: Porter Sargent, 1973, pp. xix-xxi.
SCHORSCH, Ismar. On the History of the Political Judgment of the Jew. New York: Leo Baeck Institute, 1977.
SHNEIDERMAN, S. L. The Warsaw Ghetto struggle. Midstream, 1978, 24, 18-27.
URBACH, Ephraim. Jewish doctrines and practices in Halakhic and Aggadic literature.   In Salo Barfon, & George S. Wise (Eds.), Violence and Defense in the Jewish Experience. Philadelphia: Jewish Publication Society, 1977, pp. 87-112.
WELLS, Leon. I do not say Kaddish. Conservative Judaism, 1977, 31, 3-6.
ZIMMELS, Hirsh Jakob. The Echo of the Nazi Holocaust in Rabbinic Literature. New York: Ktav, 1977.

ALICE L. ECKARDT, Ph.D., Lehigh University, Maginnes Hall 9, Bethlehem, Pennsylvania 18015, U.S.A.

16. Compliance and Oblivion: Impaired Compassion in Germany for the Victims of the Holocaust

Dieter D. Hartman

I was born in Weimar, Germany, in 1935, received my Dr. iur. from Gottingen University and my Dr. rer. soc. from Tubingen University, and from 1971 to 1981 had a teaching assignment for political science at Tubingen University. Gradually over the years, my interest moved from constitutional law and political theory to Nazism and its impact on my own generation and, finally, to the Holocaust.

Many Germans want the Nazi Holocaust and its victims to pass into oblivion.

Much may have changed in this country since the fall of Nazism, but as far as human individuals are concerned, emotional reactions of indifference to suffering link the present to the past.

This paper deals, briefly, with emotional reactions of Germans to the Nazi Holocaust and its victims. The focus will be on the stunted capacity for compassion and its psychosocial development.

Even Today There is an Absence of Genuine Sympathy for the Jewish Victims

Popular emotional reactions to Nazism and the Holocaust cover a wide range of patterns, from the pathetic to cool detachment, and from helpless silence to eloquent self-justification. Bewildered eschewal is to be found and irate self-pity, gross indifference and self-righteous rage. Neo-Nazism is rejected as a matter of course. But over and again there recurs one common reaction: rare indeed is to be found any sign of genuine sympathy for the victims. I do not know how to prove this. It sounds ill suited for a scholarly paper. But this is what I have experienced in my country all my lifetime. Seldom have I heard a word of sympathy for the Jews.

This fact in turn makes the facts of the Holocaust itself ring true.

Callous indifference also marked the emotional responses of most Germans during the Nazi period itself (Kershaw, 1981). Without undue generalization, it might be held that most people were neither anti-Nazi nor ardent antisemites. A vast majority of Germans, however, did not care for whatever happened to the Jews of Europe. They would not join in pogroms, but neither would they protest any.

Very rarely did the Nazis meet with any kind of principled opposition. And it is precisely this fact which so widely is glossed over today. Few people will flatly deny that there ever was a Holocaust. But denial and extenuation minimize responsibility for the tragedy.

The Nazis never met with any difficulties in mustering their executioners from virtually all social classes, all professions and all paths of life (Hilberg, 1961, 1980). The Nazi system could rely on ready compliance and on ruthless administrative proficiency. The Nazi appeal to violent antisemitism may have failed, but it turned out to be unnecessary when it came to administrative genocide. The Holocaust was executed by legions of subservient administrators. All too many of them went out of their way to do more than their so-called duty required of them (Hilberg, 1981). Very few of them took advantage of any opportunity for passive resistance. The planning and execution of the Holocaust allowed most of its minor execution- ers to perceive themselves as having been just bystanders, reluctant cogs-in-the-wheel, or indeed some kind of victim themselves. The Holocaust appeared to be just a marginal episode in their lives, and their silence bespoke no remorse.

More often than not, Germans stood unmoved by all the suffering they saw. People in general were not sadists. But most of them proved unable to be really moved by the victim's fate. Compassion was beyond too many Germans' reach.

Compliance with Nazism was determined by many factors, cul- tural, political, and economic (Kren & Rappoport, 1980; Merkl, 1980; Sabini & Silver, 1980; Baum, 1981; and see Sanford & Comstock, 1971; Kelman, 1973). Such factors range from the impact of Nazi propaganda, the war situation, and economic despair, to downright police terror. These factors are past and gone. But oblivion, denial, and extenuation are there today. This points to deeply rooted emotional impairments (A. & M. Mitscherlich, 1967).

So many peoples' capacity for compassion is crippled. The ca- pacity for compassion seems to be stunted in its development not only by instances of cruel early suffering, but also by derision and disregard of helpless pain. Suffering so often is justified, gloss- ed over, ridiculed, or bluntly denied. A great many people live through highly private ordeals in their childhoods. But they are not allowed to know about their emotional scars (Miller, 1980). They go on in their adult lives to fear weakness and scorn softness. It is difficult for them to attain mature self-respect. They dis- tance themselves from the tender voice of mercy. Mutilated self- respect stunts the capacity for empathy; it leaves little space or energy for active concern for other people. There is instead much hidden rage. Hurt self-esteem and corresponding vengefulness of course play leading roles in the power of the Nazi persuasion. Nazism allows its henchmen to feel untouched by human frailty. Many people never develop an inner image of a loving and compassionate mother or father. All too often, not only did they have no such parent, but there was nobody else to restore the broken image of the human heart.

Research

Social science research of course requires that we go beyond vague and sweeping generalities (for some case studies see Dicks, 1972). But it has to face some particular difficulties. For when we try to understand so complex and highly personal an emotional reality as the stunted capacity for compassion, it is difficult to resort to rigorous methods. We cannot exactly explain or even describe one single individual's emotional life. We can only strive for some informed understanding. Our insight gained into Nazi compliance must be left open to serious questioning. However, factual knowledge is only part of our task. Whatever we pass to future generations will evoke strong emotions. To learn about the Holocaust means to learn how to cope with painful and unfamiliar emotional involvement. This is so for both teacher and students (see Schatzker, 1980).

Research into Nazi compliance must resort to psychoanalysis (Loewenberg, 1975) even though one of the more controversial subjects in modern social science is whether psychoanalysis should be applied to matters of history and politics.

Only recently have psychoanalysts turned to the reverberations of Nazism in clinical experience. In West Germany both partners of virtually all ongoing psychoanalyses either lived through Nazism or were brought up by people who somehow were involved. But we still know little about the impact of Nazism on both doctor and patient Bergmann & Jucovy, 1982, pp. 159-244; Grubrich-Simitis, 1981).

To focus on the individual may tend to underrate political factors. Stunted compassion reflects living conditions and a political culture that foster fear of weakness, overall mistrust of people, dependence upon benevolent authorities, and contempt for the weak and miserable. A psychohistory of the Nazi compliance has to assess the significance of German history, Christian culture, and capitalist economy. These are touchy issues. The latter in particular is highly controversial in current social science and likely to be avoided in research that, after all, has to observe academic rituals. But, again, seeming reservations about the proper treatment of broad factors of culture and economy may conceal some trace of denial and extenuation, because in effect they avoid asking questions about some possible Nazi legacy in present-day society.

Societal factors, on the other hand, may in effect serve to minimize and belittle suffering and individual responsibility. A case in point is the poor contribution of Marxist theory to understanding the Nazi Holocaust. We should not speak about Nazism and keep silent about antisemitism. Much talk about German Fascism goes without ever mentioning the Jews. (Some years ago, I delivered a public address on the lessons of Nazism and mentioned the persecution of Jews just once and in passing).

By glossing over antisemitism, science very subtly sides with the perpetrators. The victims had to die because they were Jews.

The Holocaust was not just one more example of human destructiveness. The very indifference shown by so many people was, to a large degree, the effect of these peoples' antisemitism. They would not have taken part in overt violence; but they consented that the Jews should be put out of sight. This is precisely what Freudian psychoanalysis would call a death wish. People wanted the Jews to be gone forever. They just never cared to know what this wish really meant. Even to talk about compliance, indifference, and stunted compassion therefore may underrate antisemitism and thus also add to minimizing the Holocaust.

Detached research may unwittingly take sides with the perpetrator. It may do so by pretending to be just an innocent bystander. While a deep chasm separates the bystander from the victims, a waning line only distinguishes him from the accomplice. The researcher should face his or her own background. A gentile German at least may have to ask whether he or she really can empathize with the victims. We hardly know what their utter dehumanization does to our feelings and perception. Nazism, beneath all its odd rituals and ideology, appealed to wishes for greatness and invulnerability. It offered to distance oneself from the weak, the vanquished, and the ugly. To identify with the vilified and the persecuted may prove to be more difficult than we would like to admit.

Some heritage of Nazism may have passed from both the perpetrators and the bystanders to their children and grandchildren. What this really means we do not yet know.

When I was a little boy, I saw Russian prisoners of war beg for bread. They offered littled wood-carved toys for it. I did not like the little toys. That is why I remember. Decades later I learned from scholarly books that millions of Russians had perished in the land of my childhood. It took me some more years to understand that I knew it all the time.

We may shun such memories and prefer research methods that evade them, but we do take sides with the Nazis when we let the Jews of Europe silently pass into oblivion.

REFERENCES

BAUM, Rainer C. The Holocaust and the German Elite: Genocide and National Suicide in Germany, 1871-1945. Totowa & London: Rowman & Littlefield, 1981.
BERGMANN, Martin S. & Jucovy, Milton E. (Eds.), Generations of the Holocaust. New York: Basic Books, 1982.
DICKS, Henry V. Licensed Mass Murder: A Sociopsychological Study of Some SS Killers. London: Chatto Heinemann, 1972.
GRUBICH-SIMITIS, Ilse. Extreme traumatization as cumulative trauma. Psychoanalytic Study of the Child, 1981, 36, pp. 415-450.
HILBERG, Raul. The Destruction of the European Jews. New York: Octagon, 1978 (orig. publ. 1961).

HILBERG, Raul. The significance of the Holocaust. In Henry Friedlander, & Sybil Milton (Eds.), The Holocaust: Ideology, Bureaucracy, and Genocide. Millwood, NY: Kraus, 1980, pp. 95-102.

HILBERG, Raul. Sonderzuege nach Auschwitz. Mainz: Dumjahn, 1981.

KELMAN, Herbert C. Violence without moral restraint: reflections on the dehumanization of victims and victimizers. Journal Social Issues, 1973, 29, No. 4, 25-61.

KERSHAW, Ian. The persecution of the Jews and German popular opinion in the Third Reich. Yearbook of the Leo Baeck Institute, 1981, 26, pp. 261-289.

KREN, George M., & Rappoport, Leon. The Holocaust and the Crisis of Human Behavior. New York: Holmes & Meier, 1980.

LOEWENBERG, Peter. Psychohistorical perspectives on modern German history. Journal Modern History, 1975, 47, 229-279.

MERKL, Peter H. The Making of a Stormtrooper. Princeton, NJ: Princeton University Press, 1980.

MILLER, Alice. Prisoners of Childhood. New York: Basic Books, 1980.

MITSCHERLICH, Alexander, & Mitscherlich, Margarette. The Inability to Mourn: Principles of Collective Behavior. New York: Grove, 1975 orig. publ. 1967).

SABINI, John P., & Silver, Maury. Destroying the innocent with a clear conscience: a sociopsychology of the Holocaust. Joel E. Dimsdale (Ed.), Survivors, Victims, and Perpetrators: Essays on the Nazi Holocaust. Washington: Hemisphere, 1980, pp. 329-358.

SANFORD, Nevitt, & Comstock, Craig (Eds.), Sanctions for Evil: Sources of Social Destructiveness. Boston: Beacon, 1971.

SCHATZKER, Chaim. The teaching of the Holocaust: dilemmas and considerations. Annals of the American Academy for the Political and Social Sciences, July 1980, 450, 218-226.

DR. DIETER D. HARTMANN, Weissdornweg 14 W 34, D-7400 Tubingen 1, West Germany.

17. A Psychological Study of Gentiles Who Saved the Lives of Jews During the Holocaust

Frances G. Grossman

Dr. Grossman is a clinical psychologist who received her Ph.D. from New York University. In addition to her private practice of psychotherapy, she is on the faculty of the Postgraduate Center for Mental Health in New York City, and on the Visiting Faculty of Vermont College of Norwich University in Vermont. Her involvement in Holocaust research began in 1967 with a psychological study of children's concentration camp art which received the Holocaust Memorial Award from the New York Society of Clinical Psychologists. The major focus of her research is on the psychological aspects of preventing future Holocausts.

The vast literature of the Holocaust contains relatively few accounts of the Righteous Gentiles, as the Christians who saved the lives of Jews during the Holocaust have come to be known. Fewer still are the systematic studies which would explain their extraordinary behavior in risking their lives on behalf of the beleaguered Jews.

This neglect is not altogether fortuitous. Oddly enough, the role played by these Gentiles in the survival of a million European Jews is a difficult aspect of the Holocaust to deal with, not only for Jews but also for Christians as well.

These saviors of Jews have been honored by Yad Vashem in the name of the Jewish people. Trees have been planted in their names in the Avenue of the Righteous in Jerusalem. However, for the average survivor, the tragedy is so immense, the bitterness toward the Christian world for its role in the genocide of the Jews so deep, that to be told that some acted differently only serves to stir up memories of what it was to be a Jew in Nazi occupied Europe, and of the many millions of Christians who either stood passively by, or actively participated in Hitler's evil work. When the subject is raised with survivors, the usual response is, "There were very few."

For Christians, these Righteous Gentiles are an awkward presence among them. Their very existence adds to the sense of guilt and shame which many feel about the Holocaust.

True, there were very few Gentiles who defied the Nazi terror to help their fellow human beings. The exact number will never be known because many perished together with the Jews they sought to save. However, even if there were only one - if one Gentile gave a Jew refuge from the Nazi death squads, we would have to know about him and understand him, if we are to learn the full meaning of the Holocaust, not only for Jews but for all of humanity.

Who waged this war? How was it that some members of our species called Germans were prepared to follow a leader who vowed to
build the Third Reich on the ruins of civilization? We are far from
having sufficient answers to these questions.

As in the field of medicine, in order to understand disease, it
is necessary to study conditions of immunity to disease. In the
case of the sickness that was the Holocaust, it is necessary to
study those individuals who appeared to be immune to the genocidal
propaganda of the Nazis, those who were so imbued with that "dirty
Jewish invention" known as compassion that they were ready to risk
their lives in order to help Jews.

For the Jews caught in the Nazi death grip, their aloneness was
absolute. No laws protected them. To help a Jew was a crime punishable by death. On the other hand if you turned a Jew over to the
Gestapo, you were rewarded with five pounds of sugar, a bottle of
vodka and a carton of cigarettes, no small haul in war time
scarcity-ridden Europe. If one were really enterprising one could
do even better. One could exact money from the Jews by promising
them a hiding place, then take them straight to the Gestapo, at
which time you were again rewarded. This was not an uncommon occurrence. To understand how fiendishly the Jews were hunted, one would
have to read the Gestapo correspondence. There was no depravity too
low, no amount of money too high, which they would no pay for captured Jews.

One survivor described the situation which existed at the time
of the Nazi occupation in this way: "The terror it was everywhere.
It seeped into every pore. To find a Christian who would help was
harder than finding a white crow." If one searched hard enough, it
was sometimes possible to find a white crow, but then the other
thing one needed was money. Most white crows wanted to be paid.
Helping Jews was very dangerous work. Dealing in Jews was one of
the few lucrative businesses during the Nazi occupation. This was
particularly true in Poland, where there were three million Jews
whom the Nazis were determined to annihilate.

The most widespread undertaking in this business of Jews was
smuggling. Without smuggling the Jews in the ghetto would simply
have starved to death. The risk was very great but it paid very
well. Chaim Kaplan writes in his Warsaw Diary (1973, pp. 350-351)
that the real profiteers among the smugglers were the Nazis
themselves.

> The victims among the smugglers fall like barley before the
> reapers, but the quantity of smuggled produce in the ghetto
> does not decline...This is not the kind of smuggling the Nazis
> abet. The real smugglers sit at home and no danger awaits
> them. The Nazi gendarmes receive vast sums of money from them
> when no one is looking, and the smuggled goods are brought in
> on loaded trucks through the four entrances that these self
> same gendarmes are guarding.

However, in every country in Europe there were men and women, small in number but great in courage, who risked everything to help Jews for no monetary gain at all. Once these people crossed the Rubicon, once they commited themselves to helping Jews, their fate, if caught by the Gestapo, was the same as that of Jews.

WHO WERE THE GENTILES WHO RISKED THEIR LIVES TO HELP JEWS?

Who were these people? Why did they do what they did? What was it in their personalities, their life histories, which enabled them to make the kind of choices they made, at such terrible risks?

They were people from all walks of life. The group that I have studied consisted of nine people, three women and six men, representing the countries of France, Holland, Belgium, Hungary, Yugoslavia and Poland. There was a merchant seaman, a housewife, a storekeeper, a Catholic monk, a French couturier, a sculptor, a nurse and serveral students (people who were students at the time of the Nazi Occupation of their country.) Seven of these people had been awarded Medals of Honor by Yad Vashem for their work in rescuing Jews. Two of the people had not been honored because their work had not been reported to Yad Vashem by the survivors. Two of the Gentiles were representative of families: a Polish miner's family and a Belgian family whose members were engaged in rescue work. Eight of these people reside in the United States in the New York area. One man, a Catholic monk, now 87 years old, lives in a monastery in Paris. I visited Father Bernoit in his monastery, talked with him at length, and we also have an extensive correspondence.

A minimum of six hours of interviews were conducted with each individual. Where it was possible (some of these people are quite old), projective tests such as the Rorschach and House-Tree-Person tests were administered. In addition, The Study of Values (Allport-Vernon-Lindzey), a paper and pencil test, was used. An ongoing relationship exists with most of these people, which makes it possible to gain much information about their lives, attitudes, and behavior.

The purpose of this study was to try to ascertain whether there were any specific factors which these individuals had in common which differentiated them from the general population, particularly from the average German. My major interest was in childhood and family relationships, the assumption being that the important choices and actions which one undertakes in adult life have their roots in one's experiences in childhood. Freud wrote extensively on the importance of childhood in the future life of the individual. This thesis is one which has been generally accepted.

The major emphasis was not on the subject's experience with or attitude towards Jews, but rather on the development of self-attitudes which are the basis of the quality of one's human relationships.

The model for my study of the Gentiles who saved Jews was another study, of German anti-Nazis, undertaken by David Levy (1946-1948) at the end of World War II. This study will be addressed in detail later in this paper.

When the subjects were asked, "Why did you do it?" (Why did you undertake this very dangerous work of helping Jews?), the usual response was, "It was the decent thing to do." However, it was a time when decency was illegal.

A Catholic nun who lived in Paris during the German occupation said that when the Germans invaded, there was a feeling of solidarity among the people. People helped each other. The Jews were in the most trouble, so people helped the Jews. She also said, "We had many problems besides the Jews. They (the Germans) took our food, they took our young men, they kept marching and waving their flags in our faces. We had no heat, we had nothing. At first we believed them when they said they were sending the Jews to work camps. But then we saw them take the children, and we knew that the Jews were not going to work camps. We knew where they were going."

A Catholic monk by the name of Father Marie Benoit, or Padre Benedetto as he was known in Italy, has become a legend for his work in rescuing Jews in France and in Italy. During the German occupation, Father Benoit became an expert forger. He spent three years forging documents for Jews, in the basement of the monastery where he lived. When he was informed that the Nazis had a warrant out for his arrest, he went to Italy and carried out his work of saving Jewish lives in that country. When Father Benoit was asked why he, a monk, was breaking the law, was he not required to render unto Ceasar that which is Ceasar's and unto God that which is God's, he replied with beautiful simplicity, "The law is unChristian." The law was, of course, equally unChristian for millions of European Christians who cheerfully followed Hitler's orders.

I once had occasion to telephone one of the Gentiles who participated in my study. I shall call him Mr. Vladeck. This man was honored by Yad Vashem for having rescued Jews from the Warsaw Ghetto and for having saved diaries and documents which he later gave to the Jewish community. His wife answered the telephone. She said to me, "You want to know why my husband did what he did? I'll tell you why. He's crazy that's why. Who else would do such a thing?" Mrs. Vladeck is a Jewish woman whose life Mr. Vladeck saved by smuggling her out of the Warsaw Ghetto.

I repeated Mrs. Vladeck's statement to a university professor who is himself a survivor of Auschwitz, and who has published books on the Holocaust. The professor agreed with Mrs. Vladeck. He said, "They were deviant, weren't they?" I reminded the professor that deviant meant different, it did not mean crazy. These people were different, but they were far from crazy.

David Levy writes of the German anti-Nazis:

The deviation (of the anti-Nazis) was in the form of liberation from traditional thinking and greater independence. It represents a deviation in people who, however, are as stable as any other group, according to their education and vocational records (p. 167).

The above is generally true of the individuals in my study. Prior to the war and their involvement in the rescue of Jews, these people lived rather conventional lives, very much within the system. At the time of their underground work, they lived as outlaws hunted by the Gestapo as were the Jews.

THE MINORITY IN THE MILGRAM STUDY WHO DID NOT CONTINUE THE SHOCKS

We get a better insight into the behavior and motivation of these individuals from the well-known study conducted by Stanley Milgram (1975) at Yale University on obedience to authority. Milgram's study was designed to answer a question which was on the minds of many people after the full story of the Nazi atrocities became public knowledge. How was it possible for some human beings to commit such atrocities against other human beings? The standard response of the Germans was, "We followed orders."

Milgram's experiment was designed to see how far people would go in following orders even if doing so meant causing pain and suffering to others. His subjects were people from all walks of life who responded to an advertisement in the newspaper asking for people who would be willing to take part in an experiment on the effect of punishment on learning.

The subjects were divided into teachers and learners. The task was a paired word association test. The teacher read a pair of words to the learner, and then read the word with four other words. The learner was supposed to pick out the correct word from memory. If he got the word wrong, he received an electric shock from 15 to 450 volts, depending on how many times he said the wrong word.

In order to compare the expected results with the anticipated results, Milgram asked three groups of people what they thought they would do. Would they continue to shock the learner even though the learner was screaming in pain and begging them to stop? They all said they would certainly stop. Then he asked another group what they thought other people would do, and they said they did not think anybody would continue to cause pain to the learner if the learner was uncomfortable. The psychiatrists in the group said they thought maybe one in a thousand would continue to shock the learners.

They were wrong. More than two-thirds of the people simply followed orders. This was not in Nazi Germany. There was no death penalty for not following orders. Yet two-thirds of the people simply continued to shock the learners from 15 to 450 volts even though the "victims were crying and begging the subjects to stop. The "victims" were actors. The subjects did not know this. Only a small percentage stopped. They would not continue to cause pain to the learners.

Some very interesting differences emerged between the two groups. When the subjects (the teachers) were asked whom they considered to be responsible for their behavior, the larger group which continued to shock the victims said, "The one who gave the order was responsible." When the smaller group which did not continue to shock the victims was asked who was responsible for their behavior, the reply was, "I am responsible for what I do." It was also found that those who refused to continue to shock the victims did not see their actions as doing something against authority. They saw it as an affirmation of some value in themselves. It was not a negative act. It was a positive, affirmative act.

Another finding was that when the screen between the learners and the teachers was removed, the teachers found it much harder to shock the victims.

So too the people in my study were for the most part their own authority. They followed an inner imperative rather than an external one when the external order was in conflict with their own morality and values.

ATTITUDES TOWARD AUTHORITY OF GENTILES WHO SAVED JEWS

Barna Kiss was a Commander in the Hungarian Army on the Russian Front. He was given 214 Jews to annihilate, to throw into the Don River. Barna took the Jews into the woods, behind the front lines, and kept them alive until the end of the war.

In speaking with one of the survivors of Barna Kiss' unit, he said what impressed him and the other Jews in Kiss' unit was not only Kiss' humanism but his sense of responsibility toward the people in his care. On a recent visit to my office, Mr. Kiss said to me, "Tell me Dr. Grossman. Why do people need a leader? I don't need a leader. I know what I want to do and what I have to do. Who needs a leader to tell me what to do?" Barna Kiss did not need a leader. He is, and always has been, his own authority.

Mme. Lorette Rolande (pseudonym) lived in a small town in Belgium at the time of the German occupation. She had a Jewish neighbor who lived across the street. Mrs. R's sister was at that time in South Africa. When the Germans came, she obtained her sister's papers, and with her sister's permission, gave them to the Jewish woman across the street. I said to Mrs. R., "Why did you do this?" She replied, "I had no choice. The Nazis were coming for her any day. And do you know, they came for her the day after I gave her the papers."

Mrs. R. of course did have a choice. She had at least two other choices. She need not have gotten involved. Or she could have denounced her Jewish neighbor to the Nazis. But for Mrs. R. there was no choice. On another occasion Mrs. R. went to a hospital and took home a newborn Jewish infant boy. Then her sister came and took the mother. When asked why she did this very risky thing, she again said, "I had no choice. If the Nazis found out about the baby boy they would kill him."

Pavel (pseudonym) is a sculptor. The first time he came to see me in my office he said that he wasn't sure he qualified for my study because he only saved one Jew, and that Jew came to the United States and unfortunately was killed in a car accident. I quoted the Talmud to Pavel which says that he who saves one life saves the world, and that he certainly qualified for my research.

Pavel is now a man in his mid-fifties. During the war he was engaged in the Resistance movement in his native Yugoslavia. Since he knew several languages, his cover in the Resistance was that he was working for the Red Cross. When the Germans came to Belgrade, they rounded up the Jews in the school house ready for deportation. One of Pavel's friends was a girl who had a Jewish boy friend. She came to Pavel and said, "Will you please help me get Hugo out of the school house?" Pavel agreed to do this. He went to his superior in the Resistance and his superior said, "Today we're not saving Jews. We're doing something else." Pavel did not like his superior's reply, so he went to someone else in the Resistance. He rounded up several Resistance fighters, who agreed to help him get the Jew out of the school house. They went to the school house with a batch of Red Cross arm bands which were to be used to camouflage Jews as Red Cross workers, and in this way they hoped to get them past the Nazi guards and out of the school house. Pavel and his friends approached Hugo, but Hugo said, "I can't go. I can't leave my mother and old grandmother." They went from Jew to Jew and it was the same story. The Jews said they could not leave their families. Finally Pavel saw a familiar face in the crowd. He did not know the man's name, but he knew that he was an ice skater. Pavel was very fond of ice skating. He would often see this man on the ice skating rink. Pavel recalled admiring this man's expertise, and that he had on occasion taught Pavel some fancy skating steps. Pavel and his friends went over to this man, talked to him and he agreed to go with them. They put a Red Cross arm band on him, and took him past the guards out of the school house. (After the war, Pavel learned that this man had eventually come to the United States and had done well, but then he was killed in a car accident).

Another example of Pavel's autonomous behavior as well as his essential humanism is the following:

In the Yugoslav Resistance there were several groups fighting each other. The Chetniks to which Pavel belonged were fighting the Partisans who were mainly led by the Communists. One day while sorting the mail, Pavel came across a letter which contained an order from his Command for the liquidation of several members of the Partisans. Pavel put the letter into his pocket, got on a horse and raced as fast as he could to the Partisans to warn the people who were on the list. When I commented that this was a very dangerous act, that he could have been killed by his own people for what he did, he stated that his only concern was that he would not get to the other camp in time to warn the people on the list. He just could not allow those people to be killed, adding some of them were people whom he knew from high school. Like Barna Kiss, Pavel was his own authority. He took orders only from himself and from no one else.

The psychoanalytic literature of the Holocaust explains that following Hitler meant replacing one authoritarian father figure with another, and in Hitler's case this was a fuhreur who permitted full expression to the formerly repressed aggressive drives. The extreme nature of the Nazis' destructive and sadistic acting out was a direct reflection of the strength of these drives developed in the authoritarian German family.

In the case of the Gentiles under study who were anti-Nazis whose family backgrounds are much less authoritarian, one would expect to find less intensity of repressed hostility, and an easier acceptance and internalization of civilized and humanistic values. This finding proved to be true of most of this group of people. The actions were not based on a negation of authority, but on a positive affirmation of internalized values.

A possible exception was Pavel who was at a point in his life when he was trying to define his own identity as well as his male role. His father, a journalist, was a Minister in the Yugoslavian Government. He had been Pavel's idol until Pavel discovered he was involved with another woman. Pavel described standing with his father at the airport in Belgrade watching with disgust the government ministers leaving the country in the wake of the German occupation, and taking everything with them including their mistresses. At that point, Pavel, dressed in a soldier's uniform, turned to his father and said, "You older people are useless. You cannot save the country. Now it is up to us the soldiers," and for the first time Pavel smoked a cigarette in front of his father.

The Milgram study also revealed that the closer the subject came to the learner, the harder it was for the teacher to inflict pain on the learner. In France, it was noted at the time of the German occupation, that when the anti-Jewish laws were passed by the Vichy Government, there was very little protest from the French people. At the same time, there was a notable increase in help to individual Jews. This is not necessarily a contradiction. Gordon Allport (1954) pointed out that antisemitism is an abstraction. People cannot readily identify with an abstraction. But they can identify with another human being. Survivors have reported that some of the people who helped them had been avowed antisemites who were moved by the plight of a Jew, and risked a great deal in order to help him.

NATIONAL CHARACTER IN GERMANY

The crucial question is, how did those Gentiles who helped Jews evolve into individuals who were able to make the kind of choices which they made, and to take the risks which they took? Why did they become saviors instead of killers?

Aurel Ende (1979, p. 250) in a study of German childhood from 1860 to 1978 writes:

Nowhere in Western Europe are the needs of children so fatally neglected as in Germany.

He cites the commonly used German word kinderfeinlichkeit, meaning rage against children, and suggests that this attitude toward children is a screen for German hostility toward all people. Ende states that there is a far greater number of suicides among German children than in other European countries. Many of these suicides occur notably when report cards are issued. "Since nearly all German children are beaten we can take for granted that German children spend the most important part of their lives in terror" p. 250).

An important factor in German childhood are the Grimm's Fairy Tales. Waite (1977) in his excellent book on Hitler quotes the poet Schiller who wrote, "Deeper meaning lies in the fairy tales of my childhood than in the truth that is taught in life."

To be sure there are some sweet and charming little stories. But the number of tales involving bizarre physical and psychic cruelty is appalling. Let us consider the following scenes taken from a dozen or so of the stories and note particularly the visual imagery they evoke in a child's mind: a queen boils and eats her own children; a young man is required to sleep with a corpse to keep it warm; a king's daughter is torn apart by bears and her mother is roasted alive; a little girl's tongue and eyes are cut out; a pretty girl is hacked to pieces and thrown into a vat filled with putrefying human remains; etc. Little Germans of many generations also learned from these stories to admire racial purity and to distrust Jews. The attitude toward outsiders...is usually one of suspicion and animosity. But hatred for Jews as outsiders is so general and so intense that the Grimms assumed it to be a natural sentiment. The Jew is a foreigner, a product of non-Teutonic culture, he dresses badly, his teeth are yellow, his smile sinister. He is a miser who delights in fleecing the good, naive peasant, he is a coward who whines when he is punished. Given the content and the lessons of these bedtime stories, it is not surprising that Hitler chose a special edition for the younger children of the Hitler Jugend (pp. 262-3).

It is also not surprising that many of the atrocities depicted in Grimm's Fairy Tales were acted out by the Nazis against their victims in the concentration camps.

In the case of Hitler himself, he was very much abused by a brutal and unloving father who beat young Adolf every day. When the father wanted Adolf to come to him, he would whistle for him as one whistles for a dog. Historians agree on what they term Hitler's authoritarian upbringing. However, they state that this was the norm in German families. It was not the norm for anti-Nazis.

The study by David Levy (1946, 1948) is one of the very few systematic studies of anti-Nazis which exists in the literature. The purpose of this study was to select anti-Nazis who would aid in the de-Nazification of Germany at the end of World War II. Levy wished to isolate "the immunity factors, which made these particular personalities resistant to Nazi influence." Levy states, "If it is possible by the present means at our disposal to determine these factors in the personality which are resistant to the influences which make for aggressive wars in Germany, we shall be in possession of a weapon of prevention. We will at least have an insurance against Nazism. To use a medical analogy, we are thereby selecting prophylactic agents immune to hostile influences."

Levy established six criteria for exploration of the history of each individual. These included paternal and maternal relationships, position in the family, crossing of religious lines, political and religious anti-Nazi influences, travel and reading.

The point of reference for these criteria of differentiation was the typical or average German childhood in the average German family. German childhood is notoriously harsh and repressive, oppressive and authoritarian. Corporal punishment is very freely used. Toilet training is very early and very rigid. The whole childhood experience is designed to create instant obedience to follow orders. Be clean and obey were the messages learned in childhood. This kind of training results in an obsessive-compulsive personality, meticulous, orderly and full of repressed rage.

Levy's subjects were a group of 21 German males who had been investigated and found to have been anti-Nazis. Eight had been active anti-Nazis. The rest were passive anti-Nazis. Levy states that it was in many ways harder to be a passive anti-Nazi than an active one. A passive anti-Nazi was one who refused to divorce a Jewish wife, or who refused to join the Hitler Youth. These individuals were constantly harassed and abused and in danger of arrest.

Levy developed a series of differentiating criteria between the German anti-Nazis and typical Germans. I am going to review these criteria and then see how the do and do not apply to my own study group of Gentiles who aided Jews.

Criteria Differentiating Between Anti-Nazis And Typical Germans

1. Paternal

The typical German father is domineering and uses corporal punishment in the discipline of his children. The child is in awe of the father and does not talk to him freely. At the table conversation is discouraged. Atypical situations were those where there was a death of the father in subject's childhood; a father did not use corporal punishment; or a father spoke freely to his children and had an easy relationship with them. Out of Levy's 21 subjects, 14 scored in this area; of our 9 subjects, 7 scored in this area. In three cases the father was absent from the home (2 divorced, 1 through death); the others had a close and easy relationship with the father.

2. Maternal

The typical German mother does not display affection for her child in the form of kissing or embracing past early childhood. The presence of demonstrable affection was scored in Levy's study as a deviation in 10 out of 21 cases. In our study, there were 7 out of 9 cases which showed a close relationship with a mother or mother surrogate. One man's parents were divorced when he was five years old. He was sent to live in a household of aunts who doted on him. He grew up to be very outspoken and self assured. In the case of Barna Kiss, there was a Nana who cared for him from the time that he was a small child. She was the joy of his life and he loved her dearly. She was very protective of him and always defended him to his parents in the case of misbehavior. In the case of Pavel, there was a grandmother who lived with them, and who, he said, was the real mistress of the household. She spent a great deal of time with him and his sister.

3. Position in the Family

An only child or a favorite child occupies a special position in the family. He receives more attention, is more subject to maternal influences, and is more likely to be protected from paternal punishment. The only child does not have the problem of sibling rivalry. He has a closer relationship with parents and the opportunity for the development of more individuality. A surprisingly large number of men in Levy's study - 11 out of 21 - were only or favorite children. In our study 5 out of 9 were reported to have been only or favorite children.

4. Crossing of Religious Lines

The average German is a member of the Catholic or Evangelical Church. He or she marries a spouse of the same faith and nationality. Marriage to someone of another faith or nationality, or of no religious denomination was considered a deviation. In Levy's group 13 out of 21 cases showed "crossing." In our study there was one marriage between a Catholic and Protestant, one French woman was married to a Jew, and on the whole, the subjects or their parents did not take their religion very seriously.

5. Political or Religious anti-Nazi Influences

More than half of Levy's subjects (12 out of 21) were influenced in their anti-Nazi attitudes by being reared in devoutly Catholic homes, or belonging to Catholic Youth Movements. Political influences were exerted by fathers who belonged to the Social Democratic or Communist Party, or through membership in trade unions. The above was not true of the Righteous Gentiles. Their backgrounds were neither strongly political in the sense of membership in left wing anti-Nazi parties, nor were they deeply religious. With the exception of Father Benoit, none were avid church goers. Jacek Lubetski (pseudonym), son of a Polish miner's family who kept a Jewish girl concealed in their home for four years during the Nazi occupation, reported that on Sunday when the priest would come around, his father would hide in the attic so that he would not have to explain to the priest why he hadn't gone to Church.

6. Travel and Reading

Travel and reading were taken to reflect the extent to which there was exposure to new ideas and people of varying cultures and backgrounds which could have contributed to the subject's anti-Nazi attitudes. Of Levy's subjects, 9 out of 21 scored in this area. This criterion was not significant in the case of the Righteous Gentiles.

None of the Gentiles reported having been avid readers. They were mainly action oriented people. Jacek Lubetski stated that there were no books in his house, although he had uncles who would come on Sunday with books on politics, economics and history, and talk to the family about these matters. Pavel came from an intellectual family and he was no doubt exposed to literature and ideas. Barna Kiss stated that he was not much interested in reading. His interests were in the outdoors and in nature. As for travel, Barna Kiss was a merchant seaman. Pavel was born in Geneva, and his family moved back to Yugoslavia when Pavel was still a young child.

Earliest Memories and Favorite Childhood Stories

To Levy's criteria, I added Earliest Memories and Favorite Childhood Stories.

Freud wrote that earliest memories are representative of attitudes and tendencies which are present in adult life. Some of these earliest memories are seen as sources of motivation of the Gentiles in their reactions on behalf of Jews.

Anna Zeelund (pseudonym), a Dutch woman, recalled with much sadness the time when she was five years old and was sent to live in a foster home after her parents' divorce. The same sadness was in her voice when she spoke about the Jews being taken away after the German occupation of Holland. "You saw the Jews leaving and there was nothing you could do." It was after witnessing the deportations of the Jews that Mrs. Zeelund joined the Resistance when whe was asked to do so by a friend.

Mme. Rolande's earliest memory is of the accidental death of her brother. Barna Kiss' earliest memory is of World War I, when his fabulous Nana rescued Barna's father from execution by enemy soldiers who had occupied the town where they lived. When Father Benoit was asked for his earliest memory, eighty years seemed to drop away and he was again a child of five with a wonderfully happy expression on his face as he told of a time when his mother was making pancakes, and she offered to let him make one. He made one, but when he tried to flip it over, it dropped and fell into the ashes on the floor - "and everyone laughed." The warmth and tolerance inherent in that memory are still very much part of Father Benoit today.

The favorite stories were significant for the absence of horror tales. Pavel recalls his grandmother telling stories to him and his sister, all of which ended on a happy note.

CONCLUSIONS

All in all, the anti-Nazis in Levy's study as well as in mine had a more humanistic upbringing than that of the average German. It was less authoritarian and more permissive of affection and communication between parent and child, as well as of autonomy, risk taking and self-expression. It was a childhood which led to greater self-acceptance, self-esteem, self-love and spontaneity of behavior. Impressive in the childhood of Gentiles in my study was the absence of violence in the form of corporal punishment.

Gordon Allport in The Nature of Prejudice (1954, pp. 298, 299) agrees with the above findings:

A home that is oppressive, harsh or critical, where the parental word is law is more likely to prepare the groundwork for group prejudice...The child who feels secure and loved whatever he does, and who is treated not with a display of parental power, develops basic ideas of equality and trust. Not required to suppress his own impulses, he is less likely to project them on others and less likely to develop suspicions, fears and a hierchical view of human relationships.

It is interesting that the Gentiles did not appear to be motivated in their rescue of Jews by political or religious beliefs. On the test "The Study of Values," most received low scores in the area of Religion and did rather well in the category of Esthetics. Pavel attained the lowest possible score on Religion. Barna Kiss also scored low in this area. Mme. Rolande received a relatively high score on Religion, although there is some question as to the validity of the test results in this case. Father Benoit attained an expected high score in this area. One Gentile, who professed to be very active in his Church, and who stated that he engaged in the rescue of Jews on orders of the superiors in his Church, attained only an average score in the area of religion but a high score in the areas of social interests, which would suggest that his church activities were more a reflection of his social needs than his religious interests.

Contact with Jews, particularly in childhood, showed some significant difference between the Righteous Gentiles and the rest of
the Gentile population. The Jews were there as neighbors and fellow
students at school. Anna Zeelund, the Dutch woman had a little Jewish school friend. Father Benoit was a Hebrew scholar, and came to
have much sympathy for the Jews. Barna Kiss was in love with a Jewish girl. Mme. Duval (pseudonym), a French woman, was married to a
Jewish refugee from Poland. When he was deported to Auschwitz, she
commited herself to helping his people.

Many of the million Jews who survived the slaughter of the
Holocaust could not have done so without the aid of Christians.
These Righteous Gentiles not only saved the remnant of a people,
they also saved the honor of the Christian world. They were deviant. But in one sense, they acted on the basis of having learned
the same lesson as did the Nazis, "Do unto others as was done unto
you." They were unique. Those who had experienced security, acceptance and love could readily empathize with another human being in
trouble. The rigid, authoritarian childhood of the average German
predisposes him to the type of personality which Hitler could easily
use for his own purposes.

Freud wrote that man is an aggressive, destructive, sadistic
and cannibalistic creature whose destructive impulses are kept in
check by a superstructure we call civilization. We have seen what a
fragile edifice is civilization; that it could be made to crumble as
if overnight; that a man like Hitler, with a murderous hatred of his
father, could succeed in murdering the conscience of an entire
nation. If this is who we are, then we are doomed.

Let people like the Gentiles we studied give us hope. How a
child is treated determines the kind of human being he or she will
be, and the way in which he or she will relate to others.

In the nuclear age, survival is the main issue for the whole
human race. The study of the Righteous Gentiles points to the fact
that what is required for human survival is change - not in laws,
but in people, more specifically in the education and child rearing
methods which so profoundly affect the nature of people.

REFERENCES

ALLPORT, Gordon. The Nature of Prejudice. Cambridge, Mass.:
Addison-Wesley, 1954.
ENDE, Aurel. Battered and neglected children in Germany, 1860-1978.
Journal Psychohistory, Winter 1979/80, 7, (3), 249-274.
KAPLAN, Chaim. The Warsaw Diary of Chaim Kaplan. Edited by Abraham
Katsch. New York: Collier Books, 1973.
LEVY, David M. Anti-Nazi criteria of differentiation. Psychiatry,
1948, 2, 125-167.
LEVY, David M. The German Anti-Nazi. American Journal Orthopsy-
chiatry, 1946, 16, 507-515.

216

MILGRAM, Stanley. _Obedience to Authority_. New York: Harper & Row, 1975.
WAITE, Robert G. L. _The Psychopathic God, Adolf Hitler_. New York: Basic Books, 1977.

FRANCES G. GROSSMAN, Ph.D., 64 Fayette Road, Scarsdale, New York 10583. U.S.A.

18. Linguicide: Concept and Definition

J. B. Rudnyckyj

*Jaroslav Bohdan Rudnyckyj (born 28.XI.1910), in Premys, founding
Head and Professor Emeritus of Slavic Studies at the University of
Manitoba; M.A. (1934) and Ph.D. (1937), University of Lviv, Ukraine;
in Canada since 1949; founding member and former President of Canadian Association of Slavists; Canadian Linguistic Association; Canadian Institute of Onomastic Studies; President, International Canadian Academy of Humanities and Social Studies; Ukrainian Mohylo-
Mazepian Academy of Sciences, and other learned societies. As member of Royal Commission on Bilingualism (1963-71), advanced and elaborated concept of "Linguicide" as a form of holocaust and genocide.*

Apart from protection of a language by constitutional, institutional, and other means, the negative attitudes of the governments
banning certain languages from public life are known in the history
of mankind. It is clear that the use of a particular language may
be forbidden for reasons of uniformity, forcible assimilation, attempted dehumanization, denationalization, etc. Sometimes it is intended to curtail the development of a dialect vis-a-vis a high prestige language, and it is forbidden in public use, in print, and in
schools. As an example, the fact might be quoted that in the latter
part of the sixteenth century, the shopkeepers of Fribourg in Switzerland were fined for using French in their commercial relations
(Laponce, 1960).

As a rule, the prohibition or restriction of a language is accomplished by administrative orders of the respective governments,
following the general negative attitude of the dominant majority to
discriminate against the language of minority. Here are some examples taken from the history of Tsarist Russia, where such orders
were officially known as "ukases." One such order was issued by
Russian Minister of the Interior, Count Peter Valuev, on June 8,
1863 (Ukraine, A Concise Encyclopedia, 1963, pp. 682-684):

The majority of the Little Russians, themselves thoroughly
prove that there has not been, is not, and never can be any
Little Russian language, and that their dialect used by the
common people, is the same Russian language, but corrupted by
the influence upon it of Poland; that the general Russian language is comprehensible to the Little Russians and even more
understandable than the so-called Ukrainian language now being
formed for the Little Russians, and especially by Poles...

Therefore, Valuev ordered the censors:

to allow to be printed in the Little Russian language only such
works as belong to the realm of belles-lettres; and to ban the

publication of books in the Little Russian language, both religious and educational, and books generally intended for elementary reading by the people.

Valuev's edict was soon followed by the Tsar's "Ukase." On
June 18, 1876, in Ems, Western Germany, Alexander II signed a secret
order of which the real author was Michael Yuzefovich, deputy superintendent of Kiev School District. The "ukase" forbade the printing
in Ukrainian of anything except historical documents in the orthography of the original, and belles-lettres in Russian (so-called
"yaryzhka") alphabet; it also forbade the importation of Ukrainian
books from abroad, particularly from Western Ukraine. This so-
called "Emskyj ukase" lasted two generations and it reached its cli-
max at the end of the last century when Ukrainian composers were
compelled to write the texts to their melodies in French...

Other linguicidal acts of Tsarist Russia were intended to Rus-
sianize the vast empire and bring it to cultural, linguistic and
political unity. Well known are the attempts of the Russian Government in 1860 to stamp out Polish by forbidding its teaching in
schools (Laponce, 1960, p. 22).

A curious example of restriction of the right to print in one's
own language is a Russian ukase at the end of the nineteenth
century which permitted publication in Lithuanian, but made obligatory, under penalty of imprisonment, the use of Russian
characters. An Italian law of 1923 forbade the use of any language other than Italian not only in public notices, legal proceedings, and official correspondence, but also in private ad-
vertising. The sight of a foreign character or the sound of a
foreign language so alarmed Italian officials that they did not
stop at prohibiting billboards in non-Italian languages; they
went so far as to prohibit German choral societies and impose
the Italianization of foreign-sounding family names.

In Canada the abolition of bilingual schools in Manitoba by an
act of the Legislature in 1916 might be termed as a linguicidal measure. The act was bitterly opposed by the French, Ukrainian and Polish speakers, but their reaction was dealt with firmly; the strongest possible opposition came from the Mennonites, a considerable
number of whom emigrated to Mexico in 1919, defending German as an
instructional language in their schools. After 50 years of "linguistic Babylonian captivity," French was re-established as an instructional language in some districts in Manitoba, and Ukrainian became
an elective subject in the high school curriculum.

Linguicide is not confined to restrictive measures only. There
are other kinds of linguicidal acts which cause the partial or complete lingual destruction of a community speaking a given language.
Some governments deliberately inflict on ethno-lingual groups conditions of cultural backwardness refusing help in their organic cultural development. As a result the feeling of "low prestige cultures"
or "low prestige languages" develop within the groups concerned and
lingual switches to dominant language occur.

In summing up, it might be stated that any attempt on the part of any society, government or institution to limit or suppress the exercise of the linguistic rights of one or any of its minority groups may be designated as linguicide. As such the linguicide is carried out by constitutional and/or institutional arrangements, administrative measures, political means, by preferential treatment of the imposed majority language in allocative decisions, or in general through social and economic pressures.

Without attempting to exhaust general or specific cases of acts aiming at linguistic destruction of lingual groups in the past and present, we arrive at the following conclusions with regard to language rights and language suppression, linguicidal measures, and linguicide:

Any of the following acts commited with intent to destroy in whole or in part or to prevent the natural development of a language or dialect should be considered as a linguicidal act:

a) KILLING MEMBERS OF A COMMUNITY SPEAKING A RESPECTIVE LAN-
GUAGE OR DIALECT (GENOCIDE);

b) IMPOSING REPRESSIVE MEASURES INTENDED TO PREVENT THE NATU-
RAL, ORGANIC DEVELOPMENT OF A LANGUAGE OR DIALECT;

c) FORCIBLY INFLICTING ON A BILINGUAL COMMUNITY CONDITIONS OF
CULTURAL DEVELOPMENT CALCULATED TO TRANSFORM IT INTO A UNI-
LINGUAL GROUP;

d) AGAINST THE WILL OF AN ETHNO-LINGUAL GROUP, DENYING THE
RIGHTS OF A LANGUAGE TO BE TAUGHT IN PUBLIC SCHOOLS, TO BE
USED IN MASS MEDIA (PRESS, RADIO, TELEVISION, ETC.);

e) AGAINST THE DEMAND OF AN ETHNO-LINGUAL GROUP, REFUSING MORAL
AND MATERIAL SUPPORT FOR ITS CULTURAL ENDEAVOURS AND LAN-
GUAGE MAINTENANCE EFFORTS.

REFERENCES

LAPONCE, J. A. The Protection of Minorities. Berkeley & Los Angeles: University California Press, 1960.
Ukraine. A Concise Encyclopedia. Vol. 1. Toronto: Toronto University Press, 1963.

J.B. RUDNYCKYJ, Ph.D., The University of Manitoba, 5790 Rembrandt # 404, Montreal-Cote St. Luc, Quebec H4W2V2, Montreal, Canada.

Part IV

Arts, Religion and Education

19. German Expressionism Heralding Genocide and the Holocaust

Luba K. Gurdus

*Luba Krugman Gurdus, a Holocaust survivor, was educated in Poland
and studied art at the Academy of Fine Arts in Warsaw. After World
War II, she came to New York and studied history of art at the Institute of Fine Arts, New York University. She worked as Director
of Research at French & Co. and at the Frick Art Reference Library.
In 1978, she wrote and illustrated THE DEATH TRAIN, a personal account of her war experience. Her present effort is centered on com-
memorating the Jewish victims of the Holocaust. She exhibits her
art works and lectures on Holocaust art. In her writing she also
emphasizes the value of Holocaust studies for the socio-historic education of the young and for a deeper insight into the problems of
genocide in the world.*

In its course of development, Expressionism came to prize emotions and its objective was the immediacy of response and the spiritual contact with mankind in an art which became "a call from man to
man."

Expressionism did not sacrifice its artistic aims while being
moral and polemic. Its exponents were not discouraged by repression
though often restricted in their artistic aims and intellectual
freedom. In its long span, the style experienced consecutive phases
of development and devised various artistic means to express its
close relationship to the turbulent history of the era. In all its
manifestations, Expressionism exposed the viles of society and the
appalling conditions, persisting in Germany. The artists, disappointed with the existing social order, called for a new system
and a new humanity. But their aims were vague and their ideas were
consumed by scepticism and doubt arising from the world of chaos and
despair surrounding them.

The major artists of the period Kollwitz, Grosz and Dix, displayed in their output a progressive awareness of the grave ills
consuming the nation. Kollwitz portrayed the social injustices
leading to a full scale war, and in its aftermath political betray-
al, economic catastrophy, rising militarism and genocide. The ideological affirmations of Grosz undergo a similar pattern. The artist
first criticized the disintegration of society and turned against
its leaders in a bitter condemnation of German aggressiveness and
militarism. He, subsequently, lashed out at the politicians, responsible for the spreading violence, hostility and discrimination,
expediently channeled into a new, even more destructive militarism.
Dix delved in the sad legacy of the lost war exposing hardships
causing bitterness and discrimination. On the whole, Expressionism
has shown that Germany with its frustrations and anxieties, of which
the style was a true reflection, was "a moral and psychological

swamp from which the fanaticism of the Third Reich was destined to emerge."[1]

With the advent of the Third Reich in Germany, Expressionist artists were harassed into isolation and inactivity. Their art works, declared decadent and degenerate, were removed from museums and destroyed. Ironically, the Nazi "purification" of German art and simultaneous condemnation of Expressionism, drew the attention of the entire world to its true value and meaning. In retrospect, we realize that Expressionist art, closely tied to the destiny of Germany, was all along imbued with an urgent message and warning. The seeds of unrest were clearly exposed in this style spanning Germany's two wars. These warning signals, heralding the outbreak of major violence, channeled into genocide and the resulting Holocaust were ignored, overlooked and suppressed.

EXPRESSIONISM AS A REVOLUTIONARY MOVEMENT

At the turn of the century, German art steeped in the rigid academic tradition of the nineteenth century, has been challenged by the emerging "Berlin Secession" which laid the foundation for modern trends in art, especially Expressionism, deriving directly from its radical resistance to the tradition and authority of the past.[2] The early symptoms of social change, caused by the Industrial Revolution which came rather late to Germany, were already apparent in Realism and in Impressionism. These styles reflected, however, the cold rationalism and positivism of an industrial society with materialistic philosophies, clearly at variance with the socio-economic ideas emerging in Germany.[3] The problems, besetting the country during the period of intense militarism and expansionism leading to World War I, saw a number of Cubists and Expressionists initiating a consciously social art. The rise of social democracy as a political movement stimulated the emergence of a dynamic art response and Expressionism became a revolutionary movement, even if on the surface it had a clearly defined program with distinct artistic aims.[4]

The movement was a cultural phenomenon which spread throughout Germany. Artists, writers and intellectuals with widely differing ideas were identified as Expressionists only because they were motivated by a common mood of polemic and revolt. Peter Gray calls the style, "the revolt of sons against fathers."[5] Expressionism reflected Germany's social turmoil and instability as well as ominous warnings of brewing unrest and revoilt. The serious problems were inflamed by aspirations stemming from social philosophies, dominated by Freidrich Wilhelm Nietzsche and Karl Marx. The former's doctrine of self-aggrandizement, thinly veiled in parables of Germanic myths, enhanced the zest for power, the latter's theory of class struggle encouraged violent action.

The new generation of writers, inspired by Hauptmann, Wedekind, Ibsen, Gorki, Doestoievski, Zola and Strindberg, produced the mystical poems of Rainer Maria Rilke and the sympathetic social novels of Heinrich Mann. The period stimulated the rebellious novels of Arno Holz, Stefan George and Franz Werfel and the explosive plays of Ernst Toller, Georg Kaiser, Ernst Barlach and Oskar Kokoschka. The latter's "Burning Bush," 1911, and "Job," 1917, were the earliest experimental dramas of the twentieth century.[6] The example of the Austrian Kokoschka, a true artist- intellectual, was emulated by George Grosz, a founding member of "New Objectivity." The latter poured his convictions into drawings while simultaneously publishing books and portfolios.[7] For a time a publishing poet, Grosz successfully expressed himself in two media, clamoring the decadence of society and shocking the public by his criticism.[8]

German Expressionist painting paralleled French Fauvism. It based its style on the structural method of Cezanne and the symbolism of Munch, Gauguin and Van Gogh. The style used light and color for the sake of drama and movement for emotional projection. It emerged in 1905, in Dresden, as "Die Brucke" (The Bridge) and was headed by Schmidt-Rottluff, Kirchner, Muller, Pechstein and Nolde.[9] In 1911, an abstract Expressionism developed in Munich and became known as "Der blaue Reiter" (The blue Rider). This trend was headed by Marc, Kandinsky and Klee. In its third and last phase Expressionism became known as "Die neue Sachlichkeit" (New Objectivity) and was headed by Grosz, Dix and Beckmann.

The members of "Die Brucke" used a representational style probing the moral and social conditions of prewar Germany. Their analytical and soul-searching art conveyed the agonies of the working classes, unemployment, hunger, sickness and grief. Ernst Ludwig Kirchner (1880-1938) and Karl Schmidt-Rottluff (1884-1976) adopted the philosophical Expressionism of the Norwegian Edvard Munch, uniquely suited for the spiritually harassed Germans of the period. Kirchner, an ideological leader of "Die Brucke" was, in addition, strongly influenced by the art of Van Gogh and the writings of Feodor Dostoievski. His art reflects the lonesomeness and isolation of modern man in hostile surroundings. His graphic work is permeated with an all-pervasive humanity and sympathy for the downtrodden ("Peasant's Meal," Woodcut, Priv. Coll.). Kirchner's figures, "illuminated from within," move singly or in groups through a world of distorted space and color and project a sense of futility and misery.

During his period of war service, the artist shared with other Expressionists a despair over Western values and a revulsion against war. Wounded in action, he was invalided and subsequently left Germany. His prolific output was confiscated and 600 of his art works were destroyed by the Nazis in 1937. A year later Kirchner committed suicide.

Schmidt-Rottluff saw in Munch a kindred spirit and shared his horror of existence and fear of isolation. The artist's terror-stricken figures are isolated behind primitive masks and shielded from the world at large ("Evening on the Sea," 1910, W. R. Valentiner Coll., Detroit).[10] In typical Expressionist manner, he identified himself with the primitivistic creatures he had projected. During the war he created a series of religious woodcuts imbued with mysticism and attesting to his escapist tendencies and his dread of violence. His pictures were condemned by the Nazis.

Another important member of the group was Emil Nolde (1867-1956), invited to "Die Brucke" because of his violent impulses, expressed in his use of color and form. The artist's fear inspiring art reflects his delight in the macabre at times bordering on the psychotic ("The Masks," 1911, Folkwang Mus., Essen). Nolde produced a series of religious pictures, marked by turgid violence of feeling and a frightening mood atuned to his mystique of "blood and soil," professed during his life. The artist's inherent cruelty is best expressed in his autobiography.[11] A pseudo-intellectual, Nolde was known for his ambitious aspirations and controversial views. His writings with dubious political overtones, betray overt prejudices. Despite his membership in the Nazi Party, the artist suffered the confiscation of his art and in 1941 was forbidden to work.

On the eve of World War I, the second phase of Expressionism emerged in Munich. The trend, lyrical and escapist in a mild, spiritual manner, projected the hopelessness of the time. Known as "Der blaue Reiter," the style was headed by Franz Marc (1880-1916), whose art, based on the example of Gauguin and Delaunay, combined dynamic Cubist form with brilliant light and vibrant color. The artist betrayed a subconscious drive to probe the inner life of animals, convinced of their pure existence.[12] Trying to equate his own feeling with that of the animal world, Marc invented the term "Sicheinfuhlen" (feeling into). The artist saw his own suffering reflected in the agonies of the horses mercilessly exposed to the violence and brutality of war. His Field Sketch Book, dated 1916, though full of abstract forms is also filled with a disturbing feeling of a world returned to the primordial.[13] Marc died at Verdun, leaving a series on the theme of horses which inspired several artists, most probably also Picasso, whose "Guernica," 1936, projecting the Spanish war horrors, is clearly dominated by a horse's primordial reaction to inflicted pain.

Marc's theory and method were adopted by other members of the group. In each case the motivation sprung from the feeling of isolation and the need to establish a contact outside the sphere of repressive reality. The Russian-born Wassily Kandinsky (1866-1944) who worked with Marc on the Blue Rider Album and Exhibition in 1911, was an outstanding theorist of non-objective art. A mystic and theosophist, he was the creator of a keen formal sensibility and a believer in the psychological and biological basis of Expressionism. Kandinsky theorized that the style is able to reproduce the intrinsic meaning of things, their soul-substance. In 1912, he published the "Art of Spiritual Harmony" and produced a series of Improvisations, conveying "soul-states." These lyrical and improvisatory works with accent on spontaneous movement and lyrical color were meant to teach the spectator to look at a picture as a graphic representation of a "mood."[14]

Another outstanding member of the group was Paul Klee (1879-1940) who in 1912 participated in the Blue Rider Exhibition. His style was still representational but became increasingly grotesque and fanciful. Klee's unique draughtmanship was of a very special kind, expressive of his own, not always immediately apparent meaning. The artist drawn to the naive, bizarre and insane, demonstrated his ability to project himself into the specific state of mind, demanded by the represented subject in the true spirit of "Einfuhlung" ("Fool in Trance," Willy Strecker Coll., Wiesbaden). Klee also produced a series of grotesque and cleverly satirical allegories in etchings, characteristic of his half-concealed irony. A stern critic of the Nazi Regime, the artist produced a number of Nazi caricatures for which he was expelled from Germany ("Hitler, ein Stammtischler"). In his native Switzerland, the artist created meaningful allusions to Jewish persecution in Germany ("Forced Immigration," 1934, Paul Klee Found., Bern).[15]

In its third and final phase, Expressionism gained new impetus and returned to the representational style reacting decisively to Germany's political and economic upheaval after the World War I defeat. The style combined a proletarian Realism with a critical Verism which brought to the surface the disappointment and bitterness which set in the aftermath of the Versailles Treaty resulting in substantial territorial cessions and extensive reparations. It also mirrored the apathy and stagnation caused by the vain efforts to revise the imposed terms and to restore the impoverished economy. New Objectivity reflects with varying acuteness the peculiar atmosphere of the period and is a valid counterpart to the contemporary literary classics of Henri Barbusse and Erich Marie Remarque.

GEORGE GROSZ

The most powerful exponent of New Objectivity became George Grosz (1893-1959), a true artist-intellectual with close ties to Expressionist writers, championing the cause of society.[16] With consummate skill, Grosz penetrated to the core of Germany's inner turmoil and exposed with analytical veracity the serious ills of its sick society.

First associated with the anarchistic Dada movement, Grosz adopted an explosive style which reflected the turbulent spirit of pre-World War I Germany and his own aggressive and rebellious personality. His participation in Dadaism was intense and without reservation as an expression of his own doubt and scepticism. The artist harboured great bitterness against the "reactionary" segments of society held responsible for the national disaster. His work was devastating, almost ionoclastic expressing the essential ugliness of sad reality.[17]

Under the impact of the first German Autumn Salon in 1913, showing German Expressionists and Italian Futurists, Grosz created his "Pandemonium, August, 1914," a street scene filled with perverted and vicious people in war hysteria which swept Germany. The artist captured the stupification of the mindless masses, hypnotized by their military leaders. In a flow of trenchant satire, he also created the "Mirror of Philistines," a strong indictment of the moneyed oligarchy which profited from the war, and his "Metropolis," a mirror of a big city with its corruption, lust and cunning. Gunther Anders states that the artist's portrayal of the postwar years was so sensitive and penetrating that many who lived at the time rely on his drawings more than on their memories of the period.[18] Politically, Grosz was associated with the left wing in Germany, convinced that only a revolution will solve the country's social problems. He first joined the Spartacists and then the Communists, convinced all along of his sacred duty "to act as a scourge upon society." With the Spartacus Uprising and the crisis of the Socialist Movement, Grosz showed the defeat in his famous "Prost Noske—The Proletariat is Disarmed," 1919. The composition portrays a German officer with a bloody saber on a heap of bodies and barbed wire. This poignant allusion to German militarism gained Grosz the reputation of being not only daring but slanderous and vicious. In fact, the artist did not hesitate to shock and horrify, pouring his convictions into provocative caricatures and following his inner compulsion to bring into the open the major ills of society. His concern and motifs were misunderstood. Accused of blasphemy for linking the German clergy to militarism, Grosz was forced to leave Germany.[19] He arrived in the United States a disappointed and bitter man.

Otto Dix (1891-1969), another founding member of the New Objectivity expressed his dramatic condemnation of German militarism. The artist never forgot his World War I experience and spent nearly two decades recreating his revulsion against war and terror. His extensive series of Trenches, Barricades and Battlefield scenes, started in the 1920s, found a monumental crowning in his triptych "The War," 1929-32. During this period, Dix also created a poignant commentary on the sad war legacy in compassionate images of war invalids and a courageous condemnation of rising racism ("Pragerstrasse," 1919). In 1933, the artist created his famous "Seven Deadly Sins" exposing Hitler's policies. More akin to the German masters of the Middle Ages than to the realistic craftsmen of his own time, Dix strengthened his message with an allegorical symbolism. In the composition, Hitler, personifying Jealousy, occupies the central stage thus leading the other sinners and assuming responsibility for their scheming.[20] The artist's work was condemned and labeled degenerate by the Nazis.

Like Dix, Max Beckmann (1884-1950) adopted Expressionism after the spiritual shock received in World War I. Under the impact of his experiences, he created his most poignant works. In his "Night," Staedel Institute, Frankfurt, 1918-19, the artist portrayed a repressive and repellent subject matter, exposing the agonizing ills of society and its sadistic impulses, "more overt than imagined."[21] Beckmann's cold realistic style conveys the morbidity, tenseness and terrifying nightmare enveloping the defeated nation.

KAETHE SCHMIDT-KOLLWITZ

The most penetrating and incisive analysis of the turbulent times was left by Germany's foremost woman artist, Kaethe Schmidt-Kollwitz (1869-1945).[22] Independent of group affiliations, she left an extensive record of social conditions about which she learned first hand through her husband Karl, professing socialized medicine. The first decisive stimulus for her socially oriented art came from Gerhart Hauptmann's play "The Weavers," 1893, dramatizing the plight of the Silesian weavers. Kollwitz followed with her cycle, "The Weaver's Revolt," 1893-97. In her six etchings, exposing the spirit of revolt, engendered by Marx, the artist expressed not only the horror of the theme but a dark almost tortuous striving for inner emotional meaning. Painfully aware of the widespread social injustice, she also represented the plight of another large segment of society in her "Peasants' War," 1902-08, based on the writings of Zimmermann and Bebel.[23] Using lithography for absolute freedom of expression, the artist showed the total dissolution of social restraint in the fifth print of the series, "The Outbreak" where a peasants' insurgence is led by a woman, bearing her own features.[24]

Embittered and disillusioned after Germany's defeat in World War I, the artist hoped that the revolution which spread across Europe at the end of the war will herald a springtime for a new Germany. Artists and intellectuals alike were captured by dreams of brotherhood and equality of men. Romantic hopes for the revitalization of society mingled with hopes of abolishing hunger and disease.[25] After the armistice of November, 1918, Kollwitz joined the Spartacus Movement advocating the dictatorship of the proletariat. The party led by Karl Liebknecht and Rosa Luxemburg, rose in revolt in which its leaders were killed. In homage to Liebknecht, Kollwitz created a powerful woodcut.[26]

For the artist and her Spartacus friends, the Weimar Republic, created after World War I, was reactionary in its inception. Convinced that the old system had not been totally overthrown, Kollwitz embarked on an anti-government campaign with a series of posters on suffering and starvation.[27] A pacifist and humanist, she basically despised war and in 1923 created her most powerful series of woodcuts, "The War."[28] Denouncing German militarism, she mercilessly exposed the blind, destructive forces plaguing the nation. In a powerful allusion to Germany's ordeal, she showed the phantoms of Poverty, Hate and Ignorance reaching for a helpless child, shielded by its mother.

With the advent of Nazism, Kollwitz saw thousands arrested, tortured and sent to camps. Her last series of lithographs, "Death and Departure," 1933, shows her obsession with death and reaction to the senseless wave of terror which engulfed Germany.[29] The cycle is not a Last Judgment in the spirit of the German Dances of Death by Holbein or Rethel, nor an Expressionist allegory by Grosz or Dix. Kollwitz created a compassionate farewell to humanity threatened by a devastating force bound on total destruction. The artist's lifelong preoccupation with death and war has risen from her genuine concern for the fate of Germany and of humanity at large.[30] Sensing the murderous tendencies of the Nazis, Kollwitz issued a last, desperate warning, heralding an indiscriminate wave of genocide which eventually resulted in the Holocaust.

NOTES

1. MYERS, L. B. S. Modern Art in the Making. New York: McGraw-Hill, 1950, p. 356.
2. WESTHEIM, P. "Berliner Freie Sezession," Deutsche Kunst and Dekoration, XIX (1916), pp. 157-180. Max Liebermann (1847-1934), president of The Prussian Academy of Art, became the founder and president of the "New Berlin Secession," a movement with an interest in emotional and symbolic problems treating such themes as the workingclass and the loneliness of man.
3. BLUM, P. von The Art of Conscience. New York: Universal Books, 1976, Chapter 7.
4. CHENEY, S. Expressionism in Art. New York: Liveright Publishing Co., 1934, pp. 75, 410.
5. GRAY, P. Weimar Culture: The Outsider as Insider. New York: Greenword Press, 1968, p. 102.
6. University of Conn. Oskar Kokoschka: Literary and Graphic Works, 06-1923. Exhibition, Jan. 24 - March 13, 1977, p. 7.
7. LEWIS, B. I. George Grosz. University Wisconsin Press, 1971, pp. 121-171.
8. Ibid, p. 38.
9. KIRCHNER'S "Group of Four Artists," 1926-27, Wallrat-Richartz, Cologne, represents Otto Muller, Erich Heckel, Karl Schmidt-Rottluff and Kirchner himself, as members of "Die Brucke" in 1913, the group's last year of existence. The early members of the group included also Fritz Bleyl, Cuno Amiet, Max Pechstein and Axel Galeen.
10. MYERS, Ibid, p. 343.
11. NOLDE, E. Das eigene Leben. Berlin: Julius Bard Verlag, 1931, v.1; Jahre der Kampfe. Berlin: Rembrandt Verlag, 1934, v.2.
12. LANKHEIT, K. Franz Marc Shriften. Koln: Du Mont Verlag, 1978, p. 98.
13. BUNEMANN, H. Franz Marc. Munich: Bruckmann Verlag, 1960, pp. 32-33.
14. REBAY, H. Wassily Kandinsky. New York: S. R. Guggenheim Found., 1945, p. 33.
15. FROMMHOLD, E. Paul Klee: The Late Years: 1930-40. New York: S. Sabarsky, 1977.
16. GROSZ, G. A Little Yes and a Big No. New York: Dial Press, Translated by Lola Sachs Dorin, 1946. Grosz wrote about his close relation with Ernst Toller, poet, rebel and dramatist who wrote "Masse-Mensch."
17. Ibid, p. 134. "Hitler was in power...a reckless wave of terror enveloped Germany. Thousands were arrested and killed. It was the beginning of the hell of concentration camps."

18. ANDERS, G. George Grosz. Zurich: Die kleinen Bucher der Arche, 1961, pp. 7.8.
19. LEWIS, op.cit., p. 221.
20. LOFFLER, F. Otto Dix: Leben and Werk. Dresden: Veb Verlag der Kunst, 1960, p. 110.
21. MYERS, op. cit., p. 353.
22. ZIGROSSER, C. Kaethe Kollwitz. New York, G. Braziller, 1951, p. 8.
23. SENEFELDER, A. The Invention of Lithography. New York: Fuchs & Lang, 1911.
24. GURDUS, L. Kaethe Kollwitz: Her Art Seen Through Her Self-portraits. Master's Thesis. Institute of Fine Arts, New York Univ., New York, 1952, p. 36.
25. LEWIS, op. cit., p. XIV.
26. MITCHELL, D. 1919: Red Mirage. London: Jonathan Cape, 1970.
27. ZIGROSSER, C. Das politische Plakat. Berlin: Plakat Verlag, 1919.
28. KOLLWITZ, H. Kaethe Kollwitz. Tagebucher und Briefe. Berlin: Gebr. Mann, 1948. Entries: Oct. 11, 1916; Feb. 26, 1920; June 25, 1920.
29. Ibid, p. 61.
30. KOLLWITZ, K. Ich will wirken in dieser Zeit. Berlin: Auswahl aus den Tagebuchern, Briefen, aus der Graphik, Zeichnungen und Plastik. Gebr. Mann, 1952, p. 156: "Der Krieg begleitet mich zum Ende." (The artist's last letter to her son, Hans, of April 16, 1945).

LUBA KRUGMAN GURDUS, Ph.D., 180 W. 58 St., New York, N.Y. 10019, U.S.A.

20. The Search for a Language: Translating Paul Celan

John Felstiner

Since 1976 I have been teaching literature of the Holocaust at Stanford University, in the English Department. I am now engaged in studying Holocaust poetry and in the process of translating Paul Celan. I hope to identify and establish the set of poems - European, Israeli, American - that emerged from the Holocaust, and at the same time to explore the writing of Paul Celan, whom I consider an epitome of this poetry. My published books are: MAX BEERBOHM'S PARODY AND CARICATURE (1972), and TRANSLATING NERUDA: THE WAY TO MACCHU PICCHU (1980).

Ich bin zu Ihnen nach Israel gekommen weil ich das gebraucht habe, "I have come to you in Israel because I needed to." With this sentence, which I have translated from his German, the European Jewish survivor poet Paul Celan began a talk here in Tel Aviv in 1969, a few months before his death, when he came for the first time to the land of Israel. I hope you'll understand if I, as a literary translator, borrow Celan's words to begin speaking to you here today.

In that 1969 talk, Paul Celan suggests why he needed to come to Israel: "I think I have a notion of what Jewish loneliness can be," he says. A little later he speaks of "taking joy in every green homegrown thing that refreshes you," and then he adds a difficult sentence that I believe must have come from the heart of his need: "I take joy in every newly won, self-feelingful, fulfilled word that rushes up to strengthen those who turn toward it." I see the fulfillment of the word working at the heart of all the forces that had drawn this poet to Israel. After all, as an exile and a poet, Celan's survival coincided with his search for a language. He took refuge in his mother tongue, yet it was the murderers' tongue as well: this choice of his, to go on in German, makes Celan's writing, to my mind, an epitome of Holocaust poetry.

Now as a translator and avid offerer of verse translation workshops, I have found how exactly and how essentially the process of translation has to do with both constituent processes in poetry: with reading - that is, hearing, absorbing, interpreting a poem; and with writing - that is, germinating, generating, completing a poem. Here of course I've reversed the poet's original order of writing and reading, since it happens that way for a translator: read first, then write.

Yet in a sense that order is not eternally reversed. Once a poet's lines have gotten deeply absorbed, transfused in me, the poet's and the translator's tasks begin to seem kindred. Having read my way back - via prosody, philology, biography, history, and dogged guesswork - to the remotest sources of a poem, I start my version from something like the poet's standpoint. In translation

the processes of reading and writing actually coincide, they inter-
animate each other. So that kindredness I spoke of, and this coin-
ciding, give the translator as writing reader or reading writer a
peculiarly revealing task.

With Paul Celan's writing I have found the translator's task at
its most challenging and revealing - especially with his later
poems, which fracture and obscure the lineaments of lyric form. Why
do they? "Every word you speak," he said, "you owe to destruction."
Born in Czernowitz, Rumania, in 1920, within a German-speaking Jewish community, Celan saw Soviet forces overrun his homeland in 1940,
then in '41, Rumanian troops plundered and brutalized the Jews, followed by an SS Einsatzgruppe obliterating the millennium-old culture, burning, torturing, shooting, deporting. Paul's parents (he
was the only child) were wrenched from the ghetto overnight; he
worked 18 months at forced labor, hearing first of his father
murdered, then of his mother.

After the war an exile in Paris, teaching German poetry, he also made brilliant translations from Rimbaud, Valery, Mandelstam,
Dickinson, Shakespeare, and many others. It heartens me that Celan
upheld the possibility of verse translation. Above all he dwelt in
- wrote poems in - the Muttersprache, the German mother tongue that
had passed through "a thousand darknesses of deathbringing speech,"
he said - the language that was literally all he had left. He became the leading postwar poet in German, though increasingly inaccessible, unattended to. In 1970 he drowned himself in the Seine
River.

Paul Celan's poetry, however idiosyncratically lodged within
his native tongue, still beckons to the translator, because every
poem he wrote remains a work in progress - or as he himself, est-
ranged and precarious, once put it: "A poem can be a message in a
bottle...that may somewhere and sometime wash up on land." A poem,
he said in his great speech "The Meridian," a poem wants to reach an
other, a "thou," a poem is making toward encounter, homecoming, messianic release from exile. Is it presumptuous to see in translation
a way of continuing that work in progress, of keeping the poem in
motion toward attentive listeners and toward some new beginning,
following Celan's meridian around to where his poem and its translation alike have their source?

Nothing he wrote has drawn me more than one poem composed in
1969, between the Six-Day War and Celan's journey to Israel. The
poem appeared in Lichtzwang (1970), shortly before his Freitod, as
the German has it, his "free-death":

DU SEI WIE DU, immer.

Stant vp Jherosalem inde
erheyff dich

Auch wer das Band zerschnitt zu dir hin,

inde wirt
erluchtet
knüpfte es neu, in der Gehugnis,

Schlammbrocken schluckt ich, im Turm,

Sprache, Finster-Lisene,

kumi
ori.

YOU BE LIKE YOU, ever.

Ryse vp Ierosalem and
rowse thyselfe

The very one who slashed the bond unto you,

and becum
yllumyned

knotted it new, in myndignesse,

spills of mire I swallowed, inside the tower,
speech, dark-selvedge,

kumi
ori.

To carry over into English and yet still respect the integrity
of Paul Celan's poem, which already bespeaks enough displacement and
loss, I won't leave you with my (always provisional) version but
will retrace my way there and back via the to-and-fro, symbiotic exchange between intepretation and translation - the process of reading and writing.

Du sei wie du

How to preserve the tensile arc of that phrase, and the modula-
tion of its vowels? We cannot tell yet whether the poet is speaking
to God, himself, or his listener, or what has dissevered du from du
so that we need this stark imperative. But we can hear how Celan's
grammar moves - how it binds - one pronoun to the next through a
terse articulation. I know two French versions of the poem. One begins Toi sois comme toi, euphonious and seemingly inevitable; yet

the other says <u>Toi sois égale à toi-même</u>, "You be equal to your-self," which tips the balance of the phrase. Celan's barest utter-ances can make so strong a call on us that in translating, one is tempted to interpret them. Whatever we may hear in <u>Du sei wie du</u>, the simplest rendering probably holds the most potential: "You be like you." For the verbal symmetry, if nothing else, holds some promise.

What English cannot manage though, as French can quite natur-ally, is a true equivalent for <u>du</u>. We have "thou" only in archaic or poetic usage, whereas the intimate pronoun marks four hundred of Celan's poems, coloring their speech and shaping their stance. Celan began to read Martin Buber intensively during the war - the lectures on Judaism, the Hasidic translations, and possibly <u>Ich und Du</u>, "I and Thou." Unfortunately a modern English version cannot re-flect the charged expectancy of Celan's du, although it can closely mime both his rhythm and vowel-sounds: <u>DU SEI WIE DU</u>, immer, "You be like you, ever."

Stant vp Jherosalem inde erheyff dich

Here two more imperatives enter, again in the second-person singular: literally, "Stand up Jerusalem and / raise yourself." Now we hear that line one may also have been addressed to Jerusalem, Zion, an exiled people. These next two lines, bearing the emphasis of italics and strange orthography, seem to have warned off their French translators, who simply transfer the Middle High German as is. But how do the words sound to German readers of Celan's poem, and how then should they sound within an English version? These questions of translation carry straight to the heart of Celan's own poetic undertaking.

The thirteenth century mystic Meister Eckhart first uttered the words. He would open his sermons with a Biblical text in Latin, then translate it into the vernacular as here, then go on to specu-lation. One such sermon caught Celan's eye, giving rise to "Du sei wie du." <u>Surge, illuminare, Jerusalem</u>, reads Jerome's Vulgate, <u>quia venit lumen tuum, et gloria Domini super te orta est</u>. We know this in the King James version of Isaiah 60, which makes a soaring alto aria and chorus in Handel's <u>Messiah</u>: "Arise, shine, for thy light is come, and the glory of the Lord is risen upon thee." The preacher's Middle High German version, <u>Stant vp Jherosalem inde erheyff dich inde wirt erluchtet</u>, made its way literally into Celan's poem - having made its way, that is, from the prophet Isaiah's preChristian Hebrew to Saint Jerome's fourth century Latin to Meister Eckhart's medieval German and then into Paul Celan's ly-ric voice, the messianic word underway and translated through time.

Eckhart considerately rendered the Latin for his flock, but Celan does not in turn adjust Eckhart's words for his own audience. Nearly every German reader would understand them, but at the same time would feel a sudden strangeness, feel displaced backward in time. Celan wanted this dialogue between one epoch and another. In

carrying us back from the present, Eckhart's German preempts by
seven centuries the spawning of words such as Einsatzgruppe and
Sonderbehandlung and Endlosung. Long before Juden raus!, as it were,
was heard Stant vp Jherosalem inde erheyff dich – words which, inci-
dentally, more than one reader of Celan's poem has taken for Yiddish
– a plausible yet painfully ironic mistake, given that language's
European fate.

If a German listener, then, would catch the sense of Eckhart's
words, they need translating into an equivalence, familiar yet
slightly inaccessible. I went to the visionary Dame Julian of
Norwich and to the mystic Richard Rolle of Hampole. My keenest
pleasure came from seeking out the early English Bibles, and then
going back to the Hebrew itself: Isaiah 60:1 and also 51:17, since
Eckhart (or the scribe or congregant who wrote down his sermon) made
a new blend of those two passages. Isaiah 60:1 opens,
which in John Wycliffe's 1382 version from the Vulgate becomes
"Rys thou...be thou lightened." And for the Hebrew of 51:17 –
קומי קומי ירושלם Wycliffe offers a striking verb:
be rered, ris thou, Ierosalem." Finally "rere" felt merely physical
and I pulled out a prosodic stop to carry the metaphoric energy of
Eckhart's Stant vp Jherosalem inde / erheyff dich: "Ryse vp
Ierosalem and / rows thyselfe."

Auch wer das Band zerschnitt zu dir hin

Each word here bristles with possibilities and problems, which
begin to resolve as one decides how to translate the pivotal noun
Band. It can mean "ribbon, band, strap," so that literally the line
reads, "Also the one who cut apart the band to you there." But the
figurative sense of Band, a "link" or "bond," may come closer to
what animates this poem. The German word Band is cognate with Bund,
meaning "covenant," or in Hebrew   , which originally meant a
binding. Once Isaiah's call to God's people has rebounded off
Eckhart and resounded through Celan's voice, Stant vp Jherosalem,
the idea of breaking and renewing a covenant comes into force.

It may well be the speaker who has severed himself from Jerusalem, from his people. Yet always in Jewish history a sinful
people, not their God, has broken the mutual covenant. Here if the
poet congruent with Isaiah, is speaking to a people in exile and
even to the Jewish dead, then the very one who slashed the bond – I
need that stressful language – must be God. This crucial ambiva-
lence must remain in translation.

inde wirt
erluchtet

The dialogue returns in italics to another prophetic imperative, "and becum yllumyned," letting us hear that Isaiah's words,
the old dispensation, have been at work all the time. I hope
"yllumyned" does not look merely quaint. To intensify the word I
have gone from translating Eckhart's wirt as "be" to a more full and
exact idea: "becum."

knupfte es neu, in der Gehugnis

Whoever slashed the bond, Celan now tells us, knüpfte es neu, "knotted it new." (I must have had Pound's "Make it new" in mind here.) This knotting it new seems too much to hope for, unless it is the very persistence of God's word that binds the covenant again. That persistence Celan found not just expressed but embodied in language. After the Holocaust, he said, "There remained in the midst of the losses this one thing: language." In exile he dwelt, he took refuge within the mother tongue itself, and every poem he wrote he wrote in mind of the dead. So to summon up a medieval German that has the prophet's Hebrew behind it constitutes the only kind of memorial that counts for him.

The one who slashed the bond, knotted it anew, and Celan can say where in der Gehugnis - in a very strange word. Virtually no German reader will recognize this term from Middle High German (and rare in that lexicon too), where its root hügen meant "think on, be in mind of, long for." Given the dictionary's three modern equivalents for Gehugnis - Erinnerung, Andenken, Gedächtnis - we find that the word means "memory" or "remembrance." Gehugnis, then, vexes translation in a revealing way. For a while I tried "memoraunce," dating from 1320 and filling out the verse rhythmically, but it came to seem too Latinate and, what's worse, too understandable. The point is, Celan leads his audience to a word they cannot know, then prints it in roman rather than italics as if they ought to know it. Possibly he wished his readers to go through something like what the translator does here. In digging for the arcane and archaic word Gehugnis, "remembrance," we perform an act of memory itself and of possible renewal. Not quite having the courage of Celan's conviction, I searched for remote but just barely perceptible terms and finally settled on early Middle English "myndignesse," akin to "mindedness" and meaning the faculty of memory. I still wonder if it is obscure enough or too obscure.

Schlammbrocken schluckt ich, im Turm

I've put more time into revising and refining precisely what the speaker recalls here, than into any other line of the poem. Translated simply - "I swallowed bits of mud in the tower" - it drains from Celan's verse the revulsion and anger and pain of exile. More must emerge. Impelling the line, strong drawn-out stresses pull the word Schlamm ("mud," "mire," "slime") into schluckt ("swallowed," "gulped"), then a vowel ties schluckt into Turm ("tower").

Schlammbrocken schluckt ich, im Turm, "mudclods I swallowed, in the tower": that will do, yet it still lacks something. Despite - or rather thanks to - my difficulty in finding a vital equivalent, I begin to feel myself edging closer to the experience behind Celan's line as I sound out phrase after not-quite-adequate phrase. "Hunks of muck I gulped" or "scum in lumps" or "chunks of sludge" go too far in miming the poet's disgust, while "scraps of slime" and "bits of swill I swallowed" risk sounding like tongue-twisters.

I need a deeper sense of the voice Celan is projecting. Both Luther's and Buber's German Bibles use Schlamm in figures of abandonment and despair: Jeremiah prophesies Jerusalem falling to the armies of Babylon and is put into a dungeon where (in the King James) "there was no water, but mire: so Jeremiah sunk in the mire." Psalm 69 makes the painfullest utterance if we remember Paul Celan's own death: "I sink in deep mire, where there is no standing: I am come into deep waters, where the floods overflow me. I am weary of my crying: my throat is dried: mine eyes fail while I wait for my God...Deliver me out of the mire." So maybe Celan is saying, "mire in lumps I gulped, inside the tower." That felt all right, until one day I recognized a constraint more essential than any other, in Schlammbrocken schluckt ich, im Turm, / Sprache...

The alliteration linking Schlamm with schluckt carries even further to a word in apposition: Sprache, "language" or "speech," supplants the mire the poet swallowed. After Schlamm and schluckt make their bitter alliteration, in Sprache they give way to what the poet cherishes, what "remained in the midst of the losses." Celan's language so engages with his agony that I feel obliged to alliterate these two lines, even if it means changing word order. Here then is one rendering, awaiting a better: "spills of mire I swallowed, inside the Tower, / Speech..."

Sprache, Finster-Lisene

Why "speech" for Sprache, instead of "language"? I would respect the sources of Sprache in sprechen, "speak," and also bring out the influence of Buber, who made speech that act by which we identify all our realities. Since the next image describes Sprache as something bordering or buttressing the dark, I think Celan meant it as language in use, in action - that is, speech.

As to Finster-Lisene, he invented the term and had never used Lisene before. In Romanesque architecture, Lisene denotes a pilaster strip, a semi-projecting column that buttresses, and later mainly decorates, the corner of a building. Lisene derives from French lisiere, "list, selvedge," a woven edge that keeps fabric from unraveling and thus by extension a margin or frontier. That figurative sense of speech as an ultimate stay against dissolution fits Celan's image, yet he loved the precise and highly unusual name of things, probably because they were not spoiled, not abused by any usage other than their own.

So if I translate Lisene at all familiarly, I am prying Celan away from the difficult purity he elected. He craved yet in his way resisted being understood. Still I myself dearly want him understood, and reluctantly, wrongly, I abandon the architectural sense of Lisene in favor of "selvedge," derived from "self" and "edge," with overtones of "savage" and of "salvage":

spills of mire I swallowed, inside the tower,
speech, dark-selvedge.

And here Celan's German ends.

kumi
ori

    Whatever displaces — and releases! — this final Hebrew couplet
from the German poem should do the same from the English poem. Like
Celan, I leave untranslated these imperatives, second-person singular, feminine of קומי ("rise") and אורי ("shine"). In Isaiah 60,
kumi ori proclaims a new Jerusalem, renewing the covenant and
returning the exiles. Since German and English transliterate the
Hebrew words אורי קומי identically, Celan's gesture in closing as he
does allows me the choice — I would almost say the grace — to do the
same and leave kumi ori as is.

    In several earlier poems, Celan moves at the end from German
into Yiddish or Hebrew, utterly transfiguring the tone of the lyric.
Possibly these moments offer him a kind of refuge. (Though what
happens, I wonder, when "Du sei wie du," exposing Celan's Diaspora
fate, gets translated into Hebrew?) As it is, I delight in not
needing to translate the poem's final words, kumi ori. I see him
breaking free in them, renewing his bond with them in messianic
speech. After a lifetime's writing dictated by loss, here at least
nothing need be lost in translation — unless the very catch of
breath between German and Hebrew has its own quality, distinct from
that between English and Hebrew.

    Celan's audience in Germany, as he well knew, had scarcely any-
one left to recognize kumi ori. For him, Hebrew was anything but
strange. He studied it as a child, after his parents' death used to
recall the beauty of the language, kept a Hebrew Bible on his book-
shelf in Paris, and in Jerusalem in 1969, recited Bialik to Yehuda
Amichai.

    In Jerusalem, Celan renewed contact with a woman he'd known
when they were young in Czernowitz, and who had emigrated after the
war. He wrote out "Du sei wie du" for this friend, and recently
when I visited her, she gave me a photocopy. Only later, on the
plane, as I was staring at this paper, I noticed that Celan had
written the two closing words not in transliterated form, as the
published version had them, but in a perfectly natural Hebrew
script. Only for her, perhaps, and only there in that city.

    Not, anyway, for his postwar German public, who must find the
Hebrew in this poem legible, barely legible and audible. Although
he could expect precious few to understand kumi ori, I think that
not only printer's limitations kept Celan from setting the words in
Hebrew characters. His listeners must have something at least to
wonder at, and should (in a utopian world) feel spurred to seek the
source.

From modern to medieval German, then back out of all this toward a yet deeper source, reversing the process of translation as if
of history itself, Celan comes finally upon words that were there to
begin with.   "Du sei wie du," as it closes, renews, a circle, a
meridian from Isaiah's   'קומי אורי through Jerome's <u>Surge illuminare</u>
to Eckhart's <u>Stant vp Jherosalem</u> and then around to the poet's (I
hope also the translator's) <u>kumi ori</u> - a circle broken by the
slashed bond knotted new, the mired mouth surviving.

<u>JOHN FELSTINER</u>, Ph.D., Stanford University, Stanford,
California 94305, U.S.A.

21. A Critical Evaluation of the Resistance of German Protestantism to the Holocaust

Chester L. Hunt

My interest in the relation of German Protestantism to the Holocaust dates back to a period of service as a Chaplain in the American army in Germany immediately after World War II. I was able at that time to interview Protestant leaders and view relevant documents. Since that time I have been teaching sociology with a stress on intergroup relations. This has resulted in a book, ETHNIC DYMANICS, written with a colleague, Lewis Walker, which examines intergroup relations in a world framework; genocide is one of the topics considered in that book.

Hochhuth's (1964) play, The Deputy, raised difficult and embarrassing questions on the conduct of Pope Pius during the Hitler era which are matched by equally awkward questions on the role of German Protestantism during the same period. Both religious groups faced what seemed to be a choice between abandoning all concern for the welfare of the Jews or suffering possible extinction of their own institutional life by a totalitarian state which had already demonstrated its ability to deal ruthlessly with religious personnel. Neither church was characterized by racist ideology, but both were compromised by a considerable incidence of antisemitism among their own clergy.

For the Catholic Church, Hochhuth may be justified in assuming that the conscience of the church is represented by the action of the Pope as the Vicar of Christ and the symbol of the church. Protestantism had no such central figure, and to disentangle the web of Protestant reaction it is necessary to look at its relation to the state, its internal organization and the struggle of various clergy to formulate a Protestant attitude. Such an analysis must perforce treat, at least briefly, both the Protestant situation before Hitler and the relation of Protestantism to the Nazi government.

PROTESTANTISM AND GOVERNMENT

Church and State Prior to Weimar Republic

The religious pattern of Germany is largely the result of historical developments within particular areas. It is the old rule, "huius regio, eius religio" - the sovereign decides the religion of his country. Under this principle, political allegiance determined religious affiliation. Thus, the division of Germany into Catholic or Protestant areas is mainly the result of the historical successes of Catholic or Protestant princes. Germany, as a whole, was religiously divided, but the individual sections tended toward a homogeneous pattern.

In the nineteenth and twentieth centuries, the increased mobility of population, coupled with a greater religious tolerance, led to some diffusion of the various religious beliefs; but even in the 1930s, there was a a large degree of religious uniformity within small territorial units. In Bavaria (except in the northern part), in the Rhineland, and in certain other districts, a majority of the population were Catholic. For the country as a whole, in 1933, Catholics comprised about 32 percent of the population; Protestants, 63 percent, Jews less 1 one percent and those not affiliated with religious bodies, 4 percent (Krose, 1937).

The Protestant Church shared the status of state church with a Roman Catholicism which had been subjected to heavy attack by Bismarck and was still hindered by various kinds of restrictions. Protestantism was the religion of the reigning family and of the Prussian state. Its hold on the masses might be tenuous, but during the Empire, its official prestige was great.

Change in Status of Protestant Church During the Republic

The collapse of the monarchy and the installation of the Republic resulted in a drastic change of status for the Evangelische Kirche. This change in governmental structure meant that the whole question of state-church relationship was open for review. The Emperor had fled, the territorial kings and dukes were deposed; hence, the government to which the church looked for guidance and support had vanished. The new regime was dominated by the Social Democrats. These, at best, were neutral to the church and often appeared to be friendly to an atheistic philosophy. Under these circumstances, Protestant pastors feared that the shift of political power might have ominous consequences for the church.

The immediate effect of the new political climate was a determined assault by the Socialists upon all ecclesiastical privileges. This attack includes every aspect of the state-church pattern: religious lessons in the schools, state financial aid, and state encouragement of church membership. The move to curtail support of religion was simply a part of the total campaign against the old regime in which the church, the monarchy, and capitalism were linked together.

On most specific proposals to restrict church privileges, the Social Democrats were defeated. Religious lessons were retained in the schools and state financial support was continued. A few years after the end of the Empire, it appeared that the Evangelische Kirche had survived the worst attacks and was making a successful adjustment to the new regime. However, this did not mean that church leaders were reconciled to the changed political order.

Hostility of Protestant Leadership to the Republic

For the official Protestant leadership, the Weimar Republic was a political regime in which their position was precarious at best. The advantages of somewhat greater freedom were more than offset by a constant fear that left-wing parties might achieve actual control of the government. Under the monarchy, the Protestant church had been closely allied with the state. In the Republic, it was more nearly in the position of a tolerated stepchild. Cooperation with Catholic political forces might safeguard ecclesiatical prerogatives, but this was hardly a consolation for the loss of an avowedly friendly government.

Protestant leadership now had to contend with a situation in which parties historically at odds held the reins of power. The political enemies of Bismarck also represented forces usually hostile to official Protestantism. The Liberals had been identified with pacifism, internationalism, and a skeptical spirit in affairs of religion. The Social Democrats were considered representatives of atheistic Marxism, while the tension between Catholic and Protestant had been too strong for a comfortable alliance with the Centre Party.

The Republic was regarded as a result of the Versailles Treaty and the Treaty was often ascribed to these three parties. They had voted in favor of the 1917 peace resolution and they assumed a dominant role in the early days of the Republic. The political atmosphere of a Republican Germany appeared invariably to strengthen these ancient enemies of the Evangelische Kirche. Under the circumstances, it is hardly surprising that the hopes of Protestant churchmen invariably turned to a restoration of the favorable conditions they had known in the Hohenzollern Empire.

Attitude of Protestant Church Toward National Socialism

The vote for the Nazis (NSDAP) came from all classes of the German people and it is impossible to analyze on a religious basis. The figures available do warrant the negative conclusion that a Protestant constitutency was certainly no handicap to NSDAP candidates. Thus, the seven districts with the largest NSDAP vote in the 1933 elections were all predominantly Protestant. Of the seven districts with the smallest NSDAP vote, three were Catholic, three Protestant and one district, Dusseldorf-Ost, almost evenly balanced on a religious basis (Hagmann, 1946). When the National Socialist Party attempted to take power in 1933, it had elected only 43.9 percent of the Reichstag deputies and still lacked the absolute majority it needed to control the government. This was overcome by the cooperation of the largely Protestant German National Party whose deputies, representing 8 percent of the Reichtang, gave Hitler the parliamentary majority.

So it is not unfair to charge that in the period between 1918 and 1933, the Protestant church leadership had been friendly to the forces working along National Socialist lines. Their encouragement of German nationalism and opposition to a proletarian socialism parallied the Nazi program. While comparatively few pastors were active Nazis, neither were the majority bitter opponents of the new order. The German National Party would have preferred the return of the monarchy, but was willing to throw its support to Hitler at a critical period. Similarly, while the bulk of the pastors preferred the monarchial regime to the fanaticism of the "new order," they did not regard the Nazi movement as dangerous to the church. The National Socialists proclaimed their support of religion, opposed the atheistic left-wing groups and promised a strong Germany. National Socialism was not the direct product of clerical political thinking, but it promised to eliminate many enemies of the church. It was at least a change from the confused pattern of Weimar democracy and few clergymen saw any reason to fear its rule.

ANTISEMITISM WITHIN THE PROTESTANT CHURCH

One of the factors which hindered Protestant churchmen from recognizing the danger of antisemitism was that suspicion of Jews was far from unknown in Protestant circles. In church circles the tendency to blame national evils upon the Jewish community had a long history. It had been fanned by numerous preachers and even some writings of Martin Luther provided a source for tirades against the Jews (Borchardt & Merz, 1938, V. 3, p. 61).

In the time of Bismarck, the preaching of the Court Chaplain Adolf Stoecker linked antisemitism with the churchly interest in social welfare. Stoecker, who wielded tremendous influence at that time, was one of the first German clergymen to attempt a religious criticism of economic life. He vigorously attacked what he considered materialistic influence in the press and a reckless disregard of community obligations by great capitalists. To Stoecker the materialism of the press was due in large part to the influence of Jewish publishers and journalists, and the exploitive tendencies of business were due to the activities of Jewish capital. Thus a movement towards social justice became transformed into an antisemitic campaign.

Although antisemitism never became a part of official church doctrine, not many pastors were inclined to challenge the milder forms of antisemitic utterances or practices. Even Karl Barth admits that he was not fully aware of the implications of Nazi antisemitism. Eberhard Bethge reports the following comments in a letter from Barth:

> It was news to me that Bonhoeffer, as I read in your biography of him, in 1933, viewed the Jewish question as the first and decisive question, as the only one, and took it in hand so energetically. I myself have felt guilty that I did not make this problem central, at least public, in the Barmen declarations of 1934 which I composed. In 1934 certainly a text in which I said a word to that effect would not have found agreement either in the Reformed Synod of January 1934 or the general synod of May at Barmen - if one considers the state of mind of the Confessors of those days. But that I was caught up in my own affairs somewhere else is no excuse for my not having fought properly for this cause (Bethge, 1974: p. 167).

Niemoeller, who eventually offered courageous opposition to the
Nazi Jewish policies was not initially disturbed by this aspect of
the Nazi program. Leo Stein, who was a prison companion and has
written a sympathetic book on Niemoeller, quotes him as acknowledging an initial tolerance of some antisemitic measures:

> ...I am certainly not free from reproach because at that time
> certain restrictions against the Jews seemed to me tolerable,
> considering the great aims the Nazis were driving at.
> What kind of restrictions do you mean?
> To keep the Jews out of political office, he replied.   I
> thought it would be for their own good. Many of our people
> identified the Weimar Republic as Jewish, and to a certain de-
> gree they were right without realizing it, for the Weimar Re-
> public was the outgrowth of the liberal spirit, to the growth
> of which the Jews had greatly contributed. So, since it was
> our policy to show that the Weimar Republic was a mistake, the
> Jews naturally came in for a large share of the discredit.
> Jews had taken office in the Republic and worked for it. It
> was unwise therefore to take Jews into the new government of
> the Reich and of the states, or to employ them in any capacity
> ...At that time I did not realize that we would have to pay for
> these restrictions with our own liberty...He who desires
> liberty for himself cannot deny it to others, lest he lose what
> he has gained. This is Germany's lesson to the world Stein,
> 1944: pp. 120-121).

If men like Barth and Niemoeller were initially undisturbed by
Nazi antisemitism, then one can assume that such an attitude was
even more typical of the majority of church.

Initial Amity Between Third Reich and Protestant Church

At the outset, it appeared that there was no reason why the
National Socialists should not establish the same type of modus
vivendi with the Evangelische Kirche that they had reached with the
political groups which represented the bulk of the Protestant church

Even the pages of "Mein Kampf" contained much that was reassur-
ing to the churches. Hitler disparaged the effort to reform religion on an early Germanic foundation, and disclaimed any intentions
to interfere in religious matters. His famous statement along these
lines quieted the fears of many anxious churchmen! "A political
leader must never meddle with the religious doctrines and inclinations of his people" (Hitler, 1935, p. 127).

From the standpoint of the church, opposition to the state was
considered both undesirable and unchristian. Lutheran theology had
deliberately forsworn any attempt to dominate the political power,
saying that the state was charged with maintaining public order
while the church was interested in the salvation of individual
souls. The two functions were considered distinct and the church
did not attempt to make the spiritual standards of the Gospel ethic
the criterion of political conduct. Further, the course of histori-

cal development had drawn church and state together in a relationship in which the church was definitely the subordinate partner.

Not only was the general attitude of the National Socialist
State and the Protestant Church conducive to peaceful relations,
but they had a wide measure of agreement on specific issues. The
major political opponents of National Socialism had also been
hostile to the Protestant Church and the nationalistic aims of the
Party were likewise congenial to a highly nationalistic church. In
spite of a strong anti-Christian wing within the Nazi Party, there
is no indication that responsible leaders desired to provoke a
state-church conflict. Similarly, there is no evidence that even a
minority of churchmen desired to overthrow the National Socialist
Regime.

As in all other conflicts between the church and state, conflict over antisemitiism first became manifest when official rules
clashed with the internal organization of the church. This took
place with the effort to apply the Aryan Paragraph to the churches.
This section was taken from the law of April, 1933 concerning quali-
fications for civil service. Since Protestant ministers were considered state officials, an effort was made to apply the antisemitic
strictures of the law to church officials. It was accepted by the
General Synod of the Church of the Old Prussian Union and by the
newly organized Deutsche Evangelische Synode (hereinafter referred
as German Christians) which professed to speak for the whole Reich.
However, its application was resisted by many of the Landeskirchen
and, at first, it was enforced only in Thuringia, Mecklenburg,
Saxony, Anhalt and Lubeck. The German Christian element favored
its universal application and continually pushed the issue
(Gotthard-Briefe, 1934).

The law provides:
(a) Only he who has the full training prescribed for his career
and will intercede unreservedly for the National State and the
German Protestant Church can be called a clergyman or official
in the church administration.
(b) He who is not of Aryan origin or is married with a person
of non-Aryan origin is not permitted to be called a pastor or
official in the church administration. Clergymen or officials
who enter in a marriage with a person of non-Aryan origin will
be dismissed.
Paragraph 3 -
Clergymen or officials who are of non-Aryan origin or who are
married with a person of non-Aryan origin will be super-
annuated (Schmidt, 1935, pp. 178-179).

This enactment was aimed specifically at Jewish converts to
Christianity. In theory, converted Jews had always been welcome in
the Evangelisch Kirche and a proselyting organization (Judenmission)
had been functioning for many years. Actually, the number who entered the fold was insignificant. From 1886 to 1932 some 19,767
Jews were listed as converts from Judaism to the Protestant Church
(Statistische Mitteilungen aus den evangelschen Landeskirchen, 1881-

1932). The total number of Jewish Christians is difficult to determine, since no records were kept of the racial origins of church
members. Estimates vary from 100,000 to one-and-a-half million.
The latter figure was calculated by the Nazi Rassenamt (office to
guard racial purity) and included families which as far back as 1880
had one Jewish relative. This estimate takes in families which had
little connection with Judaism and until the Nazi era had never
thought themselves different from other Christians.

The number of pastors of Jewish descent was even smaller than
might be expected in ratio to church membership. An editorial in
the Deutsches Pfarrerblatt gives the number of active Protestant
pastors of Jewish descent in 1933 as twenty-nine or about .0019 of
the total German Protestant pastors. The same article estimates
that only 98 pastors of Jewish descent had served the Protestant
Church since the time of the Reformation (Deutsches Pfarrerblatt,
1933). In the period between 1935 and 1939, Pastor Maas arranged
for the emigration of Jewish pastors. He found a total of fortyfive
clergymen listed as non-Aryan, some of whom were classified in this
way because they had married Jewish wives (Maas interview).

Even taking the most generous estimates, the number of non-
Aryans was only a fraction of the total membership of the
Evangelische Kirche. There seemed to be no prospect of mass Jewish
conversions and the annual addition of a few hundred Jewish converts
brought the church little prestige and considerable embarrassment.
Both from the viewpoint of the material gain of the church and the
influence of the surrounding culture, the pressures in favor of religious antisemitism were strong.

Nor did many of the German churchmen relish the role of opponents of antisemitism. Thus Martin Niemoller while defending the
right of Jewish clergymen to hold their positions, advises them to
remain inconspicious for the sake of preserving harmony among the
brethren.

The question can be solved in this way: that we may today expect the clergymen of Jewish origin, for the sake of the existing 'weakness,' keep reserve to prevent any scandal. It would
not be good today, if a pastor of non-Aryan origin engaged in
an office in the church government or in an especially high
charge in the People's Mission, but it is not possible to make
a law of it, because an action in this direction means a refusal of the Christian freedom which can never be forced by
law, but only by love (Bekenntnisse, 1934, p. 96).

An even greater caution is shown in the statement of General-
superintendent Kalmus in one of the first protests against the application of the Aryan Paragraph to the church. It will be noted
that the only part of the law which he objects is the forced removal
of pastors already consecrated by the church.

We understand and appreciate the regulations of the state and
acknowledge also that the Protestant Church has reason to be

attentive in keeping pure the German race; therefore, we agree with paragraph one, but it is our opinion that the regulations of the state can not be simply transferred to the church. Therefore, the General Superintendents are obliged to propose the cancellation of paragraph three (Die Evangelische Kirche in Deutschland und die Judenfrage, 1945, p. 36).

In view of the initial cautious approach of the church to the Jewish question, it is interesting to note that in the face of increasing pressure, the position of the Confessional group became more pronounced.

The German Christians attacked the Jewish Christians as insincere and hypocritical. To them, a Christian Jew was simply a hypocrite attempting to conceal his Jewish nature under the cloak of Christianity. Gradually, all classes of Jews were being stripped of protection and it was logical that those in the church should be no exception. Jews with a record of military service or even of friendship with the Nazi movement were being placed in the persecuted group. Hence, churchmen attempting to defend Jewish converts were put in the position of providing a final refuge for the hated element.

Such a project as the Christian Mission to the Jews sought to convert and incorporate them in the membership of established churches. Carrying out this policy inevitably brought the church into direct conflict with the antisemitic policy of National Socialism. On the other hand, it was difficult for even the German Christians to deny the privilege of conversion to those Jews who might respond to the Christian message. The plea for a separation of Jewish Christians from the rest of the church was presented as a means of maintaining the opportunity of Christian worship and at the same time avoiding conflict with the Nazi racial policies.

Further support for the complete separation of Jewish converts from Aryan Christians came from churchmen who felt that the church had been corrupted by a Jewish materialism which threatened both church and state. In their opinion, the subject of race was not specifically dealt with in the Scriptures, and hence, the church was justified in following state direction.

Against this viewpoint, the Third Synod of the Confessional Church of the Old Prussian Union replied with a defense of the right of the church to admit all who desire to be Christian. Occasional hypocrisy is not a sufficient reason to deny the universal character of the Gospel, nor can racial and political reasons alter the essential nature of the church.

...If the church would refuse the baptism of a Jew because of race political reasons, then it would claim a power over the sacrament which is not given to it. It is bound to the mission of Christ. The realm of Christ in which we are adopted by baptism does not know the differences of race and sex which have their limited meaning in the natural sphere of this world.

There is, in Christ, no Jew or Greek or German! (Immer, 1933, pp. 24-25).

For practical reasons the proposal for a separate Jewish-Christian church was difficult, if not impossible, to carry out. The converted Jews were too small a group to maintain separate churches, and in any event, no avowedly Jewish group could long survive in the Third Reich. On theological grounds, Confessional churchmen also rejected the idea of a segregated church and proclaimed their right to accept converts as individuals, rather than as members of a national group.

The treatment of Jewish converts became a major issue in the struggle between the Confessional Church and the German Christians. The former group stoutly resisted any discrimination against allegedly non-Aryan Christians, while the German Christians sought to make German antisemitic measures as effective within the church as they were in other institutions.

Protests and proclamations by Confessional churchmen against repressive measures were offered shortly after the beginning of the Nazi regime and continued through the war period. These protests were hardly sufficient to stem the tide of antisemitism, but they testify to the failure of the state to completely regiment the Christian churches.

In the early days of the Nazi regime, church protests were mainly concerned with discrimination against the Christian Jews. Later, as the persecution of all classes of Jews became more severe, the Confessional protests also condemned the entire basis of antisemitism.

In 1936, when the state was trying to apply the Nuremberg Law its full force, the leadership of the Confessional Church sent a memorandum of protest to Hitler.

If blood, race, nationality and honor, get the rank of eternal values, then the Protestant Christian is forced by the first commandment to refuse this valuation. If the Aryan man is glorified, so God's Word testifies the sinfulness of all people If they want to force the Christians to antisemitism within the National Socialist Weltanschauung which obliges to hatred of Jews, then the Christians have to oppose this with the Christian commandment of Christian charity (Die evangelische Kirche in Deutschland und die Judenfrage, p. 152).

In 1939, the state ordered the complete segregation of Jewish Christians. At this time, Bishop Marahrens, who was often regarded as too close to the Nazi position, denounced the measure as "unacceptable from the standpoint of the Lutheran confession" ("Die Evangelische Kirche": pp. 167-168).

Simultaneously, the leadership of the Confessional Church sent its pastors a pulpit proclamation. This statement criticized the

German Christian attitude and urged the churches to trust in Christ regardless of the power of those who ignored the Gospel.

State Antisemitic Measures

The pressure against the Jews continually mounted and meanwhile restrictive police measures against the Confessional Church made it more difficult for that body to defend its Jewish members. In 1937 Martin Niemoller and many other leading Confessional pastors were imprisoned. Following this, offerings were forbidden in the churches, religious lessons in the schools attacked, and meetings of Confessional leaders greatly restricted.

Jewish Relief Activities of Confessional Church

The verbal attacks of Confessional churchmen on antisemitism were supplemented with charitable activities. Active relief measures were carried on by numerous individuals and church organizations after 1933.

These efforts continued until 1939, when the rigid application of the Nuremberg Law, regardless of religious faith, forced the establishment of separate institutions for Christian Jews. At this time, the relief efforts were carried on in a setup under the leadership of Pastor Gruber, known simply as "Buro Pfarrer Gruber" (Boyens, 1980).

The Buro had branch offices carrying on similar activity in Heidelberg, Breslau and Kassel. The work of this organization was soon complicated when the mass deportation of the Jews began in February of 1940. At the beginning, the Buro attempted to help the deportees, but this attempt ended when Pfarrer Gruber himself was imprisoned on the 19th of December, 1940 ("Die Evangelische Kirche"). First, he was imprisoned at Sachsenhausen and later transferred to Dachau. In the beginning of this period, the branch offices were allowed to continue and Pastor Werner Sylten, a colleague of Gruber, attempted to keep the organization in operation. Pastor Sylten was imprisoned in 1941 and died in the concentration camp at Dachau in 1942.

Pastor Maas of Heidelberg, who had long been active in Jewish relief activities, met with similar difficulties. He had worked as liaison man between Germany and The Committee for World Alliance for Promoting Friendship Through the Churches. Until the beginning of the war, he made yearly trips outside Germany and facilitated the escape of hundreds of German Jews. At times he was able to work legally, on other occasions he had to resort to the bizarre type of underground activity in which every anti-Nazi became involved. In this manner, he was able to function as a link between the German Church and men in other countries, particularly in England, who were willing to offer sanctuary to Jewish refugees. From Germany, the refugees fled to Bloomsbury House in England, which had become the center for the work of the Christian Church among the Jews. Bloomsbury House in turn was sustained through the activities of the Bishop of Chichester and other English clergymen.

Maas had been an active opponent of antisemitism since the beginning of his ministry and this activity inevitably brought him into conflict with the Nazi regime. However, he had been pastor of a large Heidelberg church since 1915, and for a time the support of his congregation was able to protect him. In 1941, however, his activities caused his dismissal from the pastorate and a few months later, at the age of 67, he was conscripted into a front-line labor battalion (Mass interview).

The Confessional Church had a committee on the Jewish question which aided Maas in his work. This committee assembled at frequent intervals to plan what action the church could take. It brought the Jewish problem to the attention of Confessional synods and supported the issuing of proclamations defending Jewish rights. The committee helped to raise funds for the support of Protestant-Jewish relief agencies and aided refugees in fleeing the country. It functioned with some degree of effectiveness until 1941 when the arrest of many of its members and government surveillance of church meetings made it impossible to continue (Asmussen interview).

Result of Confessional Stand

From the beginning of the Nazi regime, the Confessional Church worked against the more extreme forms of antisemitism. This action included material relief, resistance to antisemitic church laws and continued protest against antisemitic outrages. The protest of the church led to unpopularity at best and, on occasion, even to imprisonment and death for its ministers.

Any hope of success in the struggle against antisemitism was slight and the only tangible effect of churchly resistance was the rescue of a few Jews and some postponement in the actual application of restrictive measures to church life. The Confessional Church could not claim to have had major influence on state policy towards Jews, but it did maintain a constant testimony that the antisemitism of the Third Reich was incompatible with Christian principle.

CONCLUSION

In retrospect, the leadership of the German Protestant Church cannot claim to have spoken against antisemitism with a united voice, and still less can it claim to have rallied even a substantial minority of its lay members in defense of human brotherhood. Most of the lay members stifled any sense of moral outrage and gave at least tacit acquiesence to the slaughter of Jews. Some of the clergy openly collaborated in antisemitic measures while others sought a nonexistent middle ground. There were others of the clergy and some of the laymen who overcame both a tradition of quietism and an imminent danger of persecution to speak out in defense of a helpless and unpopular minority. In terms of the immediate issue, their stand had little effect. In terms of the moral position of the

Christian church, their stand gives substantial evidence of the reality of ideals in a world blinded by brute power and overwhelming violence.

Revisionist scholars tend to criticize the church as being primarily concerned about its institutional interests. Yet it is impossible for any organization, even a religious one, to ignore questions of its own survival. As Beate Ruhm von Oppen points out, "Questions of the role of institutions are very important, including naturally the question of self defense of institutions and the cost and benefits, both to members and nonmembers...of course there were moments when the defense of the institution was in conflict with the defense of faith and humanity. But to make those moments into a comprehensive indictment of these institutions strikes me as wrong, irresponsible and unhistorical" (von Oppen, 1974, p. 61).

From a standpoint of perfectionist consistency, even the Confessional Churchmen fell far short of the ideal. Compared to leaders of other groups, however, their resistance is impressive. Karl Barth summarized it:

> In proportion to its task the church has sufficient reason to be ashamed that it did not do more; yet in comparison with those other groups and institutions (the German universities and schools, the legal profession, business, theater and art, the army and the trade unions) it has no reason to be ashamed; it accomplished more that all the rest (Barth, 1945, p. 193).

The essential question, though, is not how the reaction of the church compares with other institutions but why all parts of German society succumbed to the forces which produced the Holocaust. When the Nazi power was at its height, the church (or at least some elements of the church) did manage to maintain an organized resistance to antisemitic policies. However much honor may be due to those who resisted at this point, the question remains as to why conditions ever came to such a pass. Although many Germans were only nominal Christians, it still is true that to a considerable extent the Protestant Church was the voice of conscience for the most prestigious elements of German society. Why was not churchly resistance to Nazism evident at a time when it might have been effective in stopping its rise? Needless to say, the same question could also be asked of political parties, trade unions, the universities and others.

In part the difficulty lay in a long tradition of separation between spiritual and political realms which hindered any churchly criticism of the state. To a greater degree the problem lay in the fact that most Protestant churchmen were so concerned with immediate issues and had interpreted these in so particularistic fashion that they were blind to the real nature of Nazism. German churchmen took the limitations of the Versailles treaty as a personal affront rather than the judgment of God. They espoused militarism, rejected pacifism and called for a strong Germany. Hitler hardly embodied the Prussian ideal, but a leader who called for the forcible correction of ancient wrongs could not be all bad. When to this was added the Nazi opposition to Bolshevism and atheistic liberalism, the attraction of Nazism is obvious. True, there were the advocates of a Germanic non-Christian philosophy and the inevitable demagogic antisemitism, but these were dismissed as the froth accompanying any new popular movement. The will to believe the best of the Nazis was so strong that it was only overcome when it was far too late for the church to turn the balance.

The church was so preoccupied with historic grievances and current problems that it could not realistically appraise the rise of a movement which became far more of a threat to the Christian church and its ideals than had any of its earlier adversaries.

Scholars today are likely to discount the validity of the concerns of the German churchmen and to assume that their shortsightedness was due to a cultural myopia which distorted German understanding of social issues and to a basic lack of humanitarianism. Such a judgment involves appraising one generation by the insight of the next. The fact that earlier problems seem trivial or irrelevant to us does not mean that an earlier generation could have been expected to view them that way.

What it does mean is that particular groups are only secure in weltaunschauung friendly to liberty of all groups. When antisemitism affected churches directly, some churchmen responded in a heroic fashion and their response was a resistance to all aspects of antisemitism, not just those that were directly church related. However, for too long they tended to minimize the extent of Nazi antisemitism and to deprecate its significance. Jews may be viewed as a sort of lightening rod which invariably attracts the attacks of those who would suppress human freedom. As is now apparent, antisemitism was not an aberrant fragment of Nazi philosophy but an indication of total direction. An earlier recognition that Jews and Gentiles were integral parts of the same body might have avoided the occasion for largely ineffective heroism in the time of extremity.

REFERENCES

BARTH, Karl. Eine Schweizer Stimme 1938-45 (Zollikon-Zurich: Ebangischer Verlag, 1945, p. 5 (Tr in Arthur C. Cochrane, The Message of Barmen for Contemporary Church History). In Franklin H. Littell, & Hubert G. Locke (Eds.), The German Church Struggle and the Holocaust. Detroit: Wayne State University Press, 1974, p. 193.
Bekentnissynode Der Deutschen Engalischen Kirche Dahlem 1934, Vortrage und Botschaft. Als Handschrift gedruckt, nur fur Mitglieder der Bekennenden Kirche. Verlag Junge Kirche, Gottingen, 1935.
BETHGE, Eberhard. Troubled self-interpretation and uncertain reception in the church struggle. In Franklin H. Littell, & Hubert G. Locke (Eds.), The German Church Struggle and the Holocaust. Detroit: Wayne State University Press, 1974, pp. 167-184.

254

BORCHARDT, H. H.; Merz, Georg (Herausgeber); & Luther, D. Martin. Schriften wider Juden und Turken. Drittes Band der Erganzungareihe innerhald der Muncher Lutherausgabe Christian Kaiser Verlag, Munchen, 1938.

BOYENS, Armin, F. C. The ecumenical community and the Holocaust. Annals of the American Academy of Political and Social Science, July, 1980, 450, 140-152.

Die Evangelische Kirche in Deutschland und die Judenfrage. Genfe: Verlag Oikumene, 1945.

GOTTHARD-BRIEFE, monatliche briefe. Jahrgang 11-13: Chronik der Kirchenwirren, Anstatt Handschrift gedruckt bei F. W. Kohler, Elberfeld.

GOTTHARD-BRIEFE, 11 (140th letter, July, 1934).

HAGMANN, Meinrad. Der Weg ins Verhangnis, Reichstagswahlergebnisse 1919 bis 1933. Munchen: Michael Beckstein Verlag, 1946.

HITLER, Adolf. Mein Kampf. Muchen: Franz Feher Nachf., Zentralverlag der NSDAP, 1935.

HOCHHUTH, Rolf. The Deputy. New York: Grove Press, 1964.

IMMER, D. Earl (Serausgeber). Wo gehen wir hin? Bericht des Bruderrates. Berlin: Verlag Unter dem Wort, 1935.

KITCHNER, Magnus, Die Neuere Kirchenaustrittsbewegung, Christliche Welt, 34 (February, 1920).

KROSE, Herman S. J. Statistik der Religionsgemeinschaften im Deutschen Reich. In den Landern und Verwaltungsbezirken. Koln, 1937.

SCHIELE, Friedrich Michael, & Zscharnack, Leopold (Herausgeber). Religion in Geschicte un Gegenwart. Tubingen: Verlag I.G.B. Mohr, 1913.

SCHMIDT, D. Kurt Dietrich (Herausgeber). Die Bekenntnisse und grundsatzlichen Reusserungen zur Kirchenfrage des Jahres 1933, 1934, 1935. Gottingen: Verlag Vandenhoeck und Ruprecht, 1934-1936, vol. 1.

Statistische Mitteilungen aus den evangelischen Landeskirchen. Gutersloh: Verlag L. Vertelsmann, vol. 1881-1932.

STEIN, Leo. I was in Hell With Niemoeller. New York: Fleming H. Revel, 1942.

VON Oppen, Beate Ruhm. Revisionism and counterrevisionism in the historiography of the church struggle. In Franklin H. Littell, & Hubert G. Locke (Eds.), The German Church Struggle and the Holocaust. Detroit: Wayne State University Press, 1974, pp. 54-68.

CHESTER L. HUNT, Ph.D., Visiting Professor, Center Asian Studies, Arizona State University, Tempe, Arizona 85281, U.S.A.

22. The Holocaust and (*Kiveyachol*) the Liberation of the Divine Righteousness

A. Roy Eckardt

A. Roy Eckardt, Professor Emeritus of Religion Studies, Lehigh University, has published articles on the Holocaust in SHOAH, ANNALS OF THE AMERICAN ACADEMY OF POLITICAL AND SOCIAL SCIENCE, THEOLOGY TODAY, and other journals. His latest book, written in collaboration with Alice L. Eckardt, is LONG NIGHT'S JOURNEY INTO DAY: LIFE AND FAITH AFTER THE HOLOCAUST (Detroit: Wayne State University Press, 1982). He has been Editor-in-Chief of the JOURNAL OF THE AMERICAN ACADEMY OF RELIGION and visiting scholar at the Oxford Center for Postgraduate Hebrew Studies. He is Special Advisor to the United States Holocaust Memorial Council, and on the Executive Board of Zachor: Holocaust Resource Center.

According to a survivor of Auschwitz, a certain story was told in that camp of death about a Hasidic rebbe who argued with a disciple, "You know, it is possible that the rebbono shel olam [Master of the Universe] is a liar." "How can that be possible?," asked the disciple in dismay. "Because," the rebbe answered, "if the rebbono shel olam should open his window now and look down here and see Auschwitz, he would close the window again and say, 'I did not do this.' And that would be a lie" (Rosensaft, 1967, p. 294).

But why would it be a lie? Does not the blame for Auschwitz fall upon human beings? Rabbi Eliezer Berkovits (1976, p. 704) of today's Jerusalem supplies a different answer, in a single sentence: "God is responsible for having created a world in which man is free to make history." This answer is unanswerable, is it not? For no human being ever asked or resolved to be born.

A MIDRASH ON DIVINE SIN

The following is a kind of midrash on the sentence of Berkovits that assumes the standpoint of human righteousness in the presence of, kiveyachol, the divine sin. (I am informed that in some Jewish thinking the proviso, kiveyachol, "so to speak," is included when the issue of the divine attributes and praxis is introduced. Here is a linguistic and substantive barrier to the idolatries of theology; it may also suggest one theological origin of Jewish humor).

1. The sole discontinuity (absoluteness) of the Shoah lies in its theological aspect.

In the context of human agony and evil, the Holocaust manifests continuity with acts of genocide (together, of course, with discontinuity), while both the Shoah and genocide stand in radical discontinuity with omnicide, since omnicide is not alone radical evil but the end of all historical evil. The intention of the Endlosung der

Judenfrage, the last answer to the question of Jews, the obliteration of every last Jew, gives the Holocaust its singularity, historically and existentially. But the absoluteness of the _Shoah_, its _singular_ singularity, is found only in the truth that the people who were to be brought to an end were the people of God. In this respect, and in this respect alone, Emil Fackenheim (Littell, 1980, p. 116) is right when he states, "Rather than face Auschwitz, men everywhere seek refuge in generalities."

2. There is no consolation for the Holocaust – for the simple, transcendently bleak reason that the infants, the children, the women, the men have suffered and are gone.

"Rachel is weeping for her children; she refuses to be comforted for her children because they are not" (Jer. 31:15). To protest that the Lord of all the universes looked upon the anguish of his people in Treblinka and Maidanek and resolved to return some of them to the land of Israel is riddled with obscenity. The victims are dead. There is no consolation for that.

Does this mean that no bond is to be found between the two realities, Holocaust and State of Israel? There is such a bond, and it is unbreakable. But it is not a causal bond, nor is it a bond of meaning. The bond is present in and through the human response to the _Shoah_, only there, yet necessarily there. "It is necessary," "Fackenheim (1978, pp. 281-282) writes, "because the heart of every _authentic_ response to the Holocaust – religious and secularist, Jewish and non-Jewish – is a commitment to the autonomy and security of the State of Israel." Is not Israel to be grasped as sublime defiance on the part of the piteous remnant from the kingdom of night, who resolved to take Jewish life into their own hands? We are met here by what Irving Greenberg (1980) calls "the third era of Jewish history," which stands for the absolutely essential rebirth of political power to replace the hell that grew inevitably out of powerlessness.

In the world after the _Shoah_ an awesome yet all-comforting paradox challenges us: to leave everything to God is to betray God; to do everything ourselves (even against God?) is to serve God.

3. Does not the nature of the Holocaust's intention bear tellingly upon, kiveyachol, the complicity of God?

We are caught up in the question of the relation between faith and history, but now we must go deeper into that question. The Nazi _Endlosung_ is profoundly paradoxical: on the one hand, it is not something entirely new (the hatred of Jews for their representation of God is a very old story) (Eckardt, 1974); on the other hand, it is absolutely new (every Jew was supposed to die). The latter fact helps to explain how just before his suicide, Adolf Hitler was fated to write a remorseful letter apologizing for having failed to exterminate the Jews. Six millions of them were murdered, yet Hitler knew that he had completely failed. Sufficient Jews were left to ensure a fresh metastasizing of the cancer of Jewishness. As Hitler wrote, with powerful if demonic truthfulness, "The Jews have inflicted two wounds on mankind - circumcision on its body and 'conscience' on its soul. They are Jewish inventions. The war for domination of the world is waged only between the two of us, between these two camps alone - the Germans and Jews. Everything else is but deception" (Scherman, 1974, p. 9).

Irving Greenberg (1977, p. 24) points out that were we to ignore or deny the theological-historical significance of the Holocaust-event, we would be repudiating a fundamental affirmation of the Sinai-covenant, namely, "that history is meaningful, and that ultimate liberation and relationship to God will take place in the realm of human events." Now of course anyone may reject out of hand the entire notion of uniquely unique, trancendingly decisive heilsgeschichtliche events. The argument would then cease. But if the rejection of the decisiveness of the Holocaust comes from someone who affirms heilsgeschichtliche responses to other events (Exodus, Sinai, Crucifixion, Resurrection, the Second Temple's destruction) but not such a response to the Holocaust, we are forced to respond, as an old saying has it: "Ein Esel schilt den andern Langohr" ("The one ass is calling the other ass 'Longears'").

In sum, it appears most difficult to rule out revelatory meaning within the Shoah - this upon the primordial ground that the historical intentionality of that event can scarcely be dissociated from what it was that made the event fatefully possible in the first place, namely, the Covenant, the setting apart of Jews as "a kingdom of priests and a holy nation" (Ex. 19:6). Presumably, God is anything but uncaring of the future, and ought to be able to foresee the consequences of his own methods and decisions. God is of course identifiable as the culprit behind all Jewish suffering, but the Shoah remains uniquely unique as a most monstrous, eschatological incarnation of that suffering. In Elie Wiesel's (1970, p. 28) Beggar in Jerusalem, a young madman, one of only three survivors who had escaped the deportation, asks: "How does God justify Himself in His own eyes, let alone in ours? If the real and imaginary both culminate in the same scream, in the same laugh, what is creation's purpose, what is its stake?"

4. An appeal to the Crucifixion and the Resurrection of Jesus is blocked: this must be asserted from a strictly Christian point of view.

The liberation of the divine righteousness is intertwined with the uncompromising honesty that Soren Kierkegaard coveted so painfully. Accordingly, we cannot attribute to God a redemption that has not taken place.

Ulrich Simon of King's College, London turns to the crucified and risen Christ for an answer to, or a means of reckoning with, the horror of the Holocaust. Simon (1978, pp. 13-14) writes: "The pattern of Christ's sacrifice, which summarizes all agonies" is "the reality behind Auschwitz." Robert E. Willis (1975, p. 506) has pointed up the unknowing irresponsibility and hence the irony in

Simon's kind of theologizing when he responds: the problem is applying the model of Christ's death and Resurrection to the Holocaust
"is that it was the very development of the church's official
Christology...that provided the charge of deicide leveled against
the Jewish people with at least quasi-official credentials...One
cannot simply proceed as though the passion of Christ provided a
symbolically innocent vehicle for coping with the Holocaust. Symbolically, it has become part of the very evil it seeks to illumi-
nate."

Differing degrees of support for Willis' reaction are forthcoming within a growing legion of contemporary historiographical
works by Christian scholars and church people in many lands. I select but one citation, from the United Methodist historian Franklin
H. Littell (1975, p. 2), a passage that encapsulates 1900 years of
relevant church history: "The cornerstone of Christian antisemitism
is the superseding or displacement myth, which already rings with
the genocidal note. This is the myth that the mission of the Jewish
people was finished with the coming of Jesus, that 'the old Israel'
was written off with the appearance of 'the new Israel.' To teach
that a people's mission in God's providence is finished, that they
have been relegated to the limbo of history, has murderous implications which murderers will in time spell out."

Again, the issue has been raised by Fackenheim (1980) of
whether in one or another of the camps of death, Jesus of Nazareth
could have become a Musselman. "Musselman" was camp-slang for an
all-too-familiar, spectral figure, described by Gerald Reitlinger
(1961, p. 122) as "a walking skeleton wrapped in a bit of blanket."
If the answer is that Jesus could not have been turned into a
Musselman, then the reputed incarnation of God in Jesus is fatefully
unrelated to the human condition. And if the answer is that Jesus
could have become a Musselman, it is thereby out of the question to
maintain that redemption has taken place.

Within our own epoch of history, the traditional Chistological
claims of the church have been subjected to an all-determining crisis. They are surrounded by huge mounds of torn human bodies and
their ashes. A message resounds in and through the shrieks of the
silent dead: "There is no redemption in this world." Do we not have
here a stern lesson of the Shoah, that if there is to be any redemption, it must lie wholly within some tomorrow?

However, there remains the question of the Resurrection. The
challenge to the proclamation of Jesus as raised from the dead by a
special act of God is quite a different one from the challenge confronting the message of the Crucifixion. Yet this other challenge
already lies implicit in Littell's allusion to the Christian myth of
supersession as comprising the cornerstone of a potential Holocaust.
The other challenge presents itself in particularly stark form in
the work of Wolfhart Pannenberg (1968) of Munich University. In his
book Jesus - God and Man, as elsewhere, Pannenberg argues that since
Jesus has in truth been raised from the dead by God, Jesus' claim to
an authority that supersedes Judaism was "visibly and unambig-

uously confirmed by the God of Israel." Note the level upon which the case is put: Controversies between Christianity and Judaism are more than simple human conflicts. God himself is a protagonist, and his very truth is at stake. The resurrection teaching purports to convey something absolute concerning the real history of God. God himself has intervened within human history to prove once and for all that the Christian faith is divinely true, and that, correspondingly, the faith of Judaism is false and displaced. In the Resurrection of Jesus Christ, God has definitively and finally acted to show that he is _for_ Christianity and Christians, and _against_ Judaism and Jews.

There is a special irony in this state of affairs because Wolfhart Pannenberg is a theologian of Germany. (I speak now, in a way, _ad hominem_. Something took place in and through the land called Germany, once upon a time. But Germany is the land of my own fathers as well, so I speak more than _ad hominem_.) The question with which we must confront Pannenberg is, how can the Resurrection of Jesus be proclaimed as a special and world-decisive salvational act of God without the Christian triumphalism that paved the road to Belzec and Sobibor? To my knowledge, no Christian theologian has answered, or sought to answer, this world-determining question. Christian supersessionary thinking, preaching, and behavior go forward, keeping alive, in effect, the Christian aspect of the foundation of the Nazi ideology and program. Christian supersessionary thinking is a carrier. It carries the virus of the last solution, the _Endlösung_ only of Jews.

Perhaps this matter can be put a little more objectively. In his recent work _The Trinity and the Kingdom_, Jürgen Moltmann (1981), another influential Christian thinker of Germany, contends that on the date of Jesus' Resurrection "the eschatological era" began. But if it is the case, as the American Catholic theologian Rosemary Ruether (1974) argues, that the basic trespass of the Christian church vis-a-vis Judaism and the Jewish people is the attempt to historicize the eschatological dimension, how then are we to continue to affirm the Resurrection of Jesus as an actual event already realized by God without at the same time perpetuating this very trespass?

5. The unforgivability of forgiveness

A final comment on behalf of the norm of human righteousness and justice at war against (_kiveyachol_) the sinfulness of God has to do with whether a measure of moral integrity is to be found amidst what appears to be sacrilege.

Elie Wiesel thus describes the genesis of his play _The Trial of God_ (1979, pp. 128, 157, 127, 133): "Inside the kingdom of night, I witnessed a strange trial. Three rabbis - all erudite and pious men - decided one winter evening to indict God for allowing his children to be massacred. I remember: I was there, and I felt like crying. But there nobody cried." As the play moves along, only a single individual can be found who is ready and willing to serve as Defense

Attorney for God. Out of thoughtfulness for those of you who have
not yet read the play, I shan't reveal that party's true identity.
I tell you only his name, his assumed name. It is Sam. The burden
of Sam's argument is this: While the events are not to be disputed,
they are irrelevant. For who is to blame for them? Human beings,
and human beings alone. Why implicate God? God's ways are just and
beyond reproach. Our duty is simple: to glorify him, to love him -
in spite of ourselves. But the Prosecutor argues that if our truth
is not God's as well, then God is beneath contempt - for giving us
the taste and passion of truth without apprising us that such truth
is in fact false. God may very well persist in his destructive
ways. This does not mean that we have to give our approval. "Let
Him crush me, I won't say Kaddish. Let Him kill me, let Him kill us
all, I shall shout and shout that it's His fault." Let the priests
chatter on about God's suffering. He is big enough to take care of
himself. We do better to pity other human beings - this from the
Prosecutor.

It is not an accident that the "death of God" thinking should
have historically succeeded the Holocaust. Berkovits (1976) concludes that within the dimension of time and history, the ways of
God are simply unforgivable. If convincing, this finding demands an
inversion of various biblical passages. Of Amos 3:2: "You only have
we known of all the reputed gods of earth; therefore, we will punish
you for all your iniquities." Of Hosea 1:9: "You are not our God
and we will not be your people." Of Hosea 14:1: "Return, O God, to
Israel your people, for you have fallen by your iniquity."

Jesus of Nazareth said: "If you are offering your gift at the
altar, and there remember that your brother has something against
you, leave your gift there before the altar and go; first be reconciled to your brother, and then come and offer your gift" (Matt.
5:23-24). Marvelous! - except when we have already murdered our
brother, in which case there is no longer a way to be reconciled to
him.

And God? Forgiveness for the transgressions of God may be possible if he can still somehow manage to leave his gifts at the altar
and go and be reconciled to his human children. He has sinned
against life, and life can only be vindicated through life. God has
one chance left to be saved. He must do two things: seek human forgiveness, and act to redeem himself. In Wiesel's work Souls on Fire
(1972, p. 107), Rabbi Levi-Yitzhak reminds God that he had better
ask forgiveness for the hardships he has inflicted upon his children. This is why, so the tale goes, the phrase Yom Kippur appears
also in the plural Yom Kippurim: "the request for pardon is recipro-
cal." Second, God is obligated - no, he is commanded - to redeem
the victims of the Shoah by raising them to eternal life with him.
This tells us that the final disposition of the trial of God rests
upon the future of God. In the meanwhile, as a teacher of Wiesel
once said to him, "Only the Jew knows that he may oppose God, so
long as he does so in defense of God's creation." (Perhaps the
Christian is eligible for a parallel calling. For only the

Christian knows that he may oppose Jesus Christ, so long as he does so in defense of Jesus' own people.)

A PRAYER FOR GOD

In his powerful oeuvre upon the Holocaust called The Tremendum, Arthur A. Cohen (1981) brings honor to those who are aware of the abyss of the tremendum in all its horror, yet whose own being "is elsewhere - on the bridge, in fact, over the abyss." The complication is that bridges point in opposite directions. Which direction is to be ours?

Wiesel's Trial of God is set on the Feast of Purim, an occasion when the innkeeper Berish (the very fellow who plays the role of Prosecutor), observes that "everything goes." And we are all to wear masks on the journey, since Purim is a day for fools, children, and beggars. Perhaps, then, we can still play together.

In The Gates of the Forest (Wiesel, 1967, p. 196), the dancing and singing of a certain Hasid remain his way of telling God: "You don't want me to dance; too bad. I'll dance anyhow. You've taken away every reason for singing, but I shall sing. I shall sing of the deceit that walks by day and the truth that walks by night, yes, and of the silence of dusk as well. You didn't expect my joy, but here it is; yes, my joy will rise up; it will submerge you."

The one direction of the bridge thus ends in a blind alley. The playing, the singing, the dancing, the joking - none can any longer be done for the sake of joy, not even the joy of Tel Aviv, but only on behalf of outrage, of defiance. As Julian Green said, "After Auschwitz, only tears can have meaning." The rebbe who tells the story of the singing and dancing Hasid admits that the song merely cloaks "a dagger, an outcry." The humor and the joy fall upon their own swords. And, worse, the Feast of Purim is powerless before the ice-hot awareness that should the unforgivability of forgiveness ever become the final word, despair will in a single moment gain dominion over all reality, and each and every human life in each and every time will become a ghastly thing. The visit by the character Gregor to the story-telling rebbe climaxes in a piteous request. "Rabbi, make me able to cry" (Wiesel, 1969, p. 197). Reinhold Niebuhr (1916, p. 112) was not a Jew. Yet he was a Jew, for he knew well that while laughter may be heard "in the outer courts" of religious faith, no mirth is allowed "in the holy of holies."

But yet, laughter can manage at least to get us to the door that leads to forgiveness. As Cullen Hightower (Corn, 1982) has written, "There are people who can talk sensibly about a controversial issue without taking sides; they are called humorists." In authentic humor we all, in a way, stand forgiven. Let us, therefore, not wholly abandon the way of Purim.

Rabbi Abraham J. Heschel (1962, p. 92) has spoken of the "overwhelming sympathy with the divine pathos" that the prophet Isaiah developed. Why not put on, then, the mask of Isaiah? The play's the thing: no one can stop us. Contrary to Berish the Prosecutor, to be sorry for God and for human beings is never an either-or: the two sustain each other. For me, the penultimate height of faith - not the final height, for that would be redemption, the reconciliation of humankind and God - the penultimate height of faith is to find oneself genuinely sorry for God.

In the Woody Allen film Love and Death, Boris Grushenko claimed that the worst thing we can say theologically is that God is an underachiever. Boris failed to go far enough. The worst thing we can say (and, for that very reason, as well as in the name of the death chambers of the Shoah, we have to say it) is that God is a klutz - the ultimate klutz - so much so that he has got himself strung out upon a cross that is never going to be taken down. He would have to go and make himself a world! Now he is stuck with it and with us, and he is left with no choice but to keep on undergoing the agony of it. For no divine sin is possible without human beings (just as no human sin could ever eventuate apart from God). By revealing and making normative for humankind certain apodictic requirements, God has only opened the way to being held strictly to account by the identical requirements. If all this is not the height of klutzyness, I do not know what is. The Creator of all the universes made radically vulnerable - and under his very own sponsorship!

Is there anybody around who is willing to attend to the anguish of God, and to give him comfort there upon his cross? We humans may not amount to very much, and we are tiny nothings in all the terrifying vastness, but we can at least manage that. Someone ought to go to the side of the eternal victim. If no one will come forward, all of existence is just a dreadful thing.

So: God is absolutely unforgivable - and we forgive him, absolutely. Bonhoeffer (1959) taught that God does not appreciate "cheap grace." Yet maybe we do - or we can - when it comes to God. Does that make us inferior to God? Well, it does not make us superior: it is not we who originated forgiveness. Forgiveness is a gift - from the beyond. And if it is so that on the day of Purim our grace is forced to go for cheap - to go, indeed, for no price at all - it is because all the available currency has been consumed in the flames of the Shoah.

Why are we to forgive the unforgivable God, and without any price and without any conditions? For no reason. Were there a reason, the Feast would be spoiled, the party would be over. And besides, there can be no reason to forgive God, not after the Shoah. However, there can be justification for doing so: Does not God yearn that we be free? As Paul Tillich (1977, p. 6) has it, "a person experiences an unconditional demand only from another person. The demand becomes concrete in the 'I-Thou' encounter. The content of the demand is therefore that the 'thou' be accorded the same dignity as the 'I' [and, we add, that the 'I' be accorded the same dignity as the 'thou']; this is the dignity of being free...This recognition of the equal dignity of the 'Thou' and the 'I' is justice...<u>Justice is the true power of being</u>." Or - can we not substitute? - "<u>love is the true power of being</u>," for at this place love and justice appear as one, within the praxis of a most strange equality.

The very prophet who knew sorrow for God claimed that "the holy God proves himself holy by righteousness" (Isa. 5:16). On the assumption that the <u>imago dei</u> and the <u>imitatio dei</u> somehow converge here, human beings too prove themselves holy by righteousness. But righteousness never comes finally into its own until it is forgiven, until everyone begins to smile and then breaks into laughter. Thus is the righteousness of God itself set free. Love between God and humankind is <u>always</u> having to say we are sorry. In this way we are empowered to do a last inversion of Scripture. Hosea 11:8: "How can we give you up, O God!" And Psalm 130:34:

If thou, O humanity, shouldst mark iniquities,
Humanity, who could stand?
But there is forgiveness with thee...

I have heard it said that at the conclusion of one of the many trials of God, after the accused had been adjudged guilty as charged, a certain Hasid stood before the assembly and said: "Let us pray." And it is further told, at the close of <u>The Gates of the Forest</u> (Wiesel, 1967, p. 223), that Gregor, whose <u>real identity</u> was that of Gavriel but whose faith had been carried off in the transports to the East, came to pray. He prayed for, among others, the soul of his father, and he prayed as well for the soul of God.

REFERENCES

BERKOVITS, Eliezer. The hiding God of history. In Yisrael Gutman & Livia Rothkirchen (Eds.), <u>The Catastrophe of European Jewry: Antecedents - History - Reflections</u>. Jerusalem: Yad Vashem, 1976, pp. 684-704.
BONHOEFFER, Dietrich. <u>The Cost of Discipleship</u>, trans. R. H. Fuller & Irmgard Booth. London: SCM Press, 1959.
COHEN, Arthur A. <u>The Tremendum: A Theological Interpretation of the Holocaust</u>. New York: Crossroad, 1981.
CORN, Ira. <u>The Globe Times</u>, Bethlehem, Pa., January 20, 1982.
ECKARDT, A. Roy. <u>Your People, My People: The Meeting of Jews and Christians</u>. New York: Quandrangle/New York Times, 1974.
FACKENHEIM, Emil L. <u>The Jewish Return Into History: Reflections in the Age of Auschwitz and a New Jerusalem</u>. New York: Schocken, 1978.
FACKENHEIM, Emil L. Open discussion on "Thinking About the Holocaust," International Scholars Conference Devoted to Historiographical and Theological Questions, Indiana University, Bloomington, Indiana, November 3-5, 1980.
GREENBERG, Irving. Cloud of smoke, pillar of fire: Judaism, Christianity, and modernity after the Holocaust. In Eva Fleischner (Ed.), <u>Auschwitz: Beginning of a New Era? Reflections on the Holocaust</u>. New York: Ktav, 1977, pp. 7-55.

264

GREENBERG, Irving. On the Third Era in Jewish History: Power and Politics. New York: National Jewish Resource Center, 1980.
HESCHEL, Abraham J. The Prophets, Vol. I. New York: Harper & Row, 1962.
LITTELL, Franklin H. A milestone in post-Holocaust church teaching. Christian News from Israel, 1980, 27, 113-116.
MOLTMANN, Jurgen. The Trinity and the Kingdom: The Doctrine of God. San Francisco: Harper & Row, 1981.
NIEBUHR, Reinhold. Discerning the Signs of the Times. New York: Scribner, 1946.
PANNENBERG, Wolfhart. Jesus - God and Man, trans. Lewis Wilkins & Duane A. Priebe. Philadelphia: Westminster, 1968.
REITLINGER, Gerald. The Final Solution: The Attempt to Exterminate the Jews of Europe 1939-1945. New York: A. S. Barnes, 1961.
ROSENSAFT, Menachem. Symposium on Jewish values in the post Holocaust future. Judaism, 1967, 16, 266-299.
RUETHER, Rosemary. Faith and Fratricide: The Theological Roots of Anti-Semitism. New York: Seabury, 1974.
SCHERMAN, Nosson. An understanding of the Holocaust in the light of the 'Sparks of Glory,' London, Jewish Observer, 1974, 9.
SIMON, Ulrich. Theology of Auschwitz. London: SPCK, 1978.
TILLICH, Paul. The Socialist Decision, trans. Franklin Sherman. New York: Harper & Row, 1977.
WIESEL, Elie. The Gates of the Forest, trans. Frances Frenaye. New York: Avon, 1967.
WIESEL, Elie. A Beggar in Jerusalem, trans. Lily Edelman & author. New York: Random House, 1970.
WIESEL, Elie. Souls on Fire, trans. Marion Wiesel. New York: Random House, 1972.
WIESEL, Elie. The Trial of God, trans. Marion Wiesel. New York: Random House, 1979.
WILLIS, Robert E. Christian theology after Auschwitz. Journal Ecumenical Studies, 1975, 12, 493-519.

A. ROY ECKARDT, Ph.D., Lehigh University, Maginnes Hall 9, Bethlehem Pennsylvannia 18015, U.S.A.

23. Holocaust: The Pedagogy of Paradox

Alan L. Berger

Alan L. Berger, Department of Religion, chairs the interdisciplinary Jewish Studies Program at Syracuse University.

My ongoing concern in studying and teaching the Holocaust is to educate students so that they may be prepared to move away from the edge of destruction. As such I strive to achieve not only an awareness of facts of the catastrophe, but to instill a sense of personal obligation for preventing its repetition. I view the university as having the moral obligation to defend against the collapse of civilization. Being married to an Israeli child of a survivor, and having children, intensifies my commitment to the perpetuation of the Jewish and human community.

Speaking in Tel Aviv on the eve of the destruction of European Jewry, Martin Buber, (1954) distressed at the "slavery of collectives" into which mankind had fallen, addressed the central paradox of education in modernity. He observed "It is an idle undertaking to call out, to a mankind that has grown blind to eternity: 'Look - the eternal values!'" (p. 110).

Although Buber's 1939 despair could not have imagined that the "Final Solution" to the "Jewish Problem" would mean the murder of six million Jews for the crime of existing, paradox is perhaps the only way to approach the abyss of Holocaust. The confusion of human freedom with divine imperatives had set the stage for mass ideological murder unequaled in history.

Paradox must be understood in a number of senses.

There is the paradox concerning whether one can or should speak at all of the slaughter. Not only is the adequacy of language severely undermined, but Auschwitz ends where it began, by denying the existence of a rational purpose and a transcendent meaning to life. Elie Wiesel (1977, p. 7), has observed that "He or she who did not live through the event will never reveal it. Not entirely. Not really." Yet one must bear witness. The obligation of the survivor is to testify. Silence and speech are the contradictory demands issuing from the death camps.

There is the paradox of education itself contributing to mass murder. Franklin Littell (1980) notes that "the death camps were built by Ph.D.s." The modern university is, he argues, facing a "credibility crisis" (p. 271). There is also the question of whether pedagogy can treat paradox. Has loss of access to the transcendent (Buber's "eternal values") restricted the vision of university education?

This essay is concerned with the paradox of education's involvement in murder, and suggests ways in which pedagogy can refrain from resorting to destruction. The questions of today dwarf Buber's pre-Holocaust anxiety. Do universities critique or mirror society? Can values be taught? Are there remedies for the millenial and destructive forms of antisemitism, and all other forms of hatred? Is teaching a job or a calling? What lessons should higher education be teaching about murder of Jews in particular and about the age of administrative mass murder in general?

THE HOLOCAUST AND WESTERN CIVILIZATION

Teaching and learning about the Holocaust also involve recognizing the paradoxical relationship existing between Judaism and Western Civilization. Ideological and moral shapers of western culture, Jews have frequently been put to the sword in the name of that culture. Yet the survival of both Judaism and Western Civilization depend one upon the other. Concerning Holocaust specificity, Elie Wiesel observes, "Not every victim was a Jew, but all Jews were victims" (Eckardt, 1980, p. 131). The Nazi murder machine, while involving others, was designed specifically for the Jews. This is a fact which some people who come after the Nazis are unable to grasp with the tenacity which the murderers themselves displayed. One example, Heinrich Himmler, observing a "liquidation," which he personally ordered, saw a blond-haired, blue-eyed youth of twenty in the condemned group.

> Just before the firing was to begin, Himmler walked
> up to the doomed man and put a few questions to him
> Are you a Jew?
> Yes.
> Are both your parents Jews?
> Yes.
> Do you have any ancestors who are not Jews?
> No.
> Then I can't help you. (Hilberg, 1917, p. 218).

Those who cannot fathom Jewish specificity but rest contentedly with abstractions such as mankind in general and the universal brotherhood of man must be confronted with the evidence.

At the same time, clearly the Holocaust has universal implications. If the Jews are Abel, the murdered brother, what of the murderers? Wiesel writes that "It was its own heart the world incinerated at Auschwitz" (1968, p. 190). Auschwitz inaugurated the age of mass bureaucratically-administered death, and mass indifference. "The Holocaust was the beginning of an era, an era of turmoil and upheaval, of irrationality and madness..." (Donat, p. 43).

Holocaust pedagogy confronts a further paradox. Either the murder of the Jews in the heart of Western culture shattered all interpretive categories and requires new modes of teaching and learning, a transformation of the educational enterprise itself - which has not as yet occurred - or the modern university, with its stress on value-free performance and technical proficiency, combined with the inherently conservative nature of education, is in the service of the devil.

MURDER AND CULTURE

One must confront the relationship of the Holocaust to the modern university.

Problem-solving modes of education which stress solutions involve refinement of skills without ethical boundaries. These modes are inherently genocidal and clash with the notion of education as a moral or initiatory experience.

Has stress on scientific knowledge and technical competence (techne) overwhelmed the prior goal of wisdom (sophia, or in Littell's words, "even logos")? What is culture's attitude towards murder?

The Shattered Paradigm

Two very different responses deserve attention. First, there is what has been termed the "shattered paradigm" approach Greenberg, 1979, p. 13). Wiesel is its leading spokesman.

Auschwitz signifies death - total, absolute death - of man and of mankind, of reason and of the heart, of language and of the senses. Auschwitz is the death of time, the end of creation (1979, p. 234).

For Wiesel the death camps signal that the covenant itself has been broken, and must be reforged. Irving Greenberg extends the shattered paradigm argument to include the secular humanist understanding of the world. He writes:

There is the shock of recognition that the humanistic revolt, celebrated as the liberation of humankind in freeing humans from centuries of dependence upon God and nature, is now revealed - at the very heart of the enterprise - to sustain a capacity for death and demonic evil (1975, p. 535).

This approach may be summarized as follows. Cherished assumptions must be rigorously scrutinized and where necessary - which is almost everywhere - abandoned as morally, politically, and theologically bankrupt. Modernity and its blandishments: academicization, bureaucratization, intellectualism, Jewish-Christian relations, scientism, technism, "no-fault" ethics and contextual morality, in short, so much of the human enterprise of the last three centuries is radically called into question.

The "shattered paradigm" view casts a long shadow over modern education. The unstated but omnipresent assumption of this view is that education serves to critique societal practices, striving for what one scholar has felicitously termed "mature iconoclasm" (Friedlander, 1979, p. 533); that values can and should be taught and that these values are ethically enriching and morally superior to the prevailing political climate; that a teacher is an ethical exemplar in deeds as well as in words; and that there was a massive pedagogical failure in modernity.

The Fulfillment of Civilization

Certain other students of the Holocaust suggest the contrary. The murder of one third of the world's Jewish people may legitimately be viewed as the "fulfillment" of Western Civilization. Hilberg's magisterial work tenaciously advances the thesis that a modern state possessing the technological skills, the bureaucratic infrastructure, and the will to exterminate a minority is literally unstoppable. The repercussions of mass murder are, moreover, ominous for the future of mankind. He writes:

A primordial impulse had suddenly surfaced among the Western nations; it had been unfettered through their machines. From this moment, fundamental assumptions about our civilization have no longer stood unchallenged, for while the occurrence is past, the phenomenon remains (1967, p. 760).

The "fulfillment" position is advanced in a lucid and provocative manner by Richard Rubenstein. He notes that the modern is, in his view, functionally godless and that dignity and rights depend solely upon power. Consequently, for Rubenstein:

The Holocaust bears witness to the advance of civilization - to the point at which large scale massacre is no longer a crime and the state's sovereign powers are such that millions can be stripped of their rights and condemned...(1978, p. 91).

This interpretation of murder builds upon the Weberian notion that history is an "Iron Cage" which leads inexorably to entrapment in rationalization while eliminating options of creativity and freedom. The creeping bureaucratization is an historical process from which the university is hardly immune, and it means that there is no provision for dissent from centrally directed policy. Nor is there a higher moral order to which appeal can be made for the righting of wrongs. In Rubenstein's words: "No cold-blooded contemporary David need worry about a modern Nathan the Prophet proclaiming the ultimacy of God's law" (p. 91). Society, in this view, cannot and will not tolerate the possibility of living either with religious or political pluralism.

The educational implications of "fulfillment" are no less ominous than those raised by the "shattered paradigm" position. Values consist of duty to the state as opposed to the obligations of conscience. There is no contradiction between civilization and extermination for those in the "fulfillment" camp.

THE COMPLICITY OF THE UNIVERSITY

The ideal of education must be to make the world a better place, to humanize its inhabitants, and to remember that, in Buber's words, "Education worthy of the name is essentially education of character" (1954, p. 104). This goal applies to the theoretical scientist no less than to the humanist. If, however, one enquires into the role of university-trained people, we find that university academics, first, aided and abetted the Holocaust and, second, ignored its lessons and denied its existence.

Under Nazi patronage research institutes were established and Ph.D. dissertations were written justifying destruction of the Jews. Heinrich von Treitschke, a nineteenth-century Professor of History at the University of Berlin, coined the infamous phrase "The Jews are our misfortune" (Die Juden sind unser Ungluck). Twentieth-century academic elites lent their prestige to Nazi Jew-hatred with a passion far exceeding that of von Trietschke. Max Weinrich's (1946) Hitler's Professors chronicles the sad tale of academic collusion with Hitler. Among those eagerly joining the Nazi bandwagon were Nobel laureates in physics, men of the social sciences, and historians. Especially prominent in the murderers' camp were the disciplines of physical anthropology, biology, and law. Nazi pseudo-racial institutes worked tirelessly against the Jews. For example, Weinrich cites the official policy of the Reichsinstitut as follows:

> German scholarship is a struggle against World Judaism! Just as the outrage of World Judaism was followed by the political and economic counterblow of the Reich, so in scholarship there will be a reply in that we continue to strengthen the anti-Jewish wing of our research work (p. 56).

University complicity in mass murder is a complex phenomenon. Littell (1980) for example, traces the shift from thirteenth-century universitas - a community (Gemeinschaft) of enquirers - to the twentieth-century specialized, research-centered multiversity (pp. 276-278). Symbolically, the modern university came into being, Littell argues, with the "triumph of the von Humboldt schemata of learning" in Europe (1809) and the Morrill Land Act of 1862 in America (p. 78). But what needs stressing is the underlying and tacit assumption of the professionalization of education: Universities reflect rather than critique societal interests.

Modernity has uncritically accepted a scientistic attitude: the premise that science and the scientific method are all that is required to improve the world. Coupled with this is the ease with which academics and intellectuals have gone into the service of tyranny (Berger, 1982). The predominance of scientism is a modern phenomenon resulting from a deteriorating understanding of science. Scientism is an incorrect belief that the scientific method itself yields all truths worth knowing. Its basic confusion is in thinking that science is synonomous with both culture and truth. There is a serious lack of clarity in modern university teaching reflecting society's confusion of means and ends, technology and culture, and knowledge and wisdom. For cut off from any notion of transcendence, scientism limits man's spiritual awareness while increasing his brazen temporal powers.

A related phenomenon is the use of language which has no moral bottom line. Language is the bearer, reflection and defense of culture. As such, it shares culture's need for an ethical dimension. But culture in modernity has become distorted. For example, in their manipulation of language, the Nazis camouflaged their murdering by resorting to bureaucratic code words. Murder was called by many names: Aktion (rounding up and, usually, murdering Jews), Sonderbehandlung (special treatment - murder), Liquidieren (liquidate), Umsiedeln (resettle), Sonderkommandos (special commandos who did the killings). Friedlander (1980, p. 110) observes that "the SS liquidated human beings the way others liquidate a business." The ease with which German culture, the flower of Western Civilization and heart of Christian Europe, metamorphized into the largest single mass murder machine in history is both example and warning.

UNIVERSITIES AS ANTI-LIFE: THE EUTHANASIA OF MENTAL PATIENTS

The anguish and moral confusion of our age is illustrated by the gap between technical skills and human values. Enshrined as a standard and taught as a value in and of itself by universities, this dichotomy has contributed to the deaths of millions. For example, a book (little known in America), which had much to do with rationalizing murder, authored by two university professors, Karl Binding (Jurisprudence) and Alfred Hoche (Psychiatry), was Die Freigabe der Vernichtung Lebenswerten Lebens: Ihr Mass und ihre Form. Appearing in 1920, the work spoke of "life devoid of value." It argued for euthanasia - which under the Nazis meant murderous pseudo-racial eugenics on utilitarian grounds. Care of the mentally retarded prevented thousands of medical and administrative personnel from doing "productive work." Physicians were henceforth to be encouraged to reverse their traditional roles; from preservers they became destroyers of life. The book was cited by defendants at the Nuremberg Trials who had participated in so-called medical experiments on Jewish prisoners in the death camps.

Murder of mentally retarded patients soon expanded to become murder of other categories of people; those with behavior problems, those with unusual physical characteristics, and others (Wolfensberger, 1981). These murders were performed by physicians, psychiatrists, and other university educated elite. Modern universities readily embraced necrophiliac activities. Seminars were held at the University of Heidelberg which dealt with means of improving the killing process. Participation in the murder program was voluntary and readily embraced. Professionals viewed this as an opportunity to showcase their skills while remaining insensitive to the sanctity of life. For example, it is reported that:

> Upon the extermination of the ten thousandth mental patient at the Hadamar Psychiatric Institution in 1941, a big celebration was held in which psychiatrists, nurses, attendants, and secretaries all participated and free drinks were provided (Wertham, 1966, p. 157).

Euthanasia was, in reality, cold-blooded murder, and it exemplifies the danger of scientism. It was mass murder, however, it was not the Holocaust. The Nazis ceased murdering their own citizens when protests began to mount from neighbors, friends and clergy. For the Jews there was no such protest.

MORAL EDUCATION AND THE HOLOCAUST

There is an inherent conflict between the moral role of education and the educational premise of the modern university whose search for solutions to problems is undertaken in a value-free environment. Questions, constantly asked and refined, are the hallmarks of moral education. Answers, frequently posited in an ethical vacuum, denote modernity. The modern university prides itself on searching for solutions to problems.

On the positive side, certain problems have proven themselves amenable to solving. For example, cures for disease, the eradication of hunger and ignorance, and the lessening of suffering fall into this category. But there is a terrible dark side of this phenomenon. Polarities must be reduced and then dissolved rather than embraced.

The Holocaust, in fact, leaves one with questions which overwhelm all attempts at response: Why did the highest levels of Christian leadership keep silent while Jews were being murdered in the millions? Why was the West apathetic - then and now? Where was God? Where was man? What would I have done in the ghettos and in the death camps? Answers deceive by their simplicity. They are too tidy, and tend to relieve us of the obligation of looking into the abyss. Greenberg has posed the ultimate moral litmus test for any attempt at answering the whys of the Holocaust: "No statement should be made that would not be credible in the presence of the the burning children" (1975, p. 529). Wiesel, for his part, insists that questions are all that may morally be permitted to man in the Age of Auschwitz.

> I have nothing against questions. They are useful. What is more, they alone are. To turn away from them would be to fail in our duty, to lose our only chance to be able one day to lead an authentic life. It is against answers that I protest, regardless of their basis. Answers: I say there are none (1968, pp. 181-182).

Answers signify the completion of a task. In our time, answers kill. Questions indicate that more enquiry is necessary.

University education appears weakest at the point which requires greatest strength - communication and demonstration of the necessity of a "universe of obligation" which embraces all citizens. The research of Helen Fein (1979) shows that only where Jews were included in this universe did their fellow citizens refrain from assisting Nazis. But how is it possible to teach compassion or responsiveness to one's neighbors, acquaintances, or especially to strangers? Buber warns of the dilemma involved in attempting to teach values without stressing character. "The worst habitual liar of the class," he notes, "produces a brilliant essay on the destructive power of lying" (1954, p. 105). Inability to empathize, to involve oneself in the human dimensions of mass murder leads to cynical indifference and grotesque forms of classification which blur the distinction between degrees of evil, and dishonors the memory of the dead. Pedagogy displays an urge towards such utterances in its taxonomical excess. For example, the social scientific typology of "retributive," "utilitarian," and "optimal" genocide loses touch with the human dimension of suffering and death. What, one wonders, is an "optimal" genocide? Is there not a different mode of educating which will assist not only in confronting the Holocaust but, equally as significant, in attempting to avoid its repetition?

OTHER MODELS: THE PEDAGOGY OF PARADOX

If the past is ignored, the future is condemned. Taalat Bey spoke of solving the "Armenian Problem" forty years before Hitler's final solution of the "Jewish Problem." We are, therefore, compelled to seek guidelines from those who have preceded us which may aid in moving away from the edge of destruction. While our technology has become increasingly sophisticated and deadly, there has been no accompanying upward spiral of human understanding. Skills of death far exceed skills of life. Living creatively and reverentially with paradox appears to be the only alternative to the death of mankind. There are two examples of paradox-sustaining cultures which deserve attention:

Archaic Hunting Cultures

Archaic hunting cultures worshipped a "Master of Animals" who protected the game as well as aiding the hunter. In a religious ethos, hunting could only be conducted according to specified ritual. There was a limit to the number of animals which were to be killed. Prior to the hunt, prayers were offered to the "Master of Animals." These petitionary utterances sought the deity's assistance in the upcoming hunt while simultaneously expressing the hunter's regret at having to kill. Eichmann's statement was otherwise, that he could jump laughing into his grave knowing that he had killed five million Jews. After the hunt, prayers were again offered, and

elaborate rituals effected whose goal was the regeneration of the
animal. Frequently the animal's bones were placed in a tree or on a
hill or other high place in hopes of assisting its rebirth. In no
case was the hunting party permitted to take more than the number of
animals needed for sustenance. It is a process unlike the situation
where prior to the dropping of the atomic bomb, a clergyman prayed
for God's blessing upon the crew for their safe return, and no mention was made of those about to become the first victims of the Atomic Age (Wertham, 1966, p. 368).

The pedagogy of hunting cultures is transmitted by elders and
shamans as sacred lore. Education in the tribal ethos is initiatory. Degrees were not granted, but the initiate's ontological status was elevated. Myth and ritual were employed to describe the
flowing and open-ended relationship between man and the divine. It
is no small irony that today the last remnants of hunting cultures
are being eradicated in the name of progress and civilization (road
building, construction, mineral exploration and the like). (See
Kuper, 1982, in his comprehensive book on genocide).

Rabbinic-Culture

Classical rabbinic culture embraced paradox in the form of midrash. Derived from the root drosh meaning "to search," "to seek,"
"to examine," "to investigate," midrash is dialectical; it recognizes that contraries must be affirmed in their separateness while
seeking to penetrate beyond and beneath literal textual meanings.
Emil Fackenheim (1970) argues that the Midrashic Framework preserves, by reflecting upon root experiences of Jewish historical existence as those in which God operates. This framework requires
that Jews live in history while simultaneously affirming that redemption will occur, "even though Messiah may tarry." Underlying
the midrashic approach is a belief that solutions to seemingly in-
solvable dilemmas will occur in the messianic age. Midrashic
thought is both fragmentary and whole.

Midrashic pedagogy involves story, parable, and metaphor. Non-
systematic in nature, this type of expression aims at comprehensive-
ness while allowing for diversity. Concerning the relationship between midrash and catastrophe, Fackenheim examines several possibilities, viz., midrashim of protest, midrashim of divine powerlessness,
and the eclipse of God. Ultimately however.

Jewish thought at its deepest level, especially vis-a-vis catastrophe, does not express itself in explanatory systems but
rather in conflicting midrashim, the goal of which is not how
to explain God, but how to live with Him (1977, p. 211).

Specifically concerning the Holocaust, Fackenheim radicalizes the
midrashic framework. He writes, "...to find a meaning in the Holocaust is impossible, but to seek a response is inescapable" (1977,
p. 211).

I offer these as examples of the possibilities of living with and teaching paradox. Our culture is neither archaic nor classical but technological and Post-Modern. While we cannot return to that which is not ours, we can learn from authentic responses to human experiences which have proven decisive. Two of the most promising contemporary responses to the Holocaust base themselves upon paradox and dialectic.

Contemporary Pedagogies of Paradox

Contemporary attempts at living with paradox are embodied in the literary works of Wiesel and in Greenberg's theology of "moment faith." Wiesel expresses the paradoxical nature of Holocaust response throughout his literary corpus and in his essays. He embraces the central kabbalistic paradox that God is a savior in need of salvation, but reshapes the sixteenth-century reply in face of the enormity of the twentieth-century crime.

> Yes, man is very strong, greater than God. When You were deceived by Adam and Eve, You drove them out of Paradise. When Noah's generation displeased You, You brought down the Flood. When Sodom no longer found favor in Your eyes, You made the sky rain down fire and sulphur. But these men here (Jews in the death camps), whom you have betrayed, whom You have allowed to be tortured, butchered, gassed, burned, what do they? They pray before You! They praise Your name! (1969, pp. 78-79).

Wiesel's view is best summarized in his response to Rubenstein's "death of God" position. Referring to the latter's "answer" to the Holocaust, Wiesel grants the pain that Rubenstein feels. It is difficult and traumatic to live in a world without the possibility of God. But, argues Wiesel, living as a believer poses far greater burdens.

> And here I will tell you, Dick, that you don't understand them (the victims) when you say that it is more difficult to live today in a world without God. NO! if you want difficulties, choose to live with God. Can you compare today the tragedy of the believer to that of the nonbeliever?! The real tragedy, the real drama is the drama of the believer (1974, p. 274).

Wiesel's protest against God is made within the midrashic framework, and sets him firmly in the Jewish tradition of protest.

Greenberg maintains that only a dialectical or "moment faith" is tenable after Auschwitz. He rejects classical theism (Eliezer Berkovitz) and atheism (Rubeinstein) because both positions provide answers which subsume the Holocaust under extant categories. Moreover, "After the Holocaust," writes Greenberg, "there should be no final solution, even theological ones." On the contrary, moment faith moves between hope and history, between "...moments when Redeemer and vision of redemption are present, interspersed with times when the flames and smoke of the burning children blot out faith though it flickers again" (1975, pp. 533-534). The pedagogical value of "moment faithful" dialectics is its "ability to live with pluralism, and without resorting to the self-flattering, ethnocentric solutions which warp religion or make it a source of hatred for the other" (p. 535).

These examples share an emphasis on openness to transcendence, and a stress on story, tale and parable. Moreover, provision is made for ritual which can transform even as it transmits.

The pedagogy of paradox demonstrates a willingness to accept the limitations of human existence and of culture. Simhah Bunem, the nineteenth century rebbe of Przysucha, observed that man should carry with him two slips of paper. On one is to be written, "For my sake was the world created." The other contains a different message "I am but dust and ashes." Modernity has erred in stressing the former in isolation from the latter. Pedagogy which is able to retain the tension or dialectic between these principles does not refrain from seeking meaning, but neither does it assume that the search is exhausted by any one mode of enquiry or that one may cease one's quest. The pedagogy of paradox reveres life and abhors idolatry - whether it be religious or political in nature. Education on this plane is character training, an initiatory experience which enlightens and illumines the initiate while simultaneously building community.

CONCLUSION: EDUCATION FOR THE SANCTITY OF LIFE

The minimum task of Holocaust pedagogy is also its ultimate goal: rediscovering the sanctity of life and the image of the divine which inheres in humanity. Universities need desperately to begin the work of recovering their spiritual health and institutional integrity. The reconstructive task means that pedagogy will cease what Buber termed its "obscuring of eternity" by focusing instead upon human responsibility. Death camps and crematoria bear horrendous witness to the truth that imaginative capacity which is not grounded in a firm sense of human obligation imperils life itself. Teaching the Holocaust means embracing both specificity and its universalistic implications. Because the Holocaust happened to a specific group, it means every group is threatened. The Jews have been history's lightening rod, but at the same time, as in Yehuda Bauer's query, "Who knows who the 'Jews' will be next time?" (1978, p. 49). Authentic universalizing involves understanding the danger of stereotypical thinking, emphasizing the perils of making certain human life "more valuable" than others, the necessity of participation in the political process, and the realization that there is no inherent conflict between culture and murder.

Technology, hatred, and ignorance combine to make the world increasingly susceptible to final solutions. Two of America's top technical schools (M.I.T. and Cal. Tech.) for example, offer no courses on either the Holocaust or genocides. Debasement of the sciences continues in a more subtle but no less dangerous manner. Holocaust pedagogy shoulders responsibility for the present and the

future, no less than bearing the weight of the past. Universities
may not be able to defuse the massive threat to human existence, but
they are under moral obligation to try. Earlier in this century,
Hitler accurately claimed that no one spoke of the Turkish genocide
of the Armenians and that no one would protest the killing of the
Jews. No less significant are the so-called little things to which
insufficient attention is paid. For example, Wiesel reports in
Night his father's reply to the decree requiring every Jew to wear
the yellow star: "The yellow star? Oh well, what of it? You don't
die of it..." (1969, p. 20). "Poor Father!," observes Wiesel, "Of
what then did you die?"

Exposing absolutism and literalism as idolatries, pedagogy can
educate for life rather than acquiesing in death. Educators need to
keep their ears, and those of their students, attuned to academic
and societal liturgy, to story, and to ritual. More than imparting
any specific vocational skills or technical competence, pedagogy in
the Age of Auschwitz is obliged to heighten moral awareness and ethical responsibility. The pedagogy of paradox is instanced by what
Wiesel has termed moral madness: an attempt at sanity, caring, and
nurturing in a world gone awry with mass indifference, dictatorships, mendacity, and weapons of death. Those who approach the
Holocaust in this manner may derive sustenance from the midrashic
admonition: "It is not your duty to complete the task, yet you are
not free to desist from it."

REFERENCES

BAUER, Yehuda. The Holocaust in Historical Perspective. Seattle:
University Washington Press, 1978.
BERGER, Alan L. Academia and the Holocaust. Judaism, 1982, 31,
166-176.
BUBER, Martin. Between Man and Man. Trans. R. G. Smith. London:
Routledge & Kegan Paul, 1954.
DONAT, Alexander. A letter to my grandson. Midstream, 1970, 16,
41-45.
ECKARDT, A. Roy. Contemporary Christian theology and a Protestant
witness for the Shoah. Shoah, 1980, 2, 10-13.
FACKENHEIM, Emil. God's Presence in History. New York: New York
University Press. London: University London Press, 1970.
FACKENHEIM, Emil. The Holocaust and the State of Israel: their re-
lation. In Eva Fleischner (Ed.), Auschwitz: Beginning of a New Era?
New York: Ktav, 1977.
FEIN, Helen. Accounting for Genocide. New York: Free Press, 1979.
FRIEDLANDER, Henry. Toward a methodology of teaching about the
Holocaust. Teachers College Record, 1979, 80, 519-542.
FRIEDLANDER, Henry. The manipulation of language. In Henry
Friedlander, & Sybil Milton (Eds.), The Holocaust: Ideology, Bureau-
cracy, and Genocide. Millwood, New York: Kraus International Publi-
cations, 1980, pp. 103-114.
GREENBERG, Irving. Judaism and Christianity after the Holocaust.
Journal Ecumenical Studies, 1975, 12, 521-551.

GREENBERG, Irving. Polarity and perfection. Face to Face, 1979, VI, 12-14.

HILBERG, Raul. The Destruction of the European Jews. Chicago: Quadrangle Books, 1967.

KUPER, Leo. Genocide. New Haven and London: Yale University Press, 1982.

LITTELL, Franklin H. The credibility crisis of the modern university. In Henry Friedlander, & Sybil Milton (Eds.), Ibid, 271-283.

RUBENSTEIN, Richard L. The Cunning of History. New York: Harper Colophon Books, 1978.

WEINREICH, Max. Hitler's Professors. New York: Yivo, 1946.

WERTHAM, Frederic. A Sign For Cain. New York: Macmillan, 1966.

WIESEL, Elie. Legends of Our Time. New York: Holt, Rinehart & Winston, 1968.

WIESEL, Elie. Night. Trans. S. Rodway. New York: Avon, 1969.

WIESEL, Elie. Talking and writing and keeping silent. In Franklin H. Littell, & Hubert G. Locke (Eds.), The German Church Struggle and the Holocaust. Detroit: Wayne State University Press, 1974.

WIESEL, Elie. The Holocaust as literary inspiration. In Dimensions of the Holocaust. Evanston: Northwestern University, 1977.

WIESEL, Elie. A Jew Today. Trans. M. Wiesel. New York: Vintage Books, 1979.

WOLFENSBERGER, Wolf. The extermination of handicapped people in World War II Germany. Mental Retardation, 1981, 19, 1-7.

ALAN L. BERGER, Ph.D., Syracuse University, Syracuse, New York 13210, U.S.A.

Part V

Toward Intervention
and Prevention

24. Extrajudicial Executions, International Alerts and Campaigning

Daan Bronkhorst

Daan Bronkhorst (1953) is a human rights researcher in the Nether-lands. He started Amnesty International's first project on means to counteract extrajudicial executions and "disappearances" committed or condoned by governments. He organized Amnesty's International Conference on Extrajudicial Executions in May, 1982.

THE CONTINUING STORY

"We have won these great victories thanks to our decision to track down and liquidate enemies in a systematic way, uprooting their important organizations at the base level." The source for this quote is an internal Khmer Rouge directive, the context that of Democratic Kampuchea under Pol Pot (1975-79). In Kampuchea, the number of political killings initiated or condoned by the government certainly ran into over a million who died from malnutrition, starvation and disease as a result of the extremely crude policies of socialist construction implemented by the Khmer Rouge. The scale of the killings presents to the world a particular form of outrage that most people hoped had disappeared with Nazism after 1945. Despite the magnitude of the horrendous events, world reaction was grossly inadequate. Some would argue that this in part was caused by inadequate information at an early stage about the killings, and undoubtedly this factor has to be taken into consideration. The fundamental problem however was the absence of international mechanisms to confront mass political killings at an early stage.

On 27 June 1980, hundreds of prisoners were reported to have been killed by the Special Defence Units at Palmyra desert prison, Syria. According to several reports reaching Amnesty International, forces flew to Palmyra and shot the prisoners as they were emerging from the prison after they had been told they were being released. Other reports state it was part of a mass escape attempt, helped by a number of guards. Estimates of the number of prisoners killed vary from 300 to over 1,000. Most of them are believed to have been members of the Muslim Brotherhood. This massive scale extrajudicial execution received only little coverage in the international media. The same applies to other instances of mass scale political killing by the government, as in Aleppo (29 February 1980), Jisr al-Shugher (9 March 1980), and Hama (23 April 1981).

It was only some months after the event that reports began to leak out about hundreds of killings in May 1980 in El Salvador, when refugees, mainly women and children, were reportedly killed by Salvadorian troops as they tried to cross the Sampul River into Honduras. Honduran troops allegedly blocked the refugees' way. One survivor told AI: "We were attacked from all sides. Two helicopters

281

attacked us from the air and more than 500 National Guardsmen blocked all exits. During the attack, more than 25 people were machine-
gunned. When I entered the swollen river, I saw seven children who
had drowned being dragged downstream." According to a testimony by
local priests, the total number of deaths approached 600. These
deaths are only a fraction of the total toll of political violence
in El Salvador, estimated at some 12,000 for 1980 only. Of these,
at least some 80% can be tracked down to killings by official,
para-military or government condoned troops and "death squads."

A WORLDWIDE PHENOMENON

In the current vocabulary of human rights, there is no commonly
accepted name for the phenomenon of murder committed or acquiesced
in by governments. Amnesty International has opted for "extrajudicial executions," i.e., killings as a means of political persecution, unlawfully and deliberately carried out by governments or
with their complicity. Another term could be "political killings by
governments."

Murder committed or condoned by governments occur in a considerable number of countries with great variation in geographical,
political and ideological characteristics. According to a news release connected with the AI 1980 Annual Report, in the period under
review extrajudicial executions had been reported in more than
thirty countries. If a longer period of time is taken, this number
increases considerably. The scope of such killings is large. It
may include massive scale killings, as in the Red Terror period in
Ethiopia, Uganda under Amin, present day El Salvador and Guatemala,
or Indonesia after the alleged coup attempt. It may include death
in custody often after prolonged torture, as in Zaire, Afganistan,
Iraq and Turkey. It may include many cases of "disappeared"
persons, of whom sometimes the bodies are found, as in Argentina,
Bolivia, Mexico, East-Timor and the Philippines. It may include
targeted police brutality, as in Bangladesh, India and South Korea.

Also large is the scope of the victims of such killings: politicians and officials (Afghanistan, Uganda, Chile) students and
schoolchildren (Guetamala, Bolivia) religious officials, journalists, displaced persons, ethnic minorities, etc.

INTERNATIONAL ALERTS

In April 1982, the Dutch section of Amnesty International organized a conference to discuss remedies to counter this phenomenon.
The meeting which brought together more than 100 human rights
workers and specialists, issued a great number of recommendations in
the fields of fact finding and research, nongovernmental activities,
intergovernmental organizations and international law, and the international context of political, military, economic and cultural
relations.

One Working Party was especially oriented on the issues of research, fact-finding and the dissemination of information. It is the last of these three interconnected items especially that is of special relevance to the issue of early warning, intervention and prevention of genocide. The issue was summarized in the introduction of Israel Charny's paper for the conference: "Beyond the romantic and I fear blind belief that many of us have in the effectiveness of information as such - if people only know what is happening they will obviously take steps to stop violations of human rights and destruction of life - there are very serious problems in how best to communicate human rights informations to people in ways that invite, guide and facilitate taking stands and taking action on behalf of human rights."

Clearly, just to present the facts is not enough. Sometimes the facts are not accepted or believed, as was the case with many of the early refugees' testimonies on Democratic Kampuchea. Sometimes the facts are well known at least in circles of human rights organizations, but they do not really reach the international opinion by various mostly political constraints. This may have been the case with e.g., the Burundi massacres of 1972; and according to Walter Laqueur's The Terrible Secret, it certainly was the case regarding the Holocaust and the German concentration camps in the early years of the war. Sometimes the facts are widely known, but no effective action is undertaken. The Amin government in Uganda was known to commit genocide already in 1973, but the regime could continue to murder its own population until overthrown in 1979. Sometimes a lot of action is indeed undertaken internationally, but the effect seems to get lost in a game of international power, as we may say regarding El Salvador, Guatemala and Argentina.

As a human rights activist, one can hardly be optimistic on the short term effects of any information presented, any consciousness-raising activity undertaken or any international action appealed for. On the other hand, pessimism will clearly be of no avail to victims, much less to potential victims. The important thing then seems to be to analyze where we should start and how we should proceed.

The basic scheme for effective, or rather as effective as possible, action may well be simple and clear:

First, we need the facts.
Second, we have to present them.
Third, we have to mobilize an action potential.
Fourth, we should channel any action according to its effects, its benefits to the people involved and its feasibility.

The most important thing to realize would be that each step should not stand isolated, and that coordination and follow-up are of paramount importance.

Campaigning against mass scale killings committed by governments is evidently primarily of a preventive nature. To elaborate on systems of early international alerts is the logical start. But there are a number of problems connected with such alerts. The following short list mentions a few of these and tries to suggest clues to a solution:

1. What Are The Signs?

In the Dutch Conference, one of the Working Parties presented a list of 25 "symptoms" which might point to a potential situation for extrajudicial executions. These symptoms include secret places of detention, increase of grave violations of human rights, placement of known violators in high positions, the creation of irregular or paramilitary troops, the elimination of human rights organizations or advocates, etc. The list is far from exhaustive or systematic. But we do see, today, that such trends indeed appear to be realized. Speakers at the conference mentioned for example the creation of "death squads" in Honduras, the forced and violent migration programs in Uganda, the militarization of remote zones in Colombia and the many deaths among prisoners in Syria.

2. Which Sources?

Sources may be ranked according to their proven reliability, history of concern and their proximity to the incident reported. Of considerable reliability would be domestic human rights groups including church sponsored groups; survivors; relatives; lawyers and documentation arising from judicial actions. With more care, we could draw from sources such as journalists and diplomats. Official government statements, while probably of the lowest reliability, are important sources of information of which NGOs must be aware in order to be able to respond. The problem of sources may well be one of resources, e.g., the possibilities to interview refugees in-depth, support to domestic human rights groups in gathering information and setting up documentation, sending of fact-finding missions, etc.

3. How To Present Information?

On the one hand, there is the need for thoroughly researched documentation, coming up to the standards of a judicial inquiry. On the other hand, such information is far from adequate for campaigning purposes. Briefly stated, in a process of consciousness raising the issue is one of turning information into action. This implies that opportunities for such action should be made clear in the presentation of the material. As a simple rule of thumb we may say that each report on human rights situations should contain recommendations and appeals for action directed towards the readership intended.

4. To Whom Should Information Be Directed?

The obvious priority would be to direct the early alerts to the people involved, i.e., the potential victims. However, in practice it rarely seems to work out in this way. What can people do? Flee

the country? Undertake action in a situation that is already extremely repressive? Go into hiding?

More often than not, a threatened group will call for international attention and support in a very early stage. It is for this
same reason that early alerts should be directed from the beginning
to those outside the country who may help to prevent the process
leading into killings by governments. This will demand concerted
efforts by governments and inter governmental organizations, plus
the total of institutions that can put pressure to bear on the
target country through political, economic and other channels.

5. How To Use The Information?

As said earlier, no information should be presented without at
least some clue as to its use by those who will receive it. To put
it in other words, information should have an action perspective.
Providing information should optimally take place within the framework of an international program. Elements that come to mind are:

. a clear name, a clear point of reference, thorough and accessible
  documentation
. regular reporting by a number of organizations, e.g., in the form
  of "logs"
. concerted efforts to develop audio-visual material
. an effective use of the media and coordinated approach towards
  journalists, especially where professional groups of journalists
  have become active in covering human rights issues
. raising consciousness at an academic level; the literature on the
  issue is as yet strikingly scarce, whereas in political and social
  science a great potential for research seems to exist
. raising consciousness in an "historic" sense; the populations of
  many countries that are far away from the scenes of large-scale
  executions nowadays have experienced situations with obvious similarities in their own recent past.

In this regard one can note that the International Conference on
the Holocaust and Genocide in Tel Aviv was a major step towards such
conscientization.

PRIORITIES

From the above considerations, some priorities can tentatively
be drawn up recommending further activities. The wording of these
is based on the recommendations brought forward at the Dutch conference on extrajudicial executions. I also give some examples in
conection with these points.

1. A Program Of Action Should Be Coordinated

There are various constraints on coordination and cooperation
among human rights organizations. Human rights organizations are
wary of their field of interest or "mandate," many academics tend to
work in a kind of solitary confinement and inter-governmental or-

ganizations are often extremely sensitive in relation with other groups. Bedsides, a grossly overlooked problem is that of coordination and direct contacts with local human rights groups in the countries concerned, who often provide a lot (information) and get back little in active support.

As an important institution in this field, we should mention the Washington-based Human Rights Internet and its Reporter. It may surprise us that this organization is unique and only in existence for five years. The multitude of actions undertaken and documents published by human rights groups is only slowly discovered. The necessity of a coordinated effort is more than evident when we realize, in the confrontation with governments and other violators of human rights, that a high degree of coordination exists among repressive forces.

2. A Program Should Have An Active Media Approach

There are many ways to present information to the press, either free of charge (press releases, briefing journalists) or paid (advertisements). The important goal is that the media cover violations of human rights, such as murders by governments, in a systematic way. To date there is only a small number of committees of journalists directly involved in human rights campaigning, e.g., the U.S. Committee to Protect Journalists, the Canada Center for Investigative Journalism, and the Dutch Amnesty International Journalists Group. Interestingly, while these committees often start with concern for fellow journalists only, their spread-off effect on media coverage in general can be high.

3. A Program Should Set Out Research Standards

There is a serious need for standards of investigation of human rights violations by governments, e.g., when the El Salvador government states it is investigating the killing of four Dutch journalists, the fact that international research standards are lacking makes it difficult to evaluate the far from satisfying results of that investigation. There should be a machinery for inviting investigation by outsiders. The standards of both judicial inquiries and social science surveys should not be incompatible with the realization of human rights investigations.

4. A Program Should Have "Spearheads" For Action

One of such spearheads could be the international transfers and trainings in the field of military, police and security technology. When people are killed, it is mostly by weapons. Though peace movements are rapidly growing in significance in Western Europe and the U.S. especially, most of their interest is in potential future wars. The mechanisms contributing to warlike situations of massive killings in a number of countries now merits much more attention. A restrictive arms policy, as suggested by the Dutch Minister of Foreign Affairs, should first of all focus on the non-transfer of arms to countries where people are killed by their own governments.

5. A Program Should Activate Early Action Mechanisms

Effective early actions can mainly be envisaged at the governmental level. In this regard we should follow closely what happens, or does not happen, in the United Nations, the Organization of American States, the European Parliament, etc. A Working Group on Enforced or Involuntary Disappearances was set up in the U.N. in 1980. Its most significant characteristic was that it undertook direct communications and actions towards governments immediately after having received notice of a "disappearance." A Special Rapporteur is now being appointed for arbitrary and summary executions. It is of the utmost importance that non-governmental organizations and the public opinion mobilize all possible suport so as to make the task of such a rapporteur a sensible undertaking. This would imply inter alia that the rapporteur would have considerable freedom and resources in gathering information and in approaching the governments concerned.

6. A Program Should Involve Professional Groups

Campaigning, to put it briefly, is the mobilization of a potential. The potential should be understood as the willingness of individuals and institutions to act when confronted with such horrendous violations of human rights as murders by governments. The way in which this potential is frustrated is less important than an analysis of how it can be mobilized.

Journalists have already been mentioned as such a group, and references have been made to the academic world. Another group that deserves our special interest is that of the military and police. Significant results have already been made in approaching the latter group on human rights issues. Some approaches undertaken regarding the former group, the military, are promising. The conference on extrajudicial executions in the The Netherlands featured a special meeting for this group. The main interest in this field is that military officials of the higher levels have many international contacts with colleagues, among them from countries where murders committed or condoned by governments take place.

DAAN BRONKHORST, Nieuwendijk 92, 1012 MR Amsterdam, The Netherlands

25. The Bottom Line in Preventing Future Holocausts

Julius Lieblein

Currently am a volunteer consultant on altruism to the Anti- Defamation League of B'nai Brith, representing them in the InterFaith Conference of Metropolitan Washington, the Holocaust Committee of the Washington Jewish Community Council, and have represented the ADL at the American Gathering of Jewish Holocaust Survivors. Was chairman of Americans for Prevention of Another Holocaust. Have written articles on Holocaust prevention and on altruism. Working career was in scientific fields. Became committed to Holocaust prevention after retirement allowed time for working on my ideas.

The main point of this paper can be bluntly stated - to prevent a Holocaust in technological societies like the United States of America. The time to do something is <u>before</u> such a point is reached - to find ways of <u>reaching</u> people so they <u>do not want</u> to participate nor acquiesce in eliminating a minority people in their midst.

This then is the "bottom line," for unless this can be done, there seems to be little hope of preventing future catastrophe. It presents us with an enormous challenge.

By a Holocaust I mean what Dr. Alex Grobman, Director of the Simon Wiesenthal Center for Holocaust Studies, characterizes as "the most extreme example of which western society - with its civil service bureaucracy, modern technology, advanced scientific and business community, centralized government and highly trained police force and military" - a society with all these features of "civilization" - "is capable of doing when mobilized for destruction."[1]

The discussion and suggestions will apply mainly to modern industrialized societies where the conditions of "civilization" specified by Grobman are prevalent.

THE CAUSES AND CONTEXTS OF GENOCIDE

I start with what might be called a "Framework for Genocide," <u>Chart 1</u>. This is a crude - almost naive - sketch showing at a glance an overall situation of how genocide can be possible. Such a sketch can indicate where understanding, intervention, and prevention might be applicable.

Chart 1. Framework For Genocide

The occurence of genocide involves a <u>dominant</u> population in the midst of which lives a <u>minority</u> ethnic or other kind of group. There are <u>relationships</u> between these groups, the dominant group exerting pressures upon the minority group. As the chart indicates,

CHART I.   FRAMEWORK FOR GENOCIDE

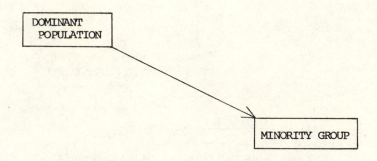

---

if these relationships deteriorate badly enough, then the stage is set for a Holocaust or genocide.

Chart II. Influence

The pressures of the dominant group upon the minority are related to the many pressures and influences that impact upon the individuals of the dominant group. Some of the important ones are indicated in Chart II.

The factors will be considered roughly in the order of awareness on the part of the individual, without going into too much detail. First come the drives and impulses of which one is largely unconscious. Of importance for understanding genocide are those natural human reactions when confronted with something strange and alien, like the practices of another culture or religion. Lack of understanding or misunderstanding at first produces discomfort and aversion. If the situation is not dealt with, these feelings are apt to grow into suspicion, fear, hostility and can end in hatred.

This, of course, points up the critical need for improving race relations and understanding of one another's culture.

Other factors that influence the motivation and attitudes of an individual without fully conscious awareness are tradition and environment - the influence of upbringing, family, friends, and community. Thus, if the individual is exposed only to bigoted attitudes from his home and surroundings, then that is bound to dominate his life-style - he knows no better.

CHART II. INFLUENCES

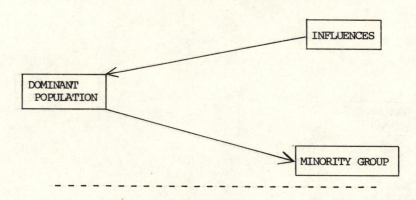

- -

INFLUENCES

INSTINCTIVE REACTION TO DIFFERENT CULTURE
    MISUNDERSTANDING–DISCOMFORT–AVERSION–FEAR–HATRED
TRADITION AND RELIGION
NURTURE AND ENVIRONMENT
POLITICAL AND SOCIAL FACTORS
ECONOMIC FACTORS

Political and social factors are of course very much in the consciousness of the individual and strongly influence behavior. This can lead to one taking actions counter to conscience or better judgment.

In certain parts of society, the influence of hate groups play a special role. Such groups can exert an inordinate amount of influence by preying upon fears and hardships, especially among disadvantaged segments of society. Unfortunately, such practices seem to work well, and result in the growing size and influence of these groups.

Economic factors have the most directly perceived impact. People who are unemployed and facing hardships with their families form a fertile field for recruitment by the hate groups. Moreover, such people are less apt to listen to their consciences or to progressive community or interreligious groups as to where their true interests lie. Of course, if economic hardship could be removed for everyone, then the climate for genocide would be greatly improved.

The aim should be to provide people with the will and means to exert the mental effort necessary to overcome the unworthy feelings and impulses.

What are these messages and approaches?

APPROACHES TO PREVENTION

These suggestions are not necessarily something wholly new – some of them are undoubtedly being practiced currently. I believe what is needed is an integrated approach that is aware that these are all directed towards a single ultimate goal – the uplifting of the human spirit so it becomes less vulnerable to the ultimate sickness that can produce a Holocaust or genocide.

These approaches take the form of effective communication of messages of various types to the entire population but especially to the dominant group.

I will make the discussion concrete now in terms of the Jews and non-Jews in the United States.

The Jewish minority group may wish to provide and convey such messages to the dominant non-Jewish group, but in view of its small size, the results will be limited. What is needed is amplification of these messages, by interposing between the two groups a body composed of the best people of good will of both the dominant and minority groups. This is represented by the additional box in Chart III.

Chart III. Amplification Of Messages To Dominant Groups

The interposing groups may consist of established interreligious bodies. These bodies are of course functioning to disseminate many good will messages throughout the non-Jewish and Jewish communities. Again, an integrated approach is needed that is not always evidenced.

CHART III.   AMPLIFICATION OF MESSAGE
TO DOMINANT GROUP

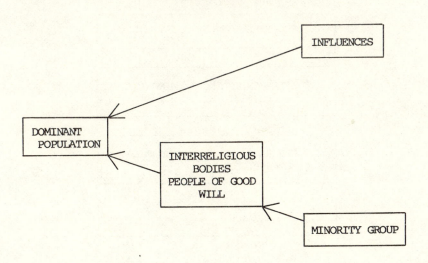

Chart IV. Approaches

1. "Downfall Of Civilization"

This message represents the "bottom line." From the Nuremberg war crime trials onwards, many outstanding thinkers have re-emphasized the warning that another Holocaust would involve and result in such chaos and devastation that civilization could not survive. If this could be made a part of the core belief of every individual, then this appeal to the most powerful motivation, survival, might serve as a "vaccine" to immunize against the viral influence of hate groups and other adverse factors such as those outlined previously.

The best way for inculcating such beliefs will have to be determined by experts in the disciplines of psychology, sociology, history, law, and related subjects.

This "bottom line" warning message is a negative one. There are some other, positive, messages that I would like to present that could strengthen the forces for prevention.

2. Self-Monitoring by Minority Groups and Empathy

Under this heading are attitudes or practices which may irritate or insult the feelings of the dominant community. The dominant group obviously can inflict bigoted attacks on a minority, but what is less well recognized is that the minority can, unthinkingly, do or say things that have a very negative effect on the dominant group.

CHART IV. APPROACHES TO PREVENTION

1. "DOWNFALL OF CIVILIZATION"

2. SELF-MONITORING BY MINORITY GROUPS, EMPATHY

3. REVERENCE FOR LIFE, ALTRUISM, HUMAN RIGHTS

4. REMEMBRANCE

If the messages are seen as valid and essential and are widely propagated by the above groups, they may be taken to heart by the tens of millions of people of good will and a bulwark can be created against the future evil of a Holocaust. A means of spreading these messages into the consciousness of the community could be through workshops, seminars, and other educational methods such as Holocaust curricula.

A recent example is a cartoon in the principal metropolitan Washington, D.C. newspaper for Jewish community interests which showed an unflattering caricature of an Arab, and the President of the congregation is saying to the Rabbi: "This is the ultimate challenge. If you can convert him, you will have the entire congregation eating out of your hand." It seems harmless enough, yet it took a letter from an Arab representative to remind us of the insulting nature of the cartoon, and to point out that Jews should be "all to familiar with the potentially dangerous consequences of stereotyping and scapegoating." This could have been revealed by an application of empathy, putting ourselves in the other's shoes. If the roles were reversed, putting a Jewish stereotype in place of the Arab stereotype, then the prejudical nature of the cartoon would have been instantly revealed. This is the type of self-monitoring that seems essential.

This idea of empathy and role reversal has much broader applicability. Jews should ask themselves: how would they feel if they were the dominant group and had living within their area a small group which seemd favored in many ways that were to be envied: health, longevity, superior education, excellence in many fields, apparently disproportionate occupancy of positions of wealth and power, carrying out strange practices such as dietary laws and observance of Sabbath that conflicted with public events scheduling and community practices? If they could get inside the feelings of others, they might be able to see how discomfort and aversion can arise, and better understand (which does not mean condone) the intolerance they encounter.

If suspicion of seemingly superior characteristics of Jews is an irritant to non-Jews, how much more so are the self-proclaimations of such things by Jews themselves. This is one case where the truth - if it be truth - hurts, and therefore should be subordinated to caring: caring for the other's feelings. Not every truth needs to be asserted if it would be hurtful to the feelings of others. Just as mercy is overriding over justice, so is caring above truth.

3. Reverence For Life, Altruism And Human Rights

Prominent on the list of prevention approaches must be high regard for human life. The Nazis in Germany had very little of this quality. Therefore, it was not difficult for them to torment and dispose of lives without any civilized restraints. If regard for life, and for human rights which give quality to that life, is kept universally and consistently high, then a Holocaust or genocide will be much less likely.

That altruism and regard for life lie within everyone of us is demonstrated by the outpouring of public feelings when the saving of life is given mass media attention. An example of this happened in January, 1982 when an airplane tragedy in Washington, D.C. claimed 78 lives. One rescuer who dived into the icy water received such spontaneous acclaim that he received a special citation by President Reagan who had him present at a session of both Houses of Congress which received nationwide television coverage.

This spirit of altruism is generally present at disasters such as when volunteers search for live victims in earthquakes. Why would they risk their lives if not spurred by the altruistic impulse? The media can abet this feeling.

The media should not hesitate to promote the concept of "altruism" when reporting instances of its occurrence. Its message might be something like: "So much of the news shows the results of evil and violence in man. But you should be reminded that there are good and altruism also, and the stories we have shown give dramatic evidence of this fact."

4. Remembrance

This has been the subject of so much effort by so many that there is not much that needs to be added. The need for remembering what happened, growing more desperate with the passing years of attrition of survivors and the corresponding increase of deniers, is very widely recognized as an essential facet of prevention of a recurrence. In fact, there are entire organizations, such as Zachor in New York City, and the United States Holocaust Memorial Council, that are largely or exclusively devoted to remembrance. However, it is less well recognized - or admitted - that remembering alone is inadequate in the absence of specific programs designed to attack the occurrence of Holocaust mentality at its source - in the minds of people who may be potential participants, or bystanders.

"SOFT" AND "HARD" APPROACHES

The above ideas - downfall of civilization; self-monitoring by minority groups and empathy; reverence for life, altruism and human rights; and remembrance - may be considered "soft" approaches to the problem of prevention, in contrast to the traditional ones that may be called "hard" approaches of direct confrontation or protest against ongoing prejudices and antisemitic acts which evidence the mentality that could produce a future Holocaust. The approaches here suggested have in common their concern with the mind of the individual - to seek to divert it from destructive paths. They thus look to the future and do not concentrate on the present-day hate phenomena. These latter are best left to the professional organizations already in the field, like the Anti-Defamation League of Bnai Brith, and others.

About such efforts I would raise two questions. To the Jewish protective agencies, I suggest that long-range strategies be developed to deal with hate groups if they should ever reach dangerous size. What could be done, for example, if hate groups should elect officials who could exert substantial influence in Congress? This possibility is not wild fantasy. In Michigan a former neo-Nazi party leader won Republican nomination for Congress, obtaining 32% or 53,000 of the votes in the general election. In the 1980 Democratic Party primary for President of the United States, a neo-Nazi candidate received 170,000 votes and raised over $2 million. Under the U.S. election laws, this entitled him to receive government matching funds of over $500,000 from the Federal Election Commission. Conceivably, then, such groups could come to power one day through perfectly democratic processes.

To the legal community in the United States, I put a second question also having to do with hate groups becoming too dangerous: must we zealously guard the civil rights of the heirs of Hitler to unlimited marching and propagating their beliefs, within the law, no matter how large they become? Can some principle be found whereby civilization can protect itself?

To those who may scoff at the soft approaches as visionary and ineffectual, I say, "Do you have a way that's better?" The problem of preventing a Holocaust is too difficult by ordinary means. We must explore all possibilities including approaches that are not usually considered.

CONCLUSION

The bottom line is, how do we appeal to the minds and hearts of the bulk of people not to yield to their baser impulses and follow leaders on the road to mass murder no matter how bad conditions are. Among these ideas that could make a difference are spreading the belief that mass murder means the end of civilized society, self-discipline by minority groups, reverence for life, empathy, altruism, human rights, and remembrance, with the media incorporating recognition of these in news broadcasts to raise public awareness, and education to be carried out through workshops, seminars and suitable curricula; all this to be carried on with the indispensable cooperation of interreligious organizations and people of good will everywhere. I appeal to you to develop your own ideas.

NOTE

1. "The virus of antisemitism will remain virulent until we face up to the Holocaust." Alex Grobman in the Los Angeles Herald Examiner, January 12, 1981, p. 12.

JULIUS LIEBLEIN, Ph.D., 1621 E. Jefferson Stree, Rockville, Maryland 20852, U.S.A.

26. The United Nations and Genocide:
A Program of Action

Leo Kuper

Given the new technologies of mass destruction, there is a greater need than ever for international protection against genocide. This is notwithstanding the United Nations resolution at its first session, which declared genocide to be a crime under international law and called for international cooperation to prevent and punish the crime. And it is notwithstanding the Genocide Convention of 1948 which was designed to liberate mankind from what the Convention described as an odious scourge that has inflicted great losses on humanity throughout all periods of history. But though the Convention has been ratified by ninety-two nations, international cooperation to suppress the crime has been withheld, and genocide has been reduced to a term of abuse in the political exchanges of Member States of the United Nations.

I recall in the 1930s my anguish at the seeming indifference of much of the outside world to the persecutions in Nazi Germany and my despair at the time of the Holocaust that so little help was extended by powerful nations. But I did not realize then that the indifference of the outside world is a perennial complaint.

Burundi

Let me take a few examples of genocidal massacres and other mass murders in the last decade. In Burundi, on independence, it seemed that the two main groups in the country, the Tutsi and Hutu people, would integrate harmoniously. But political rivalry soon took an ethnic form, and escalated, through repression and massacre, to genocide. In 1972, in reprisals against Hutu massacres, the Tutsi slaughtered some 100,000 Hutu. The educated were a special target for revenge, with the massacres reaching down to young Hutu school children, who were seized in their classrooms and brutally murdered. And there were further massacres in the following year bringing the total number of deaths to an estimated two to three hundred thousand.

Now the policy of the United Nations and of western diplomats was that the Organization of African Unity should be primarily responsible for initiating action in conflicts within its region. But the official position of the Organization was supportive of the Burundi regime, and the United Nations itself took no effective action. It is against this background that we can understand the complaint to African heads of state by a Movement of Progressive Burundi Students studying in Belgium. They said there was nothing in world history, outside of Hitler's Nazi movement, to compete with Burundi oppression. "And the peoples in Africa say nothing. African Heads of State receive the executioner Micombero and clasp his hand in fraternal greeting...Are you waiting until the entire Hutu ethnic group of Burundi is exterminated before raising your voices?" (See Lemarchand and Martin 1974; Kuper, 1977, pp. 87-107 and 197-208; and Kuper 1982, pp. 162-165.)

Uganda

Or let us take the example of Uganda where Amin came to power in 1971, and immediately started murdering his countrymen. Most of the murders were of political opponents, real, or imaginary, and so would not fall under the United Nations definition of genocide. But there were also genocidal massacres of ethnic groups. Yet Amin continued under the protection of the Organization of African Unity and of the United Nations Commission on Human Rights for most of the period of his rule, until he was overthrown in 1979 in a war with Tanzania (Martin, 1974; International Commission Jurists, 1977).

We can readily appreciate the despair of the Ugandan people, left undefended while a brutal dictator massacred a quarter of a million of his unfortunate subjects. It was this despair, which a succeeding President of Uganda expressed in an address to the General Assembly of the United Nations in September 1979. He referred to the commitment of the international community to human rights, as set out in the United Nations Charter, and his people's expectation of solidarity and support from the United Nations in their struggle against the fascist dictatorship. But for eight years they had cried out for help in vain. Their cries seemed to have fallen on deaf ears. The United Nations looked on in embarrassed silence as the tragedy unfolded and the Amin regime continued with impunity to commit genocide. For how long, he asked, would the United Nations remain silent while governments represented within the organization continued to perpetrate atrocities against their own people.[1]

Cambodia

During the same period, the Pol Pot regime in Democratic Kampuchea was engaging in large scale systematic massacres in the interests of establishing its version of a Communist Utopia. A French missionary, who was present at the brutal evacuation of the inhabitants of the capital, and later interviewed many refugees, complained that even the United Nations turned a deaf ear, and he quoted the bitter comment of a Khmer friend, that there were societies for the protection of animals in France, and factories for the manufacture of dog and cat foods. Were Cambodians less than animals, that no one condescended to defend them? (Ponchaud, 1978).

The massacres in Kampuchea, like the Ugandan massacres, were largely political, but there were also ethnic massacres, and a genocidal campaign against Buddhism and against a Muslim tribal group, the Cham. Perhaps as many as two million or more were murdered or died of starvation and disease or as a result of the harsh conditions of living imposed in the labor camps. Yet there was no effective United Nations action. As for the Commission on Human Rights, it decided almost three years after the first massacres, and under great pressure from western governments, that it would initiate a study of the human rights situation in Democratic Kampuchea with the cooperation of its government. The effect of this decision was to postpone action in relation to ongoing massacres until the next meeting of the Commission, that is, a postponement for a whole year. It is a decision which defies belief, as does the continued recognition by the United Nations of the Pol Pot regime as the legitimate representative of the Cambodian people (Ponchaud, 1977; Hildebrand and Porter, 1976; Kiernan and Chanthou, 1982; & Shawcross, 1979).

Bangladesh

As a final example, we have the genocidal massacres in East Pakistan (Bangladesh). Here, an escalating dispute between the Bengalis of East Pakistan, seeking self-determination, and the government in West Pakistan led to a massive onslaught by the Pakistan Army. The government of Bangladesh claimed that three million of its people were killed in the ensuing massacres. In addition, millions of Bengalis sought refuge in India, placing an intolerable burden on its government. But the Commission on Human Rights refused to act on a complaint by twenty-two nongovernmental organizations. And as for the Security Council, it only took up the issue almost nine months after the first massacres when war had broken out between India and Pakistan. But even at this late emergency stage of the conflict, the Security Council was paralyzed by the veto. Draft resolutions floated round like autumn leaves. And notwithstanding a resolution by the General Assembly, the Security Council was only able to arrive at a face-saving decision, when the issue had already been settled on the battlefield by the capitulation of the Pakistan army.[2]

By way of comment on these proceedings, I can do no better than refer to the frustration and disgust felt by United Nations' delegates at the inability of the Security Council to agree on a form of action, when confronted with a major conflict. There are repeated expressions of this disgust in the course of the General Assembly debate.

> Despite all the appeals made to it and the gravity of the situation, the Security Council once again has demonstrated its impotence, that is, the powerlessness of the United Nations...I should like to declare - and I am aware that this statement is supported by the whole of the United Nations - that, in not adopting any decision, the Security Council has not acted on behalf of the United Nations, has not acted on behalf of all its members, has not acted on behalf of a world public opinion which is troubled and dismayed at the turn of events...
> No one who watched over the weekend the proceedings of the Security Council on the Indo-Pakistan dispute could have left the Security Council chamber without a feeling of sadness, deep disappointment and frustration. I am sure we all recognize that we have before us a human tragedy of very great proportions and therefore the performance of the Security Council in the face of such human tragedy - a performance which we all saw - was nothing short of irresponsibility...

I come with a feeling of sadness and anguish - sadness as a member of the Council because of the failure of that main organ of the United Nations to exercise its primary responsibility for the maintenance of peace and security while there was still time to do so even before the last three days of anguish because, while the world Organization continues its deliberations, people suffer and die in the Hindustan subcontinent.[3]

THE UNITED NATIONS

I do not need to labor the point with further examples. The failure of the United Nations to extend protection against genocide and mass murder is sufficiently well-known. Part of the difficulty is that the United Nations lacks adequate power for enforcement of its resolutions. But the main difficulty is a failure in the political determination to use the power with which it is vested. The core of the problem is that the crimes of genocide and of large scale mass murder are generally commited by governments; and the United Nations is an organization of governments, not of peoples of the world, as the Charter proudly proclaims. The result is that in the general councils of United Nations bodies, the offending governments enjoy the protection of regional or ideological alliances, or they are protected as clients of the superpowers. In the Security Council, under conditions of the cold war, and a divided world, action against a client state of one of the superpowers is almost certain to be frustrated by a protective veto. In the Indonesian genocidal massacres of the people of East Timor, the Security Council did succeed in passing a resolution, but took no steps to enforce the resolution.

Of course, the United Nations record is not entirely negative. The Secretary-General usually becomes involved, at a level of diplomatic exchanges and good offices, and the United Nations can be relied upon to extend humanitarian relief. Peacekeeping forces in some cases must certainly have restrained mass murder. In some cases, too, the United Nations has taken action against genocide, as for example, in the case of the Ache Indians in Paraguay (Kuper, 1982) and at its last sessions, in 1982 and 1983 the Commission on Human Rights and its subcommissions passed resolutions concerning the threatened genocide against members of the Baha'i faith in Iran.[4] The resolutions did not use the term genocide, but the submissions documented a pattern of systematic persecution, highly reminiscent of the first stages in the Nazi persecution of Jews. Moreover, in the last years, under the courageous and highly principled leadership of the former Director of the Division of Human Rights, Mr. Theo. van Boven, the Commission has taken up many cases of gross violations of human rights. There have also been some encouraging developments in the procedures for protection of human rights.

The United Nations thus offers some potentialities for action against genocide and mass murder. But the obstacles are deeply embedded in the structure of international relations. Hence, the potentialities for action within the United Nations need to be acti-

vated from the outside, as they have been in the past, by the international nongovernmental organizations with consultative status.
Moreover, given the past record of the United Nations, it is clear
that pressures exerted within the U.N. need to be supplemented by
action outside its framework. Thus the comments which follow are
divided between possibilities for action within, and outside of, the
United Nations.

TYPES OF GENOCIDE

The Genocide Convention defines genocide as one of a number of
acts "committed with intent to destroy, in whole or in part, a national, ethnical, racial or religious group, as such." It differentiates the means of destruction, but does not distinguish between
types of genocide. From the point of view of prevention and protection, however, it is crucial to distinguish between the varied forms
of genocide.

Where genocide arises in the course of international warefare,
the Security Council could, in theory, invoke sanctions. In practice, however, as we have seen, the Security Council is almost certain to be paralyzed by the veto. In some cases, regional intergovernmental organizations might be more responsive. Apart from this,
individual nations, or groups of nations, could apply diplomatic and
other pressures. As a last resort, there remains the possibility of
forceful humanitarian intervention. But the prospects for effective
action against genocide in international warfare are not very promising, as long as the Security Council is paralyzed by its internal
divisions. Meanwhile, nuclear armament greatly increases the threat
of genocide in international conflicts.

Domestic Genocides

Most genocides, at the present time, arise on the basis of internal divisions within a society and not in the course of international warfare. I will refer to these as 'domestic' genocides. They
are a phenomenon of plural societies, that is to say, societies with
persistent and pervasive cleavages between ethnic, racial or religious groups.

Plural societies are societies which one may regard as being at
risk of genocide, particularly when: (1) there is a superimposition
of differences, so that, for example, two groups in a country are
differentiated by ethnicity, culture, political status and economic
structure; (2) there is extreme discontinuity between the groups in
such dimensions as social and physical segregation, membership of
political parties and of religious and other organizations; and (3)
there is a tendency, by reason of the superimposition of difference
and the discontinuities, for conflicts to spread readily from one
domain to another, so that the society rapidly polarizes along the
lines of cleavage.

A common contemporary form of 'domestic' genocide corresponds
to the genocides of colonial times. This is the annihiliation of

indigenous groups in the course of economic developments, the so-called 'victims of progress.' It is widespread, and tends to be accepted as an inevitable development. Often a genocidal process is involved, rather than a deliberate intention to commit genocide.

The hostage or scapegoat genocides continue to take a heavy toll. Under this heading, which I do not regard as very satisfactory, I include the Turkish genocide against Armenians, and the Holocaust. The most current example is the threatened genocide against the Baha'is in Iran. The victims are generally of different religion from the majority ruling group, and distinctive in other ways; they have usually been subject to discrimination and hostility in the past; and they are vulnerable, and hence readily available as scapegoats in times of crisis. A contemporary form of the persecution of these groups is mass expulsion, as for example, of Chinese from Vietnam, and this can assume genocidal proportions when the outside world is unwilling to receive the refugees. Given the pressure of expanding populations on limited resources, mass expulsions are likely to be a continuing, and perhaps an increasing, threat to the survival of minority groups.

The most destructive genocides in the last two decades have arisen out of struggles for power between groups in plural societies (as in Burundi), or in struggles against discrimination or in response to claims for self-determination in the form of a measure of autonomy, or secession (as in Bangladesh). Decolonisation has resulted in many plural societies, since the colonial powers arbitrarily grouped together different peoples, with little concern for their integration in a unified society. The adjustment of group relations in the process and aftermath of decolonisation has often been a source of violent confrontation and massacre.

Mention must also be made of genocidal massacres perpetrated in the course of political mass murder by tyrannical regimes. I have in mind the genocidal massacres of Buddhist priests and of the Cham people in Democratic Kampuchea, and of Lango and Acholi in Uganda, under Amin, to which reference has already been made.

INTERNATIONAL ACTION AGAINST GENOCIDE

Turning now to international action against genocide, there are many procedures available within the United Nations. Some are applicable to genocide in general; others are specifically related to particular forms of genocide. In my paper for the Minority Rights Group on International Action Against Genocide (Kuper, 1982, pp. 13-14), I have surveyed these procedures and mention them only briefly here.

Complaints of genocide would normally be channeled through the Sub-Commission on Prevention of Discrimination and the Commission on Human Rights, either under confidential procedures, or increasingly in public session. The public discussions are certainly more effective, since Member States are sensitive to international opprobrium, as shown by the great pains they take to defend themselves.

In addition, Member States can raise complaints in the General Assembly, and in other bodies, such as the Social and Humanitarian Committee, since genocidal massacres raise humanitarian issues calling for emergency action. Where there is a threat to the peace, the Security Council is the appropriate forum. And indeed, genocides generally threaten the peace, with a flow of refugees, and other repercussions, in neighboring countries.

Organizations within the United Nations orbit, such as the International Labor Organization, World Health, etc., also provide a forum through which such specific issues may be raised, as flow from the genocidal massacres and are relevant to the organization's goals. And parallel intergovernmental regional organizations, for example, the European Parliament, or the Organization of American States, may be helpful in exerting pressure against offending governments.

In regard to the forms of action related to specific forms of genocide, an important new development is the establishment of a Working Group in the Sub-Commission to deal with issues of discrimination against indigenous populations. This should be a channel for some measure of protection against the anihilation of small indigenous groups in the course of predatory economic development.

There is also in preparation a declaration on the protection of minorities which may give rise to a Convention. And a recent report on massive exoduses by the former High Commissioner for Refugees makes a number of recommendations which, if adopted, would contribute to protection of hostage (scapegoat) groups against this form of persecution.[5]

Finally, the reassertion of the applicability of the right to self-determination in post-colonial societies, and some detailed specification of possible forms of autonomy, might assist interregional organizations and interested governments in mediating potentially destructive conflicts arising between groups in plural societies.

Some possibilities for action within the United Nations look well into the future, but they are not a target for present endeavor. Given the unwieldy bureaucratic procedures of the U.N., its deep cleavages, and protective stance toward offending governments, there is a need for some supranational institutions to transcend the present limitations. Talk of punishing the crime of genocide is relatively meaningless without an International Penal Court. The establishment of such a court has been intermittently on the agenda of the U.N. from its earliest days. Perhaps it may ultimately eventuate. A more promising possibility, at any rate in the relatively near future, is the establishment of the office of High Commissioner. This is presently on the U.N. agenda, and has fair support. A Commissioner, with high status and executive powers, could, hopefully, make some contribution to restraining the outbreak of genocidal violence.

Any campaign in the United Nations against genocide would need the support of nongovernmental organizations with consultative status. In the past, they have taken the initiative against gross violations of human rights, and they will certainly continue to do so in the future. But much can be gained by a coordination of effort in a sharply focused attack on genocide. The recent campaign conducted by the Baha'is is a model of what can be achieved within the U.N. by concentrated effort. Of course, the Baha'i campaign was assisted by the general unpopularity of the Iranian regime, and by the access of Baha'i communities throughout the world to governments of the countries in which they live.

Outside of the United Nations, many strategies are available to nongovernmental organizations. Laurie Wiseberg and Harry Scoble (1982) in an excellent discussion of an international strategy for NGOs analyze the human rights function of these NGOs as they relate to fact-finding, dissemination of information, techniques of mass action and humanitarian relief. They conclude with an emphasis on the need for a coordination of effort in campaigning against extra-legal executions.

In the Minority Rights Group paper on International Action Against Genocide, I have also referred to a wide range of available strategies for activating an international alert against impending genocides. The first step would be representations to the offending government, since genocides generally involve governments, either as active agents, or as condoning, or failing to take preventive action. If these should fail, then all possible means of pressure and persuasion would be brought to bear.

These means would include activating different organs of the U.N. and related organizations, directly and through national delegations, and making representations to national governments and to interregional organizations for active involvement; seeking support of the international press in providing information and commentary; enlisting the aid of other media, and of demonstrations, to call attention to the threat, or actuality, of genocidal massacre; asking religious leaders, in appropriate cases, to intercede, since a surprising aspect of the genocides is that the murderers and the victims are mostly of different religions; and generally, initiating campaigns of appeal by members of the public along the lines of Amnesty International campaigns. Finally, there are the sanctions which can be applied through public support, by means of economic boycotts, the refusal to handle goods to or from offending States, and selective exclusion from participation in international activities and events. Representations would also be made to governments, or campaigns mounted, to enlist their support in the application of sanctions.

The organizational base would be a small activating secretariat, working in cooperation with networks of nongovernmental organizations. The gathering of information is, of course, crucial. A major source would be nongovernmental organizations themselves. In

addition, the support of journalists would be needed, both for re-
ceipt and dissemination of information. I think too that a network
of academic research support could be established to provide information on situations which would seem to call for an international
alert. An important resource would be the Early Warning System proposed by Charny and Rapaport (1982). And finally, the Secretariat
would be open to receive communications from all sources.

Support would also be invited from committed individuals, and
from interested organizations not falling within the human rights
network. It should be possible to involve religious groups because
of their humanitarian concerns, and because of the intimate relation
between religion and genocide. Hopefully, strong support would come
from groups which have themselves suffered the overwhelming catastrophy of genocide, and now add to their commemorations help to
others similarly threatened, by way of a LIVING MEMORIAL to assist
the survivors of contemporary genocides, and to mobilise an International Alert, as necessary, to prevent future genocides.

There is, at present, a movement under way to establish an organization for this purpose under the name INTERNATIONAL ALERT. In
this way, we would hope to add to the days of mourning and of dedication and of remembrance of past genocides a living memorial for
aid to our fellow human beings against the all too prevalent scourge
of contemporary genocide.

NOTES

1. A/34/PV. 14, pp. 2-5.
2. International Commission of Jurists, The Events in East Pakistan,
1971, Geneva, 1972; Indian Ministry of External Affairs, Bangla Desh
Documents, Madras, B.N.K. Press, 1971; and Anthony Mascarenhas, The
Rape of Bangla Desh, Vikas Publications, 1971.
3. A/2002, 5-6, and A/2003, 6 and 26.
4. E/CN.4/1982/L.   See also Baha'i International Community, The
Baha'is in Iran, New York, 1982.
5. Sadruddin Aga Khan, Study on Human Rights and Massive Exoduses,
E/CN.4/1503, dated 31 December, 1981.

REFERENCES

CHARNY, Israel W.   In collaboration with Chanan Rapaport.   How Can
We Commit the Unthinkable?: Genocide, The Human Cancer. Boulder,
Colorado: Westview Press, 1982,Chapter 13.
HILDEBRAND, George, & Porter, Gareth.   Cambodia - Starvation and
Revolution. New York: Monthly Review Press, 1976.
KIERNAN, Ben, & Boua, Chanthou.   Peasants and Politics in Kampuchea
1942-1981. London: Zed Press, 1982.
INTERNATIONAL Commission of Jurists. Uganda and Human Rights,   Re-
port to the United Nations, Geneva, 1977.
KUPER, Leo. The Pity of It All.   London: Duckworth, 1977, pp. 87-
107 and 197-208.

KUPER, Leo. Genocide. New Haven: Yale University Press, 1982. MARTIN, David. General Amin. London: Faber, 1974. PONCHAUD, Francois. Cambodia Year Zero. Harmondsworth: Penguin, 1978. SHAWCROSS, William. Sideshow: Kissinger, Nixon and the Destruction of Cambodia. New York: Simon & Schuster, 1979. WISEBERG, Laurie, & Scoble, Harry. An international strategy for NGOs pertaining to extra-legal executions. Paper presented at Amnesty International Conference on Extra-Legal Executions, Amsterdam, 1982.

LEO KUPER, Ph.D., Department Sociology, University California, Los Angeles, California 90024, U.S.A.

27. Reason and Realpolitik: International Law and the Prevention of Genocide

Louis René Beres

Louis René Beres is Professor of Political Science at Purdue University. Born in Switzerland in 1945, he is the author of many books and articles dealing with nuclear war and human rights. Educated at Princeton University, his most recent books are MIMICKING SISYPHUS: AMERICA'S COUNTERVAILING NUCLEAR STRATEGY (Lexington Books, 1983), and APOCALYPSE: NUCLEAR CATASTROPHE IN WORLD POLITICS (University of Chicago Press, 1980). Professor Beres is an active member of such groups as Physicians for Social Responsibility, The American Committee for East/West Accord, The Committee for National Security and the World Policy Institute. At the moment, he is completing work on a book dealing with international law and the prevention of genocide, a work that stems as much from his personal involvement with the Holocaust as from his academic expertise as a legal scholar.

Goethe's Faust begins with a "Prologue in Heaven" wherein Mephistopheles speaks to God of enduring human imperfection:

> The little god of earth remains the same
> queer sprite
> As on the first day, or in primal light,
> His life would be less difficult, poor thing,
> Without your gift of heavenly glimmering;
> He calls it Reason, using light celestial
> Just to outdo the beasts in being bestial.

As Goethe suggests, humankind's inclination to evil is not new. Nor is its passion for adapting intellect to the invention and manufacture of dreadful engines of destruction. Small wonder, then, that Mephistopheles goes on to complain that since "men drown in evils...I find it boring to torment them."

Goethe is telling us, of course, that our species moves inexorably toward unreason on its own account. There is no need for satanic intervention. Humankind can be counted upon to ensure the triumph of oblivion - the prototype of all injustice - on its own. These observations have a special meaning in understanding the immediate problem of genocide and its prevention by international law.

Although legal scholars may understand that genocide has always been prohibited by international law (in the words of the Genocide Convention, "Genocide is a modern word for an old crime"), the post-World War II criminalization of genocide has been especially explicit and far-reaching. Building upon the norms established by international custom, the general principles of law recognized by civilized nations, the writings of highly qualified publicists, various treaties and conventions and the overriding principles of natural law, this criminalization has taken place under allied and U.N. auspices and has flowed almost entirely from the universal reaction to the Holocaust.

Prior to 1945, no principle of international law was more widely revered in practice than the idea of "domestic jurisdiction" on matters relating to human rights. On these matters, the rule of non-intervention was effectively absolute. Thus, what went on within one state's own borders was effectively no one else's business.

In theory, of course, the idea of absolute non-intervention had already been shattered by a number of pertinent treaties and conventions before World War II. Both the Treaty of Westphalia in 1648 (ending the Thirty Years War) and the so-called Minorities Treaties after World War I did undertake to protect specific groups within states from inhuman treatment. During the period between these norm-making agreements, the Treaties of Vienna (1815) provided for abolition of the slave trade - abolition that was reinforced by provisions of the Brussels Anti-Slavery Conference (1890). And the Geneva Convention of 1864 prescribed specific patterns for the treatment of the sick and wounded in time of war. Yet, no truly universal, comprehensive and codified protection of human rights existed before 1945.

After the Second World War, the Nuremberg Tribunal was established and in session (1945-1949). Based upon its Charter (the London Charter of 1944), this specially-constituted international tribunal brought charges on three categories of crime under international law: crimes of war; crimes against peace; and crimes against humanity. It was from this last category of crime - crimes against humanity - that the full criminalization of genocide drew its sustenance and from which the right and obligation of states to intervene in other states when human rights are in jeopardy was established. According to the British Chief Prosecutor at Nuremberg:

> Normally international law concedes that it is for the State to decide how it shall treat its own nationals; it is a matter of domestic jurisdiction....Yet, international law has in the past made some claim that there is a limit to the omnipotence of the State and that the individual human being, the ultimate unit of all law, is entitled to the protection of mankind when the State tramples upon its rights in a manner that outrages the conscience of mankind....The fact is that the right of humanitarian intervention by war is not a novelty in international law - can intervention by judicial process then be illegal?[1]

In creating a greatly-strengthened human rights regime, principal responsibility fell upon the newly-formed United Nations. Beginning with a General Assembly definition and resolution in 1946 affirming the law-making quality of the Nuremberg judgment and principles, the U.N. went on to complete a Convention on the Prevention and Punishment of the Crime of Genocide on December 9, 1948. This

Convention, which removes any doubts about the lawlessness of genocide, entered into force (1951) when a sufficient number of signatory states had deposited their instruments of ratification. Cur-
iously, the United States (Senate) has still not ratified this vital
Convention. largely out of a misplaced fear of surrender of sovereignty.[2]

Taken together with other important covenants, treaties and declarations, which together comprise a human rights "regime," the
Genocide Convention represents the end of the idea of absolute
sovereignty concerning non-intervention when human rights are in
grievous jeopardy. The Charter of the United Nations - a multilateral, law-making treaty - stipulates in its Preamble and several
articles that human rights are protected by international law. This
stipulation was reaffirmed by major covenants in 1966 and by the
Helsinki Final Act in 1975. Of course, the U.N.'s Universal Declaration of Human Rights (1948) must also be considered an integral
part of the human rights regime. Although this Declaration is not,
strictly speaking, a law-making document, it does articulate "the
general principles of law recognized by civilized nations" (a proper
source of international law under Article 38 of the Statute of the
International Court of Justice) and it does represent an authoritative elucidation of the law of the Charter.

In light of codified expressions of the international law of
human rights, it is abundantly clear that individual states can no
longer claim sovereign immunity from responsibility for gross mistreatment of their own citizens. Even the failure to ratify specific treaties or conventions (e.g., the United States and the Genocide Convention) does not confer immunity from responsibility, since
all states are bound by the law of the Charter and by the customs
and general principles of law from which such agreements derive. In
the words of former President Jimmy Carter before the United Nations
on March 17, 1977:

The search for peace and justice also means respect for human
dignity. All the signatories of the United Nations Charter
have pledged themselves to observe and respect basic human
rights. Thus, no member of the United Nations can claim that
mistreatment of its citizens is solely its own business. Equally, no member can avoid its responsibilities to review and to
speak when torture or unwarranted deprivation of freedom occurs
in any part of the world.

The international regime on human rights also establishes, beyond any reasonable doubt, the continuing validity of natural law as
the overriding basis of international law. This establishment flows
directly from the judgments at Nuremberg. While the indictments of
the Nuremberg Tribunal were cast in terms of existing positive law
(i.e., law enacted by states), the actual decisions of the Tribunal
unambigously reject the proposition that the validity of international law depends upon its "positiveness" (i.e., its explicit and
detailed codification). The words used by the Tribunal ("So far
from it being unjust to punish him, it would be unjust if his wrongs

were allowed to go unpunished") derive from the principle: <u>nullum crimen sine poena</u> (no crime without a punishment). This principle, of course, is a flat contradiction of the central idea that underlies "positive jurisprudence" or law as command of a sovereign, the idea of <u>nulla poena sine lege</u> (no punishment without a law).

In fact, the tendency to disassociate the law of nations from the law of nature and to identify international law exclusively with positive law did not really appear before the nineteenth century. Prior to that century, few scholars indeed were willing to advance the idea of international law detached from natural law.

The idea of natural law is based upon the acceptance of certain principles of right and justice that prevail because of their own intrinsic merit. Eternal and immutable, they are external to all acts of human will and interpenetrate all human reason. This idea and its attendant tradition of human civility runs almost continuously from Mosaic Law and the ancient Greeks and Romans to the present day.

ENFORCEMENT OF INTERNATIONAL LAW

Granted, there are now explicit and codified rules of international law that pertain to genocide, but what can be done about their effective enforcement? Indeed, doesn't a consideration of post-World War II history reveal several instances of genocide (the Cambodian case being, perhaps, the most far-reaching and abhorrent)? Where was international law?

To answer these questions, one must first recall that international law is a distinctive and unique system of law. This is the case because it is decentralized rather than centralized; because it exists within a social setting (i.e., the world political system) that lacks government. It follows that in the absence of central authoritative institutions for the making, interpretation and enforcement of law, these juridical processes devolve upon <u>individual states</u>. It is, then, the responsibility of individual states, acting alone or in collaboration with other states, to make international law "work" with respect to genocide.

How can this be done? In terms of the law of the Charter, it is essential that states continue to reject the Article 2 (7) claim to "domestic jurisdiction" whenever gross outrages against human rights are involved. Of course, the tension betwen the doctrines of "domestic jurisdiction" and "international concern" is typically determined by judgments of national self-interest, but it would surely be in the long-term interest of all states to oppose forcefully all crimes against humanity. As Vattel observed correctly in the Preface to his <u>The Law of Nations</u> in 1758:

But we know too well from sad experience how little regard those who are at the head of affairs pay to rights when they conflict with some plan by which they hope to profit. They

adopt a line of policy which is often false, because often unjust; and the majority of them think that they have done
enough in having mastered that. Nevertheless, it can be said
of States, what has long been recognized as true of individuals, that the <u>wisest</u> and the <u>safest</u> policy is one that is
founded upon justice

With this observation, Vattel echoes Cicero's contention that
"No one who has not the strictest regard for justice can adminster
public affairs to advantage." But how are we to move from assessment to action, from prescription to policy? Where, exactly, is the
normative juncture between the theory of human rights as pragmatic
practice and the operationalization of that theory?

Under the terms of Article 56 of the Charter, member states are
urged to "take joint and separate action in cooperation with the organization" to promote human rights. Reinforced by an abundant body
of ancillary prescriptions, this obligation stipulates that the legal community of humankind must allow, indeed <u>require</u>, "humanitarian
intervention" by individual states in certain circumstances.   Of
course, such intervention must not be used as a pretext for aggression and it must conform to settled legal norms governing the use of
force, expecially the principles of <u>discrimination</u>, <u>military neces-
sity</u> and <u>proportionality</u>.3 Understood in terms of the long- standing distinction between <u>jus ad bellum</u> and <u>jus in bello</u>, this means
that even where the "justness" of humanitarian intervention is
clearly established, the means used in that intervention must not be
unlimited. The lawfulness of a cause does not in itself legitimize
the use of certain forms of violence.

The legality of humanitarian intervention (<u>jus ad bellum</u>) has
been well established for a long time. While the theory of international law still oscillates between an individualist conception of
the state and a universalist conception of humanity, the post World
War II regime of treaties, conventions and declarations concerning
human rights is necessarily founded upon a broad doctrine of humanitarian intervention. Indeed, it is the very purpose of this regime
to legitimize an "allocation of competences" that favors the natural
rights of humankind over any particularistic interests of state.
Since violations of essential human rights are now undeniably within
the ambit of global responsibility, the subjectivism of state primacy has been unambiguously subordinated to the enduring primacy of
international justice.   In place of the Hegelian concept of the
state as an autonomous, irreducible center of authority (because it
is an ideal that is the perfect manifestation of Mind), there is now
in force a greatly expanded version of the idea of "international
concern."   In the words of McDougal, Lasswell, and Chen, (1980,
p. 211):

The general community is made competent to inquire into how a
particular state treats, not merely aliens, but all individuals
within its boundaries, including its own nationals.   Indeed,
given the facts of global interdependence and the intimate
links between peace and human rights, much of humankind appears

today to have come to the opinion that nothing could be of greater "international concern" than the "human rights" of all individuals.

Within the current system of international law, external decision makers are authorized to intercede in certain matters that might at one time have been regarded as internal to a particular state. While, at certain times in the past, even gross violations of human rights were defended by appeal to "domestic jurisdiction," today's demands for exclusive competence must be grounded in far more than an interest in avoiding "intervention."

Intervention is not always impermissible; any assessment must always be contingent upon intent. Where there is no interest in exerting "dictatorial interference," but simply an overriding commitment to the protection of human rights, the act of intervening may represent the proper enforcement of pertinent legal norms. This concept of intervention greatly transforms the exaggerated emphasis on "domestic jurisdiction" that has been associated improperly with individual national intepretations of Article 2 (7) of the Charter and, earlier, with Article 25 (8) of the Covenant of the League of Nations. By offering a major distinction between the idea of self-serving interference by one state in the internal affairs of another state and the notion of the general global community's inclusive application of law to the protection of human dignity, it significantly advances the goal of a just world order.

The importance of the changing doctrine of "intervention" to the shift in global "allocation of competences" was prefigured by the Tunis-Morocco case before the Permanent Court of International Justice in 1923. In this case, the Court developed a broad test to determine whether or not a matter is essentially within the "domestic jurisdiction" of a particular state:

The question whether a certain matter is or is not solely within the domestic jurisdiction of a state is an essentially relative question: it depends upon the development of international relations.

Although this test is hardly free of ambiguity, it does clarify that the choice between "international concern" and "domestic jurisdiction" is not grounded in unalterable conditions of fact, but rather in constantly changing circumstances that permit a continuing adjustment of competences. It follows that whenever particular events create significant violations of human rights, the general global community is entitled to internationalize jurisdiction and to authorize appropriate forms of decision and action.

Where conditions are judged to permit "humanitarian intervention," say McDougal and his associates, the general community "...may enter into the teritory of the defaulting state for the purpose of terminating the outrage and securing compliance with a minimum international standard of human rights," (p. 239). This doctrine of humanitarian intervention echoes E. Borchard's prior formulation in 1922 (p. 14):

> Where a state under exceptional circumstances disregards certain rights of its own citizens, over whom presumably it has absolute sovereignty, the other states of the family of nations are authorized by international law to intervene on grounds of humanity. When the "human rights" are habitually violated, one or more states may intervene in the name of the society of nations and may take such measures as to substitute at least temporarily, if not permanently, its own sovereignty for that of the state thus controlled. Whatever the origin, therefore, of the rights of the individual, it seems assured that these essential rights rest upon the ultimate sanction of international law and will be protected, in last resort, by the most appropriate organ of the international community.

The actual practice of humanitarian intervention on behalf of beleagured citizens of other states has ample precedent, prefiguring even the current world legal order. One of the earliest recorded cases of such intervention concerns an event that took place in 480 B.C., when Gelon, Prince of Syracuse, after defeating the Carthaginians, demanded as one of the conditions of peace that they abandon the custom of sacrificing their children to Saturn. In the nineteenth century, the high point of positivist jurisprudence, the humanitarian intervention of Great Britain, France and Russia in 1827 was designed to end Turkey's particularly inhumane methods against the Greek struggle for independence. Similar aims, inter alia, provoked U.S. intervention in the Cuban Civil War in 1898. Ironically, perhaps (in light of post-World War II relations between the United States and Cuba), this intervention was intended to put an end, in the words of the joint resolution of April 20, 1898, to "the abhorrent conditions which have existed for more than three years in the island of Cuba; have shocked the moral sense of the people of the United States, have been a disgrace to Christian civilization...."

Other cases come to mind as well. In 1902, on the occasion of persecution of Jews in Rumania, the United States - while not a signatory of the Articles of the Treaty of Berlin (protecting the Balkan minorities) made a case for humanitarian intervention. If, said Secretary of State Hay, the United States was not entitled to invoke the clauses of the Treaty, "...it must insist upon the principles therein set forth, because these are principles of law and eternal justice" (De Visscher, 1968, p. 127).

As we have seen, humanitarian intervention is one way of giving effect to the enforcement of anti-genocide norms in international law. Another way involves the use of courts, domestic and international. Under Article V of the Genocide Convention, signatory states are required to enact "the necessary legislation to give effect to" the Convention. Article VI of that Convention further provides that trials for its violation be conducted "by a competent tribunal of the State in the territory of which the act was commit ted, or by any such international penal tribunal as may have jurisdiction."

Here, there are some special problems. First, apart from the European Human Rights Court at Strasburg, no such international penal tribunal has been established. The International Court of Justice at the Hague has no penal or criminal jurisdiction.

The International Court of Justice does, however, have jurisdiction over disputes concerning the interpretation and application of a number of specialized human rights conventions. Such jurisdiction is accorded by the Genocide Convention (Article 9); the Supplementary Convention on the Abolition of Slavery, the Slave Trade and Institutions and Practices Similar to Slavery (1956, Article 10); the Convention on the Political Rights of Women (1953, Article 9); the Convention Relating to the Status of Refugees (1951, Article 38); and the Convention on the Reduction of Statelessness (1961, Article 14). In exercising its jurisdiction, however, the ICJ must still confront significant difficulties in bringing recalcitrant states into contentious proceedings. There is still no way to effectively ensure the attendance of defendant states before the Court. Although many states have acceded to the Optional Clause of the Statute of the ICJ (Article 36, Paragraph 2), these accessions are watered down by many attached reservations.

Second, courts of the states where acts in violation of the Genocide Convention have been committed are hardly likely to conduct proceedings against their own national officials (excluding, of course, the possibility of courts established following a coup d'etat or revolution). What is needed, therefore, is an expansion of the practice of states after World War II - a practice by states that had been occupied during the war - of seeking extradition of criminals and of trying them in their own national courts.

Let us briefly review the basic contours of this practice:

After the Second World War, three judicial solutions were adapted to the problem of determining the proper jurisdiction for trying Nazi offenses by the victim states, solutions that were additional to the specially-constituted Nuremberg Tribunal.

The first solution involved the creation of special courts set up expressly for the purpose at hand. This solution was adopted in Rumania, Czechoslavakia, Holland, Austria, Bulgaria, Hungary and Poland.

The second solution, adopted in Great Britain, Australia, Canada, Greece and Italy, involved the establishment of special military courts.

The third solution brought the Nazis and their collaborators before ordinary courts - a solution accepted in Norway, Denmark and Yugoslavia. This solution was also adopted by Israel, although -

314

strictly speaking - the State of Israel did not exist at the time of the commission of the crimes in question.

In the future, I would suggest that there need be no war or occupation to justify the use of domestic courts to punish crimes of genocide.There is nothing novel about such a suggestion since a principal purpose of the Genocide Convention lies in its explicit applicability to non-wartime actions. Limits upon actions against enemy nationals are as old as the laws of war of international law. But the laws of war do not cover a government's actions against its own nationals. It is, therefore, primarily in the area of domestic atrocities that the Genocide Convention seeks to expand pre-existing international penal law.

Going beyond Article VI of the Genocide Convention, which holds to the theory of "concurrent jurisdiction" (jurisdiction based on the site of the alleged offense and on the nationality of the offender), any state may now claim jurisdiction when the crime involved is genocide. There is already ample precedent for such a rule in international law, a precedent based upon the long-standing treatment of "common enemies of mankind" (hostes humani generis) or international outlaws as within the scope of "universal jurisdiction."

The case for universal jurisdiction in matters concerning genocide is further strengthened by the difficulties surrounding extradition. In this connection, the best example is the case of Israel in the apprehension, trial and punishment of Adolph Eichmann. In 1950, Israel enacted the Nazi and Nazi Collaborators Punishment Law. In this enactment, Israel did nothing different than other states that had been occupied during the war, although - of course - the State of Israel did not exist at the time of the commission of the crime.4 Yet, its subsequent efforts to obtain certain major war criminals (e.g., Joseph Mengele) from Argentina and elsewhere via extradition were improperly rebuffed.

Why were the refusals to extradite contrary to international law? For the most part, these refusals were grounded in the argument that the crimes in question were of a "political nature." Although there is a "political offense" exception to the international law of extradition, this exception is explicitly precluded by the Genocide Convention in cases involving crimes against humanity. Moreover, under the formula, extradite or prosecute, the states refusing extradition were obligated to prosecute the alleged offenders themselves. Needless to say, no attempts at prosecution were ever undertaken.

In rendering its judgment on Adolph Eichmann, the Israeli court built upon a reaffirmation of natural law, noting that there may be special occasions and circumstances for which the law, for want of foresight, failed to make provision. Moreover, citing an important case from English law, the Israeli court offered a vital conceptual distinction between retroactive law and ex-post-facto law. Drawn from Blackstone's Commentaries, this distinction held that "ex post facto laws are objectionable when, after an action indifferent in itself is committed, the legislator then, for the first time, declares it to have been a crime and inflicts a punishment upon the person who has committed it....Here it is impossible that the party could forsee that an action, innocent when it was done, should afterwards be converted to guilt by subsequent law. He had, therefore, no cause to abstain from it and all punishment for not abstaining must, in consequence, be cruel and unjust." In the Eichmann case, of course, the laws involved did not create a new crime and it certainly could not be said that he did not have criminal intent (mens rea). The accused's actions were hardly "indifferent" and they were assuredly considered crimes at the time of their commission by all civilized nations.

With respect to the issue of superior orders, the classical writers on international law had long rejected that doctrine as a proper defense against the charge of war crimes. The German Code of Military Law operative during the war provided that a soldier must execute all orders undeterred by the fear of legal consequences, but it added that this would not excuse him in cases where he must have known with certainty that the order was illegal. This view was upheld in an important decision of the German Supreme Court in Leipzig in 1921. According to the Court, a subordinate who obeyed the order of his superior officer was liable to punishment if it were known to him that such an order involved a contravention of international law.

The defense of "superior orders" was also rejected at the Einsatzgruppen Trial undertaken by an American military tribunal. According to the tribunal: "The obedience of a soldier is not the obedience of an automaton. A soldier is a reasoning agent. It is a fallacy of widespread consumption that a soldier is required to do everything his superior officers order him to do. The subordinate is bound only to obey the lawful orders of his superior."

Ironically, Goebbels himself spoke against the plea of superior orders during the war. In an article in the German Press on May 28, 1944, he wrote: "No international law of welfare is in existence which provides that a soldier who has committed a mean crime can escape punishment by pleading as his defence that he followed the commands of his superiors. This holds particlarly true if those commands are contrary to all human ethics and opposed to the well established international usage of warfare." It was the bombing of Germany by the allies to which Goebbels referred, and he was attempting to justify the Nazi practice of shooting captured Allied airmen.

ANTI-GENOCIDE NORMS AND THE REAL SELF-INTEREST OF STATES

We all know, however, that states are typically animated by forces other than an acutely moral imagination and that the presumed requirements of realpolitik invariably take precedence over those of international law. It follows that before the progressive codification of anti-genocide norms can be paralleled by the widespread re-

finement and expansion of pertinent enforcement measures, individual
states must come to believe that international legal steps to prevent and punish genocide are always in their best interests. Drawing upon the Thomistic idea of law as a positive force for directing
humankind to its proper goals (an idea that is itself derived from
Aristotle's conception of the natural development of the state from
social impulses), we need to seek ways of aligning the anti-genocide
dictates of the law of nations with effective strategies of implementation - i.e., strategies based on expanded patterns of "humanitarian intervention," transnational judicial settlement, and domestic court involvement.

To accomplish this objective, primary attention must be directed toward harmonizing these strategies with the self-interested behavior of states. Here, it must be understood that the existence of
even a far-reaching human rights regime is not enough. Before this
regime can make productive claims on the community of states, the
members of this community will need to calculate that such compliance is in their respective interests. Ultimately this sort of
calculation will depend, in turn, on the creation of a new world order system - a planetary network of obligations stressing cooperative global concerns over adversary relationships. The centerpiece
of this new world order system must be the understanding that all
states and all peoples form one essential body and one true community.

Recently, this idea has been advanced with particular lucidity
and persuasiveness by Saul H. Mendlovitz who argues that "to think,
and act as a global citizen is essential to world order inquiry and
praxis" (p. 14). Basing his analysis and prescriptions on the idea
that a global civilization is rapidly emerging and that global citizenship is prerequisite to the creation of a harmonious world order, the central thrust of our concerns, we are told, must be "to
develop a global interest perspective which will ultimately compete
with, replace or combine in some new way with national interest
theory."

Our task, then, must be to discover ways to make the separate
states conscious of their vital planetary identity. With such a redefinition of national interests, states could progress from the dying forms of realpolitik to the primordial power of human unity and
interdependence. Since all things contain their own contradiction,
the international legal order based upon competitive nationalism
could be transformed into an organic world society.

Will it work? Can humankind be expected to grasp this calculus
of potentiality, reaffirming the sovereignty of reason over the
forces of disintegration? Can states be expected to tear down the
walls of competitive power struggles and replace them with the per-
meable membranes of spirited cooperation?

Perhaps not! But there is surely no other way. The Talmud
tells us, "The dust from which the first man was made was gathered
in all the corners of the world." By moving toward a new planetary
identity, the peoples of Earth can begin to build bridges over the

most dangerous abyss they have ever known. Hopefully, even in this absurd theater of modern world politics, human beings will choose life rather than death. Stripped of false hopes, and without illusion, man may yet stare at the specter of genocide with passionate attention and experience the planetary responsibility that will bring liberation.

But how might such responsibility come into being? How, exactly, might a system based on conflict be transformed into a cooperative world public order of human dignity? How can we meet the challenge of "planetization"? What particular transition strategies need to be examined?

To answer these questions, we need to focus on the shaping of a new political consciousness. In this connection, special attention must be directed to the overriding obligations of natural law and to the corollary subordination of national prerogatives to essential human rights. The false communion of modern states is inwardly rotten, time-dishonored and close to collapsing. A communion based on fear and degradation, its mighty efforts on behalf of power and aggrandizement have occasioned a deep desolation of the human spirit. To unhinge this "communion" while there is still time, international angst must give way to real community and humankind's store of international ideals must yield a gentle and new harmony.

The problem, then, is largely the place of the state, both in the arena of planetary interaction and in the lives of its own citizens. Before we can move toward a new and effective anti-genocide regime in international law, the longstanding bellum omnes contra omnes must give way to a new affirmation of global singularity and solidarity. States, like individual persons, are cemented to each other not by haphazard aggregation, but by the certainty of their basic interdependence. Beneath the diversities of a seemingly fractionated world, there exists a latent oneness. With the manifestation of the "one in the many," states may begin to aim at particular goals and objectives in harmony with all other states. Unlike anything else, this manifestation can endow the search for planetization and freedom from genocide with real potency.

The problem of the omnivorous state, subordinating all moral sensibilities to the idea of unlimited internal and external jurisdiction, was forseen brilliantly in the 1930s by Jose Ortega y Gasset (1932). Ortega correctly identifies the state as "the greatest danger," mustering its immense and unassailable resources "to crush beneath it any creative minority which disturbs it - disturbs it in any order of things: in politics, in ideas, in industry." Set in motion by individuals whom it has already rendered anonymous, the state establishes its machinery above society so that humankind comes to live for the state, for the governmental apparatus: "And as, after all, it is only a machine whose existence and maintenance depend on the vital supports around it, the State, after sucking out the very marrow of society, will be left bloodless, a skeleton, dead with that rusty death of machinery, more gruesome than the death of a living organism" (p. 121).

Rationalist philosophy had derived the idea of national sovereignty from the notions of individual liberty, but cast in its post-Westphalian expression, the idea has acted to oppose human dignity and human rights. Left to its own nefarious devices, the legacy of unimpeded nationalism can only be the subordination of all human concerns to the imminent ends of the state. Ultimately, as Lewis Mumford has observed, all human energies will be placed at the disposal of the military "megamachine," with whose advent we are all drawn unsparingly into a "dreadful ceremony" of worldwide human sacrifice.[5]

The state flees reason because it flees intimate awareness of itself. And this awareness, of course, is informed by the always latent potential of humankind to produce evil. In the final analysis, it is in the fatal synergy of ineradicable human inclinations with expanding national power that makes genocide possible.

HUMAN INCLINATIONS TO EVIL

These human inclinations are illuminated brilliantly by Israel Charny's (1982) new book, How Can We Commit The Unthinkable?: Genocide, The Human Cancer. Seeking a better understanding of humankind's destructiveness, Charny convincingly disposes of the idea that only psychopaths are capable of genocidal behavior. "By not pushing our deepest weaknesses off into a realm of pathology or sickness, we invite ourselves to acknowledge these terribly difficult parts of ourselves and master them" (p. 22).

Frightening as it may be to contemplate, it is altogether likely that the capacity to commit terrible evil lies latent in all human beings. And this capacity, in an extraordinarily ironic kind of complementarity, is bound up very closely with our all-encompassing fear of death. According to Charny's lucid analysis:

> Much of our utterly depraved destructiveness may well have its roots in natural processes where we originally seek nothing more than to feel alive. Yet, because there is so much we do not know about how to manage the natural processes of life and its everpresent counterpart, death, many of us move ineluctably towards illness, insanity, and all manner of evil deeds, including the destruction of others (p. 45).

Charny's thesis, of course, stands in diametric opposition to Freud, who saw evil as a fatality born of base motives. It has much in common, however, with Hegel's view that evil arises from good intentions and Ernest Becker's argument that evil flows from the "logic of the heroic," from the worldwide acceptance of a formula in which killing of "outsiders" placates invisible powers of extinction by expiation. As Becker (1975) points out in Escape From Evil:

> Men cause evil by wanting heroically to triumph over it, because Man is a frightened animal who tries to triumph, an animal who will not admit his own insignificance, that he cannot

perpetuate himself and his group forever, that no one is invul-
nerable no matter how much of the blood of others is spilled to
try to demonstrate it (p. 151).

It is, if we accept the position of Charny and Becker, among
others, man's ingenuity rather than his animal nature that heaps
evil upon the world. Tortured by the knowledge of his own mortality
and by the prospect of extinction with insignificance, man seeks to
transcend this unbearable fate through culturally standardized hero
systems and symbols. Searching for an heroic victory over death by
trafficking in pure power, man inevitably produces evil. And he
produces evil in pursuit not of debased ideals but for purity, good-
ness, and righteousness. Says Becker:

Hitler Youth were recruited on the basis of idealism; the nice
boy next door is the one who dropped the bomb on Hiroshima; the
idealistic communist is the one who sided with Stalin against
his former comrades: kill to protect the heroic revolution, to
assure the victory over evil. As Dostoevsky saw, killing is
sometimes distasteful, but the distaste is swallowed if it is
necessary to true heroism: as one of the revolutionaries asked
Pyotr Verhovensky in The Possessed, when they were about to
kill one of their number, "Are other groups also doing this?"
In other words, is it the socially heroic thing to do, or are
we being arbitrary about identifying evil? Each person wants
his life to be a marker for good as his group defines it. Men
work their programs of heroism according to the standard cultural scenarios, from Pontius Pilate through Eichmann and
Calley (pp. 150-151).

Understood in these terms, evil is also - as Sartre says in
Saint Genet - a projection. Its commission, however odious, is always in response to greater wrongdoing. It is born of the search to
escape from evil.

The all-powerful state prods people to choose evil with pure
heart. Since they do evil for the sake of the good, i.e., for the
state, they will inevitably look upon themselves as sanctified evil-
doers. The hater, the potential genocider, is a person who is
afraid, not - to be sure - of his scapegoats, but of himself, of his
fate, of change, of his instincts. Left to his own devices, he is
merely a coward whose tendency to murder is censured and forbidden.
Encouraged by politics, and protected by the glorious anonymity of
the mob, this tendency knows no bounds. A pitiless stone who once
dared to kill only in effigy, he now becomes part of a furious tor-
rent of real destructiveness.

We must not permit the state to provide this kind of encouragement. To meet this objective, we first need to consider how power
is structured internally within states and how it is exercised between them. Above all else, this means a search for ways of minimizing violence and degradation by elites against their own citizens
and by governments against each other. And this search must be
tutored by the understanding that there exist important connections

between these different arenas of power, i.e., elites who maintain internal rule by violent means of coercion are also inclined to view such coercion as the principal instrument of interaction with other states, and vice versa.

One important manifestation of this nexus is large-scale scape-goating by the state. No other practice, perhaps, is as closely associated with the dynamics of international statecraft. Faced with dissidence and disaffection at home, and unwilling to respond to the causes of dissatisfaction by enlarging the prospects for social and economic justice, the state often redirects everyone's attention from domestic affairs to foreign ones. Here, the state "solves" its overwhelming internal problems by making justice a matter of triumph over an external enemy and by focusing on a heroic foreign cause.

Another important manifestation of this nexus is the unwilling-ness of certain states to intervene on behalf of oppressed peoples within other states where such intervention is viewed as geopoliti-cally self-defeating. Nurtured by a social-Darwinian conception of world politics and by a tenacious commitment to the exigencies of realpolitik, such unwillingness subverts the peremptory obligations of international law and perpetuates the primacy of positivist juris-prudence over the requirements of justice.

Before the realism of anti-genocide ideals can prevail in glo-bal society, the major states in that society must learn to escape from the confines of such a limited context for choosing policy options.

"When I get to heaven," said the Hasidic Rabbi Susya just before his death, "they will not ask me, 'Why were you not Moses?' but 'Why were you not Susya?'" When the major world powers confront the consequences of their ongoing geopolitical strategy, their peoples will not ask, "Why were we not saints?" but "Why did we act in a fashion contrary to our own unique potentiality? Why did we abandon our ideals and our interests at the same time?"

THE EVOLUTION OF A PLANETARY IDENTITY

Our task is to make separate states conscious of their emerging planetary identity. With such a revisioning of national goals and incentives, states can progress to an awareness of new archetypes for global society.

To succeed in this task will be very difficult. But it need not be as fanciful as some would have us believe. Before we take the shroud measurements of the corpse of human society, we must un-derstand that faith in the new forms of international interaction is a critical step toward their implementation.

A new evolutionary vanguard must - in the fashion of the grow-ing worldwide movement against nuclear weapons and nuclear war - grow out of informed publics throughout the world. Such a vanguard must aim to end the separation of state interests from those of its citizens and from those of humanity as a whole.

If this sounds grandly unpolitical, it is because politics as usual cannot prevent genocide. And if it all sounds hopelessly idealistic, it must be recognized that nothing could be more fanciful than the avoidance of far-reaching system transformation. Frank and Fritzie Manuel (1979) point out in their excellent study of utopian thought that the truest forms of realism now lie in the imaginings of idealists, not the imaginings of paradisaical fantasies, but embryonic expectations that carry within themselves the seeds of their own verification:

> Paradoxically, the great utopians have been great realists. They have an extraordinary comprehension of the time and place in which they are writing and deliver themselves of penetrating reflections on socioeconomic, scientific or emotional conditions of their moment in history...Their knowledge serves them as a springboard for a jump into a future which could be either a total negation of the present or so sharply lateral that others would at first glance consider it chimerical, fantastic, improbable - in a word, utopian. There is an almost inevitable inclination in a utilitarian society to value most those utopian visionaries whose "dreams came true," not the best criterion for judgment. The short-term prognosticator can be a bore. He is merely a meteorologist, useful in planning an outing or a military invasion (p. 28).

Having said these things about utopian thinking, we must also consider the prospects for improved enforcement of anti-genocide norms within a fully centralized system of world law. In such a system, the states in world politics would begin to exist with an authority above them. They would, therefore, co-exist within a hierarchy of institutions and officials that would apply rules in a relationship of superordination and subordination. Unlike the existing decentralized international legal order, which is typically characterized as a law of "coordination," this centralized system of world law would be based upon the creation of supranational centers of power and authority. In other words, we are speaking here of world government.

Students of genocide must consider the human rights implications of a potentially emergent sytem of world law, a system based upon the centralization of sovereign authority. At the initial stages of such consideration, special attention would need to be directed to such questions as: (1) Does centralized or "vertical" world law offer greater promise for the international human rights regime than the existing decentralized or "horizontal" world legal order? (2) Can there be any realistic hope for replacing the long-standing dynamics of decentralized legal relationships with more centralized dynamics? (3) Just how much military force, if any, must be transferred to the supranational authority? (4) Might the supranational authority secure compliance with its dictates without the threat or use of force?

Gabriela Mistral, the Chilean poet who won the Nobel Prize for Literature in 1945, once wrote that crimes against humanity carry within themselves "a moral judgment over an evil in which every feeling man and woman concurs." At this time in our history, the best hope for preventing such evil lies in universal compliance with the complementary imperatives of national interest and anti-genocide norms. With such compliance, the legal community of mankind could still replace its historic incapacity for humane interaction with a planetary ethos of human dignity and global renewal.

NOTES

1. See The Charter and Judgment of the Nuremberg Tribunal: History and Analysis, Memorandum submitted by the Secretary-General, United Nations, General Assembly, International Law Commission, Lake Success, New York, 1949. p. 71.
2. The Genocide Convention has been before the U.S. Senate since 1949. The Convention was transmitted to the Senate by President Truman on June 16, 1949. Notwithstanding American failure to ratify, it has been in force since January 12, 1951, 90 days after the requisite 20 states had ratified it. With the exception of President Eisenhower, every U.S. president since Truman has endorsed ratification of the Convention. When Great Britian ratified in 1970, the U.S. remained the only major Western democracy to have refused ratification. The Soviet Union ratified the Convention in 1954.
3. The idea of proportionality is contained in the Mosaic lex talionis, since it prescribes that an injury should be requited reciprocally, but certainly not with a greater injury. As Aristotle understood the lex talionis, it was a law of justice, not of hatred - one eye, not two, for an eye: one tooth, no more, for a tooth.
4. In response to the issue of Israel's non-existence at the time of the Holocaust, Gideon Hausner - who prosecuted Adolf Eichmann before the Jerusalem District Court - makes the following point:

> The argument that Israel did not yet exist when the offenses were committed was highly technical. She could certainly, as a member of the family of nations, claim her right to share in the universal jurisdiction over crimes against humanity. Moreover, the State of Israel had grown from the Jewish community in Palestine, which had been internationally recognized since 1917, under the Balfour Declaration and later under the Peace Treaty, which gave it the status of a "Jewish National Home." Palestinian Jews had fought under their own flag in World War II; postwar Israel had been recognized by the Western Allies as having been a cobelligerent and had been invited to join them in terminating the state of war with Western Germany.

See Hausner's Justice in Jerusalem (New York: Schoken Books, 1968), p. 315.
5. See Mumford's The Myth of the Machine: The Pentagon of Power (New York: Harcourt Brace Jovanovich, 1970), a book that climaxes a series of studies that began with Technics and Civilization in 1934. Mumford identifies the wholesale miscarriage of "megatechnics" that has misdirected our human energies and brought us closer to a permanent state of degradation.

REFERENCES

BECKER, Ernest. Escape From Evil New York: Free Press, 1975.
BORCHARD, E. The Diplomatic Protection of Citizens Abroad or the Law of International Claims (1922), p. 14.
CHARNY, Israel W. How Can We Commit the Unthinkable?: Genocide, the Human Cancer. Boulder, Colorado: Westview Press, 1982.
MANUEL, Frank E., & Manuel, Fritzie P., Utopian Thoughts in the Western World. Cambridge: Harvard University Press, 1979
McDOUGAL, Myres; Lasswell, Harold; & Chen, Lung-Chu. Human Rights and World Public Order: The Basic Policies of an International Law of Human Rights. New Haven and London: Yale University Press, 1980.
MENDLOVITZ, Saul. The Struggle for a Just World Order: An Agenda of Inquiry and Praxis for the 1980s. New York: Institute World Order, World Order Models Project, Working Paper Number 20, p. 14.
ORTEGA y Gasset, Jose. The Revolt of the Masses. New York: Norton, 1932.

LOUIS RENE BERES, Ph.D., Purdue University, West Layayette, Indiana 4707, U.S.A.

28. From Theory to Application: Proposal for an Applied Science Approach to a Genocide Early Warning System

Ephraim M. Howard and Yocheved Howard

Yocheved Howard, M.S., M.S.W.: Private practice in marital and family therapy and group therapy. Experience includes work with Holocaust survivors and children of Holocaust survivors. As a result of personal background and interests, is strongly committed to doing everything possible to prevent any genocidal activity - because every one may affect my people.

Professor Ephraim M. Howard: Process consultant in personal inter-relationships and industrial operations. Have been personally committed to prevention of all genocidal activities since entering concentration and death camps shortly after they were 'opened' by Allied troops at the end of World War II. These feelings were reinforced on learning of slaughter of all of my European relations in Kamenets Podolsk, a few days before its liberation by the Czech Legion.

Yocheved and Ephraim Howard were Co-Directors of the First International Conference on the Holocaust and Genocide, Yocheved Howard as Program Chairperson, and Ephraim Howard with responsibility for Organization.

Introduction

The authors show how to develop a Genocide Early Warning System (EWS) within realistic expenditures of time and funds. Genocide early warning has been desired because of the belief that if adequate warning existed, sufficiently in advance, the impending disaster could be mitigated or possibly even averted. Charny and Rapaport (1982), Payne, (1973), Ross (1982), and others have already outlined much of the philosophical underpinning required as a basis for a Genocide EWS. The authors have used an applied science approach to show how to develop such a system. From the material presented it is possible to prepare the operative proposal and request for funding.

Definition of Genocide

As stated in the title, this paper provides the basis for a concrete proposal for a Genocide EWS. The term genocide used herein refers to actual events of mass murder and NOT to any other violations of human rights, political rights, nor even to deliberate attempts to destroy a people's cultural identity. To extend the use of the word genocide to undesirable sociological processes, as some authors are currently tending to do, is to alter its meaning beyond identifiable boundaries.

Systems and Models

The terms 'systems,' 'applied science approach,' and 'model' used herein are much in vogue in the social and behavioral sciences as well as in the physical sciences, and accordingly many authors use them as common terms. We believe the applications described herein will be better understood if the background and development of these concepts are briefly outlined.

Before World War II, problems were generally resolved by separating the overall problem into its separable components and utilizing simple cause and effect linear relationships for solution of each of the problem elements. The component solutions were then summed to provide the overall solution, and this procedure was generally found adequate. However, about the beginning of World War II people became increasingly aware of the compounding effects of the interactions among the problem components. They realized that it was not valid to simply ignore the interactions among the several elements of the complex problems being encountered, and that often these interactions actually dominated the choice of solutions.

The new approaches developed for the solution of complex problems during this period were known by many names, e.g., systems studies, applied science approaches, operations research and others. However, the basic framework was the same in all cases: a clear statement of the process being studied, the determination of the specific elements entering into that process; clearly defined boundaries, or the range of limits of variation acceptable in solutions of the problem; and a knowledge of the interactions involved among the several elements entering into the process.

A typical example of the complex problems resolved during World War II was the solution of how to most efficiently transport supplies from the United States to combat areas. The outcome desired was maximum delivery in minimum time and at minimum cost. In development of the solution, it was assumed that all supplies were available and awaiting shipment from U.S. coastal ports. Thus the elements to be considered were: shipping required to carry the supplies; speed and maneuverability as well as capacity of each of the ships available; performance characteristics, numbers available and both defense and attack tactics of submarines which attacked shipping in the areas to which the supplies were to be delivered; performance characteristics and tactical performance characteristics, numbers and tactical usage of aircraft available for convoy defense at the beginning (coastal U.S.) and end of each trip; and weather and sea conditions anticipated along each of the various routes available for shipping.

As a result of such studies, it became possible, for the first time in history, to determine the quantities and availability dates of supplies together with a realistic estimate of 'costs' in manpower and equipment required for the delivery and insurance of its safety. Similar methods were used to plan the convoy defense tactics, and ultimately even the total process involved in manufacturing and moving the supplies to the shipping points. The success of the new methods was proven in all applications.

These systems/applied science approaches necessitated the development of new analytical and mathematical techniques to cope with the multiplicity of details and interactions which had to be considered. In turn, the increase in the necessary complexity of some of these techniques (notwithstanding the simplicity of the basic concepts) together with the increase in numbers of equations which had to be solved simultaneously, forced the development of the electronic computers and data reduction systems which now enter every phase of our lives. The application of these sophisticated tools also forced greater clarification of task and element definitions which also made for clearer understanding of the problems to be resolved.

The basic definition which has evolved for a system is, "A system is a whole which functions as a whole by virtue of the interdependence of its parts." From this follows the synergistic concept that, "The whole can be greater than the sum of its parts." Also, it is then apparent that the analysis of systems must of necessity focus on the interdependence between the elements of the problem.

With this definition and the associated concepts, it was clear that many of mankind's organizations such as families, institutions, communities, and even nations also could be considered as systems. As a consequence, the new analytical methods were applied to sociologic studies and the accuracy of the mathematical representation, or model, was validated in many ways. From studies of the models, comments were made which were indistinguishable from those made by sociologists who had earlier or were concurrently studying the same human relationships. Examples of such comments (based only on model studies - but verified in vivo) were: "The degree of organization varies, of course, as does the robustness of these systems"; "The organization, per se, is the fundamental problem to study"; "We must make the shift to dynamics, emergence and complex interactions and feedback cycles"; and one also began to hear and speak of "...the pathology of such systems." Accordingly, from von Bertalanffy's papers in 1950 to date, numerous papers and books have been written to show how the system concepts could be applied to sociological studies. The use of these concepts in considering the idea and in developing the reality of a Genocide EWS is therefore a logical consequence.

DETERMINATION OF SPECIFIC COMPONENTS TO BE CONSIDERED IN DEVELOPING A GENOCIDE EARLY WARNING SYSTEM

It appears that most, if not all, genocides follow essentially similar paths, starting with promulgation of the idea that the intended victims are less than human and proceeding to their final slaughter. Charny and Rapaport (1982), Payne (1973), Ross (1982) and others have separately published various analyses of the different phases in genocide and indicated 'steps' in the development of the genocidal process. In some cases, the 'causes' underlying each 'step' are also indicated. In others, some means of labeling is provided to identify the conditions of having reached a 'step' or phase in the process.

Typically, in Robert Payne's studies, he stated that mass slaughter throughout history "obeys predictable laws and assumes predictable stages, despite outward differences." He gives specific stages as: 1) The future victims are lulled into a sense of security; 2) The death blow; 3) The victims recover from their paralysis; 4) The military mounts another massacre; 5) The victims begin to organize; 6) The military mounts a third massacre; 7) The victims 'bites off the enemy's hands and feet' (the tide begins to turn against the killers); and 8) The final massacre (the killers continue relentlessly up to their final breath).

In their study, Charny and Rapaport adapted Smelser's (1963) concept of collective process but elaborated it and adapted it specifically to genocide. They proposed the following categories: 1) Societal forces supporting human life versus societal forces moving to destruction of human life (cultural values and tradition - structural processes and institutions - human rights status); 2) Key historical, economic, political, legal and social events and transitions; 3) Formation of genocidal fantasy and ideology; 4) Precipitating factors or context; 5) Mobilization of means to genocide; 6) Legitimization and institutionalization of genocide; and 7) Execution of genocide and experience denying mechanisms.

From these and others in the literature the stages or steps required for development of the mathematical model on which the Genocide EWS is based may be developed.

THE TRANSFORMATION: FROM THEORY TO PRACTICE

The first step in establishing the Genocide EWS is to complete an extensive literature search. The examples cited above are a few of those in which the 'path' of genocide are 'tracked.' In particular, several writers have extensively documented the various steps in the process of the Holocaust, the archetypal genocide. This alone may provide an adequate original basis.

After completion of the review of existing literature, the first 'model' must be developed. The mathematical model (or more simply 'model') is a mathematical scheme which interconnects the mathematical symbols correlated to the historical events (i.e., which represent them in this context) in a precise and consistent way. Since the genocide process appears to be essentially linear and Smelser's idea of a value added process applies (i.e., "each stage in the process adds its value, but only as the earlier stages combine according to a certain pattern can the next stage contribute its particular value"), more attention needs to be paid to the sequencing and to the delineation of each phase.

Judgment of the researchers will be involved in delineating each phase or step in the genocidal process. Also, their judgment will be involved in attempting to determine some unit of measure which can be used as a 'weight' (measure of importance) and/or in selection of 'marker points' which delineate the beginning or end of each step in the genocidal process.

By assigning a numerical value to each phase, it will then be possible to determine the total numerical value, i.e., the sum of the numerical values for the phases or fractional parts of phases which have passed at any point in the genocidal process. It will also be possible to determine the numerical value beyond which the genocidal process appears to take on a life of its own and proceed irrevocably. This point will probably be considered as the critical point in establishing a Genocide EWS. Prior to reaching this critical point, the genocidal process appears to be a continous (and reversible) function of time.

Prior to the development of Catastrophe Theory, in the 70's, (see Zeeman, 1977; & Woodcock, 1978), such events which appear to be continuous up to some point and then undergo a drastic and seemingly irrevocable change could not be followed mathematically. The process could be explained or understood only up to the discontinuity and after some point when it again became continuous. However, the entire idea of the discontinuity was not explainable. Use of this theory makes it possible to follow such processes throughout their course. Accordingly, it will be useful in determining the 'critical point' in the process beyond which the action is irreversible and proceeds at an ever-increasing pace. Obviously, the alarm provided by the Genocide EWS must be sounded before this critical point is reached.

Adjustment of Weights and Model Validation

Initially, the determination of 'weights' to be assigned to each phase of the genocide process is essentially arbitrary and can be based on any decision process. However, after the establishment of the first model, as discussed above, the weights will need to be adjusted (or the model changed, or both) if incorporation of data from other genocides do not provide consistent results. Adjustment of weights, or model modification, must be done using mathematically consistent processes. As each additional case of genocide is matched to the model, and the corresponding changes are made, a continued improvement of the model as a predictor will result. The more one validates the model with data from other genocides, the greater the confidence one will develop in its use as a predictor.

This proposal is based on over twenty years of personal experience of successfully estimating costs for development of models of complex processes in several fields. In all cases, successful models resulted (i.e., they closely represented the outcomes of the processes involved), and in almost all cases, the development was within the time and cost estimates proposed. Although no one process was exactly the same as any other process, the variation of processes and the success in estimating development requirements, as well as the successful project completions themselves, provides a high degree of confidence. Some projects for which models were developed included an intercontinental ballistic missile system; establishment of a sanitary system for a large county in California; establishment of mobile hospitals for an army in the field; design of an overall transportation system for a large metropolitan area; and development of a system to predict population growth and the corresponding changes in housing and service requirements for a kibbutz.

Based on what we already know, a Genocide Early Warning System is feasible. Such a system is readily derivable using basic techniques of applied systems, and its development is relatively cheap in terms of both cost and time required. The saving of ANY lives at all, in the first impending genocide, would amply repay any expense involved in developing such a system. Accordingly, it is hoped that as a direct result of The International Conference on the Holocaust and Genocide, the direct effort of implementation of a Genocide Early Warning System will begin.

REFERENCES

BUCKLEY, W. Sociology and Modern Systems Theory. Englewood Cliffs, N.J.: Prentice-Hall, 1967.
BUCKLEY, W. (Ed.), Modern Systems Research for the Behavioral Scientist. Chicago: Aldine Publishing Co., 1969.
CAPRE. F. The Tao of Physics. Boulder, Colorado: Shambala Publications, 1976.
CHARNY, Israel W. In collaboration with Chanan Rapaport. How Can We Commit the Unthinkable?: Genocide, The Human Cancer. Boulder, Colorado: Westview, 1982.
PAYNE, Robert. Massacre: The Tragedy of Bangla Desh and the Phenomenon of Mass Slaughter Throughout History. New York: Macmillan, 1973.
ROSS, R. W. DPs and Refugees, the Allies and the Jews, 1945-1950. Address at the International Congress on the Holocaust and Genocide, June 1982, Tel Aviv, Israel.
SASIENI, M. A., & Friedman, L. Operations Research. New York: John Wiley & Sons, 1959.
SMELSER, N. Collective Behavior. New York: Free Press, 1963.
WOODCOCK, A., & Davis, M. Catastrophe Theory. New York: Avon Books, 1978.
ZEEMAN, E. C. Catastrophe Theory: Selected Papers 1972-1977. Reading: Benjamin, 1977.

EPHRAIM M. HOWARD, Ph.D., & YOCHEVED HOWARD, M.S., M.S.W., Kibbutz Hazorea, Israel

29. World Genocide Tribunal: A Proposal for Planetary Preventive Measures Supplementing a Genocide Early Warning System

Luis Kutner
with the collaboration of Ernest Katin

Luis Kutner: L.L.B., J.D. Member, Illinois Bar. Founder and Chairman, Commission for International Due Process of Law, Congressional nominee, Nobel Peace Prize. Consul for Ecuador, Chicago; Consul General for Guatemala; Special Assistant Attorney General, State of Illinois; Former Visiting Associate Professor, Yale Law School. Author of many books and journal articles; author of WORLD HABEAS CORPUS, THE LIVING WILL, and THE RIGHT TO DIE WITH DIGNITY. National Chairman, Senior Citizens Crime Commission; World Advocates Center, World Court of Public Opinion, World Court of Human Rights.

Ernest Katin: Member Minnesota, Illinois and Israel Bar Associations. J.D. University of Minnesota Law School, 1958; Ph.D. Political Science, University of Minnesota, 1962, Instructor Political Science, University of Minnesota, 1953-4; Assistant Professor Political Science, Chicago State College South, 1964-5. Law Clerk to the Honorable James G. Parsons, U.S. District Court, Chicago, 1967; Assistant Legal Counsel, Office of Economic Opportunity, Great Lakes Region, 1968-9; Former Assistant Legal Advisor, Municipality of Tel Aviv-Yafo, 1972-79. Author and collaborator of articles on American constitutional law, World Habeas Corpus, human rights and other miscellaneous topics.

This paper proposes the establishment of a World Genocide Tribunal, adopted by treaty-statute, to try and punish perpetrators of acts of genocide.

The proposed Tribunal would apply international law, including the Convention on the Prevention and Punishment of Genocide and other human rights declarations, conventions and treaties and the Helsinki Accords, directly on the individual, whether violator or victim, and function as a guardian of human liberty and the sanctity of life, giving constructive notice to terrorists and tyrants that no abuse of human beings will be tolerated by the international community.

The Tribunal, functioning jointly with a Genocide Early Warning System or World Ombudsman, would initiate appropriate preventive measures. It would be empowered to hear petitions by individuals or groups and to take action to prevent or mitigate potential genocidal actions.

Individuals arbitrarily detained in genocide-related action would be conferred with the right to petition for Writs of World Habeas Corpus, the internationalization of the Common Law Writ.

The world's weak and dispossessed would be provided with redress and protection from the powerful. The Tribunal would be a legal breakthrough for public world order, constituting a ligament for
human dignity and freedom.

BACKGROUND IN INTERNATIONAL LAW

The proposal for a World Genocide Tribunal is considered within
the context of the present state of international law as developed
since 1945 as an effective solution leading towards a legal world
order.

During the 1930s the protection of human rights was primarily a
matter for domestic concern. Hitler, by asserting the sovereignty
of the state was free to persecute German Jews and dissidents with
impunity (Kutner, 1967, p. 23). By the end of World War II the
need for providing for the international protection of human rights
became apparent. However, the present world system for the protection of human rights and the prevention of genocide remains ineffective. Under the prevailing post-Westphalian system, based on state
sovereignty, the individual remains an object and not as subject of
international law (Lane, 1978). Mass killings and gross violations
of human rights continue virtually unchecked. But within the context of the prevailing decentralized world order, the adoption of
declarations, conventions and covenants have made the protection of
human rights a growing matter of international concern.

This was first expressed by the London Agreement and accompanying Charter of August 8, 1945 which were the constitutive authority
for the International Military Tribunal at Nuremberg and subsequently by the adoption of the Convention on the Prevention and Punishment of Genocide. The Convention was intended, in part, to fill the
lacunae in the Nuremberg judgment which had limited its jurisdiction
to war crimes and crimes against humanity committed in times of war
as distinguished from crimes against humanity committed before the
war (Bassiouni, 1979). The movement for the Convention resulted
from a one-man crusade by Dr. Raphael Lemkin who had coined the term
"genocide" to describe the mass murder of people for religious or
racial reasons (Lemkin, 1944).

On December 11, 1946, the General Assembly of the United
Nations adopted a resolution, unanimously and without debate, which
affirmed that genocide is a crime under international law, called
upon the member states to enact the necessary legislation for the
prevention and punishment of the crime, and the Economic and Social
Council was requested to prepare a draft convention. At the same
session, the General Assembly, acting on the request of President
Truman, reaffirmed the principles of the Nuremberg Tribunal and established a Committee for the Progressive Development of International Law and its Codification - which became the International Law
Commission - and was charged with drafting a code of offenses to international law. An ad hoc committee was charged with preparing a
charter for an international criminal court (Ferencz, 1981).

On the one hand, the General Assembly called for a Convention and for measures to deal with genocide in peace time. On the other hand, it encompassed the outlawing of genocide within a separate context applicable both to peace and war (Robinson, 1961).

The Convention, as adopted by the General Assembly on December 9, 1948, confirms that genocide is a crime under international law. Article 2 defines genocide as any of the five acts enumerated therein "committed with intent to destroy in whole or in part, a national, ethnic, racial, or religious group as such." The acts include:

(a) killing members of the group;
(b) causing serious bodily or mental harm to members of the group;
(c) deliberately inflicting on the group conditions of life calculated to bring about its physical destruction in whole or in part;
(d) imposing measures intending to prevent births within the group;
(e) forcibly transferring children of the group to another group.

Unlike the prior preparatory draft of the United Nations Secretariat, the Convention does not include cultural genocide (Robinson, 1961). Aspects of cultural genocide are covered within the purview of other conventions. The Convention, accordingly, limits genocide to such actions which imperil the physical and biological survival of members of the group.

In contrast to the General Assembly Resolution and prior drafts, political groups and economic and similar groups are excluded from the purview of the Convention. The inclusion of political groups in the prior draft was regarded as a major obstacle to agreement as to international jurisdiction and to having the Convention accepted.

The essential element in the crime of genocide is intent. The actual destruction of the group need not occur. The Convention requires proof of a state of mind indicating intent to destroy in whole or in part the group as such. It is unclear as to whether an attack on an individual because he is a member of a group would constitute genocide where the individual did not have the ability to commit genocide.

Genocide is aimed not only at the total, but also at the partial destruction of the group. It will be for the courts in each instance to determine whether the number was sufficiently large to constitute genocide. However, the murder of an individual could be considered an act of genocide if it was part of a series of similar acts aimed at the destruction of the group.

Article 3 lists as punishable, in addition to genocide, conspiracy to commit it, direct and public incitement to commit genocide, attempts to commit it, and conspiracy therein.

As provided by Article 4, persons committing genocide shall be punished "whether they are constitutionally responsible rulers, public officials or private persons."

A basic obligation of the contracting parties, as embodied in Article 5, is the undertaking to enact "the necessary legislation" to give effect to the provisions of the Convention and, in particular," to provide effective penalties for persons guilty of genocide..." Article 5 does not provide for uniform measures to be undertaken by all signatories. The term "necessary legislation" has been invoked by some governments to contend that existing legislation would suffice and that special legislation is unnecessary.

The basic shortcoming of the Convention is the absence of an international tribunal to try offenders. Since Article 5 established the obligation of the signatory states for punishment of acts of genocide, the primary jurisdiction would be in municipal courts. But it was apparent when the drafting of the Convention was first considered that domestic jurisdiction would not suffice, as municipal courts would not be inclined to try government officials and heads of state. Accordingly, the Secretariat Draft provided for trial by an international tribunal in certain instances. Some states opposed international jurisdiction, contending that the judgments of such courts would not be implemented and an international criminal tribunal did not exist. Accordingly, the subsequent Ad Hoc Committee Draft merely made reference to a competent international court while not specifying the tribunal and the instances in which it would function.

Article 6 of the Convention provides for trial "by a competent tribunal of the State in the territory of which the act was committed, or by such international penal tribunal as may have jurisdiction with respect to those Contracting Parties which shall have accepted its jurisdiction."

The Convention in Article 9 provides for compulsory jurisdiction by the International Court of Justice as to disputes between the contracting parties relating to "the interpretation, application or fulfillment of the...Convention, including those relating to the responsibility of a State for genocide or any of the other acts enumerated in Article III..." The "dispute" shall be submitted to the International Court of Justice at any request of any of the parties to the dispute.

Article 9 does not confer standing to individuals to appeal to the International Court.

Since the Court's jurisdiction is limited only to disputes between states, it may not pronounce formal judgments on persons, even if they are members of governments or are constitutionally responsible rulers. The limitation is only on whether a state carried out its obligations under the Charter.

334

The Soviet Union and the states of the Soviet bloc have adopted a reservation in ratifying the Convention that Article 9 is not
binding on them. A considerable number of other states have made
similar reservations.

Though the Convention does not provide for reservations, the
International Court determined in an Advisory Opinion (International
Court of Justice, 1951) that a state which maintains a reservation
may be a party to the Convention if the reservation is compatible
with the object and purpose of the Convention. If a party to the
Convention objects to a reservation which it considers incompatible
with the object and purpose of the Convention, it can consider that
the state making the reservation is not a party to the Convention. A
number of states have objected to the reservation by the Soviet
bloc.

Besides recourse to the International Court, a contracting
party may also, in accordance with Article 8, call upon a competent
organ of the United Nations to take appropriate action for the prevention or suppression of acts of genocide.

International enforcement through the General Assembly or the
Security Council is ineffective. The Third World majority in the
General Assembly will permit the adoption of a resolution only in
selected instances. Moreover, such a resolution would not have legal effect. As to the Security Council, assuming the veto would be
resolved, any coercive action must, in accordance with the Charter,
be related to acts or threats of aggression. Appeal to the Human
Rights Commission would merely result in reporting the matter.

The basic weakness of the Convention remains the lack of an effective enforcement mechanism. The absence of an international tribunal to adjudge perpetrators of genocide makes the Convention ineffective.

At its first session, the International Law Commission undertook a study towards the establishment of an international judicial
organ for the trial of persons charged with genocide or other crimes
over which jurisdiction will be conferred on it by international
convention and concluded that the establishment of such an organ was
both desirable and feasible. The Commission report was considered
by the General Assembly which appointed a Committee on International
Criminal Jurisdiction to prepare draft conventions and proposals relating to the establishment of an international criminal court.

The Committee, meeting in 1951, prepared a Draft Statute for an
International Criminal Court. The General Assembly, after subsequent deliberations, appointed another Committee to reconsider the
Draft in accordance with comments by governments and the Assembly.
This Committee, meeting in 1953, prepared a revised Draft. The Assembly postponed consideration of the proposed Statute pending the
report of the Special Committee on the Question of Defining Aggression and the Draft Code of the Offenses Against the Peace and Security of Mankind (Robinson, 1961). A general definition of aggression

was formulated in 1972. Recently, the General Assembly has indicated renewed interest in the establishment of an International Criminal Court (Ferencz, 1981).

The proposed Draft Statute of the Court made no specific reference to genocide but only to "crimes under international law, as may be provided in conventions or special agreements among states parties to the present statute." Accordingly, if the Statute were to be adopted, a special agreement would need to be adopted for the Genocide Convention to apply.

The Draft Code of Offenses Against the Peace and Security of Mankind, as prepared by the International Law Commission includes the crime of genocide as defined in the Convention with certain modifications (Robinson, 1961). The Code also includes acts defined as crimes against humanity by the London Charter without the qualification that they be committed in connection with the waging of war.

Since the Genocide Convention was adopted in 1948, over eighty states have ratified it. But no international tribunal has been established to try offenses under the Convention nor as to other areas of international criminal law.

The Genocide Convention sought to provide international protection for powerless minority groups. The main significance of the Convention is that the crimes of genocide, as contained in Articles 2 and 3 have become matters of international concern and are not within the matters essentially within the domestic concern of the state (Robinson, 1961).

Though the Convention may be regarded as having binding legal effect among the parties to it subject to any reservations made by the parties, the crime of genocide has come to be regarded as outlawed as part of the general principles of international law. The outlawing of genocide has become a universal obligation (International Court of Justice, 1951, International Court of Justice, pars. 33-4, 1970; International Law Commission, 1976).

The Genocide Convention, adopted in 1948, was the first of a series of human rights conventions. It may be regarded as both a human rights convention and a criminal law convention. It was adopted in the framework of the United Nations Charter and may be regarded to be interrelated with other human rights conventions subsequently adopted by the United Nations. These include the Convention on the Elimination of All Forms of Racial Discrimination, the International Covenant on Political and Civil Rights, The Convention Against Discrimination in Education and other conventions and declarations. Whilst the Genocide Convention focuses on the physical survival of the group, The International Covenant on Political and Civil Rights provides for the right to the life of the individual. Other conventions and declarations provide for cultural protection of the group and for protection from racial and religious discrimination. The adoption of human rights declarations and treaties constitute a new mode of international law-making with each international instrument having an incremental effect (Blum and Steinhardt, 1981).

THE CONTINUATION OF TERRORISM AND GENOCIDE

Despite the proclaimed existence of human rights internationally, individual human rights continue to be denied worldwide with the practice of torture and arbitrary detention undertaken by most of the world's governing authorities. The denial of human rights have included acts of genocide. The problem is to develop machinery for the protection of human rights and most imperatively for the physical protection of the individual and the group.

Acts of genocide have been characteristic of the twentieth century, and are an ever-present threat to mankind. The genocide of the Armenians by the Ottoman Turks in the early part of the century set the pattern for the Holocaust.

Similarly, Bolshevism, believing in the eschatalogical emergence of a new and different type of world order, justified any and all action transcending morality to achieve their goals, including total solutions (Cohen, 1961; Agus, 1963). The techniques of the Turks and Bolsheviks were copied and adapted by the Nazis (Watson, 1981).

The mass murder perpetrated in Kampuchea by the Khymer Rouge in the name of revolution is illustrative of the genocidal impact of totalitarian ideology. In Iran, Khoumenism is the emergence of an Islamic anti-western movement propelled by another eschatological outlook intolerant of non-believers and a disdain for the value and dignity of human life.

International terrorism is a development closely related to Nazism and totalitarian ideology with eschatological connections.[1]

Terrorism is a replica of Nazism in that it is based on group hatred and contempt for the enemy who is regarded as a nonhuman so that to kill him is not murder but elimination. It is a form of genocide (Lador-Lederer, 1974). An international terrorist network has developed, aided and abetted by the Soviet Union, Libya and other governments. A linkage has existed between the PLO, the Italian Red Brigade, Baeder-Meinhof, the Basque Separatists, the Irish Republican Army and various Neo-Nazi and racist groups (Sterling, 1981; Ben Canan, 1981). Antisemitism remains a potential genocidal threat. The antisemitic stereotypes remain dangerously dormant in western culture and find expression in "anti-Zionism," particularly in the Soviet Union and at the United Nations. Jews and Jewish institutions in Europe have become the targets of terrorist attacks. Jewish communities in Iran, Ethiopia and Argentina may be in danger (Ettinger, 1978; Roth, 1982; Granach, 1981; Netzer, 1982; Shenker, 1980.)

Since World War II, genocidal actions were committed in Indonesia, Tibet, Brazil, Guatemala, Bangladash, Burundi and elsewhere. Indigenous populations are threatened by extinction and discrimination and are victims of gross violations of human rights (Horowitz, 1976; Kuper, 1981). Over 850 million people in the world may be considered to be among the dispossessed groups and live below any acceptable level of decency (Van Boven, 1981).

The basic human rights problem today is the security of human life and the need to stop deliberate violations of the right to life. Instances of mass killing continue to occur including the one million killed in Kampucheau, and over a quarter of a million persons were killed and tortured in Uganda under Idi Amin. Atrocious killings took place in Equatorial Guinea. Thousands of political murders continue to take place in El Salvador and Guatemala. Thousands of persons in Argentina and elsewhere were made to disappear involuntarily with indication that thousands have been killed (Van Boven, 1982).

Genocide and mass murder are perpetrated within the context of an international system which is tolerant of such actions. The victims, as were the Jews and the Armenians, are isolated and vulnerable. Instances of genocide since World War II indicated that the isolation of the victims was related to the tolerance of other states towards the perpetrators (Fein, 1979).

The Genocide Convention brought genocide into world perspective. The penalization of genocide by whomsoever committed and the characterization of the "crimes against humanity" in the London Charter deviated from the traditional principle of regarding only states as parties to conflicts of international bearing. With this, the law reaches beyond whatever criteria classic international law postulated as the rationale (Lador-Lederer, 1974).

The international law of human rights can protect the individual only if it is directly related to him. He must, as a human being, have the right to petition an international tribunal empowered to adjudge his rights and to bring violators of international law to justice. The international community must bring its combined power to bear on the violators (Jessup, 1980).

Presently, the international implementation of human rights is at the rudimentary state. Reliance is placed on reporting of violations by the Human Rights Commission and other United Nations bodies and by exercise of the good offices of the Secretary General who has interceded in cases of serious violations (Ramcharan, 1982). Proposals to establish a High Commissioner of Human Rights to function as a World Ombudsman to handle complaints have been resisted. An effective international adjudicatory body to which individuals and groups may appeal for redress is lacking.

Some institutions are emerging, such as the Committee on the Elimination of Racial Discrimination, established in pursuance to the Convention on the Elimination of Racial Discrimination, and the

Human Rights Committee, established in accordance with the International Covenant on Political and Civil Rights.

Jurists and legal scholars have, since World War II, proposed the establishment of an international criminal law tribunal to try violators of what may be regarded as a growing body of international criminal law involving piracy, the slave trade, white slavery, counterfeiting, narcotic trafficking, and other activities in addition to genocide (Green, 1980; Ferencz, 1980; Wingspread Conference, 1971). But, as in the Genocide Convention, jurisdiction to try and punish offenders of international criminal law is conferred on state authorities. As to genocide, the prospect that an offender will be punished is most unlikely as in most instances the governing authority has instigated or aided and abetted in the commission of the genocidal acts. Effective punishment of international terrorists is frustrated by the complicity of certain state authorities who contend that the terrorists are "freedom fighters" acting in the name of self determination, stressing the ends rather than the means.

On the other hand, global interaction and the growing interdependence among states has led to vastly increased cooperation. Shared goals of public order transcend the interests and boundaries of the national state with the evolving emergence of a community of mankind (Falk, 1981; Symposium, 1981; Ferencz, 1982).

The Genocide Convention and the other human rights declarations and conventions reflect these shared values. The constitutions and municipal legislation of all governments contain provisions against racial discrimination, protection from arbitrary arrest, torture and summary execution (Hevener and Mosher, 1978; Maki, 1980). The conventions comprising international criminal law also reflect shared values.

The state in the modern world has failed to fulfill its major function - to provide physical security and well being to the individual. Transnational agencies are essential for human survival.

A WORLD GENOCIDE TRIBUNAL

A step in this direction would be the establishment by treaty statute of a World Genocide Tribunal to directly try perpetrators of genocide with authority to take appropriate preventive measures. It would be conferred with obligatory jurisdiction by the signatories of the Genocide Convention. The proposed tribunal would function both as a court to try violators and as a judicial body acting to protect individual and group rights.

As a criminal court the tribunal would be conferred with jurisdiction to try crimes against the peace as defined in Article 6(a) of the Charter of the International Military Tribunal for the Trial of the Major War Criminals of August 8, 1945; war crimes as defined in Article 1(a) of the Convention on the Non-Applicability of Statutory Limitations to War Crimes and Crimes Against Humanity of November 26, 1968; genocide, as defined in the Genocide Convention and other relevant conventions; and conventions relating to acts of terrorism and such other crimes for which international law makes individuals internationally responsible and which the parties to the Convention may regard as appropriate. To eliminate doubts as to what may be considered genocide within the definition of Article 2 of the Genocide Convention, the statutory convention establishing the proposed tribunal should expressly include all forms of mass killings as punishable.

The Tribunal would apply both to crimes committed in the course of war and in peace time. In applying the Genocide Convention and related instruments in the context of the humanitarian laws of war, the Tribunal would determine, _inter alia_, what constitutes acts of military necessity and defense as opposed to genocide and crimes against humanity as affecting the civilian population. The Tribunal should also consider the issue of war preparation and the development of weapons of mass destruction.

The Tribunal would be authorized to try perpetrators of acts of terrorism and would be able to assess responsibility as to acts of international terrorism. As an independent body it would be enabled to pierce the veil of elusiveness of responsibility. Government authorities of states from whose boundaries terrorist actions had originated should be regarded as having "constructive notice" of the acts involved and thereby bear responsibility (Kutner, 1970). State authorities should be determined guilty of complicity of particular Genocidal acts of terrorism where they have knowingly permitted or encouraged terrorist-linked organizations to operate within their boundaries. The Tribunal would be authorized to try individuals committing acts of terror where the municipal authorities indicate an unwillingness or inablility to try the perpetrator.

The Tribunal's criminal jurisdiction would be limited as to offenses and sanction but with ability to expand. The protective and humanitarian nature of the proposed Tribunal should be stressed rather than its penal nature, thereby making it easier to subsequently expand its jurisdiction.

Though functioning as a court or judicial entity, the Tribunal, like the European Commission and Court of Human Rights, would have investigative and conciliatory functions. It would be authorized to act pursuant to complaints by governmental authorities, groups, and individuals and would be enabled to initiate proceedings on its own initiative. An appendange to the Tribunal would be a corps of international Attorney Generals with investigatory and prosecutorial functions. Another appendage would be a mediation or conciliation service.

The Tribunal would have jurisdiction with regard to acts of genocide referred to if for adjudication by state authorities who are unable or unwilling to try the perpetrator, or on the initiative of other states who are parties to the convention, by petition of groups or individuals, or by the Tribunal acting on its own initiative where it is apparent that the perpetrator will not be brought to justice by any municipal authority.

The Tribunal would also function as part of an international ombudsman system to undertake preventive measures. It would operate in conjunction with a proposed GENOCIDE EARLY WARNING SYSTEM which would collect and report to the global community information as to threatened or ongoing cases of genocide and major human rights violations throughout the world (Charny and Rapoport, 1980; Charny, 1982). Data would be collected from news gathering agencies regarded as objective and from various specialized agencies or organizations which investigate and report cases of genocide and other human rights violations. The data would be compiled, analyzed and classified. The Tribunal would station observers throughout the world who would conduct objective on-site investigations. Instances of pending genocide or of serious human rights violations would be dealt with appropriately.

An important function of the Tribunal would be to focus public attention as to possible acts of genocide. Silence, secrecy, apathy and indifference are the prerequisites for tyranny, brutality, injustice and oppression. The desire of the bureaucrat and those with vested interests to keep acts of brutality and injustice a secret is a common universal phenomen (Kutner, 1970; Morse, 1967; Feingold, 1979; Gilbert, 1979). Instances of genocide have been ignored by a world that did not care - or did not know how to respond. Some cases of genocide were virtually unknown until many years subsequently. By adjudicating cases of genocide, the Tribunal would dramatically bring the case to the attention of the global public. It would, thereby, apply law as a means of communication.

Adjudication by an impartial body would be particularly effective in verifying that genocide is occurring or has occurred within a particular state. Generally the state authorities will attempt to deny or cover up acts of genocide. Reports as to mass killings may be greeted skeptically or rejected.

By exposing genocide, the Tribunal would be a catalyst to marshall world public opinion. In contrast to the politicization and selective morality characteristic of existing United Nations institutions, the Tribunal would function impartially and objectively without regard to ideology or geography. International experience has demonstrated that impartial international adjudication is feasible (Franck, 1967).

The Tribunal would be enabled to assess responsibility for acts of genocide in each particular case, both with regard to the perpetrators and as to the role of government officials. Responsibility may not be confined merely to the particular state authorities. The government leaders of a more powerful state should be deemed responsible for the genocidal acts committed by an allied or client (surrogate) state, particularly where it has provided military and political support and has not protested. International agencies which fail to take preventive action may also share in the responsibility.

The World Genocide Tribunal would also apply civil remedies in undertaking preventive or anticipatory measures as to situations which may ultimately develop towards genocide. In assuming this function it would adjudicate violations of the nonpenal human rights declarations and conventions, including relevant provisions of the Universal Declaration, the International Covenant on Civil and Political Rights, the Convention on the Elimination of All Forms of Racial Discrimination, the United Nations Declaration on Torture and, where appropriate, the European Convention on Human Rights and the American Convention on Human Rights. The Tribunal would be authorized to issue Writs of Prohibition to order that actions conducive to genocide, such as torture, racial and religious incitement and discrimination, kidnappings and mass killing cease and desist.

The Tribunal would also be authorized to apply the Writ of World Habeas Corpus to inquire into the arbitrary detention of individuals or groups of individuals in contexts which may involve a background to genocide. World Habeas Corpus, first conceived by the author Luis Kutner in the wake of the emergence of the Nazi regime, proposes to universalize the common law judicial writ of habeas corpus as a summary remedy to order the release of individuals illegally detained. The concept of World Habeas Corpus envisages the ultimate establishment of regional international tribunals empowered to hear petitions from or on behalf of individuals arbitrarily detained and to issue writs for their release.

World Habeas Corpus, based on principles of international due process of law and natural principles of justice, as implied in the International Covenant on Civil and Political Rights and other Conventions, may be applied to all forms of illegal detention and restraint and particularly in the context of genocide. The proposal for World Habeas Corpus has the support of jurists and legal scholars and is a fundamental requirement for human justice (Katin, 1969; Kutner, 1970).[2]

The World Genocide Tribunal could appropriately function as an adjunct to implement the "Basket III provisions" of the Helsinki Accords - those provisions of the Helsinki Accord dealing with human rights as initially considered at the Conference on Security and Cooperation in Europe as convened in Helsinki in 1975 and the subsequent conferences in Belgrade in 1977-78 and in Madrid in 1982-83. The Wording of Provision VII of the Accords implicitly includes adherence to the Genocide Convention.

Though the Helsinki Accords are not a legally binding document, the Principle VII provision involve legally binding obligations which are made the proper concern of all participants (Henkin, 1977). The matters dealt with therein are not solely within the domestic jurisdiction of each of the states - as the Soviet Union contends - nor beyond appropriate inquiry or recourse (Jonathan and Jacques, 1977). As such, these provisions may come within the purview of a duly constituted international tribunal. As the Honorable Arthur J. Goldberg stated in a letter to the author, Luis Kutner, "It goes without saying that a World Genocide Tribunal would be in conformity with the spirit, if not the letter, of the Helsinki Accord" (Goldberg, 1981).

As a supplement to follow up conferences, a World Genocide Tribunal would be an effective means for calling attention to serious violations of the Helsinki Accords where potential situations leading to genocide may arise.

The World Genocide Tribunal's determination that genocide or mass murder is taking place in a particular state would legitimize humanitarian intervention. Such a determination may form the basis for multilateral intervention with United Nations sponsorship as occurred in the Congo.

The Tribunal would also have an educational function. The significance of the Eichmann trial, in particular, was its educational effect in providing a renewed world-wide awareness of the Holocaust and of genocide. An adjunct to the Tribunal would be a unit which would undertake psychological, sociological and anthropological studies of human behavior as to propensities towards the commission of genocide which would recommend measures to forestall such tendencies.

The Tribunal, by directly applying criminal law to the individual violator and adjudging him while at the same time providing a hearing to the world's oppressed, would create a new context for international order which would encourage attitudes and behavior patterns conducive to humanity. It would be a means for practical implementation of the rights expressed in the Genocide Convention and other internationally binding human rights instruments.

The basic function of the Tribunal, like all courts - whether municipal or international, is to make judicial determinations, to communicate legal fact. The problem of enforcement and compliance must always depend upon other agencies. In most instances there is compliance to judicial decisions, both municipally and internationally. Most government authorities prefer to adhere to the rule of law. Law is adhered to for various psychological reasons and may be regarded as essentially persuasion.[3]

The expectations for human dignity expressed in the human rights declarations and covenants and pronouncements by statesmen and jurists have been thwarted. The continued suppression of human rights provoking terrorism and counter-government anti-terrorism creates a dangerous and explosive situation worldwide. The very existence of mankind is endangered. The establishment of a World Genocide Tribunal would represent an imperative breakthrough for world public order.

A precedent for the establishment of a World Genocide Tribunal, or an international criminal tribunal, may be considered in the action of the Secretary General in appointing an international commission to hear the complaints of Iran in the course of the hostage crisis. The Commission in effect functioned quasi-judically

in hearing testimony and gathering evidence with regard to the gross
violations on human rights by the Shah. The precedent points to the
possibility of the Secretariat appointing an ad hoc Genocide Tribunal or to investigate gross violations of human rights (Green,
1980).

The establishment of a World Genocide Tribunal would constitute
an important advance in the development of the rule of law. In world
history, from time to time, the rule of law has been ignored or violated by iron-willed narcissistic or psychotic rulers; but it is the
only ligament that permeates the ever-enlarging domain of the purposes and society of man. It seeks to buttress faith in an order of
reason out of a chaotic universe of which man is a part in his quest
for individual security, opportunity and meaningful peace.

NOTES

1. Hausner, Gideon J. Interview: Forgetting is a luxury. Newsview
June 14, 1981, 14-15. "The twentieth century started in anarchism,
drifted into Nazism and is going out in terrorism. There is a connection between these three phases of our century. In all three
cases there is a shared belief in the possibility of total solution
and a complete disregard for the value of human life."
2. Quincy Wright in "Steps in the Realization of World Habeas Corpus," in Luis Kutner (Ed.), The Human Right to Individual Freedom,
pp. 159-66, stated: "World Habeas Corpus, which would provide an international remedy against arbitrary arrest and detention of individuals, is a fundamental requirement of human justice" (p. 164)
Myres S. McDougal in "A Practical Measure for Human Rights," in the
same book, pp. 90-93, writes: "The policies implicit in the writ of
habeas corpus are, for example, so fundamental to a decent human existence, and so universally demanded in diverse legal systems, that
a concerted effort to institutionalise the process on a transnational scale would be regarded more in the nature of consolidation than
of innovation" (p. 91).
The Honorable Arthur J. Goldberg has written in the Foreword to the
same book: "The idea of world wide habeas corpus internationally recognized and enforceable in an appropriate international court can
only be applauded by those who are dedicated to the rule of law and
the attainment of lasting peace for the very term "rule of law" or
"due process of law" implies a procedure such as habeas corpus, a
means whereby official detention can be challenged and if not justified on the basis of valid laws, terminated. With the advent of international habeas corpus and the universal respect for human rights
that it would encourage, a long stride toward a peaceful world would
be taken" (p. 7).
3. Ailot Anthony, The effective ends of law, Valpariso University
Law Review, 1981, 15, 229-42: "I would submit that the idea of the
binding character of norms is unnecessary for an analysis of them,
that the term 'binding' corresponds to no phenomenon in the real
world, and that we would be better off without it. People conform
to laws for a variety of reasons: those reasons lie in the realm of
psychology and not of justice. Law is persuasion: sometimes we sub-

344

mit to it because we believe we have a duty to do so; and sometimes because we believe that it is positively to our advantage; but in each case we conform because we are persuaded" (p. 236).

REFERENCES

AGUS, Jacob B. War crimes and the Judeo-Christian tradition. The Minnesota Review. Winter 1963, 3, 205-19.
AILOT, Anthony. The effectiveness of law. Valpariso University Law Review. 1981, 15, 229-42.
BASSIOUNI, M. Cherif. International Law and the Holocaust. California Western International Law Journal, 1979, 9, 201-305.
BEN-CANAN, A. Fatah maintains joint camps with Nazi organizations in the U.S. Maariv, July 8, 1981, 10.
BLUM, Jeffrey M., & Steinhardt, Ralph G. Federal jurisdiction over human rights claims: The Alien Tort Claims Act after Filartiga v. Pena Irala. Harvard International Law Journal, 1981, 22, 53-113.
BUERGENTHAL, Thomas, & Hall, J. R. (Eds.), Human Rights, International Law and The Helsinki Accords. Montclair, N.J.: Allanheld, 1977.
CHARNY, Israel W., & Rapaport, Chanan. A Genocide Early Warning System. The Whole Earth Papers, No. 14. East Orange, N.J.: Global Education Associates, 1980.
CHARNY, Israel W. How Can We Commit The Unthinkable?: Genocide, The Human Cancer. Boulder, Colorado: Westview Press, 1982.
COHEN, Norman. The Pursuit of the Millenium: Revolutionary Messianism in Medieval and Reformation Europe and its Bearing on Modern Totalitarian Movements. New York: Harper & Brothers, 1961.
ETTINGER, Shmuel. Anti-Semitism in Modern Times. Morhavia: Sifrat Hapoalim, 1978 (Hebrew).
FALK, Richard A. Human Rights and Sovereignty. New York: Holmes & Meir, 1981.
FEIN, Helen. The treatment of genocide in U.S. sociology textbooks. Patterns of Prejudice, March-June, 1979, 13, 31-6.
FEINGOLD, Henry L. The Politics of Rescue: The Roosevelt Administration and the Holocaust 1939-45. New Brunswick: Rutgers University Press, 1970.
FERENCZ, Benjamin. An International Criminal Court: A Step Toward World Peace. Vols. I and II. New York: Oceana, 1980.
FERENCZ, Benjamin. The draft code of offenses against the peace and security of mankind. American Journal International Law, 1981, 75, 674-679.
FERENCZ, Benjamin. The future of human rights in international jurisprudence: an optimistic appraisal. Hofstra Law Review, 1982, 10, 379-400.
FRANCK, Thomas M. Some psychological factors in international things. Stanford Law Review, 1967, 19, 1217-1247.
GOLDBERG, Arthur J. Letter to Luis Kutner, November 9, 1981.
GRANACH, Yochanan. Anti-semitism in the modern world. Gesher, Winter 1982, 133-140 (Hebrew).
GILBERT, Martin. Exile and Return: The Emergence of Jewish Statehood. London: Weidenfeld & Nicholson, 1978.

GREEN, Leslie C. New trends in international criminal law. Israel Human Rights Year Book, 1981, 11, 9-10.

GREEN, Leslie C. International criminal law and the legal process. International and Comparative Law Quarterly, 1980, 29, 567-580.

HENKIN, Louis. Human rights and domestic jurisdiction. In T. R. Buergenthal & J. R. Hall (Eds.), Human Rights, International Law and the Helsinki Accords. Montclair, N.J.: Allanheld, 1977, 21-40.

HEVENER, N. K., & Mosher, S. A. General principles of law and the U.N. on political and civil rights. International and Comparative Law Quarterly, 1978, 27, 596-613.

HOROWITZ, Irving Louis. Taking Lives: Genocide and State Power. New Brunswick: Transaction Books, Rutgers the State University, 1976.

INTERNATIONAL Court of Justice Reports, 1952, 15, International Court of Justice Yearbook 1950-1, 88.

INTERNATIONAL Court of Justice Reports, Case Concerning the Barcelona Traction Light and Power Company Ltd., 1970.

INTERNATIONAL Law Commission, Report on the Work of Its Twenty-eighth Session, 3 May-23 July 1976 (GAOR Supp. No. 10 (A/31/10) - a commentary on its draft articles on State Responsibility, Article 3 (c) and Commentary.

JESSUP, Philip C. Revisions of the international legal order. Denver Journal International Law and Policy, 1980, 10, 1-10.

JONATHAN, Gerard Paul, & Jacques, Jean Paul. Obligations assumed by the Helsinki signatories. In T. R. Buergenthal & J. R. Hall (Eds.), Human Rights, International Law and the Helsinki Accords. Montclair, N.J.: Allanheld, 1977, 43-77.

KATIN, Ernest. The advocate as lawyer: Luis Kutner and the struggle for due process. University Miami Law Review, 1969, 23, 397-462.

KUPER, Leo. Genocide. London: Penguin Books, 1981.

KUTNER, Luis. World Habeas Corpus, human rights and world community. De Paul Law Review, 1967, 17, 3-43.

KUTNER, Luis. World Habeas Corpus: ombudsman for mankind. University Miami Law Review, 1970, 24, 342-388.

KUTNER, Luis. Constructive notice: a proposal to end international terrorism. New York Law Forum, 1973, 10, 325-50.

LADOR-LEDERER, J. J. A legal approach to international terrorism, Israel Law Review, 1974, 9, 194-220.

LANE, Eric. Mass killing by governments, lawful in the legal order? International Law and Politics, 1979, 12, 239-77.

LAQUER, Walter. The Terrible Secret: The Suppression of the Truth About Hitler's Final Solution. New York: Little Brown, 1980.

LEMKIN, Raphael. Axis Rule in Occupied Europe. New York: Carnegie Endowment, 1944.

MAKI, Linda J. General principles of human rights law recognized by all nations; freedom from arbitrary arrest and detention. California Western International Law Journal, 1980, 11, 272-313.

MORSE, Arthur D. While Six Million Died. New York: Random House, 1967.

NETZER, Amnon. Iran and Iranian Jewry three years after the revolution. Gesher, Winter-Spring , 1982, 96-111 (Hebrew).

RAMCHARAN, B. G. The good offices of the United Nations Secretary General in the field of human rights. American Journal International Law, 1982, 76, 130-141.

346

ROBINSON, Nehemia. The Genocide Convention: A Commentary. New York: World Jewish Congress, 1961.
ROTH, Stephen. Antisemitism in the western world today. Gesher, Spring 1982, 31-45 (Hebrew).
SHENKER, Barry. Anti-Zionism and anti-semitism in the Iranian revolution. Research Report No. 2, Institute of Jewish Affairs, February, 1982.
STERLING, Claire. The Terror Network. New York: Holt, Reinhart & Winston, 1981.
SYMPOSIUM. The future of human rights in the world legal order. Hofstra Law Review, 1981, 9, 337-592.
VAN BOVEN, Theo. Report to the United Nations Sub-Commission on the Prevention of Discrimination and Protection of Minorities. Human Rights Internet,1981, 7, November-December, 1981, 246-247.
VAN BOVEN, Theo. Address to the 38th Session United Nations Commission on Human Rights. Human Rights Internet, 1982, 7, Jan.-Feb. 1982, 462.
WASSERSTEIN, Bernard. Britain and the Jews of Europe 1930-1945. London: Oxford University Press, 1979.
WATSON, G. Rehearsal for the Holocaust? Commentary, 1981, 71 (6), 60-63.
WINGSPREAD Conference Center of the Johnson Foundation. The Establishment of an International Criminal Court, A Report of the First International Criminal Law Conference. Racine, Wisconsin, 1971.

LUIS KUTNER, J.D., Chairman, World Habeas Corpus, 105 W. Adams Street, Chicago, Illinois 60603, U.S.A.

ERNEST KATIN, Ph.D., 48 Hagibor Haalmoni Street, Tel Aviv 67321, Israel

Part VI

Epilogue: The International Conference on the Holocaust and Genocide, June 1982

30. The Holocaust and Its Lessons: Excerpts From the Keynote Address to the International Conference on the Holocaust and Genocide

Franklin H. Littell

Franklin Littell, Professor in Temple University's innovative Department of Religion, has been the moving force behind more than eighty conferences on the Holocaust in cities across the United States. He was the Founder of the National Institute on the Holocaust. At Temple University he founded the first graduate program in America leading to a Ph.D. with a major in Holocaust studies. He is the author of THE GERMAN PHOENIX (1960), and THE CRUCIFIXION OF THE JEWS (1975); and co-editor of THE GERMAN CHURCH STRUGGLE AND THE HOLOCAUST (1974), and REFLECTIONS ON THE HOLOCAUST (1980).

In approaching the subject of the Holocaust, even after many years of work, I feel an intense sense of constraint. What right does a gentile - and perhaps especially a professing Christian - have to enter such a sensitive area, such holy ground? Isn't it better, perhaps, to keep still?

When we remember those who perished in the heart of Christiandom, within the lifetime of many of us here, silence is at least a decent tribute to the dead and to the feelings of those who survived.
Who dares to speak of such terrible things?

There are those among us - friends and colleagues among the survivors - who say that no one but a survivor can understand how cruelty, abandonment, and human indifference together create an experience so terrible that no outsider will ever plumb its depths. Elie Wiesel speaks to us of silence. Andre Neierhas published a sensitive and brilliant book, his latest, on The Silence of the Word. But how else shall we learn, how else shall we teach, except by bringing the story of the Holocaust and its lessons into a form of words? There is a weighty truth, a profound religious truth, in the Holocaust, and its warnings of the future, that we must sound.

There is another constraint when we approach the fire of the Holocaust. I remember David. When he was carrying on his partisan warfare, his young men one time heard him say in homesickness, "Would that I had water to drink, of the well that is by Bethlehem's gate!," and because they loved him, three crept through the enemy's line and came back with water from that well. But then David seeing what they had done, poured it out as an oblation. "For is not this the blood of those that went in peril of their lives?" When we listen to those who tell us what they know, we shall never drink easily of this well. We must never lose the quality of awe and the sense of overpowering mystery.

We are beginning to move – with care, with sensitivity, with
respect to the feelings of the other – toward an understanding of
how to tell the story of the Holocaust, in all of its power and mass
and uniqueness. With even greater care and concern, we are beginning to draw some of the lessons thereof.

Although most of us here are involved with articles and books,
with the "black snow" of footnotes, let us never forget that confronting the Holocaust is not a "head trip." The healing will come
only as the prayers and psalms, the hymns and liturgies – among Jews
and Christian at the congregational level – show that we have passed
beyond stuttering and stammering into speaking our profound recollection and re-enactment and confrontation.

At Passover time, our brethren in the Jewish community remind
themselves and their children, "Let it be to you as when the Lord
delivered you out of slavery in Egypt." The time is coming when we
shall learn from the Holocaust survivors to say, "Let it be to you
as a messenger," a messenger of something terrible that happened,
something that must be merged into the human experience as a healing
event emerging from the shattering recollection.

The rabbis have taught generation after generation that "to
have faith is to remember." It is in that context that we remember,
and when we remember we cannot keep silent.

Who shall speak? Who dares to speak of such things? Elie
Wiesel has has told of the single survivor of a Jewish community in
Eastern Europe. The round-ups came. First the neighbors and
friends, and then the other members of the family were taken. One
alone was left, and he took a vow never to tell of the terrible
things he had seen – lest God in His righteousness, overhearing,
might in judgment and wrath pull down the pillars of the universe.
Years later, he is confronted by a young man who has tried everything, who is bored, contemplating suicide. The survivor breaks his
oath to tell what he knows about the gift of life, about the meaning
of life and death. He breaks his oath to save a life. Let it be
emphasized first of all, as we open this conference, that we have no
moral right to speak of such things except in the context of saving
life.

The second thing about speaking is this: we speak because we
cannot keep still. We speak under compulsion. Remember the words
of Jeremiah, where the prophet cries out, "When I say I will speak
no longer in His name, then there is as it were a consuming fire
shut up in my bones, and I am wearing with forebearing and I cannot
contain." We are compelled to tell the story, and we are compelled
to begin to draw some of the lessons – for the sake of life.

GROUND RULES FOR WORKING ON THE HOLOCAUST TOGETHER WITH OTHER EVENTS
OF GENOCIDE

Since the beginning of work on the Holocaust it has been clear
that – if we are to approach the Holocaust in its uniqueness, and

yet relate it intelligibly to analagous experiences of other people and nations - there are three ground rules, all of which, fortunately, are being observed in this conference.

1. **The first ground rule is this: the group that tackles the problematic must be inter-faith.** Along with the Jews, there must be Roman Catholics and Protestants involved, and preferably too the ancient Christian communities that were never under either Rome or Constantinople. The reason for this ground rule is simple: the temptation on the gentile side is to flee into some banality about "man's inhumanity to man," to chatter about the Brazil Indians or the "poor Palestinians" - anything to avoid the uniqueness and the direct impact of the Holocaust.

Emil Fackenheim has shown in his essays, again and again, how the temptation - especially among gentiles - of those who can't face the Holocaust is to find some generalization or abstraction to concentrate on. Such flight from the issue sounds owlishly wise, especially in academic circles, but the real point is that it is a device to avoid talking about a discrete terrible event in all its true power.

I trust that Jewish colleagues will forgive me if I say that on the other side of the partnership we run from time to time into a kind of preciousness. Sometimes the attitude seems to be that the Holocaust is casa nostra: "What are those goyim doing here, talking about our thing?!"

We need to work together because the meanings of the Holocaust can never be perceived, at any level, if gentiles are left to their banal generalizations and Jews are left to a self-destructive preciousness.

2. **The second ground rule for such conferences and concerns is that for effective dialogue, we need an international representation.** Some of the most important work on the meanings and the lessons of the Holocaust has come out of Europe. Minimally, for a good conference or research project, we must have scholars and community leaders from Israel, from the German Bundesrepublik, and from North America working together.

Observance of this second ground rule keeps us from allowing the Holocaust to be treated as a purely nationalistic concern - as though, for instance, only Israelis have a right to speak and only Germans carry guilt.

In fact, the single most important statement by Christian churchmen has come out of West Germany. In January, 1980 a judicatory body, a Synod of one of the largest and wealthiest Protestant churches in Europe, issued a statement of extraordinary importance. It is an official position paper of that church, not a pamphlet or a book by an individual. Let me summarize the findings:

352

The Provincial Synod accepts the historical necessity of at-
taining a new relationship of the Church to the Jewish people.
The Church is brought to this by four factors:

1. the recognition of Christian co-responsibility and guilt
    for the Holocaust;
2. the new Biblical insights concerning the continuing signi-
    ficance of the Jewish people in salvation history, in-
    sights gained during the Church struggle with Nazism;
3. the insight that the continuing existence of the Jewish
    people, its return to the Land of Promise, and also the
    creation of the State of Israel, are signs of the faith-
    fulness of God toward His people;
4. the readiness of Jews, in spite of the Holocaust, to en-
    gage in encounter and common study and cooperation.

Let us say that even though we have in Roman Catholic and Protestant seminaries in the United States - for example an inter-semi-
nary program led by Professor F. Burton Nelson (who is here in this
conference) in the Chicago area - a very significant development,
and even though the American Baptist Churches in the United States
have made Yom Ha'Shoa an official date in their denominational cal-
endar, we have not had at the official level - from any denomination in the United States - anything comparable to this statement
coming from the Evangelische Kirche des Rheinlands.

We can learn from each other, and we must learn from each
other, across national lines.

3. The third ground rule is that conferences, seminars and
other efforts of this kind need to be inter-disciplinary. If you
look at the pedigrees of the various presenters and discussion leaders here, you will find every known academic discipline, I think,
and several - I won't say "unknown" - that are at least unusual.
This also is healthy. Unless we have this kind of cooperation, the
theologians are going to discuss the Holocaust as another problem of
"theodicy," and the sociologists are going to treat it as a problem
of race relations, and the political scientists are going to talk
about the problem of misuses of governmental powers, etc. We shall
all lose the essential truth, namely, that as far as academics are
concerned, the Holocaust was a bitter and legitimate fruit of the
modern university and confronts the whole university, in all of its
sectors.

Thus, it must be emphasized that when we are speaking of such
things we need each other. Jews and Christians need each other. We
need each other coming from the various diciplines. We need each
other in terms of international concern. Genocide - God pity us! -
is not and never was a German invention. Genocide is the besetting
and central sin of the Twentieth Century, which is the Age of Genocide. The century opened with the slaughter of 60% of the Armenian people, the oldest Christianized nation of history, at the hands
of the dying Ottoman Empire ("the Holy Muslim Empire"). It then

reached its maximum point to date in the destruction of one third of all then living Jews - in the heart of Christendom.

Let me say in passing that I am very glad to see our brethren from the Armenian community here. We have had some peculiar pressures applied in this conference to remove the subject of the Armenian massacres, but we have withstood them. Political difficulties will always arise when truly important matters are on the docket. Thus, every conference of this kind is in itself a case study of the problem in itself of dealing with the Holocaust and genocide.

In 1975 we held the 60th Year Memorial Conference on the massacre of the Armenians. The place was New York and the general chairman was Archbishop Manoogian of the Armenian Church of America. As he opened the conference, he said very simply: When our people were being slaughtered, the so-called civilized world was largely indifferent. And then the tradition and practice of genocide built up to that terrible thing, the slaughter of 6,000,000 Jews - again, for the most part, passively accepted by the nations.

Archbishop Manoogian's opening statement was an honest one and a sensitive one. Its theme was not, "Why talk about the Jews? - look at us" - as we have sometimes heard from other groups, like American Poles or members of the Ukrainian League in America insisting that there is too much talk about the Jews and not enough about other victims of the Nazis. Rather he put the tragic genocidal events of the Twentieth Century in their proper perspective, seeing that genocide is a problem of concern to all persons of conscience. The question is not who can outdo the other, who can claim some special preeminence in suffering and disaster. Rather he asks how we can combine our forces to deal with a threat so real that we do not know this evening what tomorrow morning's newspaper or radio may bring us - in report of some new outbreak of mass slaughter somewhere on our small globe.

OVERCOMING DENIALS OF GENOCIDE TO TELL THE STORY AND ITS LESSONS

We have to confront denials. We have to learn not only to work fraternally to strengthen each other in facing difficult things; we have to deal with denials which come in all shapes and sizes.

There are the "historical revisionists," with a well-financed quarterly journal and a series of conventions. Melvin Mermelstein, who is here - one of the heroes of our cause in facing these people and getting their public obscenities punished - can tell you about them. "Historical Revisionism" is the latest and one of the most effective weapons developed by a long-time fascist and antisemite named Willis Carto. For thirty years, Carto has praised Adolf Hitler and done what he could to promote hatred of the Jews and spread contempt for democracy.

We have too the problem of religious repression. Let me speak frankly. The number of gentiles still dodging the issue is legion. But let us also take note that there are even Jews who don't want

354

the Holocaust dealt with. When in 1969-70 Dean Hubert Locke (also here) and I set up the first Scholars Conference - which was for three years thereafter the only American conference - we approached one of the major American Jewish "defense" organizations to get help in mimeographing and mailing. We were told, "Forget the Holocaust. It is counter-productive in Christian/Jewish relations. Bury it!"

This fall we will hold our 8th Annual Philadelphia Conference on Teaching the Holocaust. Last year one of our regular participants, a teacher in a Hebrew school, told of the difficulties she had had in being released from her teaching duties to attend again. The new head of the school, a rabbi, denied her permission. She said, surprised, "Why?! I've gone every year..." He said he didn't want the Holocaust taught. She asked why, and he said, "Because it makes God look bad..."

It is imperative in spite of all these denials to tell the stories of the Holocaust and all other genocides. In each case we need particularly to gather the testimonies of survivors, and also of liberators - those who were there (especially when we are aware in the case of the Holocaust that both the survivors and liberators will soon pass from the scene). We need the primary source-testimonies of all witnesses; their reports are indispensable and will grow more so in years to come.

When we move beyond refuting the denials. We have to tell the story in the various vernaculars open to us - music, poetry, theatre, novels, scholarly research in the different disciplines. We must help each other to find the forms and words that convey in full impact the uniqueness and also the lessons of the Holocaust. The Holocaust is, first, a terrible story in history to be remembered, but then we must also draw some of the lessons it brings to us.

We meet "in the fullness of time." In 1975, when we were starting to teach the Holocaust in the high school system of Philadelphia, I wrote colleagues in Israel and West Germany for suggestions. I was astonished to discover that the first systematic teaching was just beginning in those countries too. From this experience I received the answer to the question so often and falsely put by newspaper and magazine people. They ask, "Why talk about these things, now forty years later?" They say, "Let's forget it and get on with present issues." Their questions miss the point. The real question is why forty years had to pass before anybody - except a few solitary scholars and poets - could deal with the Holocaust.

We find the answer in reflecting upon other "epoch-making," formative watershed events.

The Holocaust is an event like the Exodus out of slavery in Egypt, or the revealing of the Way (Torah) at Sinai - an event of such mass, sheer mass - what Emil Fackenheim calls an "epoch-making event" in human history - that forty years had to pass before people could begin to measure and discuss its impact.

Now the subject is breaking open, and we need to help each other to tell the true story in all of its power and uniqueness, and at the same time to relate it to the experience of other peoples and nations in a meaningful way. And, if we would be honest, we must accept personal confrontation.

THREE CREDIBILITY CRISES

1. The Holocaust is a credibility crisis for Christianity. The crisis and the apostasy occurred in the heart of Christendom. The murder was commited by baptized Christians - never rebuked, let alone excommunicated. Adolf Hitler was a Roman Catholic, paying his church taxes to the end. Hermann Goering died a Protestant, paying his church taxes to the end. And now those of us who are professing Christians have to ask the meaning of this in terms of the credibility of Christendom.

2. The Holocaust is a credibility crisis for the modern university. These crimes were not commited by ignorant, superstitious, illiterate savages off in the bush - people we've always looked down at across our long, educated noses. The Holocaust was planned, supervised and rationalized by Ph.D.s and M.D.s and professors. The question forces its way to the surface: Is there any evidence that the Medical School at Temple University, the Law School at Harvard University, the School of Education at Columbia University are - in terms of morals, ethics, and commitment to life - doing any better than was done by Tuebingen or Heidelberg in 1924, 1925, 1926? The questions that arise for the university - and most of us here are university people - are very serious indeed.

Why is a Nazi sympathizer, who has made a fortune lying about the Holocaust, still on the faculty at Northwestern University? Why is there another such person still on the faculty of the University of California San Diego? I have spent all my life both in the church and on the campus, and I love them both. But I will tell you why. The reason is that the professors are just like the Teamsters when it comes to accepting responsibility. We are long on academic freedom and short on academic discipline.

The time is at hand when we must not only consider how to tell the story of the Holocaust in the history departments, religion departments, classes in literature, and in law schools. We need also to confront the pressing question of how all professionals, in school and afterwards, have to draw implications from the Holocaust for their everyday professional work - as individuals and as national and international associations for professional people who have the stewardship of power which education gives them in the modern world.

We need to develop an Early Warning System, as Dr. Israel Charny has written. It is not yet a science if you simply have people who can make an accurate report on a cholera epidemic. It becomes a science at the point where there are a number of people who have studied carefully enough to be able to predict that, given

356

certain circumstances, you are going to have a cholera epidemic. We need to identify the factors that go into a potentially genocidal situation. We need to develop the predictive function which can make an Early Warning System feasible.

The axiom is this: <u>the German Nazi Party was a terrorist movement years before it became a criminal government with the power to commit genocide.</u> In 1923, at the time of the "Beer Hall Putsch," when the judges let Ludendorff and Hitler go with a slap on the wrist, excuses could be found. Everyone was confused, trapped in economic inflation, surviving in the shadow of World War I and the Russian revolution. But what excuse is there today for those who take a frivolous attitude to the threat poised by terrorist movements, movements which – if they come to power – will certainly commit genocide?

3. Finally, I want to say that <u>the Holocaust is not only a credibility crisis for the church and for the campus; it is also a personal credibility crisis.</u> Every one of us, each of us in this conference – in his or her association, congregation, labor union, university and/or other community – has to rethink those societal structures in terms of building together the kinds of restraints and controls that impede and finally make genocide impossible.

This does not mean simply passing resolutions! We preachers and teachers are great at passing resolutions that have no binding power. It means, rather, building those structures of controls within our universities and our professions by which persons are educated to commitment to life – not simply in the techniques of technically competent barbarians. We need learning communities where there are maintained, in daily actions and practices, the commitments that sustain life rather than destroy it. Mengele had (has?) two doctorates. What kind of a university was responsible for that?

These are the questions you and I must face. A personal confrontation is demanded of all of us. Let me assure you that if you do confront the Holocaust, and allow it to confront you, nothing is ever the same again.

Many of you know the name Hannah Senesh. I think often of her and her generation. She was a young patriot who parachuted into an area now Hungary to help the remnants of the Jewish community find their way down through the escape routes of the Balkans. The Nazis caught her and they tortured her and she died. She was 23 years old. She was a poet as well as a patriot, and she left a poem:

To die, to die in youth – no, no, I did not want it.
I loved the warmth of sun, the lovely light.
I loved song, shining eyes, and not destruction.
I did not want the dark of war, the night.
No, no. I did not want it.

You and I who are yet alive - through no special merit of our own - must ask ourselves when we speak of life and death: What am I doing with the gift of intelligence, the strength, the power of life which I have been spared? Am I prepared to commit my education, conscience, will, and my time to save life? Or will I float towards the inevitable destruction that is planned for us all - unless we unite to tell the story and to fight genocide. Our answers to this confrontation will determine our own credibility.

REV. FRANKLIN H. LITTELL,Ph.D., P.O.B. 172, Merion, Pennsylvania 19066, U.S.A.

31. Why Remember? Suffering as a Link Between Peoples

Shahe Ajamian

His Grace Archbishop Shahe Ajamian completed his higher studies at the University of Brussels (Belgium), from which he graduated in 1950 as "Licencie en Philosophie et Letters." He obtained his Doctorate in Philosophy in 1953; his thesis was: THE ARMENIAN COMMENTATORS OF ARISTOTLE. He was elected General Secretary to the Bishops' Council convened in 1969 in Etchmiadzin (Armenia), and was entrusted with the scientific translation of the Bible into modern Armenian. In 1975, Archbishop Ajamian was elected a member of the Central Committee of the World Council of Churches.

Why remember?

Why think about a genocide sixty-five years old, and a Holocaust forty years old?

Why remember that we have suffered death and devastation? Why call back to our soul the memory of women and children starving in the searing desert, or reduced to ashes in Hitler's gas chambers, with all their sinister anonimity?

My first answer is a logical one: we have to remember in order to live. "Death not comprehended is mortality, death perceived is immortality." If we do not comprehend the death of a million and a half Armenians and the death of six million Jews; if we, the "remnants," do forget, then their deaths will be mortality for us. But if we perceive the meaning of their death, we can aspire to immortality.

We are assembled here not only to remember but also to comprehend the nature of our suffering as two people who were subjected to the abomination of devastation because they wanted to live their own life, their own way, we as Armenians, and you as Jews. That is the main reason for our suffering: we want to be what we are and pay the price of being different.

Another answer to the same question, this one more pragmatic, is that we are concerned lest another megalomaniac may say, "Who remembers the Jews?," as Hitler said, "Who remembers the Armenians?" But the real answer in my mind today is: we remember because it is impossible to forget! Simple and naive perhaps, but still an expression of the deep reality of Jewish or Armenian consciousness.

"The memories of our garden in Kharkom are haunting me so often...Dear sister, I am depicting in my paintings our garden and I am recreating its green carpet and the life it exuded. Is it possible for the son to forget the soil which has given life to him...?"

These lines are quoted from one of the many letters that the American-Armenian painter, Achille Gorki wrote to his sister from Chicago where he lived.

In another letter he complains that when he speaks about his country, they accuse him of chauvinism. And he explains: "We have lived and felt the blood of our people coursing through our veins, the blood which has stained the hands of the Turks, the massacres and the 'catastrophe,' our swan song, the martyrdom of our comrades and our relatives in the bloody fight, our abandoned homes, the destruction of our country, the death by starvation of my mother in my arms..."

In his last letters, he laments: "It is not easy, no, it is absolutely impossible...My dear ones, remember the mountains and the plains. Sing a song to Van. Sing about the apricot trees, and the lark. Sing a song..."

He had fled Van, his native town, as a child, with his three sisters and their mother; had arrived in the United States in 1919, had lived there and recreated in his paintings his world; but "it is not easy, no, it is absolutely impossible...," and in 1945, he committed suicide.

Why was he remembering? What was he remembering? He was remembering for a very simple reason, that, humanly speaking, it is not easy, it is impossible to forget...

"If I forget thee, O Jerusalem, may my right hand forget its cunning. May my tongue cleave to my palate, if I remember you not, if I place not Jerusalem above my chief joy."

The verb "to remember" is not even strong enough to express the feeling of that shadow of death which enveloped a whole population of a whole land, the land of their forefathers; the feeling that darkens every day of your existence and the sorrow that is the distinctive sign in the eyes of your children. And the song on your lips can only be the echo of the lamentation of the moutains and plains, the apricot trees and water springs of a nation to which you belong, a nation which has known a full, creative life, a unique cultural heritage, a religion - all far, far away now, destroyed, abandoned, waiting.

To remember for the Armenian is his way of life. It is a daily suffering because he is in exile. And in exile, he cannot be existentially a complete Armenian. But when he contemplates the 2,000-year-long suffering of the people of Israel who knew how to remain loyal to their God-given heritage, this suffering gives birth to hope. Israel is the supreme example, the promise that as long as a nation considers itself in exile, suffering is its fate, but not its destiny, revival and regeneration on its land is not merely a utopian promise in the form of an impossible dream, but an achievement integrally linked with its will to live its own identity.

This phantom of the Holocaust has enwrapped in its black pall the blue skies of this country and remains ubiquitous in the Israeli consciousness: each time a prime minister speaks about secure borders and the necessity to safeguard Jewish lives, it is the phantom of the Holocaust that speaks through his mouth. Because the Holocaust is not a fact of the past, but a possibility in our world of violence and nuclear armament, to remember is not only a moral obligation towards the memory of the martyrs but a duty towards the coming generations. It is imperative today to stand firm and say to all the world that the monster of genocide is still alive in our midst: doesn't Turkey even deny this historical fact of the Armenian genocide?

Why remember? Because silence is still diplomacy and political considerations are still prevailing over moral values silencing the conscience of the world leaders to the point of denial, which is simply a promise of another potential genocide.

This has been our history from the day Noah's ark landed on the summit of Mt. Ararat: a series of alternate floods and rebirth. That history is the history of the land of Ararat, Armenia. The difference between our history and yours is that our ark is still drifting in the waters of the flood and there is no sight of any dove on the horizon coming back with an olive branch, while "comfort" has been given to the Jewish people and Isaiah's prophecy sounds like a nuptial song:

But you shall be called "my delight,"
And your land "espoused,"
For the Lord delights in you
And makes your land His spouse. (62.4)

That fact that Noah, "the good man and blameless," the "truly just," landed on Mt. Ararat meant, in Armenian tradition, that the Armenian people "belong" to the Bible from the very beginning because they consider themselves the "sons of Tagormah," grandson of Japhet by Gomer.

If one goes today to the old capital Ardashad in the plain of Ararat and looks towards the mountains from the monastery of Khor-Virab, the ancient fortress, the two majestic summits of the Great and Small Massis seems so near that one would not hesitate to start climbing towards that snow-covered peak where the Bible locates the ark. This extraordinary view would transport him back in time and space and he would imagine that he was seeing perhaps Noah, his sons and their wives coming down towards him. He would even hear that voice bestowing his benediction on "seedtime and harvest, cold and heat, summer and winter, day and night..." He would visualise the first gesture of Noah as he built an altar to the Lord and chose from every clean animal and every clean bird to offer sacrifices (Gen. 8.20).

This same gesture is the most familiar one for Armenians, repeated every festive day in Armenia around the sanctuaries, on the mountains, where "the sacrifices of communion" takes place, according to the rite described in the third chapter of Leviticus. Families gather to offer lambs in sacrifice, besmirching the stones of the sanctuaries with the blood of the holocaust and then consummating the ceremony with songs and dances, expressing the communion of life between the faithful and their God. This "communion" sanctifies the land, the first harvest and the most spotless animals being offered in holocaust, consecrating a mystical union between the land, the people and God.

In the sermons of St. Gregory the Illuminator, the Christianisation of Armenia in the first years of the 4th Century is construed as a return of the sons of Tagormah to the God of Noah, with the establishment of a new covenant between the Armenian people making them "children of God" and the Lord. The hymn dedicated to St. Gregory describes him in the same terms: "The Great Pontiff, messenger of the word of the real God, offered the lord a new nation, purified from its sins, and invited to partake of the glory of the heights of Zion."

The sign of that new covenant on the newborn is the baptism, called in Armenian "the seal," because the canon established by St. Gregory stresses that the newborn must be brought to the Church on the eighth day of his birth, to be anointed with chrism on all his body, and to become a "son of Abraham."

On this understanding is based the life of our church, celebrating the seasons, the days and hours in the innumerable churches and monasteries of Armenia, consecrating the land of Ararat and glorifying it as the "height of Zion," as the bride of the Song of Songs.

From the 4th Century on, our history developed as a succession of battles, fought for the protection of that faith in God. "The Great War" which raged in the 5th Century against the Zoroasterian Persians, who wanted to obliterate the character of Armenia, witnessed not only a fierce armed resistance but also an undeniable affirmation of faith, which made the Battle of Avarair a glorious religious clebration and the heroes who lost their lives, saints.

Describing the commander-in-chief of the Armenian forces, Vardan, on the eve of battle, the historian says: "Holding the Holy Book in his hand, he read aloud for everyone to hear about the valiant character of the Maccabees and with moving eloquent words he explained to them the nature of their struggle against the king of Antioch. Although they encountered death in battle, the memory of their bravery survives yet, not only on earth, but in heaven as well."

The Bible, The Holy Book, as we call it in Armenian, always remains open in our hands so that we may learn from it our religiously founded national way of life.

Speaking about the same Persian king, the historian says: "Although he dealt thus unjustly with all nations, he persecuted the Armenians more than all the others because he found them to be the most zealous adherents to the worship of God... "And zealously they answered him saying: 'He who thought that we donned Christianity as a garment has now discovered that, as people cannot change the colour of their skin, so he cannot and will never succeed in changing our minds...'" As long as we lived on our land, in the words of the same historian, our struggle was the "preservation of the God-given laws of our land."

We suffered countless deaths in the fight for the preservation of our land and the God-given laws of that land. But our resistance by the "arms of the soul" was always triumphant: in our faith in God, we kept our culture. Many invading waves of Asian conquerors reached as far as our mountains. Sometimes they could be stopped. Many times they engulfed the country and devastated it, but they could never subdue us culturally or religiously, as befell all the Christian national churches of the Middle East, all of whom became Arabic-speaking minorities.

Even the Arab incursions at the advent of Islam, which enveloped in their culture all the Coptic, Greek, Roman, Syriac and Aramaic speaking Christians, and converted them in their great majority to Islam, or tolerated them as Arabic-speaking Christian minorities, failed before the Armenian's obstinate belief in their unique national entity. The Armenians under Arab rule, and later under Turkish rule, for many centuries remained faithful to their culture, like the monasteries built on the impregnable rock of their mountains. Their church, their culture and their national identity formed an unbreakable unity because the Armenian church is, and has always been, a national church.

In the year 401, a monk called Mesrob invented the Armenian alphabet. The hymn dedicated to this saint says:

Like Moses, Lord Vartabed,
You brought the Book of the Law
to the land of Armenia,
Enlightening with it the Sons of Torkom (Targomah).

The alphabet was invented for the unique purpose of translating the Bible into Armenian and making the laws of God known to the "sons of Targomah." Religious tradition even says that the monk Mesrob saw "not in a dream, neither with open eyes, but with the senses of his heart, the right hand of God writing the letters of the alphabet on the dark wall of his cell..."

The vision of St. Mesrob, like the vision of Moses on the Sinai, brought to the Armenian people the Law, the Bible translated into their tongue. With the "vision" of the alphabet and the translation of the Bible was ushered in the golden age of the Armenian civilization, by the Church, in the Church and for the "people of

God," the Church. The Church thus became the unifying link between a land, a people and a faith. The Christianisation of Armenia was seen as the admission by the God of Abraham, Isaac and Jacob of all nations to His Kingdom. It is the identification of each nation with the New Israel. It is the choice God made about Israel extended to each nation. It is the light of the Biblical faith lit in the path of every nation. It is the redemption of a nation on its own land, in its own culture, towards its own vision.

This is the way the Armenians understand the Bible. And the Bible made them a nation, because they saw in the land of Ararat the promised land, which, by its characterisation, became the Holy Land.

Do I have to tell you what immense suffering such a concept signifies? So many links in the sensitivity of a people, developed for so many centuries, with all the risks of ruptures at certain moments of crisis, are an open invitation to tragic happenings. So many loyalties demand great courage and endurance.

We learned to suffer bravely because of our loyalty to God and ourselves. And we won. We survived. But today our suffering is of a different nature and we look again to the Bible for inspiration. Our land is divided: one small part is the Soviet Socialist Republic of Armenian, from Ararat to the east where three million Armenians are struggling hard for their national existence, strong in their faith, perpetuating their cultural heritage. But the Holy Mountain, with the greatest and most cherished part of our homeland, lies desolate on the other side of the border devoid of Armenian life, suffering since the Genocide, the martyrdom of the cultural heritage left in ruins.

Our suffering is more acute because we do not know how to organise a life of resistance in the diaspora. The rupture we experienced since the dispersion of our people after 1915, between our past and our present, the faith of our fathers and the question marks tearing us apart, the slow death of our national language in foreign lands, this rupture has created in our soul an obsessive doubt: "Are we condemned to disappear?"

It is this obsession that fosters our fighting mood and consciousness that only a return to the land of our ancestors can guarantee our national survival.

I have to conclude at this point: Isn't suffering and death in our own land a better life, a greater joy than all the promises and material successes of a life in exile?

ARCHBISHOP SHAHE AJAMIAN, POB 14001, Jerusalem, Israel

32. Round Table Discussion Following Briefing on the Conference Crisis

Following the Opening Keynote Address, conference participants were invited to reassemble, sitting in the round in the Hilton Ballroom, for a briefing by chairman Israel Charny on the crisis which had threatened to close the conference down following threats by Turkey on Jewish lives. The story of the Turkish demands to remove the Armenian subject from the conference, and the efforts of the Israeli government to close the conference down received worldwide publicity, and is covered fully in THE CONFERENCE PROGRAM AND CRISIS published earlier by the Institute of the International Conference on the Holocaust and Genocide. What follows here are some of the gripping spontaneous responses of conference participants to the briefing.

ISRAEL CHARNY: I'm going to call on a person who is here among us but who is going to speak about why he cannot be among us. This man is a moving spirit behind many important creative efforts to study the Holocaust. He himself is a survivor and his work derives from the authenticity of his own experiences. His name is Jack Eisner and he heads a foundation which awarded the conference a series of funds, some of which were received months ago, and some of which arrived a few weeks ago, but before the check cleared back in the United States, payment was stopped on it - and we had already spent the money. Nonetheless, he has asked to speak to us tonight.

JACK EISNER: I think the immense amount of detail revealed in the last half hour, a blow-by-blow description of the proceedings of the last several weeks, rather obscured the significance of the issue.

I do thank the chairman for allowing me to make a statement. I did not prepare the statement deliberately for I wanted to speak to you spontaneously and let my heart and mind talk to you. Yes, I did wholeheartedly and enthusiastically support this great idea, this conference. I, the survivor, the product of mankind's insanities; I, the child of the Holocaust; embraced all the principles, the aims, the foundation of this conference, all of its ideals as me. My whole being is so much what this conference stands for. Yet, only recently and so suddenly, I withdrew my support and my participation in this conference for reasons that I would not like to detail here and now, reasons that failed to satisfy me the human being, the member of the human race, but fully satisfied me, the Jew.

Sadly and unfortunately, there is a division between me the Jew and me the member of the human race. They are at odds. For hundreds of years, we Jews struggled to merge these two. We struggled sincerely all through the centuries. But that effort was completely shattered and destroyed in the Holocaust for a long time to come. And therefore my deeds are a product of the Gentile environment.

I am the product of Western Christian civilization; I am the reflection of post-Holocaust mankind. It is not my desire to be and to act and behave and counteract the way I do, but I must confront reality. It is what the Gentile wants, what Western Civilization, Christianity, confront me with, and I have to face the facts, and as a Jew behave accordingly in order to survive.

I hope that this conference is only a beginning. I hope that the immense efforts of those involved in arranging this conference will someday in the future reach full satisfaction, especially Dr. Charny who has so selflessly and untiringly worked to bring it to reality. I hope that this conference will continue in a much greater scope in a country, in a geographic location, among a people that can afford to be more magnanimous and generous than the young struggling State of Israel. Thank you.

ALICE ECKARDT: I'm Alice Eckardt from Lehigh University. I think I can speak for Roy at this point. We have for a long time totally committed ourselves to a position that we never in any way want to be responsible as individuals, and as Christians, for any harm coming to any Jew, that we as Christians, both as individuals and as members of a community, have a special responsibility for seeing that Jewish lives are preserved and protected. Now I find myself in a very strange situation. I didn't know any more than the two New York Times stories before we left home, and I'm only beginning to get a little bit of the seriousness of the threats now that we are here, and I am wondering if we, and perhaps some of my colleagues are wondering the same thing, if we are in fact doing the very thing we have said we would never do.

ISRAEL CHARNY: I think we're going to continue hearing statements and questions and then have some responses rather than my being the carrier of the Torah with direct answers to each question. Thank you Alice.

HELEN FEIN: I'm Helen Fein from New York. Some of you know me as a scholar, as the author of "Accounting for Genocide," but I'm also an activist and widely concerned with human rights, whether they are prisoners of conscience, victims of genocide, Ethiopian Jews, Soviet Jews, Argentinian Jews who have disappeared among 15,000 other Argentinians, and others. I have two questions:

Firstly, the commitment to the Armenians is not a question of friendship or tact. Our commitment is first to truth. We cannot discriminate between politic and not politic in truths. We can't erase events that have occurred. Turkey's problem is a function of Turkish denial. It's not a function of what I do as a Jew, it's not a function of what my Armenian colleagues do.

The second question is whether accomodating to threats is really the correct strategic response of Jewish leadership. There

366

are some situations where accomodation may be a strategic necessity, and one should not fall for the people who label it automatically as appeasement. But my suspicion from the study of the Holocaust, and from working with Amnesty International, is that the more publicity one can bring, the more focus different parties can bring against the potential victimizer or spokesman of the threat, the safer the probable victim will be.

FATHER CARROL: My name is Father Charles Carrol of the Episcopal Diocese of Colorado. The question before us is as old as "Am I my brother's keeper?" and everyone of us must answer this question in his own way. I agree with the last speaker, that the Turkish government has brought the genocide of the Armenians more to our attention, and through us to the attention of those countries in which we live, than they ever would have by allowing those who were invited to speak to us to do so quietly. But I'd like to talk for a moment about the threat made to the Jewish community in Turkey. One of the men who fashioned my life and spirit was Karl Dietrich of Harvard. Karl came from Germany to the United States at the end of World War I and he retired as Eaton Professor of Government a little over ten years ago. During the Nazi years he spoke up against National Socialism at every opportunity, from every public platform, in the course of his lectures at the university, and over any number of broadcasting stations in Boston in the immediate environs.

Finally, word came to him that if he persisted, actions would be undertaken against his family in Germany, a mother, three brothers and one sister. He never once abandoned his position. Once in later years, I asked him why; he said, "The threats would never have been carried through, because they would only have brought greater publicity." He also said, "The Gestapo never touched one of them and they all lived to the war's end."

So I would ask those of you who are Jews whether relenting to this pressure of the Turkish government constitutes a proper answer. Obviously, there are those among you who feel very keenly that it does, and I know well enough that there are many who are not here with us, who represent a large segment of American Judaism, because they shared the opinion that it was wise to relent.

I simply would like to say that there is another view. That other view is that one dare never submit to terrorism, in any form, at any time, without inviting still greater threats and forcing us to still more abject submissions in the future.

FRANCES GROSSMAN: I'm Dr. Frances Grossman of New York. I'm not a survivor of the Holocaust, but I'm a survivor of pogroms which took place before the Holocaust, events of which I have no conscious recollection, but these are events which shape my life. Now I came here Tuesday afternoon. Tuesday morning, I received a telephone call from the office of the Consul General of Israel, as I think many people did, telling me of Elie Wiesel's telegram suggesting that I not come. Now my reaction was that I felt an affront to me and my dignity as a Jew that I should be bullied this way not to come to a meeting. It reminded me of the stories my relatives told me of the old "shtetls" in Russia, where the Jews were told by the goyim what they should or shouldn't do or there will be a pogrom.

Is Israel a ghetto or a state that it can be threatened with pogroms? It seems to me that we're through all that. What was the Holocaust about? What is the State of Israel about if it can be threatened with terror or pogroms if we don't acceed to somebody's wishes? There's something terribly, terribly wrong in that, terribly offensive, offensive to my dignity as a Jew, let alone as a human being. There is no way I would have stayed away from this meeting.

However, I do have trouble with the name of this conference, Holocaust and Genocide. I believe it should have either been a Conference on Genocide or a Conference on the Holocaust. The Holocaust is a specifically Jewish/Christian issue which the Christian world has not been able to come to terms with. The Holocaust is the result of this inner Christian struggle when one cannot accept part of one's self. As Freud said, antisemitism is a neurosis of civilization, of Christian civilization. The Holocaust is a result of that neurosis, and it's a specific issue which has to be dealt with specifically. A conference on genocide I think is acceptable and certainly one I would attend. But I have trouble with joining the Holocaust and Genocide. Thank you.

JACK MOTLEY: My name is Jack Motley. I am from Cambridge, England, and I am at this conference because I received out of the blue an invitation to come to it. Now, I'm not a Jew, and I'm not an intellectual. My profession is that I'm a retired railway porter and I'm just an ordinary working class person.

All I want to say is that I appreciate that there are people in many countries where nations and races are being destroyed, for instance, Brazil and the Indians, and I believe that we have to be conscious that this is a real problem that faces many people. Therefore I am glad that the conference is being held. It may have been a mistake to hold it here in Israel, but, on the other hand, because of what has happened to the Jewish people, it seems to be a good place. Wherever it is, one has to stand up and be counted. Because it happened to you, you should be prepared to say it's not going to happen to us again, or to anybody else in the world. I'm glad the conference is being held.

NILI: I'm going to introduce myself to you in a strange way by only giving you my first name which is the most significant thing for now. It's Nili. I was named for an underground group in Israel, an underground group during the First World War when the Ottoman Empire was still in power here and the British were trying to get the power. This group believed that by helping the British, we would be helping ourselves get a state, a country, a home. One of the members of the group was Sarah Aronson who during her travels in Turkey saw the massacre of the Armenians and was so impressed, angered, touched, and horrified, that she felt she had to write about it and speak about it. I was brought up on these stories, which is why it wasn't strange at all for me to realize that this conference, being a genocide conference, was going to include issues dealing with the Armenian massacre.

Hearing what has gone on here now, I am reminded of the saying of the great sage Hillel who said, "If I am not for myself who is for me, if I am for myself alone what am I, and if not now, when?" Hearing Dr. Littell's talk, and hearing what we've been saying now, I'm wondering if it's forty years in the desert we've been wandering in order to be able to talk about the issues of the Holocaust. What have forty years done for us in terms of learning the lessons of the Holocaust? Why is it that now, with all the hindsight we have, and the things we feel we should have done, or people could have done and didn't do, we still seem to be prevented from doing things now to keep such Holocausts from happening again.

A group of Jews is being threatened overtly, not by hints, not by any subtle means. The Turkish government said they would do something to the Jews there. What hurts the most and what insults the most is to hear that leaders who have the power to speak out, who have the power to be examples for their constituencies, don't have the courage or the convictions that they seem to profess. I felt very insulted when I heard the warm wishes of some of these leaders for our conference but that they would not be here with the courage of their warm wishes. How can a real leader stay passive and not do anything instead of going forth and leading the people that he is responsible for?

RICHARD HOVANNISIAN: My name is Richard Hovannisian and I'm from UCLA. I'd like to say that I'm speaking here as an individual and only as an individual. I feel very uncomfortable speaking here this evening because of the topic that I and a number of other people here will be speaking about, that is the Armenian experience which is at the center of the controversy of this conference.

I'd like to say nonetheless that I'm not sure whether I should express sorrow and regret, thanks, outrage, hurt, or perhaps optimism. My sorrow is that once again the victims have become the victimizers, the Armenian victims today are placed in a position of victimizing others by having their name mentioned. That's what I would assume from Mr. Eisner's talk - the feeling he has and many others must have is that they do not want to jeopardize their own people in such a situation. In that sense I must express sorrow that I have in my own little way been a cause, because the threats that came forward because of my topic, are a cause for partial disruption of this conference.

I also want to say thank you because there are people with courage and conviction enough to go forward despite the threats, and despite the great difficulties, not only financial, but moral, professional, and other.

I want to express outrage because the denial continues and the strength of the denial comes from organized governments. It is an outrageous situation. It is outrageous that the Israeli government has been put into sad straights.

Finally I should say, I'm hurt in a sense that this had to happen, because the Armenians and people who are Armenian scholars have understood the Jewish Holocaust almost the same way as they felt it on their own skin. The identity of the two people has been so close, their experiences have been so parallel. Each is, of course, unique, at a different time and different place, but nonetheless they have so much in common. Therefore, it is hurtful to think that conditions have been created where one group has to feel that it has to make a choice. I want to express optimism that regardless of divisions among us, divisions outside this hall and within this hall, that at least we are present and here gathered in a society and in a state where dissension can be held, and where a conference can continue to proceed despite official withdrawal. For that I am thankful and optimistic.

CHESTER HUNT: I am Chester Hunt, a sociologist from Western Michigan University, mainly interested in the Holocaust. I am concerned about one aspect of this discussion. The Turkish government today is not the Turkish government of pre-World War I. My understanding of the Turkish government is that it is one of the very few Moslem governments who has been relatively friendly to Israel, and I think that is certainly something to be said for it. Frankly, I am disturbed because there have been several reports recently of Turkish diplomats who have been assassinated in cold blood by Armenian nationalists, and I wonder if it is possible for this conference to say that it is not only concerned about the question of the experience of the Armenian people at the time of the massacre but is also concerned about the terroristic acts of Armenians today. I wonder if that kind of statement might make this conference appear less as one that is insensitive to the concerns of the Turkish government, concerns that on the face at least seem to be very legitimate. Thank you.

RABBI MARC TANNENBAUM: I come to this microphone with considerable reluctance. I am one of those representative Jewish leaders who have been referred to, who had accepted very early on when the first conception of the program was set forth and agreed to take part in the program as actively as I could. My name is Rabbi Marc Tannenbaum. I'm the National Interreligious Affairs Director of the American Jewish Committee. I accepted at the outset because the conception of this conference conformed to a basic conviction I have had over the past 30 years in my professional work in Jewish-Christian relationships and ecumenical work, that the time is past due to recognize that the Nazi Holocaust ultimately led to the destruction of 35,000,000 other people. Of course, the Jewish people were singularly chosen by the Nazis as a matter of the official policy of a government for final and total extermination, a policy that was not addressed to any other people. However, I am persuaded that the Nazi Holocaust is not a Jewish obsession. It is not some kind of perverted Jewish hang-up. Within the realities of the Holocaust, there are insights and lessons that the entire human family must learn of the capacity of demonism when joined together with the most advanced technology of lethal destruction, to bring us ultimately, God forbid, to a global Auschwitz. Therefore, I felt this conference not only merited my own personal involvement, but called forth my obligation to involve my organization and its apparatus throughout the world.

Let me say at the outset that what has just been said about the profound empathy that Jews have shared with Armenians and that Armenians have shared with Jews is not simply an abstraction. In 1975, when Archbishop Manoogian, who was the Patriarch of the Armenian Church of North America began to organize the commemoration of the massacre against the Armenian people, he came to me and said, "Will you help us arrange for this observance? We have little experience organizationally in arranging for these observances, and the Jewish people obviously have far more experience than we have." I agreed at once to do so. In fact I brought my entire staff to the Armenian Cathedral in New York, and they sat literally for months with Armenian churchmen and scholars and helped arrange every detail of the Armenian program to commemorate the massacre of the Armenian people.

I came to this conference even though I was aware of the facts of all of this turmoil that has been going on literally weeks and days before the conference was to be held, and there were all kinds of conversations and indeed pressures and threats and counter-threats, the Turkish Government to Armenians, Israel, etc., I really don't want to get into the details for reasons that are wise and prudent. Some decision was made not to risk the possibility that the lives of hundreds of people, not in Turkey, but others whose lives would be affected by the response of the Turkish government, would be imperiled. That certainly is a legitimate concern which one has to deal with responsibly. I do not want it on my conscience that I contributed to the death of any single human being.

I really am concerned about another issue, and I'm risking standing up here speaking in my personal capacity and in no way for the American Jewish Committee. I'm troubled by the surrealism of this discussion. There is something unreal about what has been happening here, what has been happening in relation to the days and weeks before this conference, what is happening here tonight. To capitulate to pressure is to invite further terrorism. There's no question about that. But the issue that we have to face, the scandal of what is taking place, is the distortion of the central conception which called this conference into being. There are legitimate reasons for wanting to examine again and again all of the dynamics of what took place in the Nazi Holocaust and what happened to the Jews. Jews do that, year after year after year in order to understand how to cope with the demonism of the Nazi evil, and there's a legitimate place to study again and again what happened to the Armenian people. But it is wrong to allow the struggle between the Turkish government and the Armenian people to become the central preoccupation of this conference. In my own experience over the past four years, I have been to Southeast Asia and have seen in Cambodia three to four million people massacred before the eyes of the world. For that to become a footnote to this conference, or not to mention it at all what took place in Sudan four years ago, where nearly a million human beings were destroyed, cannot make sense. Where is Uganda in our agenda where more than 500,000 black Christians have been massacred? One could go through every continent of the earth, Africa, Asia, Latin America today, where hundreds of thousands of Indians are being destroyed, liquidated.

We will in fact capitulate if we allow the Armenian issue to remain the central preoccupation. I say this in all veneration and reverence for my dearest friends in the Armenian church, and I say this out of respect to some of the Turkish Ambassadors who have come to us to talk about other issues and their legitimate concerns about Armenian terrorists who have massacred now some 30 Turkish Ambassadors, for that is also a legitimate concern. It seems to me the essential question for us is to get back on the main track of the conference, not to reenact what happened in Armenia in 1915, not to reenact what happened in Nazi Germany, as painful as that is for us, but to learn what happened in both of those episodes that have relevance for a world today in which there are massacres taking place on every continent of the earth, where human lives are being destroyed.

The central preoccupation must be what can we do to try to put an end to the kind of destruction that is taking place in violence and terrorism and massacres and torture in almost every continent on the earth. If we allow ourselves to become preoccupied solely with the past, we will in fact be guilty of contributing to the kind of callousness, apathy, and indifference and evasion of the magnitude of the challenge that we face today. If we want to honor the victims of the Armenian massacres, if we want to honor the memory of the six million Kdoshim, and another thirty-five million human beings who were killed in the Nazi Holocaust, the task for us is to look at these events not as a hitching post to the past but as a guiding post to the future. I beg you as someone who will be sitting by virtue of official ukase at the sides of this conference, but whose heart and soul is at the center of this consultation, to turn to the task of the here and now. That is the challenge for human survival, that is the challenge to the deepest values that Jews and Christians and Moslems and others share.

If we value human life, we will find ways to stand up against the massive dehumanization the massive callousness that is taking place, and above all against the ultimate obscenity, the ultimate possibility of a nuclear holocaust, God forbid, in which all of us will become victims. If we're able to do that, this conference can yet be saved. If we cannot do that here now, then it will have to be done again elsewhere where there is a much more balanced and proportioned way of looking at these issues. But I tell you, both Armenians and Jews and Turks and others have a stake in moving away from the past to what faces us in everyday's newspaper. Human

lives are being destroyed day after day after day, and if we are believing Christians or Jews or Moslems or others, that is our central
moral task at this conference and in the days and months ahead of us
as citizens of the 20th Century.

SHAMAI DAVIDSON: This is one of those moral dilemmas in which
nobody emerges unscathed. For three years, we labored to produce a
conference on Holocaust and Genocide. From the very outset, the
name Archbishop Shahe Ajamian appeared on our organizing committee;
by chance alphabetically, his name was the first. On the many
brochures which we sent out, in this country and throughout the
world, the Armenian question was obviously going to be discussed.
At no time did the Israeli government or any other official body in
this or any other country question the correctness of what we were
doing.

Six weeks ago, we were suddenly informed that what we were doing was dangerous and that the Israeli government therefore felt
that this conference should be canceled. We were ready to cooperate
in every way with the postponement and relocation of the conference,
but this was something that we were unable to do on our own. We did
not have the mechanism, the ability, the money at this stage to re-
locate this conference. Unfortunately, negotiations proceeded for
many weeks without any satisfactory result and there was no possibility of any process being created in which this conference could be
transferred.

This conference, therefore, had to go on, and I believe that
the government recognizes this conference had to go on. The government did everything in its power to reduce the danger of this conference in the terms which they understood to be dangerous. These are
questions which I do not feel that we can evaluate. I think that as
citizens of this country and as visitors to this country, we have to
respect the expertise of the Foreign Affairs Ministry of this country about what constitutes a danger for Jewish or Israeli interests.
So I think we have to respect what they then proceeded to do which
was to remove any official support or any official sponsorship of
the conference. They succeeded in doing so, and what has been left
is a meeting of academics and scholars, and concerned individuals
who will discuss genocide and Holocaust without any official sponsoring or backing whatsoever, without any financial help, without
any university sponsoring in this country. I respect what they have
done, but I feel that they should respect, and they probably do, our
right as scholars and academics and concerned people within the
framework of free speech to discuss the topics which we will be
discussing during the next few days.

33. Conference Summation Panel and Round Table

The final session of the International Conference on the Holo-
caust and Genocide was convened, like the briefing session on the
opening night, sitting in the round in the Hilton Balllroom. A re-
markable attendance level has been maintained throughout the Confer-
ence, and this Summation Panel and Round Table too was attended by
several hundred people. What had the Conference covered? The major
"Track Leaders" of the Conference - John Felstiner (Co-Chair with
Sidra Ezrachi), Franklin Littell, John Sommerville, Leo Kuper, and
Shamai Davidson - present their summaries, and then the audience of
participants offer their critical observations, thoughtfully and
emotionally.

ISRAEL CHARNY: We are posing two questions tonight to our
chair-persons and then we shall invite the remarks of all of you in
the audience.

The first question is: In the field of knowledge in which you
are working - political science, sociology, international relations,
philosophy, literature and arts, wherever it may be - what are some
of the major conclusions that you would confirm for inclusion in our
knowledge base about the Holocaust and genocide at this time? The
second question: What are the major challenges, problems, frontier
questions, and gripping issues which you would identify in your
field in our struggle to understand more fully what we all know, ultimately, we cannot understand fully, but have to keep working towards - the nature of the Holocaust, the nature of the genocidal
process, and the future that we all face around these issues?

JOHN FELSTINER: I have been working as co-chairperson of the
Literature and Arts Track (with Sidra Ezrachi).

In our presentations and discussions we talked first about
Holocaust literature, including European, Israeli, and American
novels, stories, poetry, plays, diaries, memoirs, and also hard
documents of the Holocaust looked at as literature. Second, we
spoke of art or visual material - we heard about and saw photography, graphic art, water colors, and so on from the ghettoes and
camps. Thirdly, we heard about films, mostly art films, and also
documentary footage, not so much the ones you saw at this conference, but ones done in the past.

In all areas, over and over again one common theme kept emerging. Our discussions kept coming back to one fundamental distinction which I think represents the current state of Holocaust studies
in art and literature, namely, the distinction between fact and fiction of the Holocaust, or reportage or documentation versus actual
re-creation of the event or the phenomenon. Whether it was the
matter of photography versus water color, whether it was novels

like The Wall, or Steiner's Treblinka which seemed to mix both reportage and re-creation, we kept coming back to that question.

As readers, critics, teachers, we face the problem of what to
look for and what to bring out. We began to feel that, given the
relative state of progress of our field, it is more important nowadays to study and reveal the ways, the forms, that mediate Holocaust
reality to us, in other words, not to be just looking for content as
such and reporting it, but to be asking how do we understand what we
understand?

We need not treat this material any longer as sacred, like Biblical text that will always exist and cannot be questioned. We can
analyze it, which also means analyzing ourselves.

This in my mind raises a question that we have not yet treated
and I think moves us into the area of what needs to be done by
people such as ourselves. It is a question often raised by people
not doing our work, and I think it needs to be treated really head
on and decisively! Is there such a thing as Holocaust literature
and Holocaust art? Of course, we know there are works of literature
and works of art that emerged in the Holocaust, but are they to be
treated differently say from Tolstoy or Picasso, and to be distinguished, and isolated in that way?

It is a very fine line. We want to say both yes and no to that
question. I most often want to say yes because I do not want to betray the particularity of the works of art that we study. I do not
want to betray that particularity in the future work that I do. If
further Holocaust and genocide is to be prevented, we cannot allow a
repetition of failures of imagination that have allowed horrors to
occur in the past.

It is a failure of imagination that lets people order mass
genocide. A failure of imagination means a failure to generate empathy with the suffering and insulted body or spirit of the single
individual. That is what literature and art convey to us, and that
is why I do not want to betray the particularities of the art that
we work with.

The larger question implied which we cannot answer today can be
subsumed by the words unique versus universal.

The question is a fierce one. For us it has to do with the
whole question of what sort of esthethic critique we mount, whether
we need an entirely new critical form for the works of art of say
Lohemei Haghettot, or whether we can treat them the way art critics
always have. The basic distinction between unique and universal
carries crucial implications for the where we go from here, because
the larger question of what humankind in general may make of the
Holocaust is really what has been at the back of our minds.

From the Armenian contributors at this conference, we learned
both of kindred and different problems about our common subject. We

learned that Armenian writers who cared to write about what happened in 1915 were isolated within the mother tongue and in exile, therefore had a very limited audience, which was not true in the case of Jews who moved into other languages such as English and French, and eventually did reach a wider audience.

We learned about British and American and European ignorance up to and including today of the Armenian genocide. Maybe some of the Armenian participants got a sense from us of developments that are still to come in their area of a really developed literature, and consciousness and study of that literature.

There is one more issue that I will end with, the question of analogy. This question is also very tied into the question of a unique or universal reading of the Holocaust. We constantly discover analogies between the Holocaust and other events. Analogies between the Holocaust and other events can be developed every day with any urgent or emergent situation in the world. Clearly the question of distinction between the particular or universal nature of what happened in the Holocaust will affect the authenticity and usefulness of these analogies, and I have no doubt that these anologies, for better and worse, are going to be central to various political events in the future.

FRANKLIN LITTELL: I am from Temple University in Philadelphia, and my Track Group was assigned the topic of pedagogical work, that is, the teaching of the Holocaust and the lessons of the Holocaust.

We had reports by specialists working with children, high school age, college and university, theological seminaries, also summer teaching, continuing education and adult study groups in communities or in congregations, so we treated all levels pretty much in our review.

It was our consensus that, in all cases, the careful training of the teachers is an important part of the enterprise. It is not just enough that courses arouse consciousness - although without that you cannot get anywhere. It is necessary to have careful arousal of conscience, and for that you need top notch teacher training programs. The teacher has the responsibility to draw certain major conclusions and to focus on major themes. It may be that among those who have worked a long time in this area, it is taken for granted that certain points stand out and that the Holocaust is self conveying or self interpreting. We were reminded that this is not necessarily true, and that the teacher has responsibility to draw out certain lessons to the attention of those who are studying the event. The point was also made that it has proved valuable to have evaluation procedures before and after the courses, and these can either be in written essay form or in questionnaire form.

Considerable stress was also given to the importance of teaching materials other than literary. We have data on the use of records, broadcasts, including those from the Hitler period, pictures, and art and article exhibits. There is very strong testimony to the value of the witness of survivors - the message of survivors, either in person or through tapes.

Reference was made to something which has become more common in Israel, but certainly can be done in any country, which is that school children are adopting one of the destroyed communities and studying its history and its artifacts, and also the testimony of survivors, which gives a specificity to the event which can be lost if you study only the broad story of all communities together. Some reference was made to the usefulness of rescued Torah Scrolls, which are present in some communities.

Participants also underscored the importance of monuments, the importance of Yom Hashoah observances by Christians as well as Jewish congregations and communities. Some communities, as in Florida, have achieved a kind of community saturation in which all of the media, and the schools, and various community services, and movie showings were used in making the whole community conscious of the importance of Yom Hashoah.

We agreed on two imperatives: The first that under no circumstances should the Holocaust be allowed to be simply a Jewish affair, or treated in that context, although obviously it is that in its specificity. It is also important that the concerns of Christians and Humanists of Conscience be brought forward.

The second imperative is that we need to move increasingly in a dialectical way between the discrete and unique nature of the Holocaust and universal concerns with genocide to all peoples, which is of course what we are engaged in at this conference when we speak of Holocaust and Genocide.

There was also some specific discussion of the Armenian experience. The Armenians have been handicapped until the last two decades for lack of known teaching sources in languages which we commonly use, French, German and English, but this is being overcome so that it will become more possible to find materials.

We came to an agreement that we need to press in professional schools, schools of education, theology, medicine, and law and the like, not just for awareness of the Holocaust, but for some specific attention to the misuses of professional roles and power: the misuse of the medical knowledge, the abuse of legal knowledge, and corruption Visenschaften - the sciences broadly conceived - which characterize the genocide in the modern age.

It is not that we just want certain things taught about the Holocaust and its lessons, or about the Armenian massacres, or about the slaughter of the Bahai in Iran, but we need to give attention to professional ethics and commitments which will help to build barriers against genocide. People who have the stewardship of power which education gives have to be trained not to agree to be technically competent barbarians who will do anything if the price is right, and to be capable of saying no in the name of conscience, as well as to do what affirmatively needs to be done. Denial besets us also in university settings. Theology and medicine and law and all our schools need to face the facts of life in terms of the age of the Holocaust and Genocide.

JOHN SOMERVILLE: The workshop on which I am reporting is called The Workshop on Nuclear Weaponry and Ecocidal Technology - Extension of the Threat of the Holocaust and Genocide to all Humankind.

The workshop makes by unanimous vote the following recommendations to the international community as a contribution to the understanding and prevention of the supreme danger of nuclear omnicide - that is the annihilation of all life:

Recommendation No. 1. In the interests of the genuine security of all humankind, it is necessary to gain the immediate agreement among all nuclear powers to a treaty of no first-use of nuclear weapons, and an immediate implementation of a freeze on the deployment, manufacture, research and development of nuclear weaponry.

No. 2. We recommend the passage of an official resolution by the United Nations confirming that any use of nuclear weapons is a crime against humanity. This would give specific expression to the illegality - the impermissability under international law - of the use of any nuclear weapons, just as gas weapons are specifically outlawed. Surely everyone knows that nuclear weapons are infinitely more destructive than any gas weapon that was ever conceived or used in conventional warfare.

No. 3. We call for a universal convention providing for the abolition of all nuclear weapons under United Nations supervision and for the prohibition of the testing, manufacture, or possession of any nuclear weapons. This is, of course, a long term objective that, in the end, may be the only certain preventive of nuclear conflict and nuclear omnicide.

No. 4. We call for greatly increased moral education, cognitive and affective, at all levels in relation to the lethal dangers not only of nuclear weapons but of nuclear power plants and the radioactive wastes which such plants produce. The objectives should be the earliest possible phasing out of all nuclear power production. This is, of course, based on the scientific fact that all nuclear power plants produce a by-product, the one substance plutonium which is necessary to create nuclear weaponry.

No. 5. We call for greatly increased attention and creative activity on the part of all the media, all the arts, all the religions and the professions in connection with the present unprecedented danger of ending the world through nuclear omnicide. Since everything human is now threatened with extinction, everything human must recognize this threat and create its own form of resistance.

All of us agreed that such a conference as ours should not be a one-shot affair, but should continue, preferably on some regular periodical basis, and with expanded inclusion, particularly of all religions, and the widest possible range of humanistic studies, skills and professions.

Finally, we of the workshop, like all the participants in this conference, wish to express our deepest appreciation to all those in Israel who worked so hard to make this pioneering international conference so highly successful.

LEO KUPER: The Track Session that we held related to Minority Rights and International Action Against Genocide.

We assumed that minorities and minority rights should be viewed from the perspective of international action against genocide. We reviewed various possibilities of action for the protection of minorities, at the constitutional level, and in international conventions for the protection of minorities.

There was some discussion of the need for a clear statement of objectives and a sharply defined focus. It was generally agreed that the focus should be on genocide and mass murder. There was no agreement as to whether the mass murder should be limited to mass murder of ethnic, racial and religious groups, or whether it should be concerned with mass murder generally.

In any case, our session was essentially action oriented, and was primarily concerned with a proposal to establish an organization for international action against genocide to act both within and outside of the United Nations when a genocide is threatened.

Discussion of the proposal emphasized a number of areas where pressure might be exerted against governments engaging in massacres. These suggestions included pressure through international aid programs, control of transfer of military equipment, a world tribunal for punishment, and humanitarian intervention. We reviewed a paper on strategies presented by Laurie Wiseberg and Harry Scoble of Human Rights Internet in Washington to the Amnesty International, as well as a publication of mine by the Minority Rights Group on available strategies.

The most effective action from a preventive point of view would call for an early warning system, such as is being developed by Israel Charny and his associates. Genocide generally develops over a period of time, and there are often early massacres and other murders which would serve as a warning. The hope would be to call for an international alert before the onset of massacres.

We discussed what might be the indicators for an early warning. We recognized that the state of knowledge is still in a beginning stage, but we did feel that on the basis of information derived from a data bank it would be possible to identify societies which are incipiently at risk. These indicators would serve to activate an international alert. It was the common concern of the members to alert, stimulate and motivate the common conscience of mankind to combat genocide and mass murder wherever committed, towards whatever group, and in whatever circumstances, for whatever reasons. We did not differentiate between particular systems of government or particular ideologies.

We wish to stress the importance of documenting recent genocide and of refuting denials of past genocide. We have heard several denials of the Turkish genocide against Armenians which is a case in point.

Finally, we strongly affirm the legitimacy and necessity of meetings such as ours. We reject all attempts to deny genocide, because public exposure and discussion of genocide are one of our most urgent tasks. We deplore the threats and pressures which have surrounded our meetings.

Functioning under duress, the organizers and participants attending the International Conference on the Holocaust and Genocide have created an outstanding human intellectual event, and we wish to express our deep appreciation of that contribution.

SHAMAI DAVIDSON: Our Track Session was entitled Psychological Issues in the Lives of Survivors and their Families.

We discussed twenty papers, and they were grouped around three themes. The first dealt with the theme of Life Cycle Studies of Survivors and their Families. The second dealt with the Transmission of the Impact of Parents' Experiences in the Holocaust to the Second Generation. The third concerned Therapeutic Considerations and Psychosocial Implications.

These are the words, the scientific words, around which we grouped our papers, but behind these papers we were trying all the time to grasp the reality. We learned through our three days of meetings that society's inability to come to terms with the bearer of the tale of human catastrophe has been slowly changing; and with that also the image of the survivor from that of a damaged individual to a person with strength from whom we can learn of the strengths in humanity to cope with disaster.

No longer does a survivor need to hide, no longer does he need to be relegated to experts so that the rest of society can remain comfortable. Today we do seek him out, and he is ready, in order to demonstrate to us that which we have to know in order to save lives. Franklin Littell said so poignantly in his opening address, we have the right to talk of these things only if our purpose is to save lives, to prevent further genocides.

When we look at the Holocaust, we begin to realize that from our studies, and preoccupations and almost-obsessions with the Holocaust, we have begun to universalize genocide. We have begun to bring it into the stream of human history and human experience. We

also have begun to accept the monstrousness and inhumanity as part
of human functioning, as parts of reality.

A special note in in order about the presence in our section
also of our Armenian colleagues. Under the incentive of survivor
studies resulting from the Holocaust, our Armenian colleagues at
last have been studying, survivors of the Armenian genocide. They
have learned from us a lot, and they are applying many of our
findings, but what maybe they do not realize, and what we are now
beginning to realize, is that we can learn from them, even though
they are just beginning in this field, precisely because they are
looking at survivors of a genocide of sixty-seven years ago. We
have survivors who are thirty-seven years old. They are looking at
survivors who are sixty-seven years old. So they have those extra
years of what it means to live with the unlivable, and those extra
years of mobilizing resources in order to continue in life.

The confrontation with survivors is one of demonstrating human
concern, and especially in order to save future human lives. We are
reaching toward communication, dialogue, and collective discourse.
We communicate with the survivor, who is an ordinary human being,
just like the rest of us, but he has within him this special experience, which we are trying to bear and share with him, although it
is unbearable and unsharable. By doing so, we maintain, foster, and
nurture human concern, and human concern is our only real barrier
against omnicide. It is when we lose this concern that it becomes
easy to press the button. We heard the special poignancy of the
survivor through their poetry and writing presented by John
Felstiner, but that is in every survivor. If we listen, it is in
the voice of the simplest survivor.

In our group, survivors in our midst began to talk to us. They
began to tell us about their problems as survivors. Suddenly there
was an emotional disarray - there was consternation - people felt
that we were not really staying true to the tasks of our workshop
and track discussion. But this emotional disarray really meant that
we were getting to the essence of this confrontation which we do not
yet know how to arrange. Only by allowing these dialogues to take
place, by encouraging these collective discourses can we move towards the nurturing of human concern.

FRANCES GROSSMAN: I have heard a great deal at this conference
about changing laws, and also from the Track Leaders tonight about
the need to change laws to prevent genocide and omnicide. Now in
Germany there were laws against murder, but when Hitler came in, the
laws were changed so that killing Jews was no longer a crime. Not
only were the laws changed, but the super ego, the content of the
super ego, was changed; instead of the Ten Commandments, such
"virtues" as murder, brutality and sadism became accepted.

It seems to me that it is not laws that we need to change so
much. We need to change people. We need to change what is called
human nature, which may really be human nurture. What we need to
explore fundamentally is why civilization produces people with so

much repressed rage that it is so easy for men like Hitler to chan-
nelize this to destructive ends. It seems to me that no matter how
many laws we make and break, it is not going to solve anything unless we do something about raising people who are not so prone to
violence.

ABA BEER: I am from Montreal, Canada. I am not a Ph.D. I am
not a professor. My only education is that I am a survivor of the
ghettoes and the camps, and tonight at the conclusion I want to make
some remarks in my own name. First of all the conference was, in my
opinion, very well organized. Serious work was done. I was very
impressed with the calibre of the leadership and of the attendance,
but I was bothered by certain attitudes, certain expressions,
certain directions which I noticed here, and I notice everywhere
else too lately.

First of all, there is a problem, in my opinion, of euphemisms,
things are not called by the right name. Now, of course, the Germans used nice euphemisms for mass murder, very innocent words. I
find the calling of the Germans "Nazis" a whitewash of what really
happened. The German nation of Ein Volk, Ein Reich, Ein Fuehrer
committed the Holocaust, it was not a party matter, it was not a
political matter. In the thirties, if somebody was put in a concentration camp because he was a member of the SPD or the KPD, this was
a political matter, it was not done by the Nazi party, it was done
in the name of the Deutsches Reiches - that was organized from the
top - the Reich President, the Reich Chancellor down to the railroad
workers, without any opposition in Germany until they realized that
the game was over in 1944.

I saw no hesitation here at this conference in referring to the
Turkish genocide - practically no one bothered to use the word Ottoman. I heard reference to the fact that the Americans dropped the
atomic bomb, nobody said that the Democrats in the United States
dropped the atomic bomb. Nor did anybody call the Japanese the
Hirohitas - they were called Japanese. For some reasons, only the
Germans all of a sudden are called some mysterious name, "Nazis."

Let me tell you that as a survivor I discovered Nazis only in
1945. Until 1945 there were no Nazis. They were all Germans, one
way or another. So in my opinion this is a corruption of language,
it is a distortion of historical facts to say otherwise. I hope it
is just innocent, and there is nothing sinister behind it.

Another thing that I am bothered by as a survivor is that by
spreading guilt of the Holocaust, by comparing what happened in Auschwitz with what is happening in Belfast, Sri Lanka, Uganda or
Brazil, it makes everybody guilty, and of course, if everybody is
guilty then nobody is guilty. I was told here one morning at a
panel session that there are many things in common between Brazil
and the Holocaust. Forgive me, ladies and gentlemen, but this is
plain nonsense. You might as well compare me with Prince Charles -
I have two arms, two legs, I have one wife and one son, so I am
Prince Charles, but there is not much more that we have in common.

382

Let us call a spade a spade. The Holocaust tragedy is very unique; by comparing it with smaller tragedies, you make it petty. I do feel compassion for people in Sri Lanka, and people in Belfast, and any suffering people. Believe me, any survivor understands their pain and anguish more than others. But by making the Holocaust a common thing as if Holocausts happen all over the world throughout the generations, you distort it. Please, I appeal to you to refrain from it. Thank you very much.

ABRAHAM TORRY: I am one of those Israelis who feel somehow uncomfortable about what certain officials of the State of Israel did to try and jeopardize the work of this conference. I am a survivor of the Holocaust and I am an Israeli citizen since 1947. I am a lawyer, and I am very much concerned about the keeping alive of what happened, what we passed through in the Holocaust. It is something terrible and incredible that the effort to suppress this conference could happen in our time. I think every government and every public body, international and national, must do their utmost to hold such conferences.

However, I do not think that it is right to put all things together, Holocaust, genocide, the Armenians, all in some supermarket. The tragedy of the Holocaust is so unique in the history of humanity that it should not be mixed up with any other catastrophe that happened here and there. There is no analogy; you cannot put things and try to find a common denominator.

I ask myself now that the conference is being closed, where are we going from here? I hear from my very good friend Advocate Braude, that there has been legally registered an Institute to continue the permanent work of this conference. It is good. I suggest that in the next years we hold a special conference for genocide, not mix them up, because you just cannot.

I also suggest that this conference resolves to set up a permanent body with the main task to keep the past alive, with special stress on the Holocaust, also with special stress on genocide and omnicide of all people, to see to it that there should be no repetition of what happened to threaten this conference exactly on the eve of its opening. I can hardly understand that people like Gideon Hausner and others canceled their appearance here after they had given their written consent; it is absolutely incredible, and impermissible, and there should not be a repetition of this. If a conference is to be held, and I think it should be held periodically, let us say every two years or three years, there should be clear commitments from those who will want to address us and submit papers, they should live up to their obligations.

I want to pay my great respect to those leaders of this conference, Prof. Charny and Prof. Davidson, who had the courage and did not give in to all the pressures, and they were almost fighting singlehanded against officials and against donors who at the last minute dared to cancel their donations or their participation. I think we owe those leaders our gratitude and thanks.

ISRAEL CHARNY: Thank you, but let us leave the congratulations aside for the moment. I want to reflect that the comments that are being heard express a special pain of people who have experienced in their own lives the awesome hell of the Holocaust, and they are saying in a way that may have no answer that there is no way of talking about the Holocaust together with other genocides. Nonetheless, this conference is precisely on the Holocaust and all other genocides. I wonder if we should not address the pain of these remarks respectfully and humbly.

JULIUS MORAVCSIK: I am Julius Moravcsik from Stanford, California. I am touched and certainly bothered by the fact that apparently people for whom I have the highest regard and highest respect feel that those of us who want to connect the issue of the Holocaust with the general problem of genocide might be disrespectful toward the millions who died tragically in Auschwitz and Dachau and other camps.

Let me try at least to explain why some of us feel that these issues should be connected, not because we feel that the experiences of Auschwitz or Dachau might be comparable to the experiences of other genocides, but for a very different reason: because we are committed to trying to see to it that these horrible deaths were not in vain. We must try to see to it that this horrible historical event, to some extent at least, can be, together with other genocides in the past, a means for our learning to diagnose and prevent genocides in general. This way we can turn the horrible event of the Holocaust into something that at least leads to some extent towards something that is a benefit to all humanity. Perhaps by linking the Holocaust to other genocides, we can prevent it from happening to any race or nationality. If we can do that, then I think that by this kind of work we are not disrespectful to the victims of Auschwitz; on the contrary, I think we pay them the deepest homage and the highest respect.

DORIS EPSTEIN: I am from Toronto. In the spirit of what was said just now, and in the spirit of this conference, I suggest and urge that we make a public statement that we deplore the threat and the pressures brought to bear to stop this conference.

MAURICE GOLDSTEIN: I am Dr. Maurice Goldstein from Brussels. I am the President of the International Auschwitz Committee.

I would like to congratulate the organizers of this conference because they put on the program Holocaust and Genocide.

Sometimes in the papers I listened to the speaker made - shall I say - a mistake, and said "the Jewish Genocide." I have to say that in Europe we never used these words. But what is the Holocaust? It is a Jewish Genocide. If our Armenian colleagues speak of "the Armenian Genocide," it is also correct, it is good.

If this was an international conference on - I translate Holocaust - the Jewish Genocide and all other Genocides, it is important
to compare all the genocides of our century, because all of us can
learn something. If we learn together and discuss all genocides, we
can better teach young people to understand this problem.

I have to say that I was shocked, and I regret that some eminent participants in this conference were not with us tonight. But
I think that the purpose of this conference has been achieved.

NILI SHIRYON: I feel that I must also speak about the uniqueness of the Holocaust. I think we need to remember that as Jews it
was not our first. If we think back to the end of the 15th Century,
and if we use the literal meaning of the word Holocaust, which is
death by fire, sacrifice by fire, we had this in the Spanish Inqui-
sition. If we think about it along the centuries until the 20th
Century, we know that there were other attempts at genocide of the
Jews, so for us this was not the first time.

I submit that we do not learn by keeping to the uniqueness of
our own experience and looking back only on our history. I think it
is important to attempt a different way of learning our lessons, by
yes comparing the Holocaust with the other genocides, certainly with
the Armenian Genocide since it is the closest in comparison to our
own. At the same time, I wish to say I am very much for keeping the
definition of the Holocaust as unique, because we cannot make what
our survivors went though not unique.

PHUNTSOG WANGYAL: I would like to speak here for two particular
reasons. One reason is that I am very peculiar, so there are a number of people who are wondering where this peculiar man came from.

My name is Wangyal. I come from Tibet, a very remote country.
I want to thank the organizers of this conference for very special
reasons, for giving me the opportunity to express that not only in
Europe, but also in Asia a genocidal process is going on.

The Chinese invaded Tibet in 1949. In 1957 they made a statistical survey of the population. At that time the population of ethnic Tibet was six to seven million. Last year, according to their
statistics, the Tibetan population is 1.7 million. Now I know very
well how the rest of them disappeared. Whether you call it genocide
or mass murder, it does not matter to me. If this continues, ethnic
Tibetans will disappear. I am especially grateful to the organizers
for giving me this opportunity, because it is very rare for oppressed people from a remote area to be able to speak to an international
forum.

The Armenian problem had much covering in this conference, and
I am very very happy about that. Now our further attention should
also be paid to suppressed and oppressed minorities who have no
voice or standing in the international community. The United
Nations is not effective because it is an organization of governments. Normally - who commits genocide? Governments, not the

people. Therefore there should be a body where individual people can bring forward warnings of genocide. If there is no place where people like me can speak, you will not know what is happening in Tibet. Thank you very much.

FATHER CHARLES CARROLL: I am Father Charles Carroll from the Episcopal Diocese of Colorado, United States of America, retired.

Perhaps I could begin by saying that I stand here tonight in the garb of a priest of the Church because of the Germans. We met here because of Adolf Hitler for one reason. But I also came here because of men such as Dietrich and Bonhoeffer, and countless others, who gave their lives because of what transpired in Germany at that time, and I would not leave here without expressing my indebtedness to them and others.

One of the men who failed to come here is also a man who has played a large part in my spiritual formation, although we know each other only from an exchange of letters. He tells in the first book that he wrote after being released from a concentration camp that there was a day when all those who were there interned were forced to march in line before a group who had been hanged – some of whom had already died. One was a little boy whose body was not of sufficient weight to speed his death as that of an older and heavier man – he was still in that twilight zone between life and death. Someone cried out behind him, "Where is God in all this?" And the answer was, "There – at the end of that rope."

Now I am not unmindful of the fact that Jesus of Nazareth was a Jew. He said at one time – whatsoever you do unto the least of these my brothers, you do unto me. I came here not only because of what did happen, but what is happening, and what can happen. I would remind you from wherever you come, that the Shma Yisrael belongs to all of us, and Thou Shalt Love The Lord Thy God With All Thy Heart, With All Thy Soul, With All Thy Might, And Thy Neighbor As Thyself, And Every Man, Woman And Child On This Planet Is Your Neighbor.

SIDNEY STOCK: I am most moved by the survivors who talked about the uniqueness of the Holocaust, and it is most understandable to me. At the same time I am very glad that this conference was organized to include other slaughters, other genocides, but I think that the particular similarities and the particular differences were not addressed. It should have been a very important part of the conference to find out what exactly were the unique characteristics of the Holocaust and what were the unique characteristics of all the other instances. As happened in the Holocaust, the Jews were one of the first victims, but it was going to continue if it was possible. Only when people are united and when people are able to talk with each other and understand each other, can oppressive governments be opposed. So long as we are vying with each other as to which of our oppressions is worse, and we are not able to listen to each other, these same things can continue.

ARCHBISHOP SHAHE AJAMIAN: I am Archbishop Ajamian from Jerusalem. I started participating in this conference as one of the organizers with Professors Charny and Davidson. Until this conference started, I had the impression that the crisis which developed in recent weeks was just due to the fact that Turkish authorities made pressure on the Israeli Government, and the Israeli Government made pressure on some official people to resign from participating in this conference.

I must say that during these days, from many things that I heard, I come to a conclusion which saddens me a bit, that there is also another reason which is another kind of uneasiness among some people when they see that this conference speaks about others.

I want here to tell you very frankly something from my heart, very deep. I tried very hard to bring to this conference Armenian scholars from all over the world. They did not want to come to associate their genocide with the Holocaust. Their attitude was similar to some attitudes expressed here: They said, each one is a different thing. Each genocide is different. Each genocide is unique in itself.

I insisted and I insisted because in my understanding, as a person who lives in Israel, those who study the Armenian Genocide should come here to Israel, and only here, to understand better the genocide of their own people. Because when we deal with the Armenian genocide, we do not deal with it only as a question of the past, as a dramatic experience that our people lived. We must try to see in it a sign of hope that life will still continue, that things will be achieved, that destruction of our people will somehow be repaired, and we see the example of that hope here in Israel, on this land by these people.

This is why we wanted it to be here so intensely with all our presence, more to hear than to say, because we have learned that those who suffered genocide do not look for compassion. Compassion is the worst thing you can give them. We have learned that silence is the best remedy. Even at this conference we have learned that people somehow do not like to hear about others' sufferings. But I wanted to say these few words, because I did not want to remain silent again.

I want you to know, my dear friends, that our Armenian group was here not to speak about our people's genocide, but to see here the light in this land and not lose our hope of living again. Thank you.

ISRAEL CHARNY: We are of necessity approaching an end, and there is no end. I have been told by a fair number of people during the last week that I have projected a basic security and assurance while the conference was going on, but I think I am going to allow myself to end on some notes of sadness and incompleteness without in any way contradicting the hope and affirmation that there have been.

I think there are many questions to which there are no answers.
As a non-survivor, I say without hesitation that I have no answer to
the cry, the feeling, the anger and outrage of survivors. I understand their call and insistence on the uniqueness of the Holocaust,
and I believe that there are many elements of objective uniqueness
to the Holocaust. At the same time, I am convinced that the Holocaust is a tragic, classic member of a family of genocides of many
peoples, for thousands of years, and I am convinced for many years
to come. I think it is the overwhelming consensus of the participants in this conference, without ignoring the cry of protest from
those who cannot join us in the consensus wholeheartedly, that we
gathered as representatives of many peoples and nations to concern
ourselves with the Holocaust and the genocides of all peoples. I
think that is a reasonable way of summing up the process of the
conference.

Now I would add that we have not solved many problems. There
are so many gaps in our abilities to understand the Holocaust and
genocides. There were reporters here today who asked, "What did you
learn in this conference, and tell us concretely what you can do to
prevent future genocide?"

We were hard pressed to answer them in clear simple statements
about how to make changes in this world to protect us from future
holocausts and from future genocides. There are times when the mass
of words and talking "about" became unreal. Certainly for those -
to return to the earlier issue - who have experienced the hell of
Auschwitz or the Armenian massacre or any other massacre, many of
the words are an abomination. The words are impotent. Our ideas,
in any case, are no more than a beginning. We are often confused in
what we say. Many times our discussions stray far off the mark, and
many times we get caught up in the sheer meaningless momentum of
having a conference for conference sake, and then we are certainly
far off the mark.

Yet I dare suggest that the experience that has taken place
here is that we have accomplished something real by virtue of the
fact that we have begun and persisted in the task of talking about,
and learning about, and uncovering denials, and staying with the
tensions of our differences. I also thing it has been important
that we were able to bear asking probing questions of many different
professions. I do not know, for example, the answer about how the
legal system could break down in Germany. Clearly every institution
in society broke down before the press of madness and ugliness of
the Holocaust. The churches stand accused, the legal system designed to protect life against murder fell apart, the political system
was an agent of destruction. And I think it is important that we
were here, representatives of the many different professions to look
at the breakdown of values in our fields, and to look ahead to what
we can try to contribute for the future.

A number of people have asked during this week what comes next?
I personally have resisted answering that in any definitive way.

There is a natural tendency for any grouping of people to create a new institution, to invest themselves with organizational life, when much of that is a bureaucratic momentum rather than a real movement forward.

I am pleased to share with you that in organizing the conference, we also quietly created a non-profit institute which we call the Institute of the International Conference on the Holocaust and Genocide. We did that for a practical reason. We knew even before the crisis that the demands of a conference - organizational and budget demands - can be at times relentless, and that if we were not careful, one of the objectives that we had, namely, to publish the proceedings, might get swept away in the press of the conference's other budget needs. The first task we assigned this Institute was to be the guardian of the publication task, and the funds for that publication task were put in the entirely different conduit of this non-profit institute. So there will be that continuity, and we look forward to publishing the proceedings in a way that is meaningfful to all of us, and for the intellectual community everywhere.

What further - I do not know. We now have a structure that will permit the consideration of further work. I think it is premature to think in any concrete way, but I do want to express the conviction that if the conference has been meaningful, as I think it has, we are going to do further work, and we will dare to think ahead in new ways especially about genocide prevention. There will be more conferences, we do not have to plan them tonight. They will come from the genuine momentum of this experience - rather than from overplanning and overorganizing at this point.

I would like to conclude with a quotation from an article by Rabbi Pesach Schindler in a symposium which commemorated the Armenian genocide. He in turn is quoting another source, - Leviticus:

> The imperative of speaking out against wrongdoing appears adjacent to the Commandment - Do not stand idly by when the blood of your neighbor is in danger. We are compelled to break the silence of anguish in order to fulfil the ultimate purpose of remembering.

I really think we have done that reasonably well at this stage, and I thank you all very much.

Index

Abdul-Hamid II, 36,88
Abrahams, Israel, 186,195
Adel, Daljit Sen, 122
Aga Khan, Sadruddin, 304
Agus, Jacob B., 336,344
Ailot, Anthony, 343,344
Ajamian, Shahe, 358-363,
  371,386
Albino, Oliver, 45
Alexander II, 218
Allardt, Erik, 11,30
Allen, Woody, 262
Allport, Gordon, 209,214,215
Amichai, Yehuda, 239
Amiet, Cuno, 230
Amin, Idi, 43,44,46,
  282,283,297,301,337
Ammende, Ewald, 75,81
Anderson, Benedict R., 46
Anders, Gunther, 228,231
Antonescu, 132
Arendt, Hannah, 179,182
Arens, Richard, 26,30,44,45
Aristotle, 316,322
Arlen, Michael J., 36,46
Aronson, Ronald, 137-146,150,
  153,160,172
Aronson, Sarah, 367
Aron, Raymond, 183,192,195
Asch, Solomon E., 166,172
Askenasy, Hans, 157,173
Asmussen, 251
Avineri, Shlomo, 186,194,195
Baeck, Leo, 195
Banks, W.C., 174
Barbusse, Henri, 227
Barlach, Ernst, 225
Barnet, Richard J., 178,182
Baron, Salo, 196
Barron, John, 46,59
Barth, Karl., 243,252,253
Barton, James, 102
Bassiouni, M. Cherif, 331,344
Bauer, Yehuda, 130,135,179,
  182,193,195,275,276
Baum, Rainer C., 198,200
Bebel, 229
Becker, Ernest, 318,319,323
Beckmann, Max, 225,228
Bedau, Hugo Adam, 45,152
Beer, Aba, 381-382

Bein, Alex, 136
Bekenntnisse, 247
Bell, Wendell, 44
Ben-Canan, A., 336,344
Berdyaev, Nikolai, 149,153
Berenger, Henri, 106
Beres, Louis Rene, 306-323
Berger, Alan L., 265-277,269,
  276
Bergmann, Martin S., 199,200
Berkovits, Eliezer, 186,195,
  255,260,263,274
Beshir Mohammed Omer, 45
Bethge, Eberhard, 243,253
Bezwinska, Jadwiga, 135
Bhusan, Shashi, 123,126
Bialik, 239
Binding, Karl, 270
Bishop of Chichester, 251
Blackstone, 314
Bleyl, Fritz, 230
Bloch, Ernst, 145,146
Blum, Jeffrey M., 336,344
Blum, P. von, 230
Bodley, John H., 44
Bonhoeffer, Dietrich, 243,262,
  263,385
Booth, Irmgard, 263
Borchardt, H. H., 243,254
Borchard, E., 312,323
Boua, Chanthou, 304
Bowen, Murray, 155,173
Boyens, Armin, F. C., 250,254
Braichevskii, M. Iu., 67,81
Braude, Advocate, 382
Bristol, Mark L., 107,108,111
Broder, David S., 126
Bronkhorst, Dan,
  281-287
Brown, Michael, 187,195
Bryce, Viscount James,
  24,30,45,102
Buber, Martin, 192,195,
  235,238,265,269,272,275,
  276
Buckley, W., 329
Buergenthal, Thomas R., 344,
  345
Bukharin, 69
Bunemann, H., 230